ehran o

Qom
o

IRAN

Faw Peninsula

UBIYAN
ARBA
o Shiraz

BAHRAIN

The Gulf

QATAR o Doha • Abu Dhabi
o
dh
UNITED ARAB
EMIRATES

Muscat
o

BIA

OMAN

SOUTH

YEMEN

Gulf of Aden

AFGHANISTAN

Illusions
of
Triumph

ILLUSIONS
of
TRIUMPH

An Arab View of the Gulf War

MOHAMED HEIKAL

HarperCollins*Publishers*

First published in 1992 by
HarperCollins*Publishers*,
77–85 Fulham Palace Road,
Hammersmith, London W6 8JB

9 8 7 6 5 4 3 2 1

A CIP catalogue record for this book
is available from the British Library

ISBN 0 00 255014 8

Photoset by Rowland Phototypesetting Ltd,
Bury St Edmunds, Suffolk

Printed in Great Britain by
Hartnolls, Bodmin, Cornwall

Contents

Introduction

Some of the calmest words spoken in the heat of the Kuwait crisis came from Zbigniew Brzezinski, formerly Jimmy Carter's National Security Advisor. At a time when the subconscious mind of the West was girding itself for war, Brzezinski described the conflict as being 'over-personalised, over-emotionalised and over-militarised'. My hope is that this book will help redress those excesses, putting the events of August 1990 to March 1991 in another light.

In the summer of 1990 the United States found itself lacking a challenge, for the first time since its emergence as a superpower. John F. Kennedy's injunction to resist the spread of Communism had been America's guiding principle, but with the collapse of the Soviet empire and the transformation of Eastern Europe that mission seemed accomplished. A new goal, threat or sense of purpose was needed. More through miscalculation than design, President Saddam Hussein of Iraq filled that need.

Few presidents can aspire to greatness, in the eyes of posterity, without having proved their leadership in a just war. The justification for the Gulf war was self-evident to most Americans and Britons, but less so to Arabs, including many in countries which supported the Coalition. President Bush emerged with his image enhanced, but most Arabs found it hard to share the West's euphoria. Now, a year after the war, it may be possible to discuss these differences without seeming to condone Iraq's actions.

It is difficult for Westerners to understand that Arabs regard themselves as members of a single nation, united by a common language and culture and living in a well-defined geographical area. Their divisions, no matter how serious, need to be seen in the context of one nation in search of its identity. That search began in 1918, when the collapse of the Ottoman Empire put an end to what had been the Arab world's main source of order for the previous 400 years. Turkey had ceased to be an effective administrative authority much earlier, but the Caliphate system of Islamic leadership, based in Istanbul, remained a strong unifying influence. Its abolition in 1923 left the Arab world almost bereft of religious and political structures to back up its cultural unity. The next half century brought four phases, each of which gave rise to new sources of division.

Three ruling families claimed the mantle, turban and cloak discarded by the Turks. The Hashemite family, descendants of the Prophet Mohammed and traditional rulers of the Hejaz, the western part of the Arabian peninsula, regarded themselves as the natural heirs. The Saud family, formerly the rulers of Najd, the central and eastern part of the peninsula, gradually brought the Hashemite territories under their control, creating the new country of Saudi Arabia in 1932. The third claimant was the Egyptian royal family. The differences between the three aspirants were never resolved, and the attempt to recreate a religious superstate ended in failure.

The second phase came after the Second World War, when hopes of democracy and greater social justice led to friction between modernists and traditionalists, royalists and republicans, cities and tribes. These trends were exacerbated in the third phase, when the Arab world became aware that the distribution of its huge oil resources gave most of the benefits to the least populated areas. As seen from the overcrowded cities, geography seemed to mock justice, increasing the anger of the poor and hungry masses.

The fourth phase was the rift caused by Egypt's decision to make a separate peace with Israel through the Camp David accords of 1978. The rest of the Arab world, with the exception of Oman, broke diplomatic links with Egypt for more than a decade, interrupting Cairo's traditional roles as a source of mainstream Arab views and a moderator of inter-Arab disputes.

During the vacuum of leadership left by Egypt's eleven-year absence from Arab councils, three powerful bodies representing different regional interests were formed, splitting the Arab world into closed political circles. The Gulf Co-operation Council, representing oil-producing tribes, was the first, followed by the Maghreb Council of North African Arabs, who were mainly interested in links with southern Europe. The Arab Co-operation Council, a shapeless creation linking Iraq, Jordan, Egypt and Yemen, was more a reaction to the other bodies than an attempt to inspire or lead the Arab world.

These and other tensions combined to produce a state of agitation in the Arab world which interacted with the frustration aroused by the Palestinian dilemma. Older strains caused by the creation of artificial state boundaries during the colonial period made matters worse.

What little hope remained of achieving genuine unity was shattered by the Gulf war, which left the Arab nation more divided and embittered than ever before. The beginning of the second oil century, as the twenty-first century will be, does not bode well for a region that possesses two thirds of the world's reserves but has yet to learn how to use it.

In the course of preparing material for this book I have spoken to many in the Arab world, from crowned kings to heads of government, from military commanders to angry demonstrators, as well as European and American politicians. All have been generous with their time, and some allowed me to see official papers. I am grateful for their trust. My thanks are also due to: Andrew Knight, executive chairman of News International, who after long discussions would always ask, in his reflective way, 'Why don't you write it?'; Pierre Salinger, former press secretary to presidents John F. Kennedy and Lyndon Johnson, and head of ABC Television bureaux in Europe, for his enthusiasm and encouragement; Andrew McEwen, a *Times* journalist, whose skill and devotion was a great help. Many friends and colleagues read the manuscript, gave sound advice and asked probing questions which were valuable in dealing with a highly-charged subject. To them and many others I am very grateful. The information for this account of the events of 1990–91 has come from many sources, but the conclusions are solely my responsibility.

Throughout the book some passages are given as direct quotations. The sources of these passages are as follows: official minutes of meetings; official state documents; personal written notes of ministers or officials from Arab League countries; records and transcripts made available to the author; interviews by the author with those named or with their close aides.

I do not claim to be neutral; any vision of events is conditioned by its viewpoint in culture, geography and time. If this book helps to de-personalise, de-emotionalise and de-militarise the reader's understanding, I will have made my contribution.

PART ONE

THE STORMY GULF

'My brother, you must decide what you want — money or the throne.'

KING FAHD of Saudi Arabia
to Sheikh Jaber, Emir of Kuwait,
September 1990

1

A Time of Strangeness

Every Middle East war has had a character of its own, a mood understood and remembered by all who lived through it. No one would forget the outrage in the Arab world in 1956 over the conspiracy by Israel, France and Britain to seize the Suez Canal. The humiliation of the 1967 war against Israel left a mark on the Arab mind, later diminished by the elation and pride of October 1973, when Egypt and Syria showed that Israel was not invincible. In the Kuwait conflict there was much anger and no pride; what the Arab world underwent was a wrenching of the soul. It was a time of strangeness.

Neither the Middle East nor the wider world had known a period like it. For several weeks, as one Arab army faced another while the Soviet Union smiled at the United States, contradictions became the only certainty, confusion the new order. The Arab world was divided as never before. It was not just that the Arab League broke in two: every individual Arab felt an inner division. Nothing illustrated this better than the reaction of a group of Egyptian and Syrian soldiers encamped in Saudi Arabia when they heard the news on 18 January 1991 that Iraq had launched its first Scud missile attack on Israel. 'Allah Akbar!' (God is great) they shouted, only to remember an instant later that they were supposed to be against Iraq. Too late – seven Egyptians and several Syrians were disciplined.

For the previous two years a succession of events had made it seem that an era of world peace was dawning. It began with the Soviet decision to withdraw from Afghanistan and the ceasefire between Iran and Iraq in August 1988, followed by the mainly bloodless revolutions in Eastern Europe in 1989. By the summer of 1990 disarmament in Central Europe was in prospect, the remaining Soviet–US proxy wars in Africa and Central America were spluttering out, South Africa seemed in the process of throwing off white rule, Western Europe was rushing towards federalism, much of Eastern Europe was suing to join the West, the fractious twin Koreas were cooing at each other, and even the Cambodian nightmare looked less hopeless. In search of parallels some recalled the 1945 Potsdam conference and the 1814 Congress of Vienna, the last two occasions when international alignments were so comprehensively reshuffled. But the comparisons were not very illuminating. Everyone sensed that a shift from one phase of international relations to another was taking place, but they still clung to the old familiar rules. On all sides there was a failure to anticipate the new ones correctly.

Amid general euphoria over these positive events, few noticed that clouds were gathering again in the Middle East. With the Iran–Iraq war finally over, many thought the region had gone quiet. That impression was reinforced in November 1988 by the decision of the Palestine National Council, the PLO's assembly, to accept the main United Nations resolutions, including the much-disputed Resolution 242, as a basis for talks on a peace settlement. In the West this was taken to mean that the PLO was keen to create the right climate for talks. But after a half-hearted response by Washington, which agreed to talks but did not take the opportunity to try to break the Arab–Israeli deadlock, it slipped to the back of the international mind. The Palestinian intifida attracted some attention, only to fade from the headlines a year later. By the spring of 1990 the West was making alarmed noises about Saddam Hussein. Iraq was already voicing strong complaints about Kuwait's oil policies. The Iraqi leader repeatedly hinted at a possibility of military action, but was not heeded. The invasion took the Western and Arab world by surprise, to the point that April Glaspie, US ambassador in Baghdad, left her post to go on holiday only two days before the tanks rolled in, convinced that nothing would happen in her absence.

The US and Soviet governments began working together within hours of the invasion. James Baker, the US Secretary of State, and Eduard Shevardnadze, his Soviet counterpart, had met in Vladivostock the previous day and were due to depart in separate directions, Baker flying to Ulan Bator in Mongolia while Shevardnadze returned to Moscow. Baker phoned to suggest another meeting in the light of the invasion, but discovered that Shevardnadze had not heard about it. The Soviet minister was, understandably, angry with his assistants for failing to inform him. The two men immediately held a second meeting which laid the basis for a degree of co-operation no one had expected, even though the world was by now accustomed to Soviet foreign-policy earthquakes. Shevardnadze, then a personal friend of Mikhail Gorbachev, had a mandate to clear out the cobwebs of the Andrei Gromyko decades. But how he would react to the invasion was not easy to guess. Iraq is a country of special concern to Moscow in a region which the Soviet Foreign Ministry saw as its own backyard.

Shevardnadze immediately recognised that the invasion put Saddam Hussein in command of a third of Middle East oil reserves, thus posing a potential threat to vital US interests. Throughout the crisis Moscow avoided saying anything that could have added to Washington's fears. It quickly became clear that there would be no superpower confrontation, but few anticipated that America and the Soviet Union would work hand in hand.

During the Suez crisis the Soviet Union had played a pivotal role by threatening missile attacks against the invading powers. Helped by American pressure, Egyptian resistance and a run on the pound, the Soviet threats forced Britain and France to back down. Over the years of the Cold War Moscow remained consistent in its support for Arab governments, even when they spurned its overtures or expelled its advisers. Many in the Arab world assumed that even if Moscow refused to help Iraq after the invasion it would at least remain neutral, and they were surprised when the Soviet Union helped the Americans to pass resolution after resolution through the UN Security Council.

Arab leaders who went to see President Gorbachev after the invasion were astonished by his attitude. He had learned of US intentions at a mini-summit with George Bush on 9 September. 'The Americans told us that they are ready to fight and they are going to war whatever happens. We can see their point of view,' Gorbachev told one visitor. Bush used their meeting on a gloomy Sunday in Helsinki to assess whether Gorbachev would hold firm to his refusal to send Soviet troops to the Gulf. He came away convinced that Gorbachev was unshakeable, having promised the Soviet people after the Afghanistan débâcle never to send Soviet troops abroad again. Bush was equally clear that Moscow would do nothing to obstruct a US military intervention. The summit ended with a show of unity at a joint press conference. It had not been a meeting of equals: Moscow would make a formal request for American aid a few months later.

A further indication of Moscow's submissiveness came in November, when Baker and Shevardnadze were putting the final touches to the wording of Resolution 678, which implicitly authorised the use of force to make Iraq comply with earlier resolutions. Shevardnadze raised no objection to the substance, only the wording. To the amazement of Arab delegations it became clear that Moscow would give Washington a licence to act, although Shevardnadze implored Baker not to insist on including the words 'use of force'. It was agreed that the resolution should be phrased more discreetly, authorising member states 'to use all necessary means to uphold and implement Security Council Resolution 660' (which demanded a complete Iraqi withdrawal). Shevardnadze did not attempt to conceal his motives. An American war against Iraq could only be embarrassing to Moscow, even if it were cloaked by multi-national support. It would be uncomfortably close to the southern Soviet frontiers, and was bound to add to the anxiety of the Soviet army, already dismayed by large reductions in conventional weapons which Gorbachev and Shevardnadze were negotiating with Nato under the Conventional Forces in Europe Treaty. No one could be sure what effect it might have on the southern Soviet republics, with their large Muslim populations. The risk of unleashing a wave of Islamic protest seemed real.

'You and me and the rest of us [here] will understand what this means. And we agree to it,' Shevardnadze told Baker, according to Arab delegates.

Any remaining doubts about the Soviet position should have been settled on 5 September, when Tariq Aziz, the Iraqi foreign minister, visited Moscow. He expected Gorbachev to take a passive line, or at least to talk in muted language. Instead the Soviet leader began by discussing the 'new thinking', and said invasions were in contradiction with it. Then he added: 'We accept, and you must admit, that the Americans have got vital interests in the Middle East.' Moscow recognised those interests and knew that Washington would use force if they were threatened. 'We [the Soviet Union] cannot do anything, so you had better calculate your position accordingly,' he told Aziz. His final remark left nothing to doubt: 'The Americans will attack you and nobody will be able to stand with you.' Aziz replied: 'We want to think that you will stand by us at least morally.' Gorbachev answered: 'What you did was an act of aggression, and we cannot and will not back you in any way. We are ready to help . . . on the basis of complete withdrawal.' From that moment the Iraqis knew they were on their own.

President Saddam Hussein had been among the first to appreciate how much the Arab world would be affected by changes in the Soviet Union. As early as the Arab Co-operation Council summit of March

1990 in Amman he predicted that for the next five years there would be only one true superpower. It is strange, therefore, that he decided to move against a US vital interest.

At the time it appeared to Arabs that the US–Soviet relationship as regards the Middle East had swung from competition to co-operation overnight, with no intervening period of coolness. In fact, however, there had been hints of change for some time, but they had not been heeded. Yasser Arafat, chairman of the PLO, had visited Gorbachev much earlier and asked him to help the Palestinians. 'The Americans are playing havoc in our region, and you should stand up to them,' he said. Gorbachev, suddenly angry, replied in fairly crude terms. 'Now look. I have opened my guts to Reagan and he saw what is there, and I saw his guts. We both know that both of us suffer [from competition between the two powers], so you shouldn't try to play us off against each other.'

The risk that Moscow's commitment to the Arabs might be fading had been in the air for some years, although many Arabs failed to appreciate the changed situation even when Moscow explained it fully. At a conference in the Soviet Union in October 1989 entitled 'Perestroika and the Third World', George Habash, leader of the Popular Front for the Liberation of Palestine, admonished his Soviet hosts for losing confidence in themselves as a great power. 'You have done well but you don't realise it. If you go on like this you are going to hurt all of us,' he said. A former secretary general of the Egyptian Communist Party said at the same conference: 'It seems to me that it is our fate to teach a new generation of Soviet youth Marxism again.' Arab delegates returned to the Middle East shocked by the changes they had seen. Another hint of Moscow's abandonment of its former role came in a meeting with President Hafez Assad of Syria, who was seeking strategic parity with Israel. Gorbachev told him: 'Your problems are not going to be solved through any such strategic points – and anyway, we're no longer in that game.' Assad went home devastated, and immediately set about mending fences with Washington. Syria's participation in the Kuwait war was another of the contradictions. Damascus wanted a strategic balance with Israel, yet helped to destroy the offensive capability of the Arab army that Israel feared most. Some Arabs, including the Iraqis themselves, considered Iraq the Prussia of the Arab world because of its emphasis on military strength.

Shevardnadze's unexpected resignation in December, and his

replacement by Aleksandr Bessmertnykh, was interpreted in Baghdad as marking a change of Soviet policy dictated by the military. This prompted Iraqis to hope for a shift in their direction, but it was not to be.

Another surprise was the extraordinary burst of activity of the UN Security Council. Baghdad had not expected much trouble from the glass palace on New York's East River, long regarded as a preserve of Third World and Non-Aligned opinion. That assessment of the UN was out of date, as Baghdad should have known. It had held good as long as the Security Council remained paralysed by the Cold War stalemate, but by 1988 the superpowers had largely stopped vetoing each other's resolutions. The Security Council played a positive role in setting the ceasefire terms for the Iran–Iraq war and in easing the Soviet withdrawal from Afghanistan. Although the Iraqi foreign service is usually competent, it seemed not to have taken this on board. Baghdad was stunned to be condemned by Security Council Resolution 660 on the same day as the invasion, followed by ten more resolutions passed in the next seventeen weeks. Señor Javier Pérez de Cuéllar, the Secretary General, was worried that they would be interpreted as giving an open-ended mandate to the Americans to use unlimited military force. He hinted diplomatically that this was not entirely a United Nations war, pointing out that General Norman Schwarzkopf did not wear a UN blue beret. But America continued to convey the impression that the military build-up was fully a UN operation. By including every country which sent even a handful of soldiers the Americans were able to talk of a twenty-eight-nation coalition.

The motives of some participants were at best mixed. A planeload of troops from the Central African Republic landed at Cairo airport and told the authorities they wanted to go to Saudi Arabia to fight. When Egyptian officials expressed astonishment, one of the officers whispered: 'We want some aid. The Americans are distributing money to those who participate, and we'd like some of it.' When they arrived unannounced in Saudi Arabia they were told they were not needed. But then the Saudis were advised (presumably by the Americans) to change their minds. Even a single planeload of troops would enable a new country to be added to the coalition tally. Another of the smaller partners was to suffer the highest casualties of the conflict, in percentage terms, though not in battle. Senegal sent a battalion, which never saw action yet lost 200 men, a third of its number. They died in a plane crash while being taken to the *Haj* at Mecca after Kuwait had been recaptured.

The extremely hard position taken by Margaret Thatcher (then prime minister of Britain) was not appreciated in the Arab world. She happened to be in the United States on 2 August, and used the opportunity to lobby President Bush. Bush had already made up his mind, but Thatcher's backing probably stiffened his resolve. Among those who noticed her influence was King Hassan of Morocco. In a meeting with President Chadli ben Jedid of Algeria he said: 'I'm worried. The Americans talk loudly, but I'm afraid of the British. They have their way of whispering and doing things which you cannot see.'

To illustrate his point, he added: 'They wanted to connect their island with the Continent, just as we are interested in linking Africa with Europe [at the mouth of the Mediterranean, near Gibraltar]. The British decided to use a tunnel. In our case engineers came to me with projects for either a tunnel or a bridge. I was immediately against a tunnel. That's the difference between us: the British wanted a tunnel because it would not be seen. We wanted a bridge because it would be visible to everyone.'

The invasion of Kuwait placed Paris in a difficult position. French Middle East policy had been based on the fact that the Arabs needed a diplomatic and commercial bridge to Europe, but regarded Britain as unfit for the role because of its colonial history. The French record was far from unblemished, especially in Algeria and Syria, but this was less fresh in Arab minds, despite France's part in the Suez attack. In the 1950s Marshal Tito, then President of Yugoslavia, suggested to President Nasser that France could be a good link with Europe for the Non-Aligned countries, given the special character of President de Gaulle. Nasser thought it worth trying and helped to put it into effect. During Valéry Giscard d'Estaing's presidency Paris built on its relations with Iraq and Libya and became a major arms supplier. The first instinct of the French after the invasion of Kuwait was to distance themselves from Washington, but as confrontation became inevitable Paris shifted its stand. Its strategic interest was the same as Washington's – oil. Although President Mitterrand attempted to bring about a diplomatic solution, nothing came of it. The hopes that some Arabs had placed in Paris were dashed, especially after French troops participated in the ground attack against Iraqi forces.

If the international scene was confused, the situation in the Arab world was close to chaotic. A group of countries which claimed to be one nation was not just divided, but was fighting itself. Under the Arab League charter the member countries were supposedly part of a military defence pact, yet Arab armies were now facing each other. Arab commanders were advising American counterparts on the strengths and weaknesses of the Iraqi military machine. General Mohamed Ali Bilal, of the Egyptian chiefs of staff, must have had mixed feelings. During the Iran–Iraq war he had been seconded to the Iraqi army and fought with them at the battle of Faw, at which an important peninsular area was liberated from Iranian forces. He became senior adviser to the Iraqi chiefs of staff and had still been in that role until two months before the invasion of Kuwait. Now he was ranged against the army he had served for so long. Initially he justified his position by saying that the mission of Egyptian forces was only to defend Saudi Arabia, but when the mission became offensive he found it difficult to adjust.

Military analysts in Washington had painted a fearsome picture of Iraq's Republican Guard, whose original role had been to protect the president but who later became the best equipped and most professional offensive unit in the Iran–Iraq war. Its prowess had been exaggerated in the West to the point that many saw it as Iraq's equivalent of Hitler's Panzer divisions. Aside from the hyperbole, this overlooked the fact that the Iraqi army had few secrets. The Egyptians knew everything worth knowing about its fighting capabilities, while the Russians and French had all the important details about its weapons. All this information was available to the Americans. Field Marshal Mohamed Abdel Halim Abu Ghazalah, the senior presidential assistant in Cairo, announced that Iraq's feared missile capability had been greatly exaggerated. President Mubarak, a former head of the air force, added: 'We were the ones who trained Iraqi pilots, and as a pilot I say they are no good. As a chief instructor I say they are no good.'

During the crisis many Arab capitals witnessed demonstrations either in support of Iraq or against US deployments. Muammar Gadaffi led a demonstration of an estimated half a million people in Tripoli in December 1990. Some people expressed their feelings in unusual ways. An Algerian woman, Fatima Ben Said, tried to name her new-born son 'Scud', because he was born on the night of Iraq's first missile attack on Israel. When her husband went to register the child the authorities said there was a law banning foreign names. The couple hired a lawyer and took the case to court, but were persuaded to withdraw on the grounds that the name would look odd. They called him Saddam instead. The West understood and feared this popular sentiment. The French banned an Algerian pop song called 'Saddam, oh Saddam' from the airwaves, while the BBC proved unresponsive to requests from Arab listeners for songs with anti-war lyrics.

Western governments, knowing that Baghdad had close links with Palestinian organisations, were worried that domestic support for the war might be eroded if bombs began exploding in their own countries. The attacks the West feared never took place, because the organisations assumed Iraq was strong enough to fight the early stages of the war on its own. The delay also had something to do with money. The Kuwait government in exile at Taif, near Jeddah, still had most of its funds at its disposal because they had been invested abroad. It had been giving money to these groups, since their primary purpose was to fight Israel. But now the gifts were accompanied by words such as: 'This war has nothing to do with you. Your time will come later when the struggle against Israel resumes. So accept the money and prepare yourselves for your real battle.' The seduction was successful: they took both the cash and the advice. At the same time Syria, which has played host to some of the groups, was advising the Americans on how to counteract their effectiveness.

Abu Nidal, who had a large base in Baghdad and an office in Libya, was granted permission to open an office in Saudi Arabia, partly as a goodwill gesture and partly to reassure him that Riyadh remained committed to the Palestinian cause. The Saudi move demonstrated an important difference of perception: the West regards organisations like Abu Nidal's as terrorist organisations, while the Arab world considers them militias in the Palestinian cause.

The confusion in the Arab world led to some strange assessments of the situation. Muammar Gadaffi, the Libyan leader, propounded a theory that Baghdad and Washington were secretly in league. During a meeting with President Chadli in Algiers on 19 August he said: 'I'm haunted by a feeling that it's all arranged. It's all a plot.' He pointed out that the US had always wanted military bases in the Middle East, and had been obsessed with the threat to the Gulf oilfields since the Iranian revolution. Their original plans to station a Rapid Deployment Force had been frustrated by Arab objections, forcing the Americans to create a central command with a headquarters in Tampa, Florida, 12,000 kilometres from the area it was supposed to monitor. 'It's all a conspiracy; they have cooked it together so as to allow the Americans to come to the Middle East with everybody's acceptance and land their forces,' he said. Gadaffi remained convinced of his theory until the fighting started.

Another strange attitude was adopted by General Mirza Aslam Beg, the Pakistani chief of staff, who sent a mechanised brigade to Saudi Arabia but at the same time accused the Americans of conducting a conspiracy against Iraq because it was a Muslim country. It was difficult to see how he could reconcile these two positions, but he was not alone in his inconsistency. The Muslim world was acting without sense, speaking first and thinking second.

President Mubarak of Egypt always liked to describe himself as a realist, and he let that aim be his guide during the Kuwait crisis. As a politician he did not like the situation; with his military background he could see war coming. His calculations as to the outcome were clear: Iraq was facing certain defeat, and he wanted Egypt to be with the winners. President Bush's decision to forgive Egyptian debts of US$7 billion helped Mubarak convince his public that Egypt's involvement was worthwhile. Ironically, Bush's generosity cost Washington nothing, as it was offset by donations collected from the Gulf oil producers, Japan and Germany.

Nowhere in the Arab world was the sense of inner confusion greater than in Kuwait. Most people had gone to bed on 1 August unaware that invasion was imminent, and had awoken on the second to find Iraqi tanks in the streets and their government already in Saudi Arabia. The Iraqi soldiers expected to be greeted with flowers and enthusiasm, having been brought up from childhood to believe that Kuwait was a part of Iraq which the colonial British had kept for themselves. Well aware of opposition demands for the ruling family to concede some of its power and permit greater democracy, they probably thought they would be welcomed as liberators. But they found no smiles, only long faces and passive non-co-operation. Kuwait had not been an oasis of calm, but it was prosperous and relatively stable; to its wealthy and somewhat indolent upper classes it was home, while its imported masses, the mainly Asian guestworkers, saw it as a temporary haven and a source of high wages. The only elements with an interest in violent change were militant Shia factions, but they were more opposed to Baghdad than anyone. Saddam Hussein had suppressed Iraq's Shia-dominated opposition party, Da'awa (The

Call) as a precaution against Iranian infiltration.

The first reaction of most Kuwaitis to the invasion was of shock and confusion. With Baghdad portraying the Iraqi troops as an army of liberation and unity, many Kuwaitis were torn between anger and feelings of Arab brotherhood. The daughter of a prominent Kuwaiti merchant, who was related to the ruling family, handed over the keys of a warehouse containing food worth one million dinars (then US$4 million) to Iraqi officers. She said it was hard for her to regard the Iraqis as the enemy; to her they looked like tired, hungry people in a mess.

After a few days resistance began to be organised. It did not last long. On 6 September the exiled Kuwaiti government issued a statement asking that it should stop, as it was provoking severe Iraqi reprisals. During the National Kuwaiti Congress held in Jeddah in late October, many leading Kuwaitis were to criticise the al-Sabah family for failing to ask for general resistance against the Iraqis.

Iraqi troops were under orders to treat Kuwaitis well, and at first they showed discipline. But for men from mostly modest backgrounds the sight of Kuwait's riches became too tempting to resist. Acts of misbehaviour began, then looting, followed by organised pillage. As they watched their goods vanish, the Kuwaitis could not have known that their absent government was beginning to feel the pinch too. While in exile it was obliged to pay bills or sign contracts totalling around US$35 billion. King Fahd told members of his family that Sheikh Jaber, the emir, eventually expressed his dismay to his Saudi hosts. King Fahd replied: 'My brother, you must decide what you want – money or the throne.' The money was spent and no more was said.

According to the Association of Arab Banks some US$9 billion was transferred from the Gulf area to Europe between 2 and 6 August. By the beginning of September the sum had increased to US$22 billion. The real total must have been greater, because at the same time Kuwaitis in London, Paris and New York were switching funds to Switzerland, fearing that the freeze on Kuwaiti assets announced by the governments of Britain, France and America might affect them. Swiss banks were unable to cope with the flood of money. One prominent Kuwaiti merchant went to the Union des Banques Suisses to deposit US$8 million and asked for a good rate of interest, only to be told that the bank did not need the money and would have to pay him less than the standard rate. He was astonished: a month earlier anyone with that much to deposit would have received red-carpet treatment. The invasion came at a time when most well-off Kuwaitis were abroad on holiday. Thousands found themselves suddenly beggars. Western banks stopped changing not just dinars but all Arab currencies. Shops in Western capitals put up signs saying that Kuwaiti cheques and credit cards were not accepted. In Cairo the dinar slumped to a fraction of its former value. It had been worth four dollars; now one dollar would buy four to six dinars. Even the richest families found themselves forced to ask their embassies to pay their hotel bills. One woman from a wealthy Kuwaiti family remarked: 'This man [Saddam Hussein] is wicked. He decided to do it in August when he knew we would all be out of the country.'

There was little evidence of other Gulf Arabs changing their lifestyle to reflect straitened times. The night after the invasion Sheik Enani of Saudi Arabia, a merchant and consultant to the royal family, lost £8 million gambling at Monte Carlo. Other members of the Saudi royal family were having 500 kilos of oysters a week airfreighted from the Orkney islands, off the north coast of Scotland. Their ostentatiously rich lifestyle, coupled with King Fahd's decision to allow Washington to send forces to Saudi Arabia, was bound to invite criticism.

The Arab world may have been split down the middle over the Iraq–Kuwait issue, but sensitivity about foreign troops in Saudi Arabia lay outside these divisions. The West assumed that Arab countries who took part in the coalition would accept the need for a Western presence in Saudi Arabia, and failed to understand the strength of Arab feelings about the Holy Lands, which contain both the Ka'aba (the House of God) and Medina, the site of Mohammed's mosque and grave.

Thoughtless jokes by American soldiers caused offence. As a plane was being loaded with bombs a CNN television camera spotted an inscription written on one of the missiles in chalk: 'Call Allah: if he doesn't reply call Jesus'. Another missile bore the message: 'Call Allah: if he doesn't reply call Schwarzkopf'.

Many were angry when fighting raged around the holy Shia shrine at Karbala ad Negef in Iraq, site of the martyrdom of Hussein, second son of Ali, the son-in-law of the prophet Mohammed. So revered is this area that burial sites command a premium of US$175, a large sum in local terms. It may seem illogical that the Americans were blamed for a fight which involved two parties, but Muslims saw their presence in the area as indicating a lack of respect for the sanctity of holy places.

The Saudis upset other Arab countries by asking for only token forces from them. Cairo offered a substantial force, and was then obliged to spend a week haggling over numbers. The Saudis said they wanted one brigade, not more. They eventually accepted 35,000, but only because General Norman Schwarzkopf said he needed them. He wanted Arab forces, not American troops, to be first into Kuwait City. The Moroccans, sensing the Saudi mood, sent only 1000 men. 'It is clear our friends do not want any more,' King Hassan remarked. One reason for the Saudi attitude was their fear that governments which sent substantial forces would later present a bill, disguised as a request for aid. Another was the fact that it would be impossible to isolate Arab troops from Saudi soldiers, posing a risk that they might spread dangerous ideas. Saudi Arabia was also accustomed to playing host to foreign Muslims taking part in the Haj, and had had serious problems with Iranians trying to stage political demonstrations in holy places.

The Americans were convinced that once Kuwait was retaken Saddam Hussein and his government would collapse. They wanted the Iraqi army to take over and form a government made up of elements from the ruling Ba'ath Socialist Party. The Saudis were entrusted with the task of selecting people who could be called upon to serve in the new government, but one of those they chose was a man known throughout the area as an arms merchant and a collaborator with the CIA. It was part of the general folly.

Everyone was miscalculating, and none more than the government in Baghdad. It was miscalculation on a grand scale, involving errors of strategy, concept and timing. Few in the Arab world denied that Iraq had valid grievances; what it lacked was the patience to solve them by the traditional Arab approach of discussion. A country with an ancient history and culture, the region's second-largest oil production (after Saudi Arabia) and with substantial armed forces had sound reasons to see itself as a regional superpower. Yet geography and economics conspired to frustrate Iraq's aims, despite ample fresh water, fertile agricultural land and a population of 16 to 17 million. The geographical shackles stemmed from the way Britain and France carved up the Ottoman Empire after the First World War, with mandates from the League of Nations. Britain repaid earlier political debts to the al-Sabah family of Kuwait by turning their city-port and its hinterland into a separate state under British protection. Baghdad could see the sea, but with the new borders it could not reach it. The Shatt al-Arab waterway was no substitute for a deep-water port. Between the waterway and Kuwait's border lay only fifty kilometres of coastline, including one small, shallow port which could not be dredged and developed because two Kuwaiti islands, Bubiyan and Warba, straddled the approaches. After independence huge efforts were made to overcome the lack of a port by building pipelines through neighbouring countries, but they proved vulnerable to arbitrary closure. The construction of a pipeline across Syria to the Mediterranean was interrupted because of the long-standing quarrel between Baghdad and Damascus. The Iraqis spent US$8 billion on a pipeline through Turkey and another across Saudi Arabia to the Red Sea, only to find them closed after the invasion of Kuwait. Everything which had been done to prevent Iraq being landlocked had failed.

Iraq's economic problems stemmed from the falling price of oil, which Baghdad attributed to overproduction by Kuwait and the United Arab Emirates. But Kuwait ignored Iraqi demands for a production cut, refused to lease the strategic islands, and prevaricated over requests that Baghdad's war debts should be forgiven. Its obduracy led Baghdad to suspect that Kuwait had secretly obtained security guarantees from the United States. Washington's motive, Baghdad thought, was to keep Iraq on a tight leash to prevent it from becoming too powerful.

Any government leading its country to war needs three conditions: a cause its people are prepared to die for; a moral, historical and legal basis for its claims; and a goal which lies within its achievable limits. Saddam Hussein could claim the first two but not the third. The belief that Kuwait was part of Iraq, and had been wrongly taken from it by the British, was deeply embedded in the Iraqi consciousness, and was a cause Iraqis would defend with their lives. The historical and legal arguments are a matter of controversy, but the Iraqis believed strongly in their case. Saddam Hussein miscalculated the impact on world opinion of the seizure of the whole of Kuwait rather than merely the parts he needed. He overestimated the Arab resolve to keep American forces out of the Gulf, overestimated Moscow's willingness to help, and underestimated American resolve.

He also miscalculated when he called together a group of foreign hostages and was filmed patting a small British boy on the head, an act which earned worldwide condemnation. It had been intended by his image-makers as a publicity stunt, presenting him as a man who cared. Television cameras followed him into the homes of ordinary people during the war and filmed him kissing their babies. This had succeeded in Iraqi terms, and officials thought they could make it work internationally, but they were wrong.

What lay behind the international response to the invasion of Kuwait? Was it, as Washington suggested, part of a new world order in which no country would be allowed to seize another's territory with impunity? No one would deny that something new was replacing something old. The end of the Cold War and the greatly increased economic challenge of Germany and Japan had changed the perspectives. Seen from the Third World, the Cold War rules had been fairly obvious: the Soviet Union and the West were competing for the Third World's favour, wealth and strategic positions and using it as their battlefield. For decades the nuclear stalemate kept motionless armies facing each other across German fields while the struggle of ideologies continued in the Middle East, Africa, Asia and Latin America. Arabs and Israelis provided the superpowers with a testing ground for their tanks, planes and guns.

Now the game was over: Gorbachev had refused to play. But did this amount to a new world order? The phrase needs some elaboration. Clearly it should mean something more than military power. A world order requires a combination of economic and military muscle with some means of asserting an example and a set of values. It was not until after the Napoleonic wars that it became possible to envisage the planet as being politically one world. Since then two world orders have emerged. The first, in the nineteenth century, was based on commerce, beginning with competition between Britain and France, subsequently joined by Germany. In Victorian times the British offered a model for other countries in literature, the press, democracy and political organisations, while the British navy patrolled the sea lanes and British ships carried British values to the rest of the world. The First World War weakened the Pax Britannica, but the United States was not yet strong enough to succeed it, and withdrew into isolationism, refusing to join the League of Nations. Under the surface, however, America was preparing itself for leadership. It took another world war to break the British economy. During and after that war the Americans elbowed the British out of their most important assets – the Middle East oil concessions. As the empire imploded the Pax Britannica fell and a Pax Americana began. While British might had been fuelled by sailpower and coal, moving cautiously to oil, American strength always depended on oil. Before the Second World War it was the world's largest producer, but the future importance of Middle East reserves was already recognised. The ready availability of oil had made automobiles and aircraft commercially viable and had spawned industries based on them; now the entire US economy came to depend on it.

American military power, manifested by nuclear weapons, represented a quantum leap from the order it replaced. But it also brought a new culture, new means of communication and its own set of values, derived from those of the British but improved. The House of Commons today is a pale shadow of the democratic processes of Capitol Hill.

Both world systems saw many challenges. Although Germany ultimately caused the collapse of the British order, by forcing it into two debilitating conflicts, it did so at no benefit to itself. France tried to compete with Britain but was forced into alliances. Later the Pax Americana faced the Soviet and East European challenges and defeated them.

The American order is currently challenged from three directions. Japan and Germany have succeeded in dividing the world into three economic empires, based on the yen, the mark and the dollar. Unrestricted trade within the European Economic Community looks likely to weaken US exports to Europe from the mid-1990s, and the EEC's links with Eastern Europe will strengthen that challenge. The rise of Iraq was a different type of problem, one more easily remedied by traditional superpower methods. Washington's response was not the start of a new world order, but a reassertion of the old one.

The old order was still valid, but some of its unwritten laws had changed. Everybody was experimenting, everybody was miscalculating. Even President Gorbachev was shocked when he heard that Iraqi troops had entered Kuwait. Everybody recognised that Baghdad had crossed a line, but that line was not well defined. The next eight months were not so much a struggle for Kuwait's sovereignty as a battle about the power and resources of the twenty-first century.

2

The Second Oil War

Thousands of words of indignation poured from Western statesmen in the months after Iraq's invasion of Kuwait. World order meant nothing, they argued, if a small country could be swallowed whole by a big neighbour while others sat on their hands. Unless the world stood up to a regional bully, the achievements of half a century would be in question. Sound as these sentiments appeared, something was missing: speechmakers were treading warily round a three-letter word, trying not to mention it. Oil became 'resources' or 'vital Western interests'. Washington and London had already decided to fight, but knew that public support would depend on how the issues were presented. If rights of states were mentioned first and Western interests second, the liberation of Kuwait became a noble cause. Reversing the order would devalue that cause while direct references to oil might reduce it to a squabble between producers. No one wanted to die defending a balance sheet. The politics of selling the use of force made it impossible for Western governments to acknowledge that the war for Kuwait was mainly an oil war.

No great struggle in modern times has had a single cause, unless viewed in simplistic terms. Oil has been a factor in a number of conflicts, but an important one in only three. The first was in October 1973, when President Sadat ordered Egyptian troops to cross the Suez Canal, knowing that the Arab attack would be followed by an oil embargo against Israel's Western supporters. The second oil war, from 1980 to 1988, pitched the region's second-largest oil producer, Iraq, against the third-largest, Iran, and gave the West a reason to send naval forces to the Gulf. Neither Iran nor Iraq would have had the economic strength for such a fight without oil revenues.

The West's readiness to fight for its Middle East oil interests dates back at least thirty-five years. The Suez crisis of 1956 marked a vain attempt by Britain and France to regain control of Europe's oil lifeline after President Nasser had nationalised the canal, the importance of which was far greater then, when supertankers had not yet been developed and there were fewer pipelines.

The failure of the Anglo – French operation was partly caused by opposition from Washington, which was beginning to treat the Mediterranean like an American lake. America's dominance of Middle East oil and its links with Israel would put it in a commanding position. When the Iraqi Free Officers group, led by Brigadier Abdul Karim Kassem, seized power in Baghdad in July 1958, Washington took it as a threat to US interests, and mobilised the Sixth Fleet. President Nasser, who was in Yugoslavia visiting Marshal Tito, decided that before returning home he should hear Moscow's views. The Soviet Union played a vital role in supporting the Arab world during the Suez crisis, but its ultimatum to Britain and France did not come until eleven days after the invasion of the canal zone. If Moscow was to stand up to the Americans, it would need to move faster. A Soviet plane collected Nasser at Poala airport,[1] near Tito's home on the island of Brioni, and flew him to Moscow for talks with Nikita Khrushchev. The Soviet leader's attitude was blunt. 'The West is imperious, they are aggressors, but they depend on Middle Eastern oil. If they feel the oil is threatened they will fight.' Khrushchev had heard this direct from the British prime minister Anthony Eden in 1956. 'Mr Chairman,' he quoted Eden as saying, 'if our Middle East oil is threatened we are going to fight. This could be a nuclear war.' He advised Nasser to reduce tension quickly. 'Talk to your friends in the new Iraqi regime. Tell them to give all the assurances possible to the Americans and British that they are not going to interrupt the oil,' he said. President Nasser passed on the advice and the Iraqi Revolutionary Command Council acted on it, announcing that oil would continue to flow and that contracts and treaties with the international community would be honoured.

Kuwait, by now an important oil producer, was beginning to seek independence, but Britain played for time. Not wanting ideas of Arab nationalism to spread there, it refused to allow Cairo to open a consulate. At the time London and Egypt were mending diplomatic fences broken in 1956. Sir Colin Crowe, head of the British interests

---

[1] Nasser was accompanied by the Egyptian foreign minister Dr Mahmoud Fawzi and the author, at that time editor of the Cairo daily newspaper *Al-Ahram*.

section attached to the Indian Embassy, put forward a request in 1958 to open five consulates in Egypt. Cairo replied by asking for Egyptian consulates in London, Liverpool, Dar es Salaam, Aden and Kuwait. Sir Colin looked startled when Kuwait and Aden were mentioned, and immediately refused. At the time Aden was still an important link in the tanker route.

Iraq had always regarded Kuwait as part of Basra province, and voiced its claim during the colonial period. Iraq became a sovereign state in October 1932 when Britain's mandate from the League of Nations ended, but the British did not leave Kuwait until 1961. As the last British units packed their bags Kuwait applied to the Arab League for membership. Baghdad could not let this pass without abandoning its claim. After informing the League that it would not recognise Kuwait's independence it moved troops to Basra, the nearest large Iraqi city to Kuwait. The rest of the Arab world united in opposing any Iraqi occupation of Kuwait and sent forces to support the new state, including some 10,000 Egyptian troops. The British delayed the departure of their last units in 1961 until Arab replacements arrived, and Baghdad eventually backed down.

Soviet fears that the Arabs might cause an East–West confrontation over oil emerged again in 1970 when President Nasser went to Moscow for talks. The Egyptians wanted to discuss arms shipments, but Leonid Brezhnev and Alexei Kosygin focused on Libya. Muammar Gadaffi had taken power the previous year and the Russians, clearly worried about his intentions, probed Nasser for information. Would he cause trouble? Did he have any influence? Moscow's refusal to tread on Western toes where Middle East oil was at stake was understandable. The Soviet Union knew that the West had spent centuries building its power in the Gulf, and could not easily be dislodged. European influence began in the fifteenth century with the first Portuguese expeditions, followed by the Dutch, French and British. The British Royal Navy, whose main mission was to keep the sea lanes to India open, gradually emerged as the dominant force, excluding military shipping from European competitors. The navy's secondary mission was to suppress the slave trade between the east coast of Africa and the Arabian peninsula and Gulf. Under this guise it virtually destroyed Arab trading fleets, branding them as pirates because slaves were often among the commodities they carried. Merchant ships were usually armed, which helped the British sustain the piracy accusation, often sinking vessels with cannon fire. Having disposed of local competition and imposed the Maritime Peace Treaty, British trading posts enjoyed a privileged position, if not an actual monopoly.

With hindsight, contacts between the British and the al-Sabah family in Kuwait in the nineteenth century can be seen as the starting point of the Iraq–Kuwait dispute. Before then Kuwait was little more than a natural harbour surrounded by barren sand dunes, with a small settlement depending on trade and fishing. The name was derived from an Arabic diminutive meaning 'little post' (in the sense of a police or administrative post).

The Sabahs were late and initially unwelcome arrivals. They and the Saudi family were part of the Atoub branch of the Eneiza tribe, but a quarrel between sheikhs of the Bedouin and part of the Eneiza tribe resulted in the Sabahs being expelled from the tribal domain in Najd at the end of the seventeenth century. They made their way to Om-Kasr in Iraq, which was under a Turkish governor, but failed to establish themselves. For hundreds of years caravans travelling on the land trading route between the Far East and Europe had passed through Iraq. The route was now less important because of the advent of secure sea lanes, but it remained active. Throughout the region some tribes made their living by running what would now be called protection rackets, forcing caravans to pay dues on each stage of their journey. Those who attempted to avoid paying were attacked. The Sabahs raided the caravans and also local villages, making such a nuisance of themselves that the governor expelled them. They turned back towards Najd and started attacking travellers on the route to Kuwait. The Kuwaitis followed the traditional course of turning the bandits into paid policemen, and gradually the Sabahs gained respectability. Later their role was extended to include protecting dependants of Kuwaiti seafarers while the men were at sea. As fishing and the merchant marine were the main industries, apart from pearl-diving, the Sabahs came to protect much of the population. This evolved into a contract under which trading families left local administration to the Sabahs, who in return agreed to stay out of commerce. It did not make them a royal family in the traditional sense; the merchants felt they had contracted the Sabahs to perform a specific function, a view still held by those families which arrived before them.

Kuwait, like Saudi Arabia, was nominally part of the Ottoman Empire, but Britain had its representatives there. The British were not pleased to find that the sheikh was flirting with the Ottomans, seeking the title of 'Kaim Makam' (deputy ruler). In 1899 there were three Sabah brothers, Garrah, Mohamed and Mubarak. After a dispute over money, Mubarak, the youngest, murdered his two brothers, then signed an agreement with the British, accepting protection (against Turkey) and surrendering the right to make agreements with other governments. The treaty remained in force until 1961, when Kuwait became fully independent and the sheikh took the title of emir. In essence it was another form of protection racket, with the effect that Kuwait had no foreign policy of its own and conducted most of its business with Britain. When oil was discovered in 1938 the concession naturally went to London, with a share reserved for American companies. The indigenous population was then still only about 25,000.

· The British brought nearly all the Gulf Arab sheikhs under their wing with similar treaties. These were not entirely one-sided, especially in areas where the tribes spent most of the year inland and visited the natural harbours only to buy and sell goods. Even Ibn Saud disliked the sea, saying it made him feel sick. The east coast of what is now Saudi Arabia was an administrative void for five or six centuries. It was not unpopulated, as there were coastal villages and nomadic tribes, but it lacked effective government. As recently as the 1920s Abu Dhabi was nothing more than an expanse of sand with the sheikh's palace, the British representative's residence, a handful of huts and little else. Dubai had a population of about 200. Oman, however, had for long periods been a powerful Arab mercantile state with its own navy and colonies in Africa and India. The Portuguese were the first Europeans to establish a fort there, but later the British brought Oman into their zone of influence, partly because it lay on the India route, partly because Zanzibar, then an Omani colony, was the main departure point for slave traders entering what Europeans then called the Dark Continent.

Apart from dominating mercantile trade, Britain's other aim in the Gulf was to keep the French in check. Napoleon and Nelson were at one time on opposing sides in the Gulf. While Napoleon sought to increase French influence by appointing a governor general in the Gulf, Nelson was serving with the Royal Navy patrolling Gulf waters, commanding a frigate called the *Sea Shore* from 1773 to 1776, long before their encounter in 1798 at the battle of Abu Qir, off the Egyptian coast near Alexandria.

The beginning of the twentieth century was a volatile period in the region. Persia was collapsing, and the Ottoman Empire falling in slow motion, while the government of India was intensely active in opposing challenges in the Gulf. It was against this background that Lord Curzon gave an address to the chiefs of Gulf tribes in 1903. Its tone expresses the overbearing presence of the British at the time and their determination not to be removed:

> Out of the relations that were thus created over the past hundred years and which by your own consent constituted the British Government, the guardian of international peace, there grew up political ties between the Government of India and yourselves whereby the British Government became your overlords and protectors and you have allegiance with no other power. Sometimes I think that the record is in danger of being forgotten and there are persons who ask 'Why should Great Britain continue to exercise those powers?' The histories of your states and your families and the present conditions of the Gulf are the answer. We were here before any other power in modern times, before any other power had shown its face in these waters. We found strife and we have created order. It was our commerce as well as your security that was threatened and called for protection. At every port along these coasts the subjects of the King of England still reside and trade. The great empire of India, which it is our duty to defend, lies almost at your gates. We saved you from extinction at the hands of your neighbours. We opened these seas to the ships of all nations and enabled their flags to fly in peace. We have not seized or held your territory. We have not destroyed your independence but have preserved it. We are not now going to throw away this century of costly and triumphant enterprise. We shall not wipe out the most unselfish page in history. The peace of these waters must be maintained. Your independence will continue to be upheld and the influence of the British Government must remain supreme.

Curzon's speech may reflect the arrogance of the imperial mind, but it does contain some truths. It was not until the British established trading posts that nomadic tribesmen began to settle. British protection treaties effectively created sheikhdoms, and later oil concessions reinforced them. Britain built a captive market, then supported the Americans in turning it into a reliable oil supplier. They wanted people who were completely indebted to them, but the British presence was not colonisation in the usual sense.

The disintegration of the Ottoman Empire led to a further

strengthening of Britain's position after the First World War. Britain and France, the dominant powers in the League of Nations because of America's refusal to join, were given mandates over areas formerly controlled by Istanbul. British officials in the Middle East settled local boundaries for administrative convenience, often in an arbitrary manner. This sowed the seeds for countless border disputes when the Gulf regained full independence, and was one of the causes of the war in 1991. Sir Percy Cox, the principal British intelligence officer in the Gulf, was an empire-builder who left his personal stamp on the Arab world. The border between Saudi Arabia and Kuwait was partly his work. He kept close contacts with tribal leaders, including the Sauds, who were then exiled in Kuwait. Their kingdom had reached its peak at the end of the eighteenth century, but was in decline until 1890, when the rival el-Rashid family gained control of Riyadh. Abd al-Aziz, son of Prince Abdul Rahman, set out from Kuwait in 1902 with 200 men to regain the throne from Ibn el-Rashid, then Emir of Najd, who was loyal to the Ottoman Empire. Abd al-Aziz's followers discovered that the emir was a man of regular habits, praying in the mosque at dawn every day and then going to his harem. After lying in wait they caught and killed him, seized his palace, declared the restoration of Saudi rule, and re-instituted the teachings of the Wahhabi sect, a form of Islam which had been adopted by the previous Saudi dynasty. Abd al-Aziz became known as Ibn Saud and ruled until his death in 1953. In the early years of his rule, the peninsula was still nominally under the suzerainty of the Ottoman sultan, but a stronger influence came from the government of India, which paid Ibn Saud a monthly salary of £5000 to protect trade routes. Gradually, however, Ibn Saud came to suspect the British of playing a double game, favouring the Hashemites, the rival clan based in the Hejaz in western Saudi Arabia. The two families had always been at odds because of religious and cultural differences. The Hashemites claim to be descended from the Prophet, while the Wahhabi sect is a puritanical movement. The Hashemites were seen by other tribes as being essentially Ottoman, even in their manners. Ibn Saud had a poor opinion of the Bedouin in general. 'Oh, those Bedouins, they know of only two good things – swords and gold,' he said. He had to deal with two different British authorities which had different views on this squabble. The government of India was mainly interested in eastern Saudi Arabia, and cared little for the western-based Hashemites. The Cairo bureau administered a large Middle Eastern area including the

Hejaz and was on good terms with the Hashemites. Ibn Saud assumed that this was British duplicity, not understanding that two agencies of the same empire could disagree. He suspected London of following a policy of divide and rule, balancing between himself and the Hashemites. His view was reinforced by the fact that Britain had installed Hashemite monarchs in other parts of the Middle East, including Iraq and Transjordan (as Jordan was known until 1949). His opportunity to strike back at perfidious Albion would come years later.

The strategic importance of Middle East oil was not fully realised until 1912, when the British navy switched from coal-fired to oil-burning boilers. Oil was already in production in Texas, but Britain wanted assured supplies in waters which it dominated. After discoveries in Persia and Iraq the British made arrangements with local rulers, paying token royalties, while middlemen tried unsuccessfully to develop Saudi Arabia's potential. An American consortium discovered commercial quantities of oil in 1938, but Saudi Arabia remained a British area of influence until the mid-1940s. The early part of the Second World War, before the Japanese attack on Pearl Harbor brought the United States into the conflict, almost exhausted Britain. Although they subsequently fought as allies, the rivalry between Washington and London was as sharp as ever, and the US took advantage of Britain's weakness to usurp its position in the Middle East. Winston Churchill wrote to President Roosevelt saying that it broke his heart to see a friendly nation using Britain's difficult situation to inherit its belongings while it was still alive. After the Yalta conference in 1945 Roosevelt went straight to Egypt to meet Ibn Saud aboard a US warship. He found the king bitterly critical of the British, partly because a request of his for silver to mint currency had gone unheeded. 'The British never keep their word,' Saud said. Roosevelt pointed out that the British were in a difficult position, but added: 'Although they are our friends we are going to deal with you.' London saw Roosevelt's trip as a flagrant theft of British influence, and although Churchill hurried to the Middle East he was unable to repair the damage. The Americans steadily elbowed the British out of all their oil concessions, apart from Persia and some minor holdings. However, Britain retained part of its regional influence for twenty years, enabling it to keep important roles in the production, distribution, and transportation of oil. In every respect the British were forced into the role of lesser partners to the Americans. Leaving aside the cultural element, the main ingredient of the so-called 'special relationship' between Britain and the United States is a shared interest in Middle East oil.

During the post-war period the Middle East overtook earlier oil production centres (the United States, the Soviet Union and the Far East) to become the most important region, producing 40 per cent of world consumption and holding 72 per cent of reserves. It took a quarter of a century for the Arabs to begin turning economic potential into political power. The first suggestions that oil should be used as a weapon came during the 1948 war against Israel, but were dismissed as absurd. Abd el-Rahman Azzam Pasha, Secretary General of the Arab League, went to see Ibn Saud to tell him that many Arabs felt Riyadh should flex its muscles. The warrior king looked astonished. 'I don't understand you. In the old days oil-shows were always there and nothing was ever said about it. We used it for medicinal purposes. Then the foreigners came and began to dig. The foreigners extracted the oil and exported it and paid me for it. Why should I punish them?' It was impossible to convince the old man.

There was more talk of the oil weapon in 1956, but a ban was unnecessary because the pipeline through Syria was blown up and sunken ships made the Suez Canal unnavigable, causing petrol rationing in Europe and forcing the West to reactivate supply lines from the United States developed during the Second World War.

When Israel attacked Egypt, Syria and Jordan in 1967 there were immediate demands for an embargo, but the Six-Day War was over before a decision could be taken. It was considered again at an Arab summit in August 1967, but King Faisal of Saudi Arabia was opposed. 'I don't think oil is a weapon. It is an asset.' He pointed out that Riyadh would be unable to help other Arab countries financially if oil revenue stopped. President Nasser, who tried to resign after the defeat of the Six-Day War but was swept back into office by public acclaim, went to the summit convinced that it would be better to use Saudi money to help Arab countries recover. Riyadh agreed with other Arab oil producers to provide £250 million sterling, half for Egypt and a quarter each to Syria and Jordan.

As the Arab world gathered its strength for a war to recover Jerusalem and territories lost in 1967, there was mounting pressure for oil to be used in the coming battle. King Faisal stood his ground until 1972, but then hinted that he might agree on certain conditions: 'We must be sure we are punishing aggressors and not ourselves.' Faisal argued that a ban would be futile unless Arab armies could sustain the fight for at least two weeks, because at any time fifteen days' supply of oil was on the sea in tankers: 'You must give us time.' He also insisted that the intention to stop exporting oil should be kept secret. The Arab world recalled the simplicity of Ibn Saud, who had been frank enough to say that he could not understand demands for a blockade. Now it faced a more cunning Saudi ruler, apparently adept at finding arguments to frustrate the popular will. But Faisal was also clever enough to judge how long to continue his opposition, and he withdrew it just before the October 1973 war. Everyone knew that Egypt was preparing to attack Israel, but the timing was a well-kept secret. President Sadat partly confided in two people, the Shah of Iran and King Faisal. Visiting the king at the end of August, Sadat said the fight was inevitable and hoped Saudi Arabia would support an oil embargo. The king doubted that the balance of power was in Egypt's favour and wondered whether Egypt and Syria would be able to fight for long enough, but gave Sadat the answer he wanted on oil. Egyptian troops crossed the Suez Canal on 6 October, and almost immediately Faisal kept his word by announcing that oil would play its part, meaning that he would accept an embargo. After a meeting of oil ministers in Kuwait on the 17 October, the first Arab oil embargo began. It was intended to strike at the heart of the West's support for Israel by showing that the Arabs could switch off the prosperity of the developed world. The practical impact on Europe (apart from France, which was exempted) was stunning, but the political blow to Washington was even greater, revealing for the first time the limitations of its influence in the Middle East.

After the war President Sadat attempted to bring about a solution to Arab–Israeli differences by offering Washington a transformed Egyptian position. He believed that making concessions at a time when the Arabs were in a strong position would have a powerful psychological impact on Washington and Tel Aviv. It was a high-risk approach which proved unsuccessful. Sadat's first surprise was Henry Kissinger's reaction to his initiative. Instead of showing interest in the concessions, as Sadat had expected, Kissinger said he could do nothing so long as the oil embargo continued. President Nixon wrote to Sadat afterwards in a similar vein, implying that America's attitude at the Geneva peace talks which were then being convened would depend on the oil situation: 'In order to make it possible for me to move decisively [at the Geneva talks] it is necessary that the discrimination against the United States which the oil embargo represents be brought to an end.' Nixon expressed dismay over a decision by Arab oil ministers on 25 December to increase production to help Japan and some European countries while continuing the ban against the US. Kissinger pressed the point in another letter: 'I want to tell you frankly that this raises the fundamental question as to whether I will be able to continue the role which you and I have discussed at length.'

For all his earlier caution, King Faisal seemed surprised by the strength of Western pressure. The Arab world was beginning to waver, as a letter from Sadat to Kissinger on 23 January 1974 showed: 'Concerning the energy problem, I have explained completely to the oil producing countries. I have told them that the United States will be more positive to the Arabs . . . accept my assurances that the problem of energy is going towards a solution.' At the time attempts to persuade Israel to pull back on the Syrian front were deadlocked for lack of US pressure on Tel Aviv. Kissinger made it clear that there would be no progress until the oil embargo against the US was lifted. Syria's President Assad was furious. President Sadat was adamant. King Faisal, determined not to be accused of letting the side down, insisted that his fellow Arabs make an official request for the embargo to be lifted, stating that they considered it to be 'in the interest of the battle'. Washington had its way, giving nothing in return except a state visit to Egypt by President Nixon, who was glad to get away from the impending Watergate storm.

The embargo was over, although many parties exploited the atmosphere of crisis to push the price of oil to previously unimagined levels. A change in Arab mentality had taken place. In the past any increases in royalties had been in tens of cents per barrel; now the price would jump by tens of dollars. The Arabs thought they had found the confidence to treat oil as Arab property, to be used to Arab advantage.

3

A Decade of Illusions

The morning after the first oil war it seemed that everything had changed. Europeans accustomed to cheap energy suddenly found their jobs, homes and cars under threat. Empty roads in Europe and silent factories in Britain reflected more drastic energy-rationing measures than anything since the Suez crisis. Many thought the West was about to lurch from recession to slump while the Middle East became the new El Dorado. It was a vision drawn in absurd clichés, smatterings of truth creating a distorted whole. The Western economy was to prove resilient while Arabs showed their unreadiness for riches. A prize of unimaginable proportions had been handed to desert people who lacked the history or the culture to absorb it, while Egypt, the centre of Arab experience and culture, received only small change. The masses who had struggled for independence and Arab control of oil production were left out. Gulf rulers now sat at top tables with European royals, while politicians, industrialists and defence salesmen danced attention. Awash with petrodollars, some sheikhs confused wealth with power, flattery with friendship. City-states created more through colonial carelessness than Arab history began to regard themselves as real countries. According to contemporary studies, a third of the Middle East's new wealth was poured into high-technology weapons, in search of a security which would prove flawed. Some countries tried to reproduce entire Western economic systems, everything from factories to racing studs, from hamburger restaurants to wheat farms (incongruously planted in irrigated sand dunes). It would take ten years to realise that money could buy the trappings of a modern society, but not its substance. It was a decade of illusions.

The scale of the oil bonanza seemed beyond the dreams of avarice. In 1970 the United Arab Emirates was earning US$230 million a year; by 1980 it was $19 billion. Algeria went from $272 million to $10.5

billion; Libya from $1.3 million to $22 billion; Iraq from $1230 million to $25 billion; Qatar from $122 million to $5.3 billion; Kuwait from $221 million to $18.6 billion; Saudi Arabia from $1.2 billion to $102 billion. After centuries of poverty the Arab world thought it was rich; it was not. The combined oil income of all Arab countries reached $220 billion a year by the end of the 1980s, roughly equivalent to the gross national product of Spain, and less than that of Italy. In real terms it was not much, but as *cash* it was dazzling; the new rich found it hard to keep a sense of proportion.

Recovering from its initial shock, the West created the International Energy Agency as a counterweight to the oil producers' cartel, with a system of reserves to insulate consumer countries against any future attempt to raise prices suddenly. Bankers were alarmed that Arab disposable income might unbalance the West's economic system. Like a rock falling from a mountain, the danger lay not so much in its size as in its unpredictable destination.

Apart from arms, some Arab money went on gambling and high living, and some was converted into paintings, sculpture and jewellery. King Faisal disapproved but could do nothing. 'Our grandfathers used camels and our fathers went by car and we and our sons use planes, but I am afraid that their grandsons will return to camels, the way they are spending their money,' he said.[1]

It was not just the rich whose values were affected. Huge numbers went abroad to work, leaving their wives to bring up the children. Their remittances introduced strange patterns of consumption which were reinforced when the men returned home with patterns of behaviour they had picked up in Saudi Arabia or the Gulf sheikhdoms. Instead of saving or setting up businesses, many bought videos, gadgets and imported food. Oil wealth disturbed old values and shook the family structure. It is no coincidence that most of the worst crimes in Egypt in recent years were committed by young men whose fathers were caught up in the oil rush.

Not only did Arabs squander their money, they even mortgaged it. William Simons, then US Treasury Secretary, persuaded Riyadh to buy Treasury bonds but relinquish the right to resell them without consultation. Normally, anyone is entitled to buy and sell bonds without asking permission, yet when the Saudis wanted to dispose

---

[1] The king made this remark to the author in June 1971.

of bonds worth $100 million they had to discuss it with Washington.

Much of the oil was in places which barely met the criteria for viability as states. A flag, a national anthem and a seat at the United Nations are only symbols; viability calls for resources and people. The sheikhdoms had the former but not the latter, and were either companies disguised as states, tribes disguised as countries, or a mixture of the two. Their borders had been partly defined by oil company representatives seeking concessions. As sheikhs had no concept of fixed territorial limits, the representatives asked tribesmen where they grazed their animals and fishermen where they landed their nets, and set the boundaries accordingly. As a result many of these countries have unresolved border disputes. These anomalies in no way diminish the legitimacy of the Gulf sheikhdoms. All are sovereign states, members of the United Nations, the Arab League and the Gulf Co-operation Council. Whatever their shortcomings in terms of viability, the political and legal jigsaw of the Middle East would be incomplete without them.

By 1973 Kuwait was a pleasant little city, and it became rich after the oil price spiral. There was a degree of sophistication, with a tradition of vigorous debate, but the Kuwaiti parliament was suppressed by the ruler for long periods. Some hoped Kuwait would develop into an Arab equivalent of the great Italian medieval city-states, but no great patron of the arts like Florence's Medici family emerged. There was a will to achieve a kind of moral authority, as Kuwait's decision to take over the funding of Yemen's education system showed, but this needed time to mature.

The hinterland of the Arab world – Egypt, Sudan, Syria, Morocco – with the mass of population, barely has enough oil for its domestic needs, and some areas have none. Only Iraq enjoys a satisfactory balance between resources and population. So unevenly is the oil distributed that national income per capita is $21,000 in the United Arab Emirates compared with about $500 in Egypt. Seeing itself as a treasury of Arab culture, with its teachers, artists, actors, musicians and singers, Egypt felt unjustly excluded from the Arab world's new-found wealth. Many wondered what exactly was the meaning of an Arab 'nation' if those at its periphery lived in palaces and those at its centre in shanties. The sheikhs, whose fathers had thought territory less important than people, reversed their priorities as their revenues increased. Wealth sowed suspicion between neighbours, especially where borders were ill-defined (as between Saudi Arabia and Oman, between Qatar and Bahrain, and between Kuwait and Iraq). Fearing attack or insurrection, every ruler wanted the capacity to fight his neighbour or suppress his people. It was an arms dealer's paradise.

A stream of bankers, statesmen and company chairmen arriving to pay homage made Arabs feel the rest of the world was on its knees. Even the mighty yen shuddered at the thought of what might have happened to the Japanese economy if the Arabs had not given Japan especially lenient treatment. Tokyo sent deputy prime minister (later prime minister) Takeo Miki to make himself pleasant, distributing pretty vases to people of influence. In the 1970s Arab money and Arab power seemed to be the same thing, and the illusion was encouraged by the Western press. Wrongly assuming that Arab unity in raising oil prices marked the beginning of wider Arab co-ordination, the media predicted a campaign to buy up Western companies. Big industrial names were said to be available for the price of a day or two's oil production. It was a fantasy, but some Arabs behaved as if it were true. Personalised Boeing 747s carried sheikhs around the world, their upper decks converted into royal bedrooms. A play in London's West End[2] featured a British oil company chairman desperate to curry favour with a visiting sheikh. He tells his wife: 'Whatever he wants, arrange it for him.' When she announces: 'Darling, he wants me,' he replies: 'Oh dear. Well, close your eyes and think of England.' The play ran for several years.

The Saudi monarch King Khaled was in poor health, and his half-brother Crown Prince Fahd (who would succeed him in 1982) already held the reins. After a fortune-teller told Fahd no harm would come to him so long as his son Prince Abd el-Aziz was near him, the crown prince insisted on taking the boy everywhere, even to the White House when he visited President Reagan in 1980. 'Go on, salute your uncle Reagan,' he said in front of the television cameras. Such an incident would have been unimaginable a few years earlier, but no one thought it odd; if anything, it was charming. The Gulf royals could do as they liked.

The illusion of power was supported by a club which some called the institution of the summit, a supra-governmental body of kings,

[2] *Close Your Eyes and Think of England*

sheikhs, emirs and presidents which met once or twice a year. They ruled the Arab world without constitutional restraints, assisted by aides and consultants who wielded immense power.

A rung below the summit came high-powered oilers of wheels and runners of errands, some Western and some Arab. The former were mostly international bureaucrats, diplomats or company chairmen, quiet, serious and hard-working, with an air of old money. The Arabs were rougher diamonds with a wheeler-dealer mentality, a mixture of palace advisers, middlemen and traders.

Among the first group were men like the Comte du Meranche, head of French external security, very much the invisible man. His precise mind seemed to have tabs on everything that mattered in the Middle East. A former army officer, he dressed with the elegance of the French aristocracy yet spoke the English of a Home Counties squire. Two armed guards always walked a few paces ahead of him. Another was David Rockefeller, prince of New York in all but title, ruling from the chairman's suite at the Chase Manhattan Bank and the offices of Middle Eastern Oil. He was full of drive, well-informed, always probing for insights. Kermit Roosevelt, grandson of President Theodore Roosevelt, was another. He originally came to the Middle East as a young journalist but moved into intelligence. He was not an easy man to listen to, as he had a bad stutter and was given to long pauses. Few would have thought such a diffident man could lead a CIA operation, yet the Shah of Iran said of him: 'I am indebted by my throne to God, my people and you.' As well as this quiet American there was also a silent German, Herr Hans-Jurgen Wischewski, minister of state, a subdued, disciplined, hard-working individual with tremendous energy, ever whispering messages in Arab ears.

Eugene Black had been head of the World Bank and then became special consultant to the Emir of Kuwait and later the Kuwaiti Investment Fund, remaining active until he died in his eighties. He was a straightforward international bureaucrat with a robust sense of humour. The Arabs pulled his leg about his former role, because it was during his term that the World Bank withdrew a loan for Egypt to construct the Aswan High Dam. A teasing song much enjoyed by Arabs celebrated Cairo's success in building the dam (made possible by Moscow) without US help.

Some Arab diplomats and middlemen now had frequent access to the highest levels of Western government. In the past it had always been the other way around. As early as the 1920s British and American

wheeler-dealers were trying to persuade Arab rulers to accept oil exploration, and some came to have great personal influence. One of them
was St John Philby, whose son Kim later defected to the Soviet Union
after working as a double agent for the British secret service MI6 and
the KGB. The elder Philby acted as a go-between for oil companies,
as he had access to Ibn Saud, the Saudi king. As the dreams of the
thirties became the realities of the sixties, a group of powerful men
assembled round each Gulf ruler, playing a complex and important
role. By 1974 every state had its secret service whose chiefs, together
with the ruler's confidants and senior officials, formed an inner administrative alliance. Beyond them there was an outer circle containing
four elements: representatives of foreign intelligence services, confidants of sheikhs and kings, oil company representatives and arms
salesmen. All these people had their roles, but the West tended to
assume that they also had influence. Some did, some did not. Feigned
influence was sometimes indistinguishable from the real thing. They
were essentially working for themselves.

The influence of senior Arab diplomats grew immensely. Prince
Bandar, son of Prince Sultan, the Saudi defence minister, had been
sent to the United States for air force training. He was a shy young
officer at first, but soon began to lobby in Washington for his country
to be allowed to buy AWACS, the giant radar surveillance planes
which had become a status symbol for rising powers. Through lobbying he acquired connections, and when he was appointed ambassador
all doors were open, including the Oval Office, whose incumbent was
already known to him. During the 1970s a secret fund, known as the
Safari Club, was created at the suggestion of the CIA, with huge sums
of Arab and Iranian money being used to finance anti-Communist
causes. The aim was to avoid President Nixon, and later presidents
Ford and Reagan, having to approach Congress for funds for covert
operations. Arabs contributed to the destabilisation of Mengistu Haile
Mariam's government in Ethiopia by funding the Eritrean separatist
movement. Arabs financed the Mujahedeen guerrillas fighting the
Afghan government from bases in Pakistan. Arab money played a role
in the Iran–Contra scandal and in US operations in Costa Rica and
Panama, and helped Jonas Savimbi's UNITA movement in southern
Angola to fight the Soviet-supported government. These and other
causes brought George Bush, then director of the CIA, into contact
with influential Arabs, including Prince Bandar. People who moved
at that level were caught up in a strange mix of ends and means,

money and power, secrecy and slaughter.

Some played many parts. Kamal Adham, a short, plumpish man with prematurely white hair, was director of Saudi intelligence, counsellor to the king and brother of Queen Effat (wife of King Faisal), as well as being an arms dealer, an oil trader and the initiator of Japan's oil deal with Saudi Arabia. He was extremely intelligent and charming, but was obsessed by the fear that Muammar Gadaffi had hired 'Carlos' the terrorist to kidnap him. At times he practically confined himself to his house and watched videos, but he was a rich source of information and indiscretions. His private plane was kept constantly at the ready and could fly anywhere with just an hour's notice to the crew.

Adnan Khashoggi, the Arab middleman best loved by gossip columnists, seemed to be in perpetual motion between President Marcos of the Philippines, the Shah of Iran, President Sadat, Gina Lollobrigida and many others. He once estimated his annual expenses at $40 million, but fell on harder times through his links with Ferdinand and Imelda Marcos, only to bounce back after court proceedings in America cleared him. His yacht *Nabilla* was a travelling guesthouse for the glitterati, complete with nightclub. He once flew 300 guests to join him and the yacht in Puerto Rico to celebrate his birthday. Everything about his set was flashy, dripping with diamonds. Another big spender, although of a different ilk, was Rafik el-Hariri, an immensely rich contractor and trader from southern Lebanon who has business partnerships with many of the most influential members of the Saudi royal family. He has a yacht the size of a large steamer and a lifestyle to match, but there is also a serious side to his personality. He and his wife, who is Palestinian, gave a fund of $50 million to finance several charitable projects in the Fertile Crescent, including higher education for poor Arab youths.

Before the Libyan revolution Yehia Omar, an Egyptian, was very active in the arms trade. After finding work in Libya as a police officer he rose to become a counsellor to King Idris. When Gadaffi overthrew the monarchy in 1969 Omar was smuggled out in the last plane to leave Wheelus, the US airbase near Tripoli. He became a counsellor to the Sultan of Oman and a good friend of Presidents Sadat, Mubarak and even Gadaffi.

It was not unusual for influential middlemen to have private planes, yachts, secure telephone systems, and homes covered in communications antennae and protected by foreign security firms.

Visitors would be met at the door by ex-Marines while being filmed by hidden video cameras. The middlemen took their guards wherever they went, and host countries rarely asked awkward questions about guns.

Many in this group gave the impression of being larger than life. Mahdi el-Tager, counsellor to the late Sheikh Rashid El-Maktoum, ruler of Dubai, became the UAE's ambassador to the whole of Western Europe. On a typical day in the 1970s he would fly to London for lunch at 10 Downing Street with Prime Minister James Callaghan, then leave for Paris for a meeting at the Elysée Palace the next day. This level of access reflected the huge improvement in the Arab world's standing after the 1973–74 oil crisis. It also made life easy for roving ambassadors; having the freedom to come and go almost as he pleased, it was sufficient for el-Tager to spend only one week a month in Europe.

El-Tager made his fortune trading in gold, and went into partnership with Sheikh Rashid. He once defined 'medium-sized' gold traders as those who had between $200 and $400 million, and in 1980 he estimated his personal fortune as about £3 billion. He used some of it to buy castles in Britain and France, including a château which had once belonged to Henry Ford II. It cost him $6 million, yet he bought it after spending only ten minutes there, not bothering to look at the bedrooms. He was also a collector, with some 6000 rare carpets and many precious stones. Visitors to his home were sometimes shown a huge pearl, one of the most important in the world, with a crust of diamonds. He kept it in a plastic bag of the type issued by airport duty-free shops, with a cigarette advertisement on the side.

People in the Arab world have always called each other 'brother', but it sounded more convincing thirty years ago than it does now. The brotherly feeling began to fall apart with the huge movements of manpower during the seventies and eighties. The lure of black gold drew vast numbers to seek their fortune in the Gulf states, and their remittances helped keep state economies afloat. By 1980 there were 1.5 million Egyptians working in Iraq, half a million in Saudi Arabia, and a million in other Gulf states, sending home earnings of about $11 billion. The cost in terms of brotherhood was high: the oil sheikhs treated Egyptians, Yemenis, Moroccans and Palestinians as second-class citizens, and the guestworkers reacted by adopting a mercenary attitude. The ill-feeling was not helped by the system of patronage in

Saudi Arabia, under which no one can work without a Saudi guarantor. The guarantors tend to be people who do practically no work themselves.

Another illusion of brotherhood, of an entirely different kind, lies in the make-up of the Saudi royal family. Immense strains over the succession and the distribution of wealth within the family threaten to tear it apart in the years ahead. Under the current succession rules, drawn up to take account of polygamy and tribalism, those sons of King Abd al-Aziz (Ibn Saud) whose mothers were foreigners or non-tribal Saudis are excluded from the succession. Those currently in line all have mothers from Saudi tribes. King Fahd, for example, is the son of a Sudairey mother, while Crown Prince Abdullah's mother is from the Shamar tribe. Within these restrictions, the rules provide for succession on a basis known as '*Al-Arshad*', meaning the 'most eligible', of the sons of Ibn Saud. No provision is made for the following generation, and the youngest of Ibn Saud's sons is now sixty-five. In the next five or ten years the Saudi monarchy will have to introduce a new rule, which will not be easy.

When Ibn Saud died in 1953 he left thirty-seven sons, who produced 191 grandsons and (up to mid-1991) 834 great-grandsons. The total family, including the descendants of brothers of Ibn Saud, but *excluding* all the women, is estimated at between 6500 and 7000. Huge stakes are at play, as whichever branch of the family succeeds to the throne will have at its disposal a fifth of the total oil revenue. The family takes its licence from a verse in the Koran: 'And know that out of all the booty that ye may acquire [in war], a fifth share is assigned to God – and to the Apostle, and to near relatives, orphans, the needy and the wayfarer, if ye believe in God.' As the absolute monarch of the country which contains Islam's two most sacred sites, the king regards himself as the Prophet's representative and feels entitled to a fifth of the money. Some would regard this as stretching the Koran's meaning, as the share was not meant for the Prophet (or his representative) personally, but was intended to finance the mission of Islam.

When the Saudi dynasty took power in the eighteenth century, and again after its restoration in 1902, it regarded the Koran as the constitution of the kingdom. No other written document was to be above or equal to it as a source of law. In the eighteenth and nineteenth centuries, taxes paid by pilgrims on the *Haj* were the king's principal source of revenue, and administering the pilgrimage was his most important duty. Under this system the one-fifth share was considered an acceptable arrangement, but the advent of oil revenue changed the picture.

The king is obliged to devote a large part of his revenue to keeping his relatives happy, or at least quiet. The iniquity of this system became clear after 1964, when King Saud was forced by the royal family to abdicate in favour of his half-brother Crown Prince Faisal. There were good reasons for the decision, but its financial impact on the family was enormous. Once Faisal took over, the glory, money and power were transferred to his branch. He was assassinated in 1975 by a nephew who was unable to endure his misfortune. Details of the king's methods of distributing wealth within the family rarely emerge, but documents showing the use of oil for this purpose have come to light. On 19 and 20 February 1980 two transfers of oil totalling one million barrels were made to Princess Modi Abdulaziz El Saud, at a price of $31 a barrel. She passed it the same day to a Lebanese businessman called Mulsoor Shafi Daddough, who sold it at about $40 a barrel, leaving the princess with a profit after paying all costs of at least $5 million. While this system may hold tensions down for the moment, younger members of the royal family are already jockeying for position, anticipating the change in the succession rules. The two elder sons of Prince Sultan (minister of defence and second in line of succession after Prince Abdullah) are already preparing themselves, and both have been strengthened by the Kuwait conflict. Prince Bandar, ambassador in Washington, claims the diplomatic laurels while Prince Khalid sees himself as the supreme military commander. Some fear that rivalry between cousins could eventually lead to civil war.

Ibn Saud's generation understood that there was an implicit contract between tribal elements and sheikhs, effectively a constitutional balance. Before oil, the tribal wealth consisted mainly of animals, while royal revenue came from taxes, earnings from pilgrims taking part in the Haj, Ibn Saud's salary from the British government, and various other sources. Although an absolute monarch, the king maintained a balance, leaving a certain amount of power to some tribes and handing a slice of wealth to others. The new generation thinks it has a right to rule, and it is becoming ruthless.

The October 1973 war with Israel gave the Arabs a better appreciation of the need for up-to-date weapons. Soviet-made Malutka anti-tank missiles and Strella anti-aircraft missiles proved highly effective against Israeli armaments. Gulf rulers were therefore anxious to use part of their oil windfall to buy the best military hardware. Between 1970 and 1980 Arabs received roughly $2400 billion from oil, and spent about $1000 billion on defence, including $155 billion on weapons. Saudi Arabia's $30 billion order in 1985 for sixty-four Tornado aircraft at £20 million each, sixty-four training planes at £10 million each, and airports, runways, equipment and spare parts was one of the biggest orders. Western governments were able to invest in research while keeping their arms factories busy, middlemen made fortunes, and bankers welcomed the order as a sound way of recycling Arab money. Many would argue, however, that the security the money bought was partly illusory, especially in the case of small sheikhdoms. Kuwait, borrowing an idea from Israel, thought it could compensate for its lack of military manpower by buying devastating air power. It spent huge sums on aircraft, missiles and training, but in August 1990 the air force was to give little return on the investment. The government tried to remove the planes to safety in Saudi Arabia rather than lose them in a hopeless fight, but was too late. Most fell to the Iraqis.

Any country enjoying an increase in income undergoes what economists call an inevitable degree of development. No one would want to discourage badly needed infrastructure improvements and better services, but the kind of development undertaken in the Gulf was of a different and more questionable order. The aim was to create modern cities from scratch, telescoping an evolution that took centuries in Europe into a mere ten or fifteen years. To a non-Arab visitor it might well appear that this was achieved, but that would be a superficial judgement. In any normal economic system decisions emerge gradually in response to specific needs or pressures. In the Gulf there was an attempt to buy entire urban and rural schemes, with all their supporting infrastructure, off the shelves of designers who had developed them for the West. The result was forests of concrete and tracts of desert transformed into greenness; impressive, if one overlooked the cost. Wheat proved ten times more expensive to produce in Saudi Arabia than the world market price, because irrigation depended on artesian wells or distilling seawater in oil-burning plants. Too much cement and too many tractors were illusions of development. It was not that nothing was achieved; what was missing was value for money. The Kuwaitis were more sensible, setting up the Kuwaiti Investment Fund to place capital of about $150 billion on foreign markets. When the oil price dropped, their investment income equalled that from oil, and during the Iraqi occupation it enabled the government in exile to assist large numbers of its citizens and place contracts for post-liberation repair work.

The pace of change was so rapid that people barely had time to adjust. In the early days Sheikh Shakhbout of Abu Dhabi kept his oil royalties in a room at the palace and complained that rats ate the paper money. The manager of a British bank tried to convince him that there was a more modern way of storing cash, and eventually the sheikh agreed to an experiment. One morning he deposited a million pounds sterling in cash, then withdrew it again before closing time. He repeated the process every day until he was satisfied. Only then did Abu Dhabi join the banking system.

In Saudi Arabia there was a tendency to build on a grand scale for reasons of pride rather than utility. The Saudi monarch prefers to be known as 'Custodian of the Two Holy Places', underlining his country's status as the birthplace of Islam, and Mecca and Medina play a big part in the country's self-image, encouraging Saudis to see themselves as natural Arab leaders. That feeling had a strange expression in 1974 when King Faisal ordered a census, but prevented its publication because it showed that Saudi Arabia contained only four million people, including one million Yemenis. The king thought the figures were beneath his country's dignity.

In the past the Arab world had arrangements to make its rulers available to their subjects, but audiences took the form of petitions rather than discussion, and focused on an individual's needs. Most areas also had family councils within the ruling circle, but no real attempt was made to consult the people. Kuwait and Bahrain were exceptions, although their lively parliaments were often slapped down by their rulers. Most Gulf countries have seen no class development; power remains either entirely in the hands of the ruler or in a tacit understanding between the royal family and the bourgeoisie. The rulers hold elections because they want to imitate the developed world, but they are usually a sham. Democracy cannot be grafted onto an old system; it has to develop gradually, marking its progress through increasing degrees of participation and expression. It may seem impressive to have a House of Deputies, but it means nothing if the deputies represent nobody. Throughout the Arab world sheikhs, emirs, kings and presidents rule and spend money without meaningful consultation or constitutional checks. Democracy remains a hope, not a reality.

After the Arabs' moral success in the October 1973 war President Sadat believed that only the United States could make Israel accept a lasting solution, a conviction which led him to hand over the reins to Washington. President Carter brought the Israelis and Egyptians together, but other Arab countries refused to participate. The Camp David agreements were stillborn.

In the years after Camp David a mood of disillusionment overtook Egypt, coinciding with increased economic hardships. Food riots in January 1977 rocked the country and threw Sadat's leadership into question. Under pressure to repair his image, the president undertook a spectacular diplomatic initiative. His visit to Jerusalem in 1977 was thought to represent a historic turning point, but it had no sequel. Many thought his hidden motive was to gain substantial US aid for Egypt, even at the cost of losing all Arab aid, but this was not so. Sadat accepted Henry Kissinger's argument that 70 per cent of Arab–Israeli differences were psychological, and that security problems would be solved if Israel felt safe. Egyptians felt a certain pride in their leader commanding world attention, but beyond that Sadat's initiative failed to gain general acceptance. It is a maxim of the Arab world that there can be no war against Israel without Egypt, but that Egypt cannot make peace without other Arabs. The illusion of peace lay in Sadat's attempt to ignore that truth.

A subsidiary illusion was that of Egyptian friendship with Washington. For years Egypt lived in hope of being rewarded for making peace, but it received little, while the switch from Soviet to American weapons proved costly. Moscow charged 1.7 billion roubles for arms supplied between 1956–1967 and 1969–1971, of which Cairo paid 500 million roubles. There is an outstanding agreement covering the balance. Between 1975 and 1990 Egypt ran up military hardware debts to Washington of $7 billion, which was repaid several times over in interest. The equipment fought no battles, nor was it intended that it should do so. The burden of debt would by now be intolerable but for President Bush's decision to wipe the slate clean in return for Egyptian co-operation during the Kuwait crisis.

*

The incumbent of the Peacock Throne personified the decade of illusions. The Shah of Iran poured money into armaments and industrialisation but drove the masses into the arms of the ayatollahs through his autocratic ways. Many encouraged his imaginings, including President Carter, who told him six months before the revolution that Iran was an island of peace and prosperity in a sea of trouble and poverty. When the Iranian revolution began, Carter was at Camp David with President Sadat and Menachem Begin discussing Israeli–Egyptian peace. There was little he could do for the Shah apart from making a sympathetic phone call. The revolution was already unstoppable, and its effects would be felt throughout the Islamic world.

4

A Return to Fundamentals

The vapours of a lost decade penetrated the soul of the Arab nation. Everywhere the masses looked they saw corruption, broken dreams, tainted values, humiliation, disorientation. 1973 was remembered as a moment of fading hope, its heroes forgotten or discredited. President Sadat, once the prince of peace, was now an angry, lonely figure, regarded with contempt by Arabs outside Egypt. With Cairo out of the equation Tel Aviv's stature increased dramatically, at least in diplomatic and economic terms, with the US looming behind it. No Arab now trusted Washington, and many distrusted each other. Damascus brooded, feeling rejected by Cairo; Baghdad was wrapped up in itself; Saudi Arabia kept quiet; Sudan and Yemen were forgotten. The Arab nation was losing its cohesion. None of the oil revenue filtered down to the streets, and the gap between rich and poor yawned wider. Sheikhs counted their gold and pretended not to notice the envy all around them. A lack of moral leadership made millions of Arab minds receptive to the call of the Iranian revolution across the Gulf, reminding them vaguely of values embedded in their faith. The disaffected masses rediscovered their religious heritage with an enthusiasm which took everyone by surprise. It was not that Islam had been neglected during the decade of illusions – more that its commandments had ceased to be taken seriously. Islam was about to renew itself, resuming its role as an anchor for millions who were spiritually adrift. It was time for a return to fundamentals.

In different circumstances Ayatollah Khomeini would have had little impact in the Arab world. A frail old man making religious broadcasts in Persian from Paris was irrelevant, or so the Arab merchants and intelligentsia thought. They failed to realise that much had changed lower down the ladder. Khomeini's message was able to cross the linguistic barrier because of a vacuum on the other side, an absence of political legitimacy among Arab leaders. None of them had been chosen by those they governed, and leaders who had had popular support were now dead. King Abd al-Aziz of Saudi Arabia had come to his throne by killing his rival, but was seen as the unifier of his kingdom. President Nasser achieved power through a revolution, yet became an inspiration for the Arab nation. Since their deaths no one of comparable stature had appeared.

A huge change in the population distribution of the Arab world was under way, emptying the countryside and pouring unusable manpower into the cities. The population of Cairo grew from four million to 8.2 million in a decade. Drawn by illusions of riches, peasants besieged the concrete oasis thirsting for work. Finding little or none, they settled down to wait on the fringes. They could see the wealth, but could not work out how to secure part of it for themselves. The ostentation of those who had it fanned the anger of those left out. Among many who worried about the trend was a prominent Italian-Swiss family which owned the most famous patisserie and food emporium in Egypt. The Groppis had moved to Cairo in the nineteenth century during a cotton boom caused by the American Civil War, which disrupted supplies from Confederate states. They did well under the monarchy until 1952, when the 'Free Officers' ousted King Farouk. They came through the fifties, a period of socialist revolution, without their business being nationalised, and continued to prosper under Nasser and Sadat. But they could not escape being observed by hungry eyes, and by the end of the 1970s the last of the Groppis wondered whether he should be more alarmed by the menace of the poor or the insensitivity of the rich. 'I don't know where all this is going to lead. We have lived here all our lives and I am afraid for the first time,' he said. A competitive spending mentality had developed among entrepreneurs, who used their weddings, or those of their daughters, to flaunt their success. A few days after catering for one large reception Groppi was approached by a customer who asked what it had cost. Instead of gasping when told that it had come to 170,000 Egyptian pounds, the customer ordered the same, but bigger. 'I want it to cost more than 200,000 pounds,' he said. Detecting the beginnings of a social catastrophe, the Groppis sold up and left at the beginning of the 1980s. Ironically the purchaser was a member of the fundamentalist Muslim Brotherhood, which promptly banned the sale of alcohol and pork. Others more adventurous than the new owner of 'Groppis'' took over the market in catering to the wealthy.

As the cities swelled they took on a structure new to the Arab

world. The centres became the preserve of the rich. They were surrounded by a small ring of the people who served them, and then by
a huge outer belt of the discontented jobless. Danger signals appeared
in Beirut, with the flight of wealth to France and the subsequent civil
wars. Cairo released its tensions more slowly, and largely escaped
serious eruptions, partly because of differences of culture and history
between Egypt and Lebanon, partly because it was a much more
homogeneous community. Sadat responded to discontent by imposing
a series of repressive laws and locking up his critics. The masses were
indifferent to these changes, having long since lost faith in socialism,
government and justice. Nor were they impressed by President Sadat's
idea that Egypt could turn its back on its past and join a richer
club of states. During the Camp David negotiations Sadat's Arab
neighbours had tried to dissuade him from making a separate peace
with Israel by offering Egypt a subsidy of $5 billion a year for ten
years. King Hassan sent Ahmed Ben Suda, chief of the royal cabinet,
to see Sadat, but the Egyptian leader scoffed at the offer: 'Do you
think I care about that? I want to join the advanced and rich! Whatever
money I'm given, I don't want to stay in that gang.' In opting out of
the Arab pack, he left the way open for Baghdad to take the mantle
of Arab leadership.

The masses were looking for new certainties, but what they found
were old ones, reminders that Islam is in essence a revolt of the poor.
The Prophet Mohammed depended on fighters from the Mustadafeen,
the exploited weak and poor, to help him overcome the hostility of
the wealthy. Mecca was ruled by the Mustaqbireen, meaning the
self-inflated rich and powerful, whose commercial interests were
threatened by the Koran, the divine message conveyed through
Mohammed. His teachings, compiled to form the Sunna, retained
their relevance through the centuries, and were a constant solace for
the oppressed. The effect of the Iranian revolution was to rekindle the
original energy of these texts through fresh interpretations.

It was by no means the first attempt to return to the essentials
of Islam, rooting out later aberrations. One of the most famous and
recent was the Wahhabi movement, which sprang up in the Najd
region in the eighteenth century and became the official Saudi sect.
It aimed to recapture the purity of Islam in its original form, rejecting
all innovations. Other revivalist movements sprang up in Sudan and
Libya, while in Egypt the Salafi movement tried to blend the basic
principles of Islam with modern ideas. Sheikh Mohamed Abdu, one

of the great Arab figures of the nineteenth century and early twentieth century, recognised that there was no contradiction between ideas of modernisation and the principles of Islam. His interpretation of modern ideas in the light of basic principles led to an evolution of the faith.

The Muslim Brotherhood was founded in Egypt in 1928 by a follower of the Salafi movement, but it took a different direction, treating Islam as a fighting force. Under the terms of the Anglo–Egyptian Treaty of 1936, Britain gradually withdrew its troops, but retained a garrison guarding the Suez Canal. The Brotherhood's military wing, known as the Special Discipline, attacked not only British troops but everything deemed symbolic of imperialism or decadence, including cinemas and clubs in Cairo. King Farouk (Egypt's last monarch) tried to use it for his own purposes, but later suppressed it. President Nasser was at first sympathetic to the Brotherhood, but eventually banned it. In the 1980s the Syrian branch was involved in conflicts with Communists and Ba'ath Party members, with many killings on both sides, until it was crushed by the Syrian army's harsh reprisals.

Islam was always a political as well as religious movement, and it also had its cultural and social side. By 1980 it was beginning to feel the influence of Muslims from Pakistan and India, where Islam had acquired a different flavour. Asian Muslims tended to take the Koran literally, while Arabs were more inclined to interpret it. Reading the texts in their own language enabled Arabs to set it in historical context, keeping in mind observations by Arab religious authorities, but Asians were less able to look beyond it – partly because other works had not been translated into their languages, but more importantly because the Arabic language was the tongue of Islam. Deprived of linguistic context the Koran inevitably takes on a slightly different character, forcing non-Arab readers to rely more on the texts than on the way the ideas are expressed. This was all the more significant in Islamabad because Islam was the *raison d'être* of the Pakistani state. As it came into existence through the partition of India into Hindu and Muslim countries at the moment of independence from Britain in 1947, a separatist or isolationist mentality was to be expected. Before partition Muslims had felt an ill-treated minority in the subcontinent, and had developed a defensive outlook. Unable to fight a numerically superior enemy, the Indian Muslim would turn to God in his conscience and prepare himself, through education, prayer and arms, for a future struggle. Partition brought a huge migration of Muslims from all over India to West and East Pakistan (now Bangladesh), but did not end the bad blood. Islam in Pakistan came to mirror the national personality, a mixture of intense nationalism, hostility towards the 'other', and a militant spirit, almost a propensity for violence. Many Pakistanis were influenced by Abu-el-A'ala El-Mawdudi, a Pakistani newsman and agitator, whose five major books, written between 1937 and 1941 conveyed these traits. All his work was translated into Arabic in the late 1950s and early sixties, and had a considerable impact on a new generation of Muslim Brotherhood members and other Arabs. His ideas were also taken up by Sayed Kotb, a member of the Muslim Brotherhood whose book *In the Shades of the Koran* was a bestseller.

Such men had an impact in big Arab cities, where the idea of Islam as a fighting force caught on more easily than in the countryside, and within a few years their ideas found substantial followings. Islam had migrated from the Arab world to the east, then returned home with an Indian accent and a strong militant message which made the masses in Cairo, Beirut and elsewhere more receptive when the Islamic revolution exploded in Tehran. The poverty belts around the big cities became a natural breeding ground for a militant, anti-elitist, anti-Western view of Islam. Amid chaos and confusion and a loss of identity among people displaced from their home villages, Islam was not just a refuge but a battle cry. The new urban poor of Egypt took their model from Islamabad and Tehran and were not put off by being on the opposite side of a long-standing religious divide.

The schism in Islam stems from a dispute which occurred a quarter of a century after Mohammed's death in A.D.632. He was succeeded by Abu Bakr, his father-in-law, followed in 634 by Umar and then Uthman. All had the title of Caliph, which means deputy. After Uthman's death Ali, son-in-law of Mohammed, became the fourth Caliph, but he was opposed by the Ummayad clan of Mecca. The dispute was settled by arbitration in favour of Mu'awiya, candidate of the rich merchants, who became the fifth Caliph and founded the Ummayad dynasty. Ali, whose period as Caliph had lasted only four years, was murdered two years later, but he remains a powerful symbol of revolt against the wealthy. His followers became known as Shias, meaning partisans, opposing the Sunnis, or traditionalists.

Shia teachings have always had a natural appeal on the impoverished Indian subcontinent, as well as in Iran and in the poorer and more crowded parts of the Arab world. Egypt is an exception to the rule, having a Sunni majority despite its high population and low average income, but the schism tends to be felt less strongly there, and may even be irrelevant to Cairo's angry millions. Ayatollah Khomeini used to say that Egypt was Shia at heart but Sunni by law, as a result of being ruled by the 'Fatimide' Shi'i dynasty, which made a great impact on the Egyptian soul and behaviour.

After the Ottoman conquest of Egypt in 1517 the institution of the Caliphate fell into the hands of the Turks. As the Turkish Caliphs spoke little or no Arabic, they tended to put off changes need to keep Islamic *'Ijtihad'* (thought) up to date, with the result that the texts became archaic. After the disintegration of the empire the Caliphate was abolished in 1923 by Kemal Ataturk, founder of modern Turkey, but there was an attempt to revive it in Saudi Arabia. The Hashemites in the Hejaz, who claim direct descent from Mohammed, had always seen themselves as natural candidates for the Caliphate, but were challenged by the alliance of Wahhibism and the Saud family, who were building a dynasty. Most other Arab countries lost interest in the issue.

Almost a year after the Iranian revolution of 1978, a radical group in Mecca seized control of one of Islam's holiest places. There is a loosely-held belief among Sunnis that at the beginning of every new century of the Hijree calendar, which takes Mohammed's migration from Mecca and his journey to Medina as its starting point, a new religious innovator comes forward to renew Islam. The fourteenth Islamic century was just beginning when Guhaiman El-Otaybi, a member of the Oteiba tribe, began preaching the appearance of a new Mahdi. He and his followers went to the Holy Shrine in Mecca at dawn, pushed aside the man who was leading the prayers, and declared the arrival of a man called Mohamed Ben Ahmed El Kahtani, said to be a descendant of the Prophet. He was coming, they said, with a new message warning against decadence and corruption in the Islamic and Arab world and against the influence of Washington and the servants of the oil companies. The rebels demanded the creation of an Islamic state in Saudi Arabia and a break of ties with the West. They had machine guns, revolvers and ammunition which they had smuggled in over the previous two months. The entire Arab world was in a state of shock. The revolt was eventually crushed with help from French anti-terrorist forces after King Khaled had approached President Giscard d'Estaing. Saudi Arabia was virtually paralysed for two weeks during the occupation.

The success of the Iranian revolution stemmed partly from the fact that many ordinary soldiers and non-commissioned officers in the Iranian army supported it. The Mecca revolt, too, had a degree of support in the local garrison, but not enough to cause a wider uprising. In Egypt, the assassination of President Sadat at a military parade in 1981 was carried out by a military–religious fraternity. Khaled Ahmed Shawki el-Islambouli, the captain who led them, belonged to a group of fundamentalists who believed they had a religious duty to kill Sadat.

In the universities, the Islamic trend captured the mood of student associations, and women students lowered their hems and adopted the veil, while Muslim Brotherhood candidates were elected to seats in the Egyptian and Jordanian parliaments and won power in municipal elections in Algeria. The Islamic tidal wave swept aside rival thought systems, especially Marxism. Arab Communists had struggled for decades to revolutionise the masses with their creed, but had found little public enthusiasm. When they saw that the old faith had reinvigorated itself and the people, achieving the effect they had long dreamt of, many Communists began questioning their beliefs. After rediscovering Islam some went on to become diehard fundamentalists.

There was much discussion in Egypt about applying Islamic principles in government, but this was something of a puzzle. What were Islamic foreign relations, or Islamic economics? No one seemed sure, but many recalled that politicians had used Islam to support their purposes in the past. President Sadat had wrapped his peace policies in militant Islamic packaging in the hope of increasing their appeal to Egyptians. A verse from the Koran, 'And if they lean to peace, go with it and depend on Allah' was displayed on banners in many parts of Egypt during the period between Sadat's visit to Jerusalem in 1978 and the signing of the Camp David peace agreement.

Some sheikhs in the religious establishment allowed themselves to be exploited by political and commercial forces. When sales of Pepsi-Cola dropped sharply because of a rumour that it contained a derivative of pigs' livers called pepsin, sheikhs came forward to assure the public that this was untrue, and sales recovered.

One of the effects of the Iranian revolution was to make people throughout the Arab world more aware of Islamic rules concerning money. According to *Sharia* law, profit and loss in normal trading is *'halal'* (Islamically acceptable), but depositing money in an interest-bearing account is *'haram'* (Islamically prohibited). The difference lies in the risk factor: the use of money to make more money without risk is regarded as *'rebba'* (usury). During the late 1970s and early 1980s many influential sheikhs gave their support to 'Islamic investment funds', which were devised as a way of investing without breaking the rules. Investors were paid variable rates of return, reflecting (at least in theory) the success of the funds, thus giving an element of risk. Some funds paid as much as 25 to 30 per cent a year, while well-known people often received 60 to 80 per cent. Even higher rates were available to influential individuals included in lists described as the *'baraka'* (the blessed).

Advertisements for the funds started to appear throughout the Arab media under Islamic slogans. A number of prominent sheikhs appeared on television to promote particular funds, confirming that investing with them was *'halal'* and describing them as 'the true Islamic way of investment'. Others were appointed by the funds as Islamic *Sharia* counsellors. The funds further enhanced their Islamic credentials by financing popular editions of religious books. Financial newspapers in the West began to report on the funds' activities, and it was widely believed that they were speculating in precious metals, real estate and currency transactions. A number of former government ministers went into their service as 'consultants', although it was later shown that they knew little or nothing of the funds' activities. By 1986 the funds accounted for 26 per cent of all advertising in the Egyptian media.

More than a million Egyptians were working in other Arab countries, and they often had difficulty in remitting their earnings to their families in Egypt. Black-market money changers performed this service, and became involved in advising customers on how to invest their money. Some of the money changers went on to create their own investment funds.

In its 1984 report, the Central Bank of Egypt pointed out that some of the funds were not investing their money but simply using new deposits to pay interest on funds received earlier. The report correctly warned that the bubble was about to burst. Nevertheless, fund owners continued for some time to enrich themselves.

The most important fund, known as Al-Rayan, went bankrupt after a scandal involving sex and drugs. There was some irony in this, as the owners, a father and his three sons, wore long beards, a symbol of piety in Islam. When their case went to court it was disclosed that they were barely literate, and alleged that they had previously been involved in illegal currency exchanges on the black market.

Of ninety-one funds created, eighty-five eventually folded, and in some cases fund owners disappeared with hundreds of millions of pounds' worth of deposits.

The Islamic revival also caused upheavals in the worlds of television and publishing. A sheikh called Mutwali el-Sharawi became a legend in Egypt and Saudi Arabia for his interpretations on television of the Koran. Neglected Islamic classics became bestsellers, although their authors had been dead for hundreds of years. Paperback editions were read avidly and sometimes memorised by heart, while expensive handsomely-bound volumes found plentiful buyers. More recent authors gained new popularity. Among them was Ali Shari'Yati, who was killed by the Shah's secret police before the revolution. His thoughts were widely quoted and even displayed on posters. One of them caught the flavour of the times: 'Islam is the most advanced of the heavenly religions but the least of them in fortune, because of the people.' This reflected a belief that the Muslim world's problems could not stem from the religion, and must therefore lie in the people themselves. Another slogan called for a revival in the cities: 'We Muslims have managed to take Islam from the heart of the city where it belongs and only recite from it at the tombs when we bury our dead.'

The influence of the 'Asian' branch of Islam was illustrated during the row over Salman Rushdie's novel *The Satanic Verses*. The Muslim minority in Britain is mainly of Asian origin, and it was they who initiated questions which were put to Ayatollah Khomeini at a prayer meeting early in 1989. Khomeini originally spoke in general terms in response to a question which did not specify Rushdie by name. He was asked whether an apostate should be killed, and confirmed that this was so. Later he was reported as having spoken in more explicit terms which were interpreted, mainly by Muslims outside the Arab world, as an order to kill Rushdie. The '*fatwa*' was not taken up or repeated by Islamic authorities in the Arab world, although Rushdie's book was condemned in the Arab press. Huge demonstrations against *The Satanic Verses* and its author were held in Islamabad, Karachi, Tehran and Dhaka, but much less interest was shown in Cairo, Damascus and Riyadh.

In 1990 there was an attempt by the Egyptian Ministry of Religious Affairs to damp down the row. Mohamed Ali Mahgoub, the minister responsible for Islamic charity trusts, went to London and attended a ceremony which was meant to restore Rushdie as a born-again Muslim and absolve him from the *fatwa*. The move was unsuccessful, as Iranian religious authorities in the holy city of Kom were not prepared to accept Rushdie's *'tawba'* (return). Many in the Arab world felt that a man who had returned to Islam should not be sentenced to death for having rejected it, but this was out of step with the Indianised general view, which held that one could not choose to abandon and return to Islam at will.

The mood of the Muslim world by the end of the decade of illusions bore no relation to the mistaken euphoria which had begun it. The smile had gone: the new look was angry, frustrated and menacing. Profiteers from Rabat to Riyadh were growing frightened, while the West drastically increased airport security checks and waited for the worst. An explosion was imminent, but not the one the West expected. Shia militancy, which might have vented its fury on merchants' homes and Western aircraft, would find its zeal and energy absorbed for the next eight years by an enemy closer to home.

5

Convenient for Some

Mile after mile of mud, trenches, corpses, shell-holes and wrecked vehicles and artillery filled the landscape of western Iran. Not since the battlefields of the Somme had there been carnage, sacrifice and courage on this scale. Fired with visions of martyrdom, a generation of Iranian youth hurled itself at Iraqi tanks and perished, sometimes tens of thousands a day. Iraqi gunners worked ceaselessly behind earthworks thrown up by bulldozers, battering a human wall which renewed itself as fast as it was destroyed. If such a battle had taken place in Europe, or between Israel and its Arab neighbours, the United Nations Security Council would have worked day and night to stop it. Instead there was inactivity, even indifference. As the West saw it, why stop two bullies destroying each other? The new Iranian regime had alienated the West by taking American hostages in the US Embassy in Tehran, causing Washington to break diplomatic links and impose economic sanctions. Western relations with Baghdad were better, but its tendency to throw its weight about in regional affairs was viewed with misgivings. It might be no bad thing, Washington thought, if Iraq's ego were cut down to size. That view was secretly shared by some of Baghdad's neighbours and supposed friends. Saudi Arabia, Kuwait, Qatar and others gave Baghdad massive financial support, but made little effort to promote a diplomatic solution. No ruler of a rich, underpopulated sheikhdom could avoid the secret hope that Iraq would emerge weakened, though neither they nor Washington wanted to see it totally defeated. The longer the fighting lasted, the better for everyone except Iran and Iraq. It was a suspiciously convenient war, for some.

In September 1980, when news of Iraq's attack on Iran reached Riyadh, King Khaled joined other senior members of the royal family in the reception hall of his palace. While the others discussed the eruption of war the king sat in silence. Then, as the conversation ended, he quoted an old verse of Arab poetry: 'Maybe the snakes will die from the poisonous stings of the scorpions.'

Many in the Muslim world have wondered whether the West was in fact as passive as it appeared to be. After a century of American, British and French plots to keep the Third World in its place, some suspected Washington of arranging the fight, in the hope that two regional lions would devour each other. Others felt that the events which led to the war were beyond the West's control. Both views are oversimplifications, but to wholly reject either of them would be misguided.

While evidence of a Western plot is limited, Henry Kissinger did remark that it was the first war in which America hoped both sides would lose. Clearly that was impossible, but whenever one side seemed in sight of victory Washington would begin secretly helping its opponent. At the outset it was totally against Iran, but only marginally in favour of Iraq. The seizure of the US Embassy in Tehran and fifty-eight American hostages in November 1979 was the most traumatic crisis of the Carter presidency. They were not freed until President Reagan came to office 444 days later, a fact which has since prompted accusations of a secret deal in which George Bush, Reagan's vice president and successor, is alleged to have played an important role. At the same time, the United States saw little advantage in Iran being defeated by its neighbour. America regarded Iraq as a dangerous state which might change the regional power balance if it won.

Washington therefore followed a zig-zag policy, helping the two sides alternately, but always on a small scale and discreetly. It favoured Iraq during the months leading up to the war in 1980 and again in 1984, when Iran had the upper hand, then moved tentatively towards the Iranian camp in 1985 and 1986, ending the war somewhere between the two. None of these shifts was apparent at the time: outwardly American policy seemed anti-Iranian and ambiguous towards Iraq. Its support for Iraq in the early stages consisted of passing information to the Saudis, who ensured that Baghdad received it. Washington's subsequent shift towards Iran came to light because of the Iran–Contra scandal and subsequent hearings and trials, which showed that the administration had flouted its own policy of ostracising Tehran by arranging secret deliveries of advanced weapons. In 1985 and 1986, after negotiations with Arab, Iranian and Israeli middlemen, the National Security Council arranged the delivery to Tehran of 1508 TOW missiles, eighteen hawk missiles and spare parts. The deliveries were made by air, with a mixture of direct shipments on board CIA aircraft and indirect operations using Israel as an intermediary. The operations were strongly encouraged and possibly manipulated by Tel Aviv, which was playing its own game of currying favour with Tehran. A report in February 1987 by President Reagan's Special Review Board noted that this happened at a time when Washington's public policy strongly deprecated arms shipments to Iran and the ransoming of hostages. The American media assumed that the main motive was to persuade Tehran to use its influence with pro-Iranian groups holding American hostages in Lebanon. The report suggested that this was only one of a number of aims, others being the strategic importance of Iran, the Soviet invasion of Afghanistan, and the influence of Tel Aviv and profit-seeking middlemen. It did not mention a US wish to avert a complete defeat of Iran by Iraq, though President Reagan stated during the hearings that there were reasons of state which could not be divulged.

If it was Washington's intention to strengthen Iran's hand, it had little impact, because of its inept handling of discussions with Iranian officials. No atmosphere of trust was established, and the weapons deliveries stopped; indeed, the Iranians returned nearly all the Hawk missiles, complaining that they were defective. The equipment delivered was insufficient to affect the outcome of the war, but it was enough to damage President Reagan's credibility. If the aim was to release hostages, that too was a failure. Only one was set free during the period.

A further element of the conspiracy theory was the role of the CIA and other intelligence services. There has never been a Middle East crisis, or even a period of Middle East peace, in which these agencies were not active. Whether they became hyperactive between 1980 and 1988 is a moot point. The Safari Club, which brought together the CIA and intelligence agencies of certain pro-Western Middle East nations, had lost a member with the Shah's fall. It was certainly active during the war, and probably used Saudi Arabia (a member) to encourage Baghdad (a non-member). At the time there was talk of a King Fahd–Saddam Hussein axis. However, the Iran–Iraq war was only partly relevant to the club's main purpose of promoting Western interests in regional conflicts. It was more interested in the Afghanistan conflict, in which it provided weapons for the anti-Soviet Mujahedeen guerrillas. The club kept a bank account in Switzerland with a continuously revolving capital of $250 million, operated with the participation of the CIA and the Saudi government. In one bizarre incident the guerrillas said they were short of mules to transport munitions over the mountains from Peshawar in Pakistan to their fighting bases. The Safari Club set up 'Operation Mule', which involved buying 10,000 animals in Cyprus and shipping them to Karachi.

Washington saw the Iranian revolution as its most serious loss since the Second World War, not excluding South Vietnam. The Shah's regime had played a strategic role as part of a ring of American fortresses surrounding the Soviet Union. As an important oil producer its stability was important to the West's economy. The fact that its armed forces had fallen into the new regime's hands intact, virtually without a fight, was deeply worrying, raising the possibility that Tehran could close the Gulf and hold the West to ransom. The stakes were even higher than during the Vietnam war. No vital US interest had been threatened by the spread of Communism on the South-East Asian mainland, where it was already deeply entrenched. American defence in Asia was based on political influence in the larger islands – Japan, the Philippines, Malaysia – backed up by bases on smaller ones (especially Guam), and after the fall of Saigon in 1972 it returned to this island-based strategy. No similar policy could have worked in the Middle East, where the US had no close island bases and no permanent bases. Any attempt to use American facilities in Turkey, which were designed for a Nato–Warsaw Pact conflict, would have caused friction with Istanbul. British bases in Cyprus would have been available for a small operation, but were inadequate and politically inappropriate if the aim had been to reverse the Iranian revolution.

Washington's frustration was apparent when President Carter visited Egypt in March 1979 and spent much of the time discussing how Iran could be 'saved'. He felt that something had to be done, but saw few possibilities. The Iranian army had collapsed, direct American intervention was out of the question, the Turks would not get involved for fear of being seen as infidels, and the Gulf states were not in a position to help. That left Iraq as the only candidate.

During the months before the Iran–Iraq war various clandestine agencies tried hard to entice Baghdad to take up arms, using the usual tools of their trade, information and disinformation. Secret documents, sometimes genuine, sometimes false, came to light at moments calculated to fan the suspicions of some and the ambitions of others. Those who wanted war probably reckoned that the powderkeg was already full: all it needed was a single spark. The roots of the conflict went right to the soul of the two peoples. Centuries of disputes between the Sunni Ottoman Empire (of which Iraq was part) and the Shia dynasties of Persia had left the border between the two countries in question. A settlement was agreed in 1975, but Iraq only accepted it under duress, causing bitterness which was to erupt five years later. The agreement was signed during an OPEC meeting in Algiers between the Shah and Saddam Hussein, who was then Vice Chairman of the Revolutionary Command Council, although he was widely seen as the real power behind President al-Bakr. It defined the border as a line down the middle of the Shatt al Arab waterway, giving both countries navigation rights. This was a big concession by the Iraqis, who claimed the whole waterway, but they had little choice. The Shah had given his backing to a Kurdish rebellion in northern Iraq, putting its guerrillas in a position so strong that Iraqi forces could not be sure of victory. He promised to stop supporting them in return for half the waterway. This was much resented by Baghdad, whose bargaining position was made weaker by the refusal of the Soviet Union, its main arms supplier, to provide adequate ammunition. Stocks for certain types of guns had fallen as low as fifteen shells, and the situation was critical. They could obtain no more than 1200 shells from Moscow, as the Russians were playing their own game in the Kurdish conflict. The Kurds and their quest for self-determination had always been the ball, never a player, in a five-sided match between Iraq, Iran, Turkey, the Soviet Union and to a lesser extent Syria. Occupying a mountainous area straddling the borders of these countries, they were supported by none and exploited by all.

At the time of the Algiers agreement Washington's sympathies were entirely with Tehran, because of the Shah's loyalty and Baghdad's links with Moscow. Saddam Hussein, however, said he could not understand why the US thought Iran was an important base for resisting Soviet expansion. An analysis of Iranian bases in the region had shown that eighteen were directed towards Iraq and only one towards the Soviet Union.

Another cause of the war which was out of Washington's control was Baghdad's fear of the Islamic revolution. By 1980 this was the main source of contention, though the Algiers treaty remained an important secondary factor. Long before his name was noticed in the West, before his sojourn in Paris and subsequent triumphant return to Tehran, Ayatollah Khomeini spent thirteen years living at the Shia holy shrines of Karbala and Najaf in eastern Iraq, and made himself unpopular with Baghdad by claiming that the sites belonged to the Shias and should not be subject to Iraqi sovereignty. Khomeini's subsequent rise to power alarmed Baghdad, which feared that he would incite an uprising by Iraqi Shias, who make up 52 per cent of the population. The Revolutionary Command Council includes members of the three main faiths represented in Iraq (Tariq Aziz, for example, is a Christian), but it is perceived as being predominantly Sunni. Saddam Hussein saw events in Tehran as an explosion rather than a revolution, and knew Iraq would feel the shock-wave first. Ayatollah Khomeini was a supra-national force with a mission to sweep away the frontiers of Islamic states, blending them into one. Khomeini told visitors from the Arab world that he could not understand the concept of nationalism; if a state was necessary it should encompass the whole Islamic nation, not just Arab countries. It was a grand if vague idea, but not a world order, not even a design for the Middle East. It was hard to see how the Arab world could have mutual defence with Indonesia, or complementary economics with Malaysia, for example. And who would an Islamic defence system be directed against? Christians and Jews? Arabs could more easily accept a strictly Arab sub-system, which would have natural human, geographical and cultural boundaries. Khomeini, however, was unwilling to listen to such objections, being totally committed to his own concept.

After toppling the Shah the ayatollahs in Tehran and Kom felt nothing was beyond their power. They began to talk of the United States and the Soviet Union as the two great Satans, while setting out to destabilise the smaller devil in Baghdad. Iraq already had a Shia opposition party called Da'awa, the Arabic word for 'The Call', which depended on financial support from Tehran. It flourished in 1979 and 1980, becoming a virtual front for spreading the Iranian revolution, backed up by the Arabic service of Tehran Radio. Iranian groups began crossing the border to blow up installations in Iraq, and Iraqis replied in kind. One target destroyed by Iraq was an Iranian relay station used for broadcasting the Arabic service. The infiltration attacks soon led to artillery duels across the frontier.

Iraq's patience was at breaking point. As Tariq Aziz, then minister of information, was about to leave for a visit to Moscow on 21 September 1980 he received a phone call from President Saddam Hussein warning him to change his route. Iran, which he would have crossed, had closed its frontiers. Aziz diverted via Turkey and at his talks with the Soviet leadership he gave warning of Baghdad's plans. Iraq, he said, could not go on being insulted daily by Iran and facing constant skirmishes.

The Revolutionary Command Council in Baghdad had come to the conclusion that the skirmishes and the border closure showed an Iranian intention to carry out some larger action. The border was only 120 kilometres from Baghdad; a surprise Iranian attack would stand a chance of reaching the capital's outskirts in a single leap. Iraq, on the other hand, would have to penetrate 600 kilometres into Iranian territory before Tehran would be threatened. Iraq's best defence, as seen by the Revolutionary Command Council, lay in attack. At dawn on 23 September 1980 a first strike was carried out by 154 Iraqi planes, followed by 100 aircraft in a second bombing run, as a prelude to land attacks on two fronts.

All went well for Iraq in the first weeks of the war, but by 1981 Iranian resistance was becoming stiffer. An Iraqi general told President Saddam Hussein: 'It seems to me we are facing mad people. They come straight at us as if they could stop our tanks with their naked bodies. The tanks crush them yet more keep coming after them.' Wearing red bands round their foreheads, Iranian youths seemed intoxicated by Khomeini's rhetoric. 'Some say the hero is the spirit of history. It is not true. The martyr is the spirit of history,' he said. Khomeini probably could not have incited his people to such mass-suicide were it not for a role-model embedded in their culture. After Mohammed's death the Shias became an organised group in the two decades which followed the dispute over who should be the fourth Caliph. Mu'awiya, who seized power after a complex struggle over differing ideas·and interests, died in 680 and seemed certain to be followed by another representative of the merchants. Ali, champion of the poor, was long since dead, but his second son Hussein led a revolt. He and his followers died in battle at Karbala in southern Iraq (one of the shrines which Khomeini proclaimed exempt from Iraqi sovereignty). Hussein was beheaded by the Ummayads, who were transforming themselves from a wealthy tribe into an energetic and expanding empire, and his head became a holy relic. As Shias did not recognise the Sunni Caliphs they created their own leaders, called imams. Hussein is recognised as the third of these (Ali being the first) and is associated with self-sacrifice. In rural Shia areas of Iraq one still sometimes sees people wearing black in mourning for Hussein, thirteen centuries after his death. His example must have been in the minds of countless young Iranians as they went to certain death.

Iraq needed weapons, and Egypt, the only other Arab country with a substantial arms industry, was the obvious source. But the two countries were barely on speaking terms, as Iraq had been among the toughest in ostracising Egypt for making a separate peace with Israel. After the Camp David agreements nearly all Arab governments broke links with Cairo, although most maintained secret contacts. A way around Baghdad's difficulty in doing business with Cairo directly was found by Egypt selling weapons to other Arab countries, which passed them on. Oman, which had held out against Arab opinion, refusing to break links with Cairo, was chosen to be the channel for sales which kept Egyptian munitions factories working at 99 per cent of capacity for much of the war. At the same time huge quantities of Soviet-made weapons bought by Egypt before 1975 were sold to Baghdad at high prices, despite Iraqi complaints that Cairo was making a profit. Iraqi purchasers found identical weapons for sale in Yugoslavia at half the price, but nevertheless continued to accept Egyptian supplies. Cairo made $1 billion a year selling its Soviet cast-offs, and was glad to be rid of them, having begun a transition to American equipment five years earlier. It used the money to re-equip its forces with Western arms. The Iraqis had no difficulty in using the Egyptian equipment, which was identical to supplies they had received earlier from the Soviet Union, but they also needed a certain amount of Western hardware. Western governments, wanting to appear even-handed, claimed that they had blocked the sale of all but non-lethal military equipment to both sides. The ban was full of holes, and many parties, both in the West and the Arab world, made use of them. The manufacturers needed End User Certificates to protect them from prosecution, but there was no difficulty in obtaining these from Zaire, whose ruler General Mobutu Seseseko worked the system to make money.

By 1984 Iran was strongly on the offensive, recapturing lost territory and seizing the uninhabited (but defended) Faw peninsula south of Basra. Arab money immediately began to pour into Baghdad as the sheikhdoms took fright at the prospect of being swept away by the Islamic revolution, while Arab newspapers began describing Iraq as 'the guardian of the eastern gates'. The influx of funds came at a time when Iraq, despite military setbacks, was starting to look like a regional superpower. While receiving arms from all directions it was also working hard to improve its military infrastructure and training. The whole of its reserves, which before the war stood at $36 billion, and a further $30 billion obtained from Saudi Arabia and other Arab countries, had been invested to create the region's strongest army.

Although dependent on foreign supplies for most high-technology weapons, Iraq was now able to produce a large proportion of its own munitions. The need for an Arab arms industry had been realised forty years earlier after the 1948 war with Israel, which exposed weaknesses in Arab capabilities. Egyptian preparations began while King Farouk was still in power, before the 1952 revolution, and increased in 1956, after the Suez attack. In 1957, knowing that Israel was trying to build an atom bomb, Cairo set up a nuclear research programme, but later abandoned it. Iraq then recruited some of Egypt's experts, including Dr Yehiah El-Meshad, who had been highly placed in the project. In the late 1970s he supervised research work based at the Osirak test reactor, which had been supplied to Iraq by France. El-Meshad was assassinated in a Paris hotel in June 1980, and the reactor was destroyed by Israeli bombing in 1981. These were serious blows, but they did not bring Iraqi research to a halt. The more it learned of Israel's progress, the more determined Baghdad became to have its own nuclear deterrent.

Egypt's programme also included developing its own training and fighter aircraft, known as the Cairo 100, 200 and 300, some of which were supersonic, and medium-range missiles, developed with the assistance of German scientists who had worked on the V1 and V2 rockets in the Second World War. Among them was Dr Wolfgang Pils, who spent a decade on the project before moving to China to help with its missile programme.

One of the most sensitive sections of Egypt's arms industry was a national research institution which included a chemical weapons division. It began by compiling a library of scientific papers on chemical weapons, but found that little had been published since the First World War. A group of scientists began work, using an insecticide factory on the outskirts of Cairo as a front. A breakthrough was achieved in 1962–63 which led to the production of large quantities of mustard gas. Further work was carried out in preparation for the October 1973 war, but a political decision was taken not to use these weapons. By then Egypt had progressed from mustard gas to a nerve gas called Sarin VX and was producing both artillery shells and bombs armed with it. Syria became a customer, spending $6 million on Egyptian chemical weapons. In the last phase before the programme was abolished, the pesticide factory was also making binary weapons, in which two chemicals are kept separate inside an artillery shell or bomb, and then combine when it is fired or dropped to form a nerve gas which is released on impact. More than fifty chemicals were involved in the manufacturing processes.

Chemical weapons were seen in different lights by civil and military circles. The horror of the First World War trenches, when mustard gas left thousands of young men permanently disabled, and those who died quickly were considered lucky, led to pressure for an international treaty banning their use. Subsequent talks on abolishing them altogether led nowhere, not least because the United States and the Soviet Union had huge stocks in their respective parts of Germany. Many Western nations claimed to have abolished the production of chemical weapons, but even if this were true it would have been irrelevant because as Nato members they could rely on American military power. In the Arab world the arguments were inextricably linked to Israel's possession of nuclear weapons. Egypt's brief experiment with nuclear research had shown that the cost of keeping pace with Israel was prohibitive. Some other way had to be found of deterring an Israeli nuclear attack, and possession of a strong chemical weapons deterrent seemed an inexpensive option. Secondly, many Arab military commanders argued that it was no more inhumane to kill with chemicals than with bullets. Some chemical weapons were designed to disable rather than kill the enemy, allowing their positions to be overrun quickly. It was argued that this would minimise loss of life and reduce damage to infrastructure. The entire programme was scrapped after the 1973 war, which President Sadat thought would be the last. In 1981 Baghdad expressed interest in the Egyptian programme and the pesticide factory's chemical weapons branch was reactivated, with a $12 million contract. President Sadat later ordered the company to stop work, but some of the scientists left Egypt and set up new facilities elsewhere. The insecticide factory still exists, but now produces medicines.[1]

Cairo's missile programme also stopped after the 1973 war, although the work was taken over by Iraq, as were some of the experts. In 1974 Egypt, Saudi Arabia, the UAE and Qatar formed a new authority with capital of $2 billion to produce short-range missiles.

---

[1] Details of Egypt's chemical weapons programme were provided by the programme's former project manager, now retired. He must remain anonymous.

This was starting to show results when the Camp David agreements caused the other three countries to withdraw, leaving Egypt alone. After that, production was reduced. Much later, towards the end of the Iran–Iraq war, Egypt, Iraq and Argentina formed a company with its principal offices in Monte Carlo and Vienna to produce medium-range missiles called the Condor 1 and 2. Preliminary studies and administration, including the recruitment of 420 staff, cost $300 million, and over $1 billion was spent altogether, but nothing was produced. The project also led to friction with Washington when an Egyptian-American engineer, acting for Egyptian military intelligence, was accused of trying to steal carbon phenolic cloth, the export of which was banned. President Bush complained to President Mubarak about it when they met on 3 April 1989, with the result that the Egyptian defence minister was dismissed.

Even if Condor had become a reality, it would have been too late to affect the Iran–Iraq war. But Baghdad had already made much progress in improving earlier missiles. Its scientists succeeded in adapting Soviet-made Scud missiles to increase their range, enabling Baghdad to hit Tehran. Their military value was questionable, but the missiles were used to great psychological effect in the last months of the war, and helped put the Iranian public in the mood to accept a ceasefire. By this time Iraq had turned the ground war to its advantage, making good its earlier losses with a display of professionalism which earned respect even from American experts. Five major battles were fought between April and August 1988, all ending in Iranian defeats. In the first of these, on 17–18 April, the Iraqis recovered the Faw peninsula, which Iran had taken two months to capture in 1986, in less than two days. In the second they retook land around Basra which Iran had seized in 1987. The original fight had lasted three weeks and had cost Iran 70,000 casualties, yet Iraq's counterblow achieved success in only seven hours. The third battle saw the recovery by Iraq of a huge undeveloped oilfield which Iran had taken in 1984. The fourth and fifth battles eliminated any remaining Iranian threat to Baghdad, and left Iraqi forces sixty kilometres inside Iranian territory. They were ready to penetrate further but were recalled by the government, and on 18 July Ayatollah Khomeini drank what he called 'the poison cup' of defeat.

The war was over, though the ceasefire did not come until August. It had been the longest 'conventional' war of the twentieth century, excluding conflicts where one party relied mainly on guerrilla tactics (Vietnam, Cambodia, Nicaragua, Angola, Afghanistan, Ethiopia and others). The cost in both human and financial terms was shattering: 420,000 dead, 210,000 taken prisoner, $US390 billion spent or lost. The rest of the world was mainly concerned about the damage to oil facilities. Terminals at Abadan and Basra were destroyed, and Iran's oil production dropped from 4 million barrels a day in 1979 to less than 600,000 barrels a day in 1981. Over the same period Iraq's production fell from 3 million barrels a day to 550,000.

Despite these setbacks, Iraq's armed forces were immensely stronger at the finish than at the start, the country's self-esteem had never been higher, and its president began to look like a regional leader.

Saddam Hussein is a product of a society which looks for strength in its leaders, and does not expect them to be compassionate. This attitude, deeply rooted in Iraqi culture, stems from centuries of conflict in one of the most turbulent regions of the Middle East. Any country's history is a product of geography and demography, but in Iraq's case the mixture is unusually volatile. Its geographical position has made it both a bridge and a battlefield between two worlds, with Europe and the Mediterranean part of the Middle East on one side, and the Asian continent on the other. The close proximity of the Caspian Sea to the north-east and the Black Sea to the north forced the caravans trading between the Far East and the Mediterranean to pass through Iraq.

In the earliest recorded times Iraq was seen as a land of civilisation, culture and education, with the emergence of the powerful kingdoms of Hamurabi and Bukhtnassar (the Nebuchadnezzar of the Bible). Later Baghdad and Cordova were regarded as leading lights of Islamic law and literature. It was in Baghdad under the Khalifa El-Maa'moon that the main works of Greek philosophy were translated into Arabic.

The difficulties of governing Iraq are suggested by a story which is taught in secondary schools throughout the Arab world. During the Ummayad Empire, which led the Arab world from A.D.661 to 750, there was much unrest in Iraq. Yazid, the Khalifa or Caliph, who was based in Damascus, sent out a ruler noted for his strength and firmness, Al-Hajjaj ben Youssef Al-Thakafi. The new ruler summoned Iraq's dignitaries to the mosque at Kufa. When they were gathered he stood silently on the podium for a whole hour before giving a speech which is considered a classic of Arab prose. It began with the words: 'Oh people of Iraq. Oh people of divisiveness and hypocrisy. The Khalifa of the Faithful has fetched his bag of arrows and, finding me to be the most solid, has decided to shoot me at you.'

Al-Thakafi proved as severe as his words promised. Fourteen years later, as he lay dying, his last words were: 'God forgive me, for I have killed one hundred thousand or more.'

Bloodshed on a large scale is a recurring theme of Iraqi history. Dr Ghassan Salama of the Sorbonne, an expert on the area, has said: 'From the mountains of Lebanon to the mountains of Afghanistan there is a distinctive smell in the air. When you think about it you will realise that it is the smell of death.'

Hundreds of years of turbulence gradually produced a measure of co-existence, without resolving Iraq's inherent contradictions. Inhabited by mainly-Sunni Arabs in its central region, mainly-Shia Muslims in the east and south, and Kurds (who are Sunni Muslims, although they are racially and culturally distinct) in the north, Iraq could never hope for lasting stability, but managed at times to keep its turmoil within limits. The Shia majority accepted rule by the Sunni minority with varying degrees of willingness, while the Kurds oscillated between states of calm and agitation.

King Faisal I, the first Hashemite king of modern Iraq, wrote not long before his death in 1933 that 'The different and conflicting components of Iraqi society need to be melted and reset again before its real metal as one people can harden to endure the test and make a real state.'

The years 1931, 1936, 1945 and 1949 saw great political upheavals and unrest in Iraq, with random arrests and mass executions. The bodies of those executed were often hung from lamp posts, bridges and in public squares as a warning to others. In 1937 the remains of seven leaders of the Communist Party were left hanging for several weeks.

Iraqis of all cultures came to expect forceful rulers, accepting the need for an iron hand whether they liked it or not. General Nuri as-Said, who dominated Iraqi politics from the 1930s to the late 1950s and held the office of prime minister seven times, was noted for his toughness. He and the Iraqi monarchy were killed in the 1958 military revolution.

Saddam Hussein was born on 28 April 1937 near Takrit, close

to the Kurdish region of northern Iraq. This is an area where the main unit is neither the tribe nor the city but something in between called the *ashera*, which means a group of families. He claims to trace his ancestry to the Imam Ali, cousin and son-in-law of the Prophet. At least 10 million people in the Islamic world claim to be *el-Ashraf*, 'the honoured ones', descended from the Prophet.

The close-knit communities around the ancient fortress of Takrit have strong military traditions which go back for centuries. Saddam Hussein, however, chose a political rather than military career. He went to school in Takrit from the ages of ten to twenty, and was recruited into the Ba'ath Socialist Party at the age of nineteen. At the time there was much debate over Arab unity and renaissance, and a feeling that Iraq, with its military traditions, could lead the countries of the Fertile Crescent.

On 7 October 1959, aged twenty-two, Saddam Hussein took part in an unsuccessful attempt to assassinate President Kassem. His intended role was to cover the retreat of the assassination group, but when the machine-gun of one of them jammed, Saddam began firing. He was hit in the leg by counterfire but managed to escape and eventually reached Egypt, staying there from 1960 until November 1963, and finishing his secondary education at Kasr el-Nil private school in Cairo. He enrolled in Cairo's Faculty of Law, and later went to Baghdad University (passing his law degree examination in June 1966).

In February 1963 President Kassem was killed in a coup led by elements of the armed forces, and Colonel Abdel-Salem Aref became president. Aref died in a helicopter crash in March 1966 and was succeeded by his brother, Major General Abdel-Rahman Aref.

By this time Saddam Hussein had undertaken a number of responsibilities within the Ba'ath Party, including establishing links with farmers, the army and Arab military organisations outside Iraq. He was one of the leaders of a coup on 17 July 1968 which ousted President Abdel-Rahman Aref and brought the Ba'ath Party to power, with Major General Ahmad Hassan al-Bakr as president and prime minister. Supreme authority lay with the Revolutionary Command Council, of which Bakr was chairman, while Saddam Hussein later became vice-chairman.

President Bakr's health and authority declined to a point where many regarded him as a mere figurehead. Much of the executive power already lay with Saddam Hussein, which gave rise to tension between his office and Bakr's entourage. In 1979, during a speech marking the eleventh anniversary of the coup, Bakr announced that he was handing over the presidency to Saddam Hussein. Bakr was given the courtesy title of 'Father of Iraq', and Saddam Hussein took office as president of Iraq and chairman of the Revolutionary Command Council on 16 July 1979.

Although the Ba'ath Party was in power in both Iraq and Syria, relations between the two countries were seldom easy. Michel Aflak, the Syrian founder of the party, was expelled from the Syrian leadership because of his sympathy with the Iraqi branch. The relationship improved in October 1978 when President Assad visited Baghdad, and plans to create a political and economic union were announced. The move was prompted by the Camp David accords and the weakening of Arab unity which resulted from Egypt's treaty with Israel. Iraq and Syria hoped to create a powerful Arab state on Israel's eastern front, but the plan fell apart when some in the Iraqi leadership tried to use the opportunity to settle other scores. One of their aims was to remove from power all those who had caused the rift between the two wings of the party. Word of the plot leaked out and many in the leadership were accused of conspiracy. One of these cracked under pressure and confirmed the suspicions. His confessions were broadcast on television during a meeting of the Ba'ath Party Congress. In 1980, a year after Saddam Hussein became president, twenty-one members of the party, including four of its leaders, were sentenced to death.

For the next eight years Saddam Hussein was mainly preoccupied with the Iran–Iraq war. When it ended, he considered that he had saved the Arab world from domination by Tehran and an unfettered Shia Islamic revolution which would have swept away the good life of the oil producers.

6

Protection at a Price

Although Kuwait came through the Iran–Iraq war without an Iranian invasion or a Shia uprising, it did not escape unharmed. Its geographical position at the head of the Gulf, forty kilometres from Iran at the nearest point, placed it within range of Iranian missiles, aircraft and armed speedboats. In 1987 the port of Abdullah was sabotaged, there was an explosion at the refinery of Shoeiba, and liquid-gas tanks were blown up, devastating an area twenty kilometres in diameter. One hundred and thirty Kuwaiti tankers and cargo ships were damaged between 1984 and 1987, some while in port but most attempting to run the gauntlet between Bahrain and Kuwait, the section of the Gulf most vulnerable to Iranian attacks and mines.

The longer the conflict dragged on, the more Iraq regarded Kuwait as an ally. From the start of the war Iraq's access to the sea had been cut off by the closure of the port of Basra and the Shatt al-Arab waterway. Unable to export its oil by sea, Iraq used its long-range Sukhoi 23 bombers to attack Iranian ports, oil installations and ships. Its reasons were those expressed in an old Arab poem: 'If I should die of thirst, let no rain fall.'

Iran reacted by attacking tankers from countries which were giving Iraq financial aid or political encouragement. Kuwaiti vessels came in for some of the severest punishment because of Iran's suspicion, later proven to be correct, that Kuwait was shipping oil to Iraq's customers, thus helping Baghdad to fulfil its export contracts.

Iraq would have been Kuwait's natural protector, but Baghdad had no means of preventing the attacks. Kuwait was unwilling to seek help from Saudi Arabia, knowing that the Saudis felt only slightly less vulnerable than the Kuwaitis.

At first the Kuwaiti government was reluctant to seek the protection of a non-Arab power. Having experienced sixty years of British protection, it was determined to avoid compromising Kuwaiti sovereignty again. This was an admirable policy, but did not make for an easy answer to Kuwait's immediate problems. The Cold War was not yet finished, and Kuwait felt that the solution was to play the two superpowers off against each other, hoping to use their rivalry to secure protection without political strings. At this stage few imagined that the Iran–Iraq war was approaching its conclusion, and there was nothing to suggest that Iraq would ultimately win. Battles were raging along a 1200-kilometre front, and Iran was still in control of some Iraqi territory.

Kuwait began approaching the five permanent members of the UN Security Council individually, asking for help. After making an initial approach to Washington, a delegation was sent to Moscow in October 1986 to sound out Soviet views. At this stage Kuwait had no intention of doing a deal with the Soviet Union, but wanted to see how it would react. Having followed pro-Western foreign policies since independence, the Kuwaitis were pleasantly surprised when Moscow offered to rent them some empty Soviet tankers. They said they would think about it.

Kuwait had already asked the US government to hire it some American tankers, but found little sign of American interest. The matter was left on one side until April 1987, when Kathleen Cocci, the State Department Desk Officer for Kuwait, held talks with Sheikh Sabah al-Ahmed al-Sabah, who was both deputy prime minister and foreign minister. Mrs Cocci saw five potential problems with Kuwait's request. First, the US was anxious to avoid anything that could lead to confrontation with Moscow. Second, if Washington granted Kuwait's appeal, Moscow might respond by offering its services to other Gulf states, thus giving the Soviets a reason for having a military presence in the Gulf. Third, other Gulf states might approach Washington, which would be unable to protect them all. Fourth, it could further complicate US contacts with Tehran. Fifth, under American law any ship sailing under the US flag would be subject to US regulations, which Kuwait might be unable to meet.

Disappointed by the American attitude, the Kuwaiti government reopened the talks with Moscow and asked if Kuwait could re-register some ships under the Soviet flag. This was not an entirely new idea. As far back as 1901, when Middle East oil was still only a smear in the sand, France had agreed to reflag a number of Omani freighters, as part of its rivalry with the British for influence in the region.

Moscow had no law against reflagging, but proposed an alternative: the Soviet Union would hire Kuwaiti tankers, use them to carry Kuwaiti oil, and sail them under the Soviet flag with Soviet protection. Kuwait accepted, and three of its supertankers operated under this arrangement (one of them, renamed the *Marshal Chekhov*, was to hit a mine).

Kuwait also approached China, but found it unwilling to help. This was hardly surprising as, although Peking had declared that it was not selling weapons to either side, it had made a $6 billion deal to sell Silkworm anti-ship missiles and MiG 23 aircraft to Iran.

When the Kuwaiti government told the US ambassador of the deal with Moscow, he asked if it was an April fool's joke. After it had recovered from its surprise, Washington dropped its objections and agreed to re-register Kuwait's ships under the US flag and escort them in the Gulf. The Kuwaitis and Americans had protracted negotiations to decide how far the protection would extend, and where in the Gulf US warships would begin and end their escort duties. The Americans were surprised to find that the emir's negotiators drove a hard bargain. When the US team requested facilities for warships escorting the tankers they were all but slapped down. They did not ask for bases or a security agreement, but were told that such requests would be rejected. Any entry into Kuwaiti waters by US warships would be treated as aggression and Kuwait would resist it with force. Kuwait also wanted it made clear that the deal was purely commercial. Washington's motives could only be strategic and political, but that did not matter to Kuwait. What did matter was that it should be able to say that Washington had accepted its terms.

Kuwait's motive for binding the Americans so tightly was to avert accusations from other Arab countries of giving Washington a foothold in the region, and to avoid worsening its already tense relations with Tehran. Sheikh Sabah again emphasised Kuwait's conditions when he visited Admiral John Poindexter, the US National Security Advisor, at the White House in 1987. 'We do not want, nor seek, nor support the presence of American military forces on Kuwait soil,' he said. 'There must be no illusion about Kuwait giving any bases.' The sheikh pointed out that the Straits of Hormuz at the mouth of the Gulf was the route for 60 per cent of oil exports, and it was therefore in world interests to protect it.

One of the difficulties for any Arab country in doing business with Washington is a fear of confidential details appearing in the US media. Arab governments, especially those from the Gulf, invariably prefer to conduct such sensitive matters in secret, and have sometimes found the Americans indiscreet. Kuwait realised that the best way to avoid embarrassment was to keep the period of secrecy as short as possible. In a note to US officials marked 'Top Secret', Kuwait suggested that if the two sides reached agreement, they should announce it publicly.

An agreement to reflag eleven Kuwaiti tankers was sealed on 19 May 1987 and announced immediately. The deal appeared to upset France, which described the US decision as 'absurd'. The French ambassador in Kuwait immediately flew to Paris to discuss the matter with his government, and soon afterwards France offered to help Kuwait. Their discussions came to nothing, partly because French law would have required the use of French rather than Kuwaiti ships. Meanwhile the US administration faced criticism of the reflagging policy from the American media, which intensified after Iraq's Exocet missile attack on the US warship *Stark*.

The US – Kuwaiti deal was seen in the Arab world as a diplomatic coup for Kuwait, which had obtained protection without sacrificing its principles. The advantage for Washington, apart from protecting oil supplies, was that Kuwait came to regard the United States as its protector. When Iraq invaded Kuwait three years later, Kuwait immediately sought American help.

Ten days after the deal, President Reagan stressed the need to protect Middle East oil supplies when he addressed the nation after a meeting of the National Security Council to discuss the Gulf situation. He said that many would find it hard to believe that US prosperity was threatened, but they should not forget the queues at filling stations during the 1973 oil embargo.

The American willingness in 1987 to take a long view was in line with its policy towards many other non-Communist countries. Like the British Empire before it, America had found that trade follows the flag, partly offsetting the costs of maintaining its influence around the globe. The relationships between the US and its two main industrial competitors, Japan and West Germany, were exceptions to this rule. Both countries had a substantial surplus in their trade with the United States, but also made direct contributions towards Washington's costs in helping to defend them.

Washington's experience in persuading other countries to meet part of its military costs was to serve it well in 1990, when Secretary of State James Baker visited a large number of countries to request contributions to the cost of operations in Saudi Arabia and Kuwait. America received foreign assistance totalling $61 billion during the war, far more than its costs, which were estimated at $35 to $40 billion. The American economy was in better shape after the war than before it, contrary to predictions at the time. Britain was a lesser beneficiary, collecting no more than $8 billion, but nevertheless it emerged with a balance of payments surplus for the first six months of 1991.

Japan and West Germany handed over $9 billion and $10 billion respectively, huge sums which did not necessarily reflect any enthusiasm on the part of the Japanese and German people for military action against Iraq. The initial responses to Baker's requests were much smaller, and it was only after Washington and London had voiced dissatisfaction that the contributions were increased. The two countries were also taken to task for failing to send troops to the Gulf, though both were constitutionally prohibited from doing so. In Japan's case the constitution which made it impossible was imposed by General Douglas MacArthur, while Germany's inability to deploy forces outside the Nato area was another relic of the Second World War.

Washington also persuaded Saudi Arabia and Kuwait to purchase $17 billion worth of military protection and used some of the money to seduce others. Egypt was offered the cancellation of its $6 billion military debt. Syria was promised both money and diplomatic advantages in return for modest military participation. Turkey allowed Western forces to operate from Nato bases on its territory, even though Iraq is outside Nato's operational area, and Turkey was never threatened. Turkey received compensation of $3.5 billion for expenditure and losses of income that did not exceed $1.7 billion.

A three-sided transaction was taking place, which required one country to pose a threat, another to offer protection, and a third to buy it. Security and insecurity have always been saleable commodities, but rarely have they been traded with such sophistication. On a more modest scale, Pakistan sells security to Saudi Arabia by hiring out two armoured divisions at a price of $250 million a year. Israel has used the same idea in reverse for forty years, selling Washington its (largely imaginary) vulnerability to annihilation by Arab armies. During the Kuwait war it sold its abstention from responding to Scud missile attacks in return for a big increase in US aid.

Market forces in protection were also in evidence between Baghdad and Kuwait in the mid- and late-1980s, even if they were tempered by brotherly Arab feelings. Iraq, a regional superpower, was well off by Third World standards but threadbare compared to its southern neighbours. By the middle of the Iran–Iraq war, the average wealth of Iraqis (in terms of gross domestic product per capita) was just under $3000, while Kuwait's was over $11,000. The Iraqis were six times richer than the Egyptians, but almost four times poorer than the Kuwaitis. Saudi Arabia was in the middle at $6000 per head. Baghdad felt that the cost of the war with Iran should be treated as an Arab regional expense, to be spread according to the ability to pay.

Iran was offering a threat, Iraq was selling security, and Kuwait and Saudi Arabia were the main customers. It was in Baghdad's interest that the Islamic revolution should appear as alarming as possible, and the greater the danger of defeat, the looser the sheikhs' pursestrings became. Their total contributions to Baghdad during the war were about $42 billion, equivalent to Iraq's annual gross domestic product. Kuwait paid between $12 and $15 billion of this (depending on the method of calculation), reflecting its vulnerability to the Islamic revolution. It paid its dues to Baghdad with good grace, and its newspapers hailed President Saddam Hussein as 'the great cavalier of Arab nationalism'.

7

An Arab World Divided Against Itself

As the last guns of the second oil war fell silent in August 1988, the Arab world emerged from its psychological trenches and surveyed its future prospects. Longing for peace, prosperity and unity, the Arabs looked across the Mediterranean and saw a model taking shape there. The Berlin Wall had not yet fallen, but the general trend was clear. The East was about to defect from itself and join Western Europe, an experiment which Gorbachev would later describe as the creation of a common European home. Some in the Middle East saw a parallel between Gorbachev's allegory and their own aspirations. They had been talking of an Arab nation for decades, and although a start was made in 1944 with the creation of the Arab League, that institution had been weakened by half a century of wars and revolutions.

Nothing had been more damaging to the search for unity than the Camp David agreement, which left Egypt cut off from the rest of the Arab world and hopelessly in hock to Washington. The debts were not merely political: Cairo was now paying $900 million a year interest on loans for buying American military equipment, with the result that its cost had gone up from the original $7 billion to $13 billion. Washington gave Cairo aid amounting to $2 billion a year, but the banks clawed half of it back. When Egypt failed to pay it fell foul of the Brooke Amendment, which prevents the US administration from aiding countries which fall behind in servicing their debts. Each dollar left unpaid cost Egypt two in lost aid. In addition, Cairo would not have qualified for certain forms of aid if it had refused to follow economic guidelines, including sharp cuts in food subsidies, imposed by the International Monetary Fund. In 1977 the effects of these measures on the lower-paid were so harsh as to provoke food riots. Many Egyptians began to question the wisdom of accepting American aid at all. Washington showed no inclination to give Egypt special treatment, despite the service President Sadat had rendered by making a separate peace with Israel. President Nixon never hid his ambition to draw the biggest Arab country into Washington's fold so that its dispute with Israel could be treated as simply a family squabble. Now that Cairo, which needed its aid, and Riyadh, which needed its protection, could be counted on not to make trouble, Washington had begun to take the Arab world for granted. What riled the Arabs most was that they had won the laurels in the 1973 war, yet Washington took the spoils.

The Soviet Union was scarcely more interested in the Middle East than Washington once the Gulf war was over. In October 1989 a close aide and confidant of President Gorbachev, with long experience of Arab affairs, said at a dinner in the Egyptian Embassy in Moscow: 'You must get used to the fact that the Arab world is no longer an important priority for Moscow. We want to concentrate on internal affairs, rebuilding our own country. Internationally, 90 per cent of our interest is in the United States and 5 per cent in Western Europe. The rest is to be divided between China, Africa, Asia and the rest of the world.' Asked if the Middle East commanded at least 1 per cent of Moscow's foreign affairs interest, he refused to be drawn.

Moscow was not entirely unjustified in this change of priorities. It could claim to have been repeatedly let down and slighted by those it had tried to help, especially Egypt. Without Moscow's help, Egypt would not have had the Aswan dam in the 1960s, nor the tanks and missiles which nearly defeated Israel in 1973, yet Cairo had allowed itself to be seduced by Washington. As early as 1956, a year after Gamal Abdel Nasser accepted Soviet military assistance, the US Secretary of State John Foster Dulles said: 'The Russians can give you arms for death. We are the only power that can give you peace and prosperity.' He was wrong: when Cairo accepted, the Israelis got peace, the Egyptians got debts, and the Palestinians got nowhere.

Alexei Kosygin, then Soviet prime minister, urged Cairo to show gratitude for Moscow's help by persuading Gulf states to invest in the Soviet Union. President Sadat did his best, but was ignored until the end of 1974, when King Faisal told him: 'We are prepared to help your friends.' It sounded too good to be true – and it was. The help Faisal had in mind was the construction of 500 mosques in the Soviet Union. Moscow was livid, and told Cairo never to mention it again. Ironically, it was not until after its change of priorities that the Soviet

Union started to receive Arab money. Kuwait gave it a $150 million loan in 1988 and a further $300 million in 1990. Saudi Arabia granted Moscow a 'soft' loan of $3 billion as thanks for standing aside during the American destruction of Iraq in 1991.

Arabs repeatedly angered Moscow by failing to inform it before taking steps which might have forced it into a collision with Washington. President Nasser nationalised the Suez Canal in 1956 without giving an advance hint to the Russians. Iraq, which had thousands of Soviet military advisers on its territory, made its plans known to Moscow only hours before invading Iran in 1980, and gave no notice at all when it occupied Kuwait in 1990.

In Moscow's eyes the height of Cairo's ingratitude came after its switch to the American camp in 1975, when it handed over a complete battery of Soviet SAM 6 missiles to Washington for research. The Americans already had a good deal of Soviet equipment captured by the Israelis in wars with Arabs, but Moscow naturally took Cairo's action as a slap in the face. Later Egypt sold most of its Soviet weapons to Baghdad without consulting Moscow, and sent other supplies to Mujahedeen guerrillas in Afghanistan, who used them against Soviet troops. It was not surprising that when Arab leaders explained their economic difficulties to Moscow the reaction was less than sympathetic. What the Arabs did not know at the time was that even if Moscow had been sympathetic, it would have had nothing to give.

Moscow was exasperated with Tehran during the Islamic revolution, when it found itself classified alongside Washington as the 'second great Satan'. In 1979 a celebrated Iranian cleric, Ayatollah Mahmoud Talakani, died after a meeting with Vladimir Vinogradov, the Soviet ambassador in Tehran. It was rumoured in the Islamic world that his tea had been poisoned. After this the Russians marked their annoyance by making themselves less available for meetings with Iranian and other Arab leaders. A further source of irritation was an Arab tendency to lecture Moscow on what it should or should not be doing. The Russians took up the Palestinian cause, thinking it would strengthen their links with every Arab capital, but when their interest waned Palestinian leaders accused Moscow of weakness for failing to stand up to American plots.

One of the effects of *perestroika* was that Arab Communists — always a small but militant minority, as the dogma had limited appeal to Arabs — fell from Moscow's favour. A group of them took part in an Arab–Soviet dialogue in May 1989 at the Octobereski Hotel in

Moscow and used the opportunity to tell their former mentors that the new Soviet foreign policy was a surrender to the Americans. After listening to a lecture about the inevitable victory of Marxism, the conference organiser, Professor Mikhail Kapitza, head of Moscow's Afro–Asian Solidarity Movement, said: 'Next time you come, please don't bring any Communists in the delegation.' This brought home to the delegation just how much had changed. Kapitza had been Stalin's interpreter and later a deputy foreign minister under Andrei Gromyko.

Moscow had wanted the Arabs' friendship, at least until recently, but it constantly felt the relationship was one-sided. It complained that Arabs treated their links with the Soviet Union irresponsibly, and showed no appreciation of the difficulties of being a superpower, nor of the risks that conflict in the Middle East could provoke an East–West nuclear war. On several occasions Soviet officials accused the Arabs of using them merely as a means of engaging America's interest. 'We are not your first choice, we are second, and we are only used to tease Washington. If you are seeking an American solution to your problems you should go direct to Washington,' they said.

The strains in the Arab world's relationships with both super-powers need not have been a barrier to an Arab political and economic resurgence, though they did not help it. A more serious obstacle lay in King Fahd's attitude to oil prices. On the one hand he wanted to increase his country's income, and on the other to avoid harming the economies of the Arab world's principal customers. In April 1989 he was quoted on Radio Mecca as saying that oil-producing countries should not push prices too far. A combination of the king's caution and OPEC's failure to make its members respect realistic production quotas caused oil revenues to tumble. By the end of the 1980s the boom was just a memory. Saudi Arabia started the decade with annual oil revenue of $102 billion dollars. By 1989 it had dropped to $18 billion. Riyadh was not only unable to implement its development plan, which needed $20 billion a year, but had to sell treasury bonds worth $20 billion to cover current budget spending. In 1989 the Saudi Arabian Monetary Authority was forced to issue bonds worth £8 billion on London markets through Saudi commercial banks. Riyadh's share of the oil-price pain was greater than other producers', but this was because it accepted production cuts decided by OPEC. Iraq's income did not drop as much as Saudi Arabia's, but its position was worse because of vast problems of repairing war damage and readjusting to peace. The oil producers' problems were immediately passed on to other Arab countries, as their manpower was no longer needed, and by 1989 large numbers of Jordanians, Egyptians and Yemenis were returning home without work. The effect was made worse by the Gulf states turning increasingly to Korean labour, which they preferred as there was no risk of the Koreans mixing with their own people and spreading dangerous ideas.

As treasuries ran short of funds, those who still had money in hand – the Kuwaitis, Qataris and Saudis – made no attempt to spread the impact of the downturn more equitably. These economic problems brought a disheartening period to a miserable close, with Arab spirits at a low ebb.

The 1980s had been a decade of humiliation in diplomatic and military matters. In 1982 the Israelis came close to occupying an Arab capital for the first time, during the invasion of Lebanon, while in the Occupied Territories Israel behaved as if Arab views could be safely ignored. Libya remained bogged down in the Chadian civil war, Khartoum was locked in conflict with the Sudan People's Liberation Army, and the Algerian-backed Polisario front continued its guerrilla war against Moroccan forces in the western Sahara. Every Arab country was under martial law or in a state of emergency for most of the time, often for reasons which had lost their validity. When President Sadat was assassinated in 1981 Egypt was still under martial law imposed on the grounds of tension with Israel, even though there had been no risk of war for the past eight years. Sadat's assassination prompted a state of emergency and the imposition of oppressive laws. Egypt later came to regard itself as a democracy, but this was more an aspiration than a reality, more an opportunity for politicians who had made their name in the 1950s to push themselves forward than a chance for younger men to develop their political talents. The actors came and went without applause, since the audience knew that the power lay elsewhere; denied a real voice in their own affairs, most Arab peoples felt impotent and angry. No one, it seemed, had benefited from the struggle against Israel except the military bureaucracy. The Arab League's self-imposed absence from Cairo and its move to Tunis, as a way of punishing Egypt for making a separate peace with Israel, reduced its status as an Arab voice in international affairs. The Arab world felt forgotten, eclipsed by Europe, its five most important capitals – Cairo, Damascus, Baghdad, Riyadh and either Rabat or Algiers (depending on whether Islam or revolution was in ascendancy)

– pale shadows of their former glory, while minor capitals on the periphery (Kuwait City, Doha, Abu Dhabi, Dubai) embellished their palaces and shut their ears to appeals for help. Small amounts of aid were passed under the table by Gulf sheikhs – $200 million here to buy wheat, $100 million there for education – but its purpose was either to keep the hungry quiet, or to buy Egypt's influence as a counterweight against Iraq. The Arab peoples no longer believed what they read in their newspapers or heard on the radio or television, no longer trusted their institutions or political parties. Frustration turned to greater violence in Palestine and to apathy elsewhere.

Divisions in the Arab world were nothing new, but signs of deeper fragmentation emerged in 1980, when the sheikhdoms formed what amounted to a club for the rich. The Gulf Co-operation Council, made up of Saudi Arabia, Kuwait, Qatar, Bahrain, the UAE and Oman was a highly damaging departure. Iraq attended a preliminary meeting in Muscat in October 1979, but the other states later withdrew into separate quarters without it. Iraq was not invited to attend further meetings, which it deeply resented. The wealthy at first felt that Iraq's presence would help them to face the propaganda war of the Islamic revolution coming from Tehran, but decided on second thoughts that they were not prepared to have an Arab revolutionary regime in their midst. Many in the Arab world had long suspected that the sheikhs were afraid of Baghdad, whatever they may have said about Arab brotherly love, but now the matter was beyond doubt. In their eyes Iraq was as big a troublemaker as Iran, even if it were the lesser of two evils if domination by one or the other was inevitable. The sheikhs hoped that when the war ended they could steer a middle course, keeping their distance from both states while retaining links with them. They kept up contacts with Tehran throughout the war, despite giving huge financial support to Baghdad. Oman, Qatar and the Emirates, which have strong trade links with Iran, were used as diplomatic channels.

The GCC was never the happiest of clubs. The small countries needed Saudi Arabia's political weight but resented Riyadh's assumption that it was the leader. Other tensions stemmed from differences of style and religion. The opulence of the Saudi royal family was out of step with the more relaxed atmosphere of Bahrain and the UAE, at odds with Oman, and far removed from the eclecticism (within Islam) of Kuwait. The royal families of Saudi Arabia, Kuwait, Qatar and Bahrain all stem from the same branch of a Najdi tribe, but this did not make for amity. The Sheikh of Kuwait said in 1990 that his country had suffered two catastrophes at once. Not only was it occupied by Iraq, but its government was obliged to spend its exile in Saudi Arabia.

The Arab Co-operation Council was another damaging development for Arab unity. It began early in 1989 when King Hussein approached Saddam Hussein with an idea for a new regional grouping, initially to be made up of their two countries and Egypt. The king thought that a marriage of Jordan's highly educated labour force, Iraq's military strength and economic potential, and Egypt's vast manpower could create a powerful entity with ports on the Red Sea, the Mediterranean and the Shatt al Arab waterway. The two men approached President Mubarak of Egypt, which was a bold move as Cairo had not yet been officially accepted back into the Arab fold. The prime minister of Egypt, Dr Atef Sidki, was given twenty-four hours to prepare a position paper reflecting Egypt's acceptance of the new council. The whole plan was decided, written and declared in three weeks, and at the last moment Yemen was brought in as well. It was presented to the Arab world with considerable fanfare on 16 February 1990, as if a great new Arab power had emerged.

The four countries had widely different reasons for wanting to belong to the ACC. To King Hussein, it seemed the only way out of an increasingly bleak situation. By the end of the 1980s relations between Jordan and Israel had reached a stalemate, and the king's contacts with the Palestinians in the Occupied Territories were almost equally frustrating. His problems with the West Bank had deep historical roots. The area was formerly part of Palestine, but was seized by his grandfather King Abdullah in 1948, when Britain terminated its mandate over Palestine. After this move Jordan (then called Transjordan) included nearly 6000 square kilometres of Palestine, including East Jerusalem. Transjordan obtained an acknowledgement of its authority over this area through an armistice with Israel in 1949. Israel occupied the area during the 1967 war, but Jordan retained important administrative duties as well as its territorial claim. In 1974 other Arab governments made it clear that they regarded the PLO rather than Jordan as the representative of the Palestinians. King Hussein resisted this at first, but reversed his position and accepted it at an Arab League summit in Rabat the same year. A resolution was passed unanimously recognising the PLO as 'the sole legitimate representative of the Palestinian people'. The king's decision had important implications for his own kingdom, because the Jordanian National Assembly had equal representation for the East and West banks, and 60 per cent of Jordan's population was Palestinian.

Many in the West assumed that the king had caved in under pressure from other Arab governments, but this was not so. 'If anyone thinks that I left the Palestinian representation to the PLO solely because of Arab pressure he would be mistaken. I gave up because there is nothing to be gained from the Israelis: they are not going to relinquish the Occupied Territories,' he said after the 1974 summit.

The risk of a Palestinian rejection of the Hashemite kingdom did not, however, evaporate. The intifada on the West Bank and in Gaza, which began in December 1987, was directed against the Israelis, but Jordan feared that it would spread to Palestinians on the East Bank, and took precautions. The intifada continued to intensify throughout the first half of 1988, resulting in international criticism of Israel, and in June King Hussein gave it his unconditional support at an extraordinary summit of the Arab League. At the same time he renounced Jordan's legal and administrative claims to the West Bank, to show that he had no wish to restore his own rule there, and said that if a Middle East peace conference was held the Palestinians should be represented by the PLO. At the time George Shultz, US Secretary of State, was promoting a peace plan based on a conference at which Palestinian participation would be confined to a joint Jordanian–Palestinian delegation with no PLO representatives.

Some thought that the king's decision was intended to remove legal obstacles to the creation of a Palestinian homeland, and when the PLO declared an independent state of Palestine in November 1988, it was widely supposed that this was what the king had intended. In fact, however, his move was prompted by years of bitterness in his links with the Palestinians and frustration in secret contacts with Tel Aviv. The notion that he sacrificed part of his kingdom to help the Palestinians was given undue importance. He was overwhelmed by the hopelessness of the situation left by the post-Camp David impasse. He could see that flexibility on the Palestinian side would not be enough to achieve a solution, because there was no give at all on the other side. The concessions demanded by the Israelis were so drastic as to make a compromise unthinkable. Others felt that the Israeli demands were merely a negotiating position, but the king was convinced that they would prove unmovable in rejecting a Palestinian state and a role for the PLO. He was also sure that they would not exchange territory for anything, not even peace. With the two sides so far apart the king felt that if he tried to bring them together he would incur the wrath of both, as had happened in the past. As he saw it, neither the Palestinians nor the Israelis had ever shown appreciation of his efforts. The Palestinians treated him almost as a traitor, as Jordanian forces had yielded the West Bank and East Jerusalem without a real fight in 1967, and he thought the role the Israelis envisaged for him degrading. After contacts with Tel Aviv and Washington he realised that the Israelis intended to continue administering the West Bank permanently, without returning any part of his former political role. 'They intended me to remain the unpaid, unthanked roadsweeper and drain-mender of Palestinian towns,' he said.

Opting out of the West Bank was the easiest course, but it had political and economic costs. Jordan had been created by the British as a buffer zone and was never a truly viable country, but its role in Arab–Israeli wars and talks, and its administration of the West Bank, had given it a voice in the Arab General Council and a role which could not be ignored. In abandoning the West Bank, King Hussein had inadvertently knocked away an important plank of his political legitimacy. One of his aims for the planned Arab Co-operation Council was to restore Jordan's influence by making it part of a larger body. The economic cost of opting out was that Jordan's responsibilities in the West Bank had entitled it to substantial aid from Saudi Arabia. When the Arab League held a summit in Baghdad in 1990, Saudi representatives transferred a sum to the Jordanian Central Bank and said: 'That's the last instalment.'

As a small country squeezed between Israel and three important Arab powers, Jordan has always suffered from anxieties about its security. Saddam Hussein has been King Hussein's only reliable neighbour, his steady friendship contrasting with threats from Jerusalem, resentment by the Palestinians, and pressure from Riyadh and Damascus. An alliance with Iraq and Egypt therefore seemed attractive. Another cause of Jordanian insecurity is severe unemployment (about 16 per cent) combined with high economic expectations created by advanced education. The proportion of university graduates in the workforce is substantially greater than the Arab average. King Hussein hoped that as Iraq recovered from the war with Iran jobs would be found for many of his people, and that Iraqi and Egyptian markets would also be more receptive to Jordanian exports. As part of a regional complex with both petroleum and agricultural exports, Amman might become an important financial market. Even the barrenness of Jordan's eastern regions could be eased if Iraq would share some of its Euphrates water. Much of this was a daydream.

Saddam Hussein saw entirely different advantages in the king's idea. Although Iran had suffered a setback, it remained a formidable neighbour. It was nearly four times larger than Iraq, three times greater in population, and eight times stronger in terms of gross domestic product (in 1987–88 the GDP of Iran was $362 billion, compared to Iraq's $45 billion). Iraq felt that an alliance with Egypt and Jordan would overcome this disparity. Baghdad also knew that once the euphoria of victory wore off, internal Iraqi divisions would re-emerge, threatening to split the country into three parts – Kurdish in the north, Sunni in the middle, and Shi'ite in the south. There was no prospect of real reconciliation between any of these parties. Further, the long-standing dispute between the two Ba'ath Socialist Parties, in Baghdad and Damascus, presented a risk of war with Syria. In that event Iraq could use the alliance with Jordan and Egypt to isolate Syria by air and land from the Red Sea and the whole of the Gulf peninsula. A further attraction was that Jordan's access to the Red Sea at the port of Aqaba had proved indispensable for Iraq's supply lines during the Iran–Iraq war, when its ships were unable to use the Gulf and the Shatt al Arab waterway was closed. This had proved a boon for both countries, increasing economic activity in Jordan to the point that 70 per cent of its external business was with Iraq.

Egypt was also an attractive partner from Iraq's point of view, despite the problems caused by the Camp David agreement. A survey of the future of the Arab nation, carried out between 1980 and 1985 by the Centre for Arab Unity Studies and involving more than 500 Arab scholars, came to the conclusion that it would be very difficult for any one country to emerge as the leader of the Arab world. The study, which ran to five thick volumes, assessed the ability to lead in terms of a combination of economic and military power, social balance and stability. On this basis Egypt was considered to have been the leader in the 1950s and sixties, but by the seventies and eighties the situation had changed and no other country had taken Egypt's place. With this in mind, King Hussein and President Saddam Hussein may have hoped to create a form of group leadership of the Arab world through a partnership with Egypt.

Another advantage was that Cairo was well placed to serve as a conduit for communication with Washington and Israel. After the new body had been formed, Egypt volunteered to ask the Israelis not to interfere with the construction of an Iraqi pipeline across Jordan to the port of Aqaba, passing within a few miles of Jordan's border with Israel. Tel Aviv accepted the request and the pipeline was built without any trouble.

Saddam Hussein also thought that Iraq's economic problems might be more manageable if it were part of a larger body. Already faced with huge debts, Baghdad needed to spend vast sums, partly to guard against a further war with Iran and partly to convert the economy back to peacetime priorities. There were also the human problems of returning up to a million men to civilian life and caring for hundreds of thousands of widows and orphans. The new body would give Iraq greater negotiating muscle in seeking financial support from the Gulf states, while the skilled labour forces of Jordan and Egypt could help the economic recovery.

King Hussein and President Saddam Hussein had little difficulty in winning President Mubarak's interest. In a country with unemployment officially at 15 per cent, but in fact much higher, with 40 per cent of the population below the poverty line, an exploding birthrate and huge tensions in the cities, a regional grouping could only be an opportunity. Iraq's reconstruction needs could offer openings for the Egyptian contracting industry and jobs for thousands who had returned home after the collapse of oil prices. The new grouping would put Egypt in a stronger position to break out of its diplomatic dependence on the United States, while improving the Arab military balance in relation to Israel. But the biggest advantage was that Egypt's isolation from the Arab world would be broken, and it would again have a chance to play a role beyond its borders. The most painful part of its ostracism had been a loss of importance on the wider stage, once it became clear that Camp David had failed to solve the Palestinian issue.

President Mubarak had no sooner accepted the plan than President Saddam Hussein proposed widening it to include Yemen, which radically altered the aims. King Hussein had visualised a group which was geographically and culturally contiguous, but Yemen was separated by a huge land mass and a cultural chasm. While Iraq, Jordan and Egypt all had Sunni ruling classes (and large Sunni majorities in the latter two countries), Yemen was dominated by the Zaidi, a branch of Shi'ism based on a belief that Zaid, a great-grandson of Ali (the

Prophet's son-in-law, who led a revolt of the poor) was the last imam. They established their rule in North Yemen in the ninth century, displacing a Sunni leadership. The reunification of North and South Yemen on 25 May 1990 created a country with a bigger population than Saudi Arabia but a much smaller area. Although there was evidence of oil deposits, large-scale production had not yet begun and the standard of living was among the lowest in the Arab world. Saddam Hussein, however, saw Yemen as a potential counterweight to Saudi Arabia, especially if it could be linked in some way with his own country. He had begun building close ties with the Yemenis, buying their loyalty with generous aid. Yemen was also indebted to him for squeezing cheap oil out of the Gulf states to supply its needs.

The inclusion of Yemen in the new body was bound to make Riyadh feel that Baghdad and others were trying to encircle it. President Mubarak immediately sensed that King Fahd would be concerned, not least because of a long history of Saudi–Yemeni tension and the fact that present-day Saudi Arabia includes areas that formerly belonged to Yemen. He asked King Hussein to talk to King Fahd and try to allay his fears, but the Saudis got wind of the planned new grouping, and when the two kings met the issue was not broached. The Saudi government is adept at avoiding difficult subjects by a variety of stratagems. King Fahd told King Hussein that he had to attend a graduation ceremony for air force officers at the time when they were supposed to talk, and suggested that they should both go. As there was no privacy King Hussein was unable to explain why he had come. Finally, on the way to the airport to go home, he said: 'Brother, I did not have the chance to talk to you about something.' King Fahd replied: 'The chance will come when we meet again.'

The ACC signing ceremony went ahead without Saudi Arabia having been informed or consulted. President Mubarak felt uneasy and decided to send his foreign minister, Dr Ahmad Esmat Abdel-Meguid, to see King Fahd. The foreign minister, a professional diplomat, waited while the king discussed other subjects and then said: 'Isn't there something you want to ask me?' The king replied: 'Everything is all right – Our brotherly greetings,' but as the meeting ended he said: 'All right, if you insist, what's this business about Yemen?' There could be no better illustration of the Arab approach to diplomacy, a world apart from the directness needed between brothers.

The four leaders of the Arab Co-operation Council came from different and contradictory worlds, with outlooks so varied that they seemed improbable partners. King Hussein was by far the most experienced, having held a somewhat artificial realm together for thirty-seven years, despite repeated assassination attempts. As a Hashemite king with a family tree stretching back to the Prophet, with an English education and a Western outlook, his perspectives were bound to be different to the others'. A man of polite manners who would be entirely at ease in an English baronial family, the king is married to a tall, beautiful American (Queen Noor) and has half-English sons by a previous marriage (to 'Princess' Toni). When he speaks in Arabic he tends to use diplomatic language with almost excessive politeness, but also with humour.

Saddam Hussein comes from the opposite end of the social ladder and represents a generation of young men from the Iraqi countryside who went to the capital in search of another world. Saddam Hussein more than anyone else created that new world, with all its strengths and weaknesses. He speaks with great directness and knows how to handle crowds, and how to use the Ba'ath Party machine to promote his own policies. He sees power as something to be kept at any cost, and does not shrink from using an iron fist.

Hosni Mubarak, a highly reserved former air force officer, did not enter politics until the age of fifty. His dedication to his work enabled him to survive the purges which touched practically all the other senior officers of his generation. A pragmatist by nature, Mubarak's approach to all problems is to decide what he wants and to set out to achieve it. He is an adequate rather than a gifted speaker, has contacts with a great many foreign leaders, and speaks good English, which helps in international affairs.

Ali Abdullah al-Saleh, President of Yemen, is another completely different personality. He belongs to the first generation of his tribe to leave the mountains and migrate to the cities. He attended a military academy for six months before joining the army and never had an opportunity to learn oratorical skills. His attitudes are those one might expect of a man who had been both a party ideologue and an officer, and he has a tendency to fear Riyadh, which tried hard to destabilise Yemen. The country's two leaders before him were assassinated, and before that the two Yemens went through decades of turbulence. Yemenis from the mountains are apt to express themselves in oblique ways, even in riddles, and some experience is often required to understand their meaning.

The Arab Co-operation Council made its mark almost immediately by forcing the rest of the Arab world to accept the return of Egypt to the Arab League. Iraq, Jordan and Yemen wrote to the other presidents and kings saying that they would not attend any further summits unless Egypt was there too. This move hijacked the agenda of the summit about to take place on 23 May 1989 in Casablanca, Morocco, which was intended to concentrate on other issues. Muammar Gadaffi said that if Egypt's return was added to the agenda Libya would quit the Arab League and break relations with any country which accepted it. Syria also objected, though not so forcefully. Before the meeting opened Saddam Hussein said that it would be insulting to President Mubarak to make him wait for a phone call, and he should be asked to attend immediately. And so it happened, without any resolution formally ending Egypt's suspension from the League being passed. It was as if the previous ten years had not happened.

The Gulf Co-operation Council also had a substantial impact throughout the decade as the voice of the rich, but both it and the ACC were flawed in concept. The first represented a dream of physical security between people who suspected each other. The only bond holding the sheikhs together was that their fears of Iran and Iraq were greater than their dislike of each other. The second was a dream of economic security between countries whose problems were not complementary. Given that all four members of the ACC had chronic economic problems, and that Iraq's hopes of prosperity lay far in the future, it was unrealistic to think that they could pull each other out of the sand. Each country had different reasons for joining, and each hoped to take more than it put in. It was an alliance of despair and frustration rather than strength, and its weakness soon became obvious. President Mubarak referred to it as a council of conspiracies two years after joining it.

If the two groups had come together in a single organisation dealing with both physical and economic security, or if the Arab League had risen above its divisions, a first step might have been taken towards adjusting to the changed Europe. As it was, the Arab nation ended the decade divided into clubs of rich and poor, unable to face the world, unable even to face itself.

There was, however, one aspect of the Arab Co-operation Council which attracted outside interest. As an economic body it seemed misconceived, as a strategic grouping it lacked coherence, but as a military organisation it might have potential. It was clear to outsiders that Iraq was keen to develop this aspect, while Egypt was reluctant.

President Mubarak felt he was being drawn into schemes which he had not envisaged and did not want, including the co-ordination of intelligence and the creation of an integrated Arab brigade. Even the possibility of such a move was enough to engage the attention of Israel. A link between the Iraqi and Egyptian armies would be significant by any standards, including those of the Israeli Defence Force.

8

The Friendless Neighbour

Tel Aviv followed plans for the formation of an integrated Arab brigade with both resignation and apprehension. The Arab world had grown accustomed to thinking of Israel as the dominant military and political power in the Middle East, but that perspective was never shared by the Israelis. As they saw it, their entire history since Biblical times had been the struggle of a minority for survival against hostile tribes. A sense of being surrounded and disliked was embedded in the national psyche long before the diaspora. As seen by Arabs, the Jews took their complexes to Europe and made themselves a people apart within their host countries, maintaining their separateness for centuries. Britain's support for a Jewish homeland, expressed in the Balfour Declaration in 1917, was the starting signal for a reverse migration which is not yet complete. With each group of European Jews that returned to Palestine, and later Israel, it became clear that the centuries had not mellowed their attitudes towards the *Goyim*, which is Hebrew for 'others'.

Against that background, it was inevitable that Israelis would regard the ACC's military activities as a continuation of a long history of confrontation. Their sense of encirclement was so strong that nothing could increase it, but talk of an integrated Arab brigade reinforced doubts about Israel's continued ability to overcome Arab forces through superior organisation, training and technology. The formula worked from 1948 to 1967, but Israel needed massive American assistance in 1973, and since then Arab forces had increased in numbers. Baghdad's performance in the final battles with Iran showed discipline and organisational abilities, and the scale and quality of its post-war rearmament looked ominous. As Tel Aviv saw it, Iraqi triumph, truculence and technology made a dangerous cocktail, especially when shared with Egypt and Jordan, even if symbolically.

Almost every development in the region from the spring of 1988 onwards increased Israel's concern. The fortieth anniversary of its foundation as a state, which fell in 1988, coincided with the more pessimistic mood. It was a time for Israelis to celebrate, but also to reflect that they remained as friendless as ever within their region. No one needed reminding that Israel's creation marked the disappearance of Palestine – from maps, but not from Arab hearts. Every Israeli born since 1967 had grown up in a climate of international criticism of Tel Aviv's treatment of Palestinians in the Occupied Territories, though its tone and level fluctuated greatly. The end of the Iran–Iraq war, which had partly distracted the Arab world from the Israeli conflict, signalled a further increase in pressure. In August 1988 most war correspondents left the Gulf, and many headed for the West Bank. Cameramen in Israel, busy since the outbreak of the intifada the previous year, found their services in even greater demand. The uprising brought the international focus back to the Occupied Territories, and public opinion in America and Europe reacted strongly to television pictures of Palestinian children armed only with stones resisting Israeli troops in Gaza, Hebron and Bethlehem.

Baghdad's support for the Palestinians boosted the morale of the intifada, giving it new energy and hope. The Israeli perspective was naturally different: Saddam Hussein was using the Palestinians to strengthen his claim to the leadership of the Arab world. An ill-advised decision by Saudi Arabia and others to suspend funding of Palestinian groups enabled Iraq to become the largest sponsor, with a donation to the intifada of $40 million a year.

The edgy mood in Israel was mixed with elation over the Soviet decision to allow mass emigration of Soviet Jews and to start mending fences with Tel Aviv. It looked like an Israeli diplomatic victory, but in fact it was due to the adroitness of American Jews in exploiting Moscow's need for US help. Sustained pressure forced the White House to make improved East–West relations conditional on concessions by Moscow to the Jews. At first most chose the United States as their destination, but Washington changed its immigration regulations, and Israel became the only feasible destination. The scenes at Tel Aviv airport were reminiscent of Ellis Island during the waves of American settlement. Soviet Jews arrived with few possessions, little money and less Hebrew to find that life in the promised land would not be easy. Israel accepted them gratefully, as they alleviated fears that Jews might soon be outnumbered by Palestinians even within the pre-1967 borders, because of the higher Arab birth rate. Even a few hundred thousand immigrants would help to defuse the demographic time bomb, but suspicions grew in the Arab world that the influx was in fact much greater. Wild rumours spread that five million Jews were on their way – an impossibility, since the total number in the Soviet Union did not exceed two million, and not all of them would want to leave.

The costs of absorption were beyond Israel's means. Washington faced a request for an additional $400 million from a country which was already its largest recipient of foreign aid, at a time when there was concern over the US deficit. The State Department played for time, hinting that it wanted a trade-off, an Israeli concession to unblock the peace process. The link was not explicit, but Tel Aviv felt squeezed by its friends.

The diplomatic noose drew tighter after an important speech by Yasser Arafat to the United Nations in December 1988. He had received a mandate from the Palestine National Council, the annual assembly of organisations which make up the PLO, to make concessions. Meeting in Algiers in November, the PNC made the biggest change of direction in its history. Israel's right to exist would be acknowledged, albeit implicitly, a peaceful solution would be sought, and the PLO would accept direct talks with Israel. Many in the movement had long recognised the need to live together with the Israelis, but the PLO's charter committed it to implacable resistance. The hardliners, including George Habash, leader of the Popular Front for the Liberation of Palestine, had held out against anything which Tel Aviv could interpret as weakness. It was the shift in the East–West power balance which forced them to think again. Moscow was still an ally, but a less-effective one. The Algiers decisions expressed a feeling that there was no real alternative. In changing tactics the PNC adopted the least unpromising approach, but few put much faith in it.

It was clear what the PNC's decisions meant, but they were expressed in a way which gave Tel Aviv room to misrepresent them. For example, anyone following Middle East politics would have realised that in accepting UN Security Council Resolutions 242 and 338 as the basis for an international peace conference, the PNC was implicitly acknowledging the state of Israel. But Tel Aviv said that was not good enough. It wanted explicit statements and a change in the PLO charter.

Sweden and other European countries realised that the PLO had undergone a fundamental change, but feared that Washington would heed Tel Aviv's doubts. Since 1975 the US had refused to hold formal talks with the PLO unless it recognised Israel's right to exist, renounced violence and revised its charter. Just before stepping down as Secretary of State, George Shultz refused Yasser Arafat a visa to go to New York to address the UN General Assembly. The Assembly sidestepped this by convening a meeting in Geneva, giving Arafat a platform from which to proclaim the PNC's decisions. The speech itself failed to satisfy Washington, but clarifications at a press conference filled in the gaps. Between the two events Swedish and other diplomats had urged Arafat to say the words Washington wanted to hear. The results were swift: Washington accepted that the PLO had gone some way towards meeting its conditions, talks resumed between PLO headquarters and the US ambassador in Tunis, and Tel Aviv expressed its bitterness and disappointment.

Many in the Arab world saw the PLO moves as an unwise concession to Israel, but Yasser Arafat replied: 'I am making these concessions to the Arabs, not the Israelis.' Arab moderates, particularly from Egypt and Saudi Arabia, had been urging a diplomatic solution for some time, arguing that the prospects of war were over and the PLO would have to accept a dialogue with the Americans. Arafat was sure that Israel would pocket any concessions and give nothing in return, but he recognised that moderates would not be convinced of this argument until concessions had been tried: 'The Israelis want territory and will never accept the idea of compromising it for peace whatever we do.' He was equally sure that no move by the PLO would dilute Washington's support for Tel Aviv.

That was a realistic analysis, but many in the Arab world were reluctant to abandon their hopes in the Israeli Labour Party and its hints of an exchange of land for peace. This would depend on Israel's internal balance of power, which was as confusing as ever, with Labour and Likud courting small parties in search of a majority in the Knesset. The government of national unity formed in December 1988 collapsed, leading to the formation of a Likud government on 11 June 1990, with Labour in opposition. Both parties maintained contacts with the Arab world, but their signals were mixed. As time passed after Arafat's speech and nothing new emerged from Tel Aviv, Israel's relations with Egypt went sour.

King Hassan of Morocco was well placed to keep in touch with Tel Aviv, as Morocco has the largest Jewish community in the Arab world, its roots going back to the retreat of Jews from Spain after the

Inquisition. The close links between Moroccan Jews and Sephardic Jews in Israel once prompted the king to remark: 'I am the only Arab who has a political party in Israel.' Shimon Peres, the Labour leader who had been Israel's prime minister and foreign minister at various times, was able to visit Morocco and Egypt, whereas Likud's Yitzhak Shamir was excluded. The king answered criticism of his meeting with Peres by saying: 'If a solution seems possible I am going to pursue it.'

When Likud formed a government in 1990, the king received two Israeli messages through intermediaries. The first, from Peres, urged him to keep up the contacts. 'I hope you will not think that because we have left the government we have lost all our influence,' it said, pointing out that Israeli foreign policy was co-ordinated between Likud and Labour through a four-man committee, with Yitzhak Shamir and Moshe Arens (then foreign minister) on one side and Peres and Yitzhak Rabin (who had been defence minister in the previous national unity government) on the other. 'So, Your Majesty, you can still contact me, you can still talk to me,' Peres concluded. The second message was a four-page letter from Shamir: 'Your Majesty, the image given of me in the Arab press is that I am very hard. It's not true.' Shamir said he had lived through the agonies of the pogroms and that friends and relatives of his had been caught up in the Holocaust. He understood the suffering of others.

> I have lived my life dreaming of a nation and a state, so I can understand the Palestinians. If you are angry over what we are doing to face the Palestinian uprising, it is not that we do not understand. We understand their dreams very well, but unfortunately here we have a conflict between two dreams . . . we agree to the Palestinians having a dream, but they should understand that it is impossible.

To many Arabs, Shamir's approach was preferable. However much they disagreed with him, at least they knew where he stood. Peres tended to hold out hope, but nothing came of it. By the time Arafat made his speech, Arab opinion was a mixture of those who had once hoped for change under Labour but were now sceptical, those who had never believed in the apparent differences between Labour and Likud, and those still willing to give Labour a chance.

In retrospect, the Arab world had deluded itself; none more than the Egyptians. Many in the Cairo government thought that Arab concessions would help bring Peres to power. Egypt dreamed of playing a role in Israeli internal politics, and at least five Egyptian politicians or ministries had hotlines to Tel Aviv. An Arab visitor was sitting with a senior Egyptian negotiator in 1984 when the phone rang. 'Ah, that's the hotline,' he said. The caller was Peres, and the negotiator addressed him as Shimon. Afterwards he said: 'We must support Peres. Let us give him concessions; it's the only way to break the coalition government.'

Everyone wanted to help Peres, but Peres was unable to help himself. Shamir might be ineffectual too, but at least he reflected political realities. The hotlines helped sustain a sense of urgency, an illusion of Egyptian influence, but so many were connected to them that they lost their exclusivity. Every Egyptian who had one was on first-name terms with the Israeli at the other end. The idea that Israeli politics could be steered from outside was shared by the Americans, but unlike the Arabs they had diplomatic and economic muscle. What they lacked was will to use it. Another illusion was the Israelis' desire to spread the circle of friendships to as many influential Egyptians as possible. Not everyone was seduced: some felt the Israelis should be kept at arm's length until they agreed to talk to the Palestinians.

Everywhere Tel Aviv looked in 1989 and early 1990 it found unpleasant surprises. It might have expected Tehran to be well-disposed towards it after the help it gave during the war. Apart from its role in the Iran–Contra affair, Israel passed information to Iran on many levels, using old contacts developed before the Iranian revolution, when the Shah sent members of the army, police, intelligence and other services to receive Israeli training. But Israel was rewarded after the war only with diplomatic slaps. Clearly feeling that Israel's help had been self-interested, Tehran took the side of the Palestinians.

Another development unwelcome to Israel was that Jordan, which had greatly strengthened its ties with Iraq during the war, moved even closer after it. There was a time when Israel felt it had the measure of King Hussein; now it was less sure. It seemed not to realise that its own actions drove him further into Iraq's arms and provoked the creation of the Arab Co-operation Council. The king was alarmed when minister of defence Ariel Sharon, a leading Likud hardliner, proposed pushing the Palestinians out of the Occupied Territories and across the river into Jordan, which would then become their national home. Israel's problem would be solved at the expense of King Hussein and his Hashemite kingdom. Sharon continued to press this idea after leaving defence and becoming minister of agriculture and later minister of housing.

Nothing worried Tel Aviv more than Saddam Hussein's evident ambitions. The road to leadership of the Arab nation lay through the Palestinian cause, and Baghdad had gone the first mile. The Israelis saw all sorts of unwelcome implications. Syria was bound to become more intransigent from an Israeli viewpoint, not out of any warm feelings for Iraq but to avoid appearing soft. Egypt would be disturbed and might lose interest in the peace treaty, which was already being strained by the stalled talks on West Bank autonomy. The overall picture would have worried any far-sighted Israeli, not least because Tel Aviv had no solution to offer. The national unity government put forward a plan on 14 May 1989 based on starting a dialogue and holding elections in the Occupied Territories, leading to a form of autonomy. It was supported by Washington but the Palestinians were hesitant because Tel Aviv refused to allow PLO members to represent them in the talks. It was clear that Israel wanted Arabs to accept the status quo, which would then gain political legitimacy.

Overshadowing all these concerns were urgent warnings from Israeli and American intelligence over Iraq's military build-up. Newspaper headlines concentrated on its chemical weapons, but these were not the most important threat to Israel, as its own large chemical capability would be a deterrent. Tel Aviv was more concerned about Iraq's nuclear research and its overall conventional weapons strength. A report in 1990 by the Strategic Studies Institute of the US Army War College said that Iraq's development of long-range missiles had to some extent offset Israel's previous advantage in that field. Israel considered trying to repeat the setback it had dealt Iraq's nuclear research programme in 1981 when it bombed the French-built Osirak reactor. After the attack Baghdad salvaged 12.3 kilograms of uranium 235, enriched to 93 per cent. A report for the US Senate Armed Services Committee said that this was 'possibly' enough for one nuclear bomb, but only if Baghdad had access to advanced techniques. Although the material was inspected by the UN's International Atomic Energy Agency, which found no evidence of military usage, the Israelis suspected that Iraq had recovered the lost ground.

After the war United Nations inspectors established that Iraq had a substantial nuclear programme, which was at an advanced stage and included research on both fission and fusion weapons (better known as atom and hydrogen bombs). The UN team estimated that

Iraq might have been able to produce an atom bomb in less than two years, but Arab scientists close to the project pointed out that this would have amounted to little more than an experiment. In order to turn the research into a military capability Iraq would have needed at least eight years, the Arab scientists claimed.

Iraq felt entitled to develop a nuclear capability, and to do so in secret, because Israel was already a nuclear power. After disclosures in London by Mordechai Vanunu, a former Israeli nuclear worker, it was estimated that Israel could have more than 100 nuclear warheads. (Tel Aviv inadvertently gave credence to Vanunu's story by sending agents of Mossad, the Israeli secret service, to kidnap him and take him back to Israel, where he remains in prison.)

The American Strategic Studies report concluded that any pre-emptive attack by Israel on Iraqi facilities would be a most dangerous gambit and could precipitate a major war in which US interests would be jeopardised. It estimated Iraq's conventional military strength as: total armed forces of one million, including an army of 955,000; 5500 reconnaissance vehicles; 1000 armoured infantry fighting vehicles; 7100 armoured personnel carriers; 300 towed field artillery pieces; 500 self-propelled field artillery pieces; 200 multiple rocket launchers. The report expressed surprise at Iraq's military abilities. It said:

> In April 1988, when the Iraqis finally took the offensive, most observers refused to accept that this was actually happening. It was assumed that the Iraqis would soon run out of steam or would fumble in some egregiously inept fashion. It seemed incredible that they could quickly develop their offensive capabilities. When it became clear that the Iraqis would win, theories emerged to explain this extraordinary turn of events; for example it was suggested that they had relied on chemical weapons, and in so doing had overcome their enemy. Another theory was that they had received help from the Soviets or the Egyptians. Examination of the evidence behind these claims reveals that by and large it is unconvincing.

The report concluded that the Iraqis were much better fighters than had been thought.

The Kuwait war would later throw doubt on the accuracy of the report and others which contained similar figures of Iraq's military strength, but they worried the Israelis, already alarmed by Baghdad testing its long-range missiles, flaunting its chemical weapons capabilities, and boasting of its strength.

The dynamics of a conflict were in place, but there was no spark, only a dialogue of implied threats by Israel and warnings by Baghdad. This seemed out of keeping with the wider international situation, at a time when Cold Warriors were folding their tents and most regional conflicts were nearing settlement. Eduard Shevardnadze, in a speech in Vienna in 1989, said:

> In close proximity to Europe, powerful arsenals are being created . . . 25,000 tanks and 4500 aircraft are deployed in and ready for combat in the Middle East, and there is a real danger of nuclear and chemical weapons appearing there. Missiles have already appeared with an operational range of 2500 kilometres. The conclusion is obvious: the process of disarmament in Europe and settlement in the Middle East have to be synchronised.

It might have been obvious to Shevardnadze, but it was not to Tel Aviv. Nothing could have been more unwelcome than such a link; the last thing Israel wanted was Middle East disarmament. It had become feasible in Western Europe because the risk of war with the East had disappeared, but in the Middle East the causes of conflict were as sharp as ever. Shevardnadze's proposal underlined a risk which had long been apparent: the more the West drew attention to Iraq's military build-up, the more Israel's forces would also come under scrutiny. If Iraq's weapons were a danger to regional security, why not those of Israel? In nuclear, chemical and missile technologies Israel was far ahead, while its conventional forces were the Roman legions of the Middle East. Western fingers pointed at Baghdad one day could be directed at Tel Aviv the next. Military strength was the only sort of security the Israelis trusted: remove it and the future of the Jewish state would be in question.

There had been an attempt to build a security based on trust, but nothing came of it. The Camp David arrangements gave a green light for Egyptians and Israelis to visit each other's countries. Both sides initially hoped this would improve the atmosphere, as it might have done if Israel had adhered to the Camp David spirit. But its failure to make progress on autonomy for the Occupied Territories prevented any blossoming of goodwill, and although thousands of Israelis visited Egypt, the atmosphere remained clouded.

In October 1985 an Egyptian soldier, Suliman Khater, manning a border post called Ras Barqua near Taba, was so incensed by the sight of Israeli tourists entering his country, looking relaxed and wearing casual clothes, that he opened fire on them with his machine-gun, killing seven and wounding ten others. Later he was found hanged in his prison cell, and there were rumours that Mossad was responsible. On 4 February 1990 a bus carrying Israeli tourists was ambushed on the road from Ismailiya to Cairo, leaving eight Israelis dead and seventeen wounded. The attackers were never found. On 25 November 1990 Ayman Hassan, a twenty-three-year-old Egyptian border guard, opened fire with a submachine-gun on an Israeli bus in the area of Ras-el-Naquab. Five Israelis were killed and twenty-seven wounded.

Hassan was sentenced to twelve years' hard labour by a military court in Cairo, which took the view that he was under heavy psychological stress. At his trial, he and his defence lawyer argued that he was provoked by the sight of Israelis crossing the border daily at a time when Palestinians taking part in the intifada were suffering what he considered harsh Israeli reprisals. Hassan also said he was upset by the behaviour of Israeli tourists in Egypt. They were often seen wandering around Egyptian shops, buying textiles, medicines and other subsidised goods, eating on street corners and behaving as if they owned the place. It did not make a good impression on the Egyptian public, although reactions as extreme as Hassan's were rare.

However much they hated the Israelis, many Arabs secretly admired their military strength. That feeling declined after the 1973 war, and contact with the tourists destroyed what remained of it. Israelis were ordinary mortals after all.

Tel Aviv began to complain that normalisation was not going as planned, which was no overstatement. Few Egyptians visited Israel, partly for cost reasons but also because Tel Aviv had not kept its side of the Camp David bargain. Among those most conspicuous by their absence were Egypt's Christians, the Copts. Jerusalem was (and is) sacred to them, yet they boycotted it from 1967 and refused to relent even when President Carter tried to persuade the Coptic Pope, Shenouda the Third, to help the normalisation programme. The Pope's advice to his people was: 'Don't go to occupied Jerusalem. We are Arabs even if we are Christians. The Egyptian Copts will never be the faint-hearted of the Arab nation.'

Jerusalem's status as one of the holiest places of three major religions has never been easy to reconcile with the Jewish belief that they alone were chosen by God and directed to live in Eretz/Israel. During his meeting with Pope Shenouda in 1977, President Carter asked: 'Your Eminence, after all, aren't the Jews the chosen people?' The Pope was very quiet. Then he said: 'Your Excellency, that is true, but you forget something. They were the chosen people because they had the first book and the first direct messenger, but when Jesus Christ came they ceased to be the chosen people, because if the Jews were the chosen people then what were the Christians?' Carter exclaimed: 'That is a new point.' If an imam had been present he might have added that after the third direct messenger arrived with the third holy book, the Muslims became the chosen people. But what matters about the 'chosen people' idea is its place in the historical, religious, mythological and cultural entirety of Israel. The Jews see all these elements as an indivisible whole. Take away the concept of being chosen or the commandment to live in Israel and the balloon bursts. This makes it difficult for any Jewish government to give up territory without undermining Israel's *raison d'être*. The Labour Party had to tread warily in proposing an exchange of territory for peace – so warily as to call its sincerity into question. It was the Labour government of Shimon Peres and Moshe Dayan which allowed the first Jewish settlements to be built on the West Bank. Most Arabs are sceptical about ideas put forward by Israeli moderates for elections in the Occupied Territories leading to self-rule. They see it as a ploy to defuse sovereignty demands by giving a form of municipal autonomy to large population centres which are already beyond Israel's effective control.

Meanwhile the killing continued. On 20 May 1990 eight Palestinians were shot dead and fifteen others injured by a former Israeli soldier at a village south of Tel Aviv, prompting riots in the Occupied Territories which left twenty dead and 700 wounded.

The more intransigent the Israelis seemed, the more the Palestinians looked for a different solution. The rise of Saddam Hussein as a strong Arab leader coincided with the darkest period of their despair. To a desperate people, unaware that the overall picture was more complicated, Saddam appeared to offer the beginnings of an alternative. The hope became a bond.

Across the Atlantic, a very different impression of the Iraqi president was forming in the boardrooms of American big business. Iraq was emerging as a regional power, and was attempting to challenge the status quo. It urgently needed a substantial increase in oil prices, but this was blocked for the moment by the refusal of the sheikhs to reduce production. Sooner or later Iraq's agitation was likely to cause a repetition of the 1973–74 price explosion, and every US industry would then see an increase in its energy costs, forcing up prices and reducing sales. In the United States, what the captains of industry think one day, congressmen and senators say the next, especially when the captains of intelligence give similar advice. As the *Washington Post* later reported, Richard Haass, the National Security Council Staff Director for Middle East affairs, felt a 'growing disquiet' that US policy was not working as expected. Pressure on Washington to focus on Saddam Hussein began to grow sharply.

9

A Second Oil Century

Addressing Congress on 20 January 1990, President Bush said that the twentieth century had proved to be an American century, and predicted that the twenty-first would be another. Few Westerners would argue with the first half of that analysis, but to Arabs something was missing. It sounded incomplete to describe the century as American without mentioning the ingredient which made it so. The United States became a superpower through being the first country to extract oil in large quantities, the first to see its wide applications, the first to have unlimited supplies when fighting a major war, the first to dominate oil markets as a producer, the first to realise that its production would be overtaken by consumption, the first to see the importance of Saudi Arabia, and the second (after Britain) to bring Middle East oil production under its hegemony. If Bush is to be proved right about the twenty-first century, the US will have to find ways to continue being first. What seems certain, however, is that the link between oil and power will continue for many more decades. Only the future will tell whether a second American century lies ahead, but a second oil century seems inevitable.

Until recently, that statement might have seemed debatable. After the increases of 1970 to 1974, when the price of oil climbed from $2 to $11 a barrel, a frenetic search began throughout the developed world for a substitute energy source. Had it succeeded, the link between power and oil would have been broken, but one by one, all the alternatives turned out to be unsafe, uneconomical, ineffective or impractical. Nuclear power, which had been in use in the United States and Britain since the 1950s, had by now spread to many other countries, though nearly all used it on a small scale to complement other sources of energy. American reactors dominated the export market, even capturing the attention of Paris, which usually tried to keep its distance from Washington. An American design concept was taken up for a vast nuclear construction programme intended to break France's dependence on Middle East oil. After many years of construction work France began to produce a higher proportion of its electricity from nuclear energy than any other European country, and for a time other capitals thought of following its lead. Then problems started coming to light. Most of France's nuclear power stations were sited beside rivers, to provide the huge amounts of cooling water they needed. The nuclear reaction turned the water to steam to drive the turbines, and afterwards it was condensed and returned to the rivers. Very little of the water was contaminated, but it was extremely hot. Entire ecological systems began to change, forms of river life usually only found in tropical countries drove out indigenous species. As power stations became older, more and more incidents of leaks and contamination of riverbeds and seashores occurred. Radioactive crabs and clams were found near the exit pipes of stations sited by the sea. Then the failure of emergency cooling systems in a huge nuclear power complex on Three Mile Island on the American east coast almost caused a reactor core to melt, which would have contaminated a heavily populated area with radioactive dust. The incident showed that the American design was inherently dangerous, in that it depended on emergency pumps which could fail, and that doubling or tripling the pumping systems was not a solution. In an attempt to avoid this defect the British tried gas-cooled reactors, but construction costs were enormous and problems with reliability and efficiency took years to correct. The outcome was public distrust of nuclear power in the United States, Britain and much of continental Europe, leading to a huge campaign for its abolition. Italy, which had only minimal sources of natural gas, coal, hydro-electric energy and geothermal power, was forced by public opinion to shut down its reactors and shelve all future plans for nuclear reactors.

Another effect of changed public attitudes was that development of a more advanced method of fission, greatly increasing the energy which could be extracted from uranium ore, was shelved. A pilot plant on the north coast of Scotland had shown it to be technically feasible, and France constructed power stations which worked on the principle, but the political climate in Britain was against it. One of the objections was that enriched plutonium, which is not only radioactive but extremely toxic, would have to be transported regularly from one power station to another, and that this could be attractive to terrorist groups looking for new forms of blackmail. This was too much for public opinion, which was already concerned about the transportation of mildly radioactive waste from ordinary nuclear power stations.

The drawbacks of nuclear power suggested that oil would have no serious challenger as an energy source for at least fifty years, perhaps a century. The United States, the Soviet Union and Europe had been competing since the 1970s to develop a way of extracting power from nuclear fusion, as opposed to fission, but the problems were so daunting that no one expected a working prototype to be built before the second or third decade of the twenty-first century.

There were dozens of other suggestions, but no solutions. Attempts were made to build cars powered by solar cells, but they worked only in brilliant sunshine and stopped if the weather was overcast. Forests of windmills were constructed in California and Scotland to exploit wind power, but their contribution to power supplies was marginal. Huge projects were undertaken in Britanny to extract hydro-electric power from the tides, and other installations were set up to produce power from waves, but both these ideas had high capital costs and modest returns. Before choosing the nuclear option France discussed a proposal to develop agricultural alcohol on a huge scale. The attractions were that the raw materials (such as sunflowers and grains) could be produced by French farms, and cars could be made to run on alcohol with minor adjustments. It would be much more expensive than oil, but this could be offset by changing the tax structure. The idea was ultimately dismissed as impractical, partly because agricultural exports were important to the French economy, and these would have been lost if huge areas of land were diverted to alcohol production. The power needs of space satellites brought about advances in the design of solar-electric cells, but high production costs limited their use to specialised applications. Many towns in Europe set up plants to burn refuse, using the heat to produce electricity or hot water. Pig farmers found that the slurry produced by their animals could be used to produce gases capable of powering small engines. Iceland, which has more geothermal energy than it can use, began looking for ways to export it, even talking of building an undersea powerline to Britain. A revival of coal was considered, but that would have meant a return to the chimney era, and the new industrial revolution was driven by non-chimney industries. Ecological objections to coal also precluded this option, as 'dirty industries' were being forced to leave the developed world. Japan transferred some of its refinery capacity to Korea for this reason. Plants developed during the

Second World War to convert coal into petroleum were returned to use, but were prohibitively expensive to run. Only South Africa took this up in a big way, mainly to protect itself from anti-apartheid sanctions. Ways of extracting oil from shale were improved, but needed a much higher oil price to make them viable.

By the end of the 1980s the developed world had realised that a practical alternative to oil did not exist and was unlikely to be found in the foreseeable future. Some governments tried to reduce consumption by imposing tougher building codes, forcing architects to design better-insulated homes that could be heated more cheaply. The savings this effected were offset by an increased demand for energy caused by the rising standard of living.

The limited success of scientific research in finding alternatives forced politicians to re-evaluate oil. Its price had risen greatly, but it was still cheap in real terms; some argued that instead of searching for a replacement, the West should put more effort into a pro-Arab foreign policy. If the Cold War had ended ten years earlier, this would have been attractive to many European governments, but until 1985–86 the possibility that the Soviet Union might try to seize the Gulf forced them to think in strategic terms.

Even at this late stage in the Cold War the two superpowers lacked information and insights about each other. In October 1989 a group of senior American and Soviet officials, past and present, met in Moscow to consider the reasons for their long-standing mutual misunderstandings. The meeting, held at the Institute of the Americas in the Academy of Political Sciences, made it clear that Soviet officials continued to underestimate the importance of the Gulf to American foreign policy, while Americans tended to misjudge Soviet thinking and intentions. Discussing the Soviet intervention in Afghanistan in 1979 and the diplomatic and economic pressures which the US subsequently brought to bear against Moscow, Anatoly Dobrynin, chief Kremlin foreign policy adviser and former Soviet ambassador to Washington, said that the decision to send troops to Afghanistan was taken hastily in response to political conditions in Kabul. Only three people were involved in the decision: President and Party General Secretary Leonid Brezhnev, Defence Minister Marshal Ustinov, and Prime Minister Alexei Kosygin. Dobrynin accused the Americans of overreacting.

Zbigniew Brzezinski, former US National Security Advisor, became angry: 'How do I know that it was only a reaction to local conditions, or that only three people were involved? I woke up one day and found a Russian army crossing international borders and going full speed towards Kabul.' He said that the National Security Council's initial assessment was that the move was a first step towards the oilfields of the Gulf. 'There was no other way we could interpret it,' he said. The row reflected two perspectives so far apart as to make mutual understanding impossible.

The American tendency to see all events in or near the Middle East in terms of their possible impact on oil supplies was conditioned by memories of the Second World War, when the United States accounted for 63 per cent of world production but had difficulty in supplying its forces in Europe and elsewhere because of harassment by German U-boats. Since that experience, the long-term security of oil supplies and sea routes had always been among the highest priorities of US foreign policy.

At the end of the war the US was still self-sufficient in oil, but it went into deficit soon afterwards, and by the end of the 1980s it was importing 50 per cent of its consumption. Japan was in an even worse position, importing 91 per cent of its total energy needs. The Soviet Union remained a big producer, but its hopes of vast new discoveries in Siberia were disappointed. Third World nations like China, Indonesia, Malaysia and Brazil, described by economists as 'sleeping giants', were beginning to awake, their economies stirring, their rural populations abandoning wood fires and water buffaloes and switching to electricity and tractors. At present 75 per cent of oil produced is consumed by the industrialised countries, but it has been estimated that rising Third World living standards will double world oil consumption in the next thirty years.[1] If discoveries of oil reserves had continued at the rate of the 1970s, this increased demand would have been welcomed, but by the 1980s the black-gold Klondike was over. Enough had been found in the North Sea to meet Britain's needs for a time and to partly supply several other European countries, but most recent discoveries were more modest. A suspicion was growing that while many secondary fields remained to be exploited, and small fields were still being found, the world's greatest treasures had already been harvested. Another huge find comparable with the oil fields of Texas or Saudi Arabia would be needed to avoid a shortage in the

[1] The estimate was made in a study by Dr Sa'eed El-Naggar, vice president of the World Bank between 1985 and 1989, for a conference in Cairo on oil needs in the twenty-first century.

twenty-first century. In April 1985 the US Department of Energy estimated, on the basis of the forecasted increase in world oil consumption, that the price of oil would rise to $80 a barrel by the year 2000 and $110 by 2010.

The role played by OPEC was becoming unacceptable to consumer countries. Thirteen oil-exporting countries, eight from the Middle East and the rest from Asia and Latin America, but all from the Third World, were making decisions which affected the jobs and living standards of the whole world. The West could cope, but India and the African countries were knocked sideways by price increases. The Arabs talked of compensating the poorest countries, but their generosity did not last long. Oil had always been under the control of one cartel or another, first the big oil companies, then the producer governments. The more irritated consumer countries became, the more they tried to influence Middle East politics.

The dangers were clear to all Western capitals by the 1980s. Washington, Paris, London, Bonn and Rome knew that their prosperity in the twenty-first century would depend on a Middle East resource which was diminishing, could not be replaced or substituted, and for which the Third World would soon be competing. The Middle East was unlikely to be able to resolve its own tensions because of the weakness of its political structures. As far back as 1974 the United States had declared that it would use force if necessary to secure the Gulf oilfields. Long before the occupation of Kuwait, the West realised that it would almost certainly have to carry out that threat sooner or later. However, no Western defence organisation seemed suited to such an operation, as Nato was confined by its charter to the north and the Atlantic and the Western European Union was mainly a talking shop, despite its small operational role in clearing mines from the Gulf during the Iran–Iraq war. The West's naval deployments during the war with Iraq were really American operations with a political cover provided by European allies to give the appearance of a multi-national effort. The presence of Denmark, Holland and Belgium, for example, was almost entirely political tokenism, consisting of only one or two minesweepers per country. France and Britain made much bigger contributions, in keeping with their interests in the Middle East, but only the United States had the huge human, economic and military resources to undertake to guarantee the natural resource on which they all depended.

The Gulf war also underlined the logistical difficulty of conducting Western operations in the Gulf without bases in the region. Although the United States and Britain had supply dumps in Oman, and the US had created a substantial military infrastructure in Saudi Arabia, with Saudi money, neither Britain nor the US could be sure of being allowed to send forces, or even land its aircraft, in the event of an emergency. The US and Britain hoped that their reflagging operations would make Arab capitals see the advantages of allowing friendly powers better facilities to protect the Gulf. However, Arab sheikhdoms were worried about Arab public opinion and the reaction of militant Arab regimes. Also, there was a fear of repeating the mistakes of the nineteenth century, when nearly all Gulf ruling families entered into protection agreements with Britain. No one needed reminding that the arguments for providing the Western allies with bases were scarcely different to those used by London a century earlier, when the dominance of the Royal Navy could make or break a sheikh's prospects of retaining power in his area. The United States and its West European partners discussed the need for a rapid deployment force to secure the Gulf, but lacked the unity and determination to work together. The United States went ahead unilaterally, basing its force in Florida, some 12,000 kilometres from the Gulf, which was bound to be a logistical nightmare in the event of an emergency. Even so, it was still the West's best and only hope of rapidly meeting a threat to Gulf oil supplies. One effect of the Gulf war and the longer-term worries about instability in the region was to bolster Washington's position as the sole remaining superpower.

10

Rendezvous in a Minefield

It is a fact of human nature that the greatness of leaders tends to be judged by the quality of their adversaries. President Nasser would have cut a smaller figure in modern history without his struggles against the Israelis, the French and the British. Winston Churchill might never have been prime minister but for Adolf Hitler. Few in the West would have heard of Ho Chi Minh but for the aggressive polices of John F. Kennedy, Lyndon Johnson and Richard Nixon. Every American president since Eisenhower has felt a need to assert himself against his Soviet counterpart, even during periods of detente. The urge to be remembered as the defender of the West has driven most post-war American presidents to exaggerate the Soviet threat. On the pretext that the price of freedom was eternal vigilance, Europeans and Americans were bombarded with information about the vast Soviet and East European forces assembled on the other side of the Iron Curtain. Most still believed this in 1985, when Mikhail Gorbachev was appointed General Secretary of the Soviet Communist Party, but the threat began to lose credibility during Ronald Reagan's second term and evaporated soon after George Bush came to office.

In June 1989 the defeat of the Communist Party in the first free elections in Poland since the Second World War was the signal for revolution throughout Eastern Europe. As the frustration of people denied self-expression for forty-five years spilled onto the streets, tired regimes vanished into history almost without a fight. The Hungarian Communist Party was dissolved in October, swiftly followed by the resignation of Erich Honecker of East Germany, and later the rest of his government. Czechoslovakia's leader Milos Jakes resigned with the entire Party Presidium in November, only days after the fall of Todor Zhivkov, the Bulgarian leader. The Timisoara uprising in western Romania prompted a fierce backlash by the Securitate, but Nicolae and Elena Ceausescu were dead before the year was out.

On 28 November Chancellor Kohl put forward a plan for the unity of the two Germanys, causing astonishment in Bonn, East Berlin and the rest of Europe. Most Western governments feared this was five years premature and had no chance of being accepted by Moscow. President Gorbachev, under pressure from the Soviet military, played for time and raised objections, but eventually agreed in return for modest political concessions. Reunification took place on 2 October 1990, the Cold War was declared over, and the fearsome image of the Russian bear which had haunted the West for decades gave way to the appealing face of a Nobel Peace Prize winner.

The huge American defence machine began to look irrelevant. Congressmen talked of a 'peace dividend', but the public showed little excitement. If the United States no longer had its vast armed forces, would it still be a superpower? Would it remain the centre of international attention? The rot was already obvious to Europeans, whose newspapers began to give less space to reports from Washington. The gloom of introspection sapped American self-confidence, prompting talk in the US media of a retreat from global responsibilities. The lack of a challenge was bad for morale, calamitous for the defence industry. With the disappearance of the Soviet Union as a credible opponent, the White House needed a new beast to slay.

Thousands of miles away, Saddam Hussein faced a parallel but not identical dilemma. The collapse of the Iranian challenge was seen as a great victory, but the problems of peace would be no easier to manage. Iraq now saw itself as a regional superpower, and wanted to assert its leadership, but it was not sure how to go about it. Unlike Washington, it had no difficulty in identifying the enemy – Israel. The problem was how to get Tel Aviv to take up the challenge. Baghdad had been supporting the intifada for months, but there was no sign that this would lead to a wider Arab confrontation with Israel. Iraq realised that it would have to raise the stakes.

Dick Cheney, the US Defense Secretary, found himself struggling to define the role of American forces when he addressed the Congress Foreign Relations Committee on 1 March 1990. The United States was attempting to combat the drugs menace and was sending forces to Colombia. 'American forces are ready to meet whatever contingency they may face.' His audience was not very impressed. Drugs were a problem, not a menace to freedom, and meeting any contingency was hardly a strategic concept. General Colin Powell, Chairman of the Joint Chiefs of Staff, said at the same meeting: 'Two of national defence policy's basic objectives are to deter military attack against the United States and its allies and other important countries and to ensure the defeat of such an attack should deterrence fail.'

He continued: 'America cannot choose between military security and economic security. The two are inextricably entwined. On a smaller but similar scale the peaceful trade and economic prosperity of a city is dependent on the vigilant presence of the local policeman . . . No city mayor would consider abolishing his police force . . . Our global military posture is designed to keep the peace.' Washington's tendency to see itself as global sheriff has exacerbated many regional conflicts in the past, but now there was nothing on the horizon. Just the opposite; the main problem was boredom.

The administration was not alone in sensing a vacuum; American think-tanks and universities began to suggest that something more fundamental than the collapse of the Soviet empire had occurred. Could it be that the chemistry of relationships between states had changed? That an order based on perpetual conflict or confrontation had given way to peaceful discussion? That the present historical era had ended?

The intelligentsia of the Arab world should have identified this as a pyramid of fantasy. During the 1980s every Middle East capital had set up strategic studies centres, often two or three competing in the same city. They were well placed to see flaws in the American argument, as nothing had changed in their own region, but they failed to do so. Instead of challenging the thesis, many began to apply it to Arab regional problems. The Arab world was soon full of proposals for solving the conflict with Israel through a mechanism similar to the CSCE (Conference on Security and Co-operation in Europe), the thirty-five-nation organisation linking Nato, the Warsaw Pact and the European non-aligned countries. But, unlike many European problems, the Arab–Israeli dispute is not just a strategic, economic or political issue. The differences reach much deeper than that. Arabs, Jews and Christians all have valid religious claims in Jerusalem; it would be impossible for any one group to abandon it even if it seemed politically expedient. Modern techniques of conflict management sometimes produce solutions when there is a shared willingness to give and take, but religious visions do not lend themselves to compromise. Convictions of faith are total and indivisible, exempt from the constraints of reasonable-mindedness. Secondly, Israelis believe that if they abandon East Jerusalem, the West Bank or Gaza, the Palestinians will try to retake the whole of pre-1967 Israel. Compromise requires a willingness to live together and share resources. Most Palestinians, other than the fundamentalists, are willing to do that; most Israelis are not, and dislike being considered part of the Middle East. In any case, even if the Israelis dropped the promised-land concept, there would not be room for both peoples to expand, because water resources are inadequate.

Between 1988 and 1990 co-operation between Washington and Moscow helped resolve a string of regional conflicts, leading some Western diplomats to suggest that a similar approach could work in the Middle East. But those conflicts which had been ended were often little more than puppet shows manipulated from Washington and Moscow, proxy wars between Communism and Capitalism. The Arab–Israeli situation was different. The wars of 1967 and 1973 took place in spite of superpower involvement, not because of it. The fear that a Middle East war might bring Washington and Moscow into nuclear confrontation precluded the games that were being played elsewhere. Arabs and Israelis might accuse each other of being manipulated, but both knew that the real forces of darkness lay in their own history. The Arab–Israeli conflict, even in its present-day rather than its Biblical form, began long before Winston Churchill first used the phrase 'the Iron Curtain'. The lack of a solution has nothing to do with any shortage of outside efforts to find one. The British tried and failed and gave up their mandate in Palestine long before the Americans were involved. There was nothing to suggest that the dispute was any more ripe for a solution than it was in 1948.

When Gorbachev talked about a balance of interest replacing a balance of power, which was Utopian even in a European context, Arab think-tanks had a field day. There was an embarrassing readiness to borrow other countries' slogans, no matter how irrelevant to Arab problems. Every new catchphrase drew the Arab imagination towards some fresh fantasy.

The dream was shattered by a speech given by Saddam Hussein at at a summit of the Arab Co-operation Council in Amman at the end of February 1990, which made the Utopians realise that the Arab masses continued to see strength, not diplomacy, as the means of change. 'From here in Amman we can see the lights of Jerusalem,' he said, and began to talk about the 'rape' of Palestine, a reference to the

Palestinians' territorial losses in 1948, with the creation of Israel, and in 1967, with the occupation of the West Bank and Gaza. At the time the slogan of Muslim fundamentalists in the Occupied Territories was 'One Palestine, from the river to the sea.' Turning to East–West affairs, Saddam Hussein said that the Soviet decline had left a vacuum. The loss of Moscow's restraining influence posed a risk that the United States would become an undisciplined force in world affairs: 'We are discouraged because we never thought the Soviet Union would kneel in front of the United States.' He predicted that the Gulf would be the main area where Washington would assert its influence, and said Arabs should be alarmed. In an implicit attack on Egypt's links with the US he added: 'There is no place for one-sided friendship . . . Some of us claim to be friends of the US . . . Either we assert ourselves or we have to kneel like the others.'

As he left the Royal Conference Centre Saddam Hussein realised that he had embarrassed President Mubarak. 'Was what I said about the United States a bit harsh?' he asked him. Mubarak told him not to worry and that he was entitled to form his own opinions, which was polite and diplomatic, but far from candid. Saddam Hussein offered an explanation: 'I had to use such strong language because we are in Amman and Jordanian television is seen in the Occupied Territories. I wanted to encourage our brothers of the intifada.'

Needing to assert himself, Saddam Hussein had attacked Israel, the most obvious target. Washington, unconsciously looking for an adversary, found the Iraqi leader apparently claiming the part. In one sense that is exactly what he was doing, as he felt strongly about the American role in the Gulf and saw himself as the Arab leader best placed to stand up to Washington. In a wider sense, the Amman speech was more a bid by Saddam Hussein for regional leadership than a challenge to Washington.

Saddam Hussein belongs to a school of Arab politics which does not differentiate between Israel and the United States. His support for the intifada was therefore a move against Washington as well as Israel. He cannot have been unaware of the risks he was running, as he said himself that Washington would be the world's sole superpower for at least five years after Moscow's abdication. In his Amman speech he said: 'We have to show them that we can stand up to them and negotiate, and not in the way some others have done before us' (a slighting reference to Egypt's talks with Washington which led to the Camp David agreements).

President Mubarak, who gave the next televised speech from the Conference Centre, tried to lessen the potential damage and to distance himself from Saddam Hussein's remarks by saying that the American role in Middle East peace was vital and should be encouraged. Relations between Baghdad and Washington, already tense, had been greatly aggravated by Saddam's speech.

11

A War of Nerves

The wooing of an adversary has parallels with falling in love. Excitement and uncertainty play a part in both. Secret messages passed by go-betweens often have a role, growing in emotion and intensity, and leading to a clearly-defined point of no return. Thus it was between Baghdad and Washington in late 1989 and early 1990. Saddam Hussein's Amman speech on 24 February marked that point, although the two capitals had been eyeing each other for many months. The process which transformed them from acquaintances to enemies took nearly a year, punctuated by accusations and denigrations, threats and warnings. A war of words evolved into a war of nerves, while most other countries, wrapped in post-Cold War euphoria, showed only moderate interest.

Saddam Hussein considers that there was a conspiracy against him which went in two phases – the first covert, the second overt – conducted by Israel, the United States and Britain. Phase one began in the mid-1980s with the Irangate affair and deliveries of missiles to Tehran by Washington and Tel Aviv. A little later, certain parties began sowing doubts in the Iraqi president's mind. He was approached by another head of state, whom he refuses to name. Some years before, in 1986, this leader had talked to the American ambassador in his country and learned of a plot by Washington, Saudi Arabia, Kuwait and other states to prevent a complete Iraqi victory over Iran and to ensure that Iraq would be divided after the war. Astonished by what he had heard, the head of state visited Saudi Arabia and confronted King Fahd, who denied it. The story appears to have been half true and half muddled, but Saddam Hussein was concerned enough to send an envoy to see King Fahd. There is no doubt that Washington wanted to prevent either side in the Iran–Iraq war from being completely defeated, and it was probably happy with the outcome, which it did not see as a clear-cut Iraqi victory. There is no evidence that Washington wanted, at that stage, to divide Iraq. It had the opportunity to do so at the end of the Kuwait war, but President Bush, more by error than design, left Saddam Hussein with enough units and equipment to hold the country together, enabling him to defeat uprisings by Kurds and Shi'ites. Whether the unnamed head of state was right or wrong is unimportant: what matters is that his message strengthened Saddam Hussein's suspicion that Washington wanted to topple him.

Tariq Aziz, Iraq's foreign minister, voiced Baghdad's concern when he visited Washington in October 1989, and this had some effect. President Bush issued an internal directive ordering the administration to promote normal relations with Iraq, arguing that this would help stability in the Middle East. He followed this with a Presidential Order on 16 January 1990 declaring that increased trade with Iraq was in the US national interest.

Bush's intentions were overtaken by events. During the first six months of 1990 hardly a week passed without an angry statement by Washington, Baghdad or Tel Aviv, punctuated by efforts by Amman, Riyadh or Cairo to smooth things over. At first other Arab capitals saw little difference between the US–Iraqi row and similar disputes in the past. Washington seemed to enjoy having a Middle Eastern *bête noire*. Yasser Arafat of the PLO, Muammar Gadaffi of Libya, Hafez al-Assad of Syria, King Hussein of Jordan and Iran's Ayatollah Khomeini had all featured in the US gallery of infamy at various times. King Fahd of Saudi Arabia was usually viewed more sympathetically, although a series of American newspaper articles in the 1980s accused him of being lazy and incompetent, a gambler, a heavy drinker and a womaniser. The king had to get Prince Bandar, the Saudi ambassador in Washington, to hire a public relations firm to improve his image.

The chronology of events is important, marking the steps towards the battlefield. None of the diplomatic pinpricks along the way was important in itself, but the cumulative effect created the climate for the Kuwait war.

11 February 1990: John Kelly, US Assistant Secretary of State, visits Saddam Hussein and warns him that the State Department's annual human rights report will contain criticisms of Iraq, particularly over the use of poison gas against the Kurds in 1988.

15 February: At 6.30 a.m. GMT the Arabic service of the Voice of America broadcasts a commentary attacking Iraq's human rights record. It says the commentary 'expresses the point of view of the State Department'.

19 February: Saddam Hussein criticises the large American naval presence in the Gulf. It was increased during the Iran–Iraq war because of US commitments to escort reflagged Kuwaiti tankers, but eighteen months have passed since the ceasefire and the US fleet is still massive.

20 February: Tel Aviv announces that certain Iraqi forces have entered Jordan, and says it will not tolerate it. Baghdad and Amman have formed a joint air force squadron, clearly timed with an eye to the Arab Co-operation Council summit.

21 February: The State Department publishes its human rights report and Baghdad reacts strongly against the criticisms.

24 February: Saddam Hussein's speech at the ACC summit in Amman, intended as a strong warning to Israel. The Iraqi leader is disappointed by the reaction from other Arab capitals. Washington, however, reads it carefully. The US Senate passes a resolution halting sales of wheat to Iraq, despite objections from the administration, which calls it inappropriate. Saddam Hussein sees the ban as an act of aggression against Iraq.

Early March: Six fixed launchers for long-range Scud missiles are detected by US military satellites at air bases near Iraq's border with Jordan, and within range of Israel. No announcement is made at the time.

9 March: Farzad Bazoft, a journalist representing the British Sunday newspaper the *Observer*, is arrested in Iraq on spying charges and sentenced to death, prompting pleas for clemency from the British, who claim he is innocent. He had been convicted of bank theft in Britain some years earlier and sentenced to two years in prison. Most Arabs would find it hard to believe that a person with such a record could become a journalist. The fact that he was born in Iran, although naturalised in Britain, and that he had made repeated visits to Iraq, strengthened the doubts. He was taking part in a visit organised by the Iraqi Information Ministry for British journalists when he left the group and went to a military installation in southern Baghdad, where a huge explosion was reported to have occurred, and where he was alleged to have collected soil samples. In order to avoid using Iraqi transport a woman friend, a British nurse working in Baghdad, drove him to the site in her car. She was arrested too but later released.

15 March: Bazoft is hanged. The *Observer* begins a campaign against Saddam Hussein.

Iraq's refusal to heed the pleas for clemency seemed justified to many Arabs. The official Egyptian press recalled the Lavon affair of

1954–55. Two Israeli intelligence officers were sent under cover to Egypt in 1954, at a time when relations between Cairo and Washington were improving. They established contact with some elements of the well-established Jewish community and organised a secret network, planting explosives in American libraries and other public places. The aim was clearly to stop the rapprochement, but they were arrested when a bomb went off prematurely outside the Cinema Metro in Alexandria, injuring one of them. They were tried and sentenced to death, and immediately pleas for clemency came from the highest levels, including President Eisenhower and the Pope. The executions went ahead, and eleven years later Israel asked for the return of their remains, as part of an exchange of prisoners between Israel and Egypt after the 1967 war. The remains were treated with honour on arrival in Israel and only then was it admitted that they had been Israeli undercover agents. The affair took its name from Pinhas Lavon, the Israeli minister of the interior who was also acting minister of defence.

17 March: Saddam Hussein is becoming increasingly agitated about the low price of oil and continuing overproduction by some of the Gulf states, who are exceeding their OPEC quotas. He visits King Fahd to press these objections.

22 March: Dr Gerald Bull, a ballistics expert specialising in very large-calibre guns, is assassinated in Brussels. There is speculation that Mossad, the Israeli intelligence service, is responsible. Bull had studied the feasibility of using a gun rather than a rocket to launch satellites, and had been working on a project for the Iraqi government, whose purposes were suspected by the West to be of a military nature.

28 March: British officials seize what they say is a packet of krytons, or electronic switches, which have been purchased in the United States for shipment to Iraq via London on an Iraqi plane. It is claimed that these are triggers for a nuclear bomb, but the evidence is inconclusive. Saddam Hussein appears on television with several krytons in his hands. 'We don't need to smuggle them and they are not for any nuclear purpose. They are solely for civilian use,' he says. The Israeli prime minister Yitzhak Shamir announces that Iraq will be attacked if it develops a nuclear capability.

2 April: Saddam Hussein's reply, in a televised address, is intended as a warning but is reported in the West as a threat. He is quoted as threatening to 'eat half of Israel with our fire' (meaning chemical weapons). What he in fact says is that Israel would 'face grave consequences if it conducted any attack against Iraq under any pretext. Israel is threatening us with a strike and they are even hinting at a nuclear strike. By God, if they did that, we are going to use what we have and I take this chance to say that we have got weapons that can face them and they can be effective enough to create a war which would eat half of Israel if they dared to attack Iraq with nuclear weapons.' He adds: 'We do not own a nuclear weapon and we do not need one and we do not aspire to have one.'

The White House describes his remarks as 'deplorable and irresponsible'.

29 March: A British press campaign reaches its height. Large sections of tube have been seized at a factory which is making them for Baghdad, and other parts are intercepted in Italy and Greece on their way to Iraq by lorry. The British believe that the tubes could be bolted together to make a large gun designed by Dr Bull, but the Iraqis claim they are parts of a chemical pipeline. The British argue that no one would make a pipeline out of gun-quality steel of such enormous thickness. (After the war a United Nations team inspected what they said was a huge gun designed to fire shells hundreds of kilometres. Most people in the Arab world thought it unlikely that the Iraqis had built the gun with the intention of firing shells, as it was too large to be moved from one site to another, and would therefore have been vulnerable to air and missile attack. Iraq needed a cheap way of launching satellites, and it seemed possible that the 'supergun' was primarily a space project.)

3 April: Israel announces the launching of a satellite called Ofok (the Hebrew word for Horizon), said to be for military intelligence. It is the first known Israeli venture into space.

5 April: Prince Bandar, the Saudi ambassador to Washington, visits Saddam Hussein in Mosul. The Iraqi leader had phoned King Fahd and asked him to send someone who could convey his views to President Bush and Mrs Thatcher. He tells Prince Bandar that he does not intend to attack Israel but wants the West's help in obtaining assurances that Israel will not attack Iraq. Prince Bandar passes on the messages but finds both Thatcher and Bush sceptical. President Mubarak conveys the same message to Israel.

6 April: President Mubarak of Egypt defends Saddam Hussein in a speech, describing him as 'a man of peace', and expressing scepticism about reports that Iraq is building a nuclear bomb.

8 April: President Mubarak proposes that the Middle East should become a region free of nuclear weapons. When a delegation of American senators visits Cairo and voices concern about Iraqi armaments, President Mubarak suggests that they should take it up personally with Saddam Hussein, and offers to arrange a meeting. Senator Robert Dole, the Senate minority leader, heading the delegation, says he would have to speak to President Bush. Later he and Bush speak on a secure line from the US Embassy. Bush discusses the matter with Brent Scowcroft, his National Security Advisor, and gives his approval. Dole faxes him a letter which the group plans to deliver to the Iraqi president, which Bush approves. President Mubarak talks to Saddam Hussein, who replies: 'All right, send them.' A special plane takes the delegation to northern Iraq on 11 April, as the Iraqi leader is on holiday at the mountain resort of Sarsank, in the Kurdish area. They meet at Mosul the following day, in the presence of April Glaspie, the US ambassador. A transcript of the meeting is later given to selected members of the Ba'ath Party and to the Egyptian government.

The American delegation's letter expresses concern about reports of Iraq's potential nuclear, chemical and biological capabilities. These weapons, it says, are endangering Iraq and pose a threat to other countries, creating unease in the area. Saddam Hussein's speech threatening the use of chemical weapons against Israel has created much anxiety. The senators urge him to stop these weapons programmes and cease making provocative statements. The letter says they have come because they are seeking improved relations, and thank him for receiving them. It is signed by Senator Dole, Senator Frank Murkowski (Republican, Alaska), Senator Alan Simpson (Republican, Wyoming), Senator James A. McClure (Republican, Idaho) and Senator Howard Metzenbaum (Democrat, Ohio).

Senator Dole tells the Iraqi leader that President Bush wants good relations but is worried about the situation. At the same time Senator Dole acknowledges that Iraq too has reasons for concern. Saddam Hussein thanks them for their frankness and says he is not angry: 'We are worried. If you are getting news about what Iraq is doing, we are also receiving news about what the United States is doing and the policies you are pursuing . . . there is a very wide hate campaign in the United States and Europe against us.'

Senator Dole interjects: 'Not by President Bush.' Saddam Hussein replies: 'I did not say that President Bush himself was participating in it, but you must realise that every campaign triggers a counter campaign.' The problem, he says, is that the US does not realise the effect that Western media campaigns have on the Arab world.

'You must know that the two of you – the United States and Israel – are provoking the whole [Arab] nation. I don't want to tell you about the misinterpretations and misunderstandings.' He points out the way his televised speech had been reported. 'Some of you may say: "Why reply?" [to the Israeli warning]. Because I felt the Arab nation needed a psychological cover against this campaign.'

Senator Dole assures him that the American government is not behind the campaign and adds that the US had been against the Israeli attack on Iraq's Osirak nuclear reactor in 1981. Saddam Hussein replies: 'Yes, I know that, but you received so many reports about it and it was done with your clear knowledge. They could not have done it without telling you.' Senator Dole replies: 'I am sorry Mr President, we did not know.'

Saddam Hussein says: 'This is a double catastrophe, because if America knew, it would be a catastrophe, if it did not know, then something must be wrong. You are supposed to know everything that is happening in the world. Either way, it is a bad thing.'

Returning to the exchanges with Israel, he says: 'If Israel attacked us with nuclear weapons, we would reply with gases. Isn't that fair?' He discloses that he has given orders to his military commanders that if they hear of an Israeli nuclear attack they are free to fire the chemical weapons right away. 'I know that the Geneva Convention – and we have signed it – is against chemical weapons, but are chemical weapons more dangerous than nuclear weapons?' He feels that the Arabs have a right to acquire weapons if Israel is doing so, and asks: 'Why should you be unfriendly?'

In another passage he touches on a fundamental point: 'Why is it that we are treated this way in the Western media? The Arabs listen every day to insults against them. Why have you allowed yourselves to be under the influence of Zionists and Zionist lobbies to this extent? Why? We want peace but we don't want to surrender. We don't want to go on our knees . . . The country which fought for eight years defending its dignity and territory is ready to continue and sacrifice more.'

He makes no secret of Iraq's missile programme and implies that the US opposition to it is inconsistent. 'You did not say anything about the Iranian missiles or the Israeli missiles.' (Iraq also claims that it has launched a rocket carrying a satellite, but does not say whether it reached orbit.)

He offers to allow them to go anywhere they wish and says he will provide a helicopter. 'See if Saddam Hussein is killing his people. Go and see the Kurds. See the installations.' Senator Dole says it is a generous offer but he will have to consult his colleagues.

Saddam Hussein raises the broadcast on the Voice of America's Arabic service and the State Department report which it reflected. Shortly after the broadcast April Glaspie, the US ambassador, was summoned to the Iraqi Foreign Ministry to be told of Baghdad's displeasure. Later she gave the ministry a curious explanation: the commentary was prepared for broadcast in another language, and had not been cleared for use in Arabic. Baghdad felt that this showed the views were authentic, even if the broadcast was a mistake. April Glaspie also sent a statement of regret to Tariq Aziz, the Iraqi foreign minister. Senator Dole tells Saddam Hussein: 'I know that you are angry . . . the man responsible for this in the Voice of America was dismissed because the US wants better relations with Iraq.' Miss Glaspie adds: 'I assure you Mr President as ambassador of the United States that this is not the policy of our government. The policy is to be friendly to you.' This was the truth, but not the whole truth. President Bush's order of 16 January still held good, but was not the only source of authority. By this time American policy had fragmented into various strands, working separately.

Senator Dole says he has seen a television report that in an area south of Baghdad the Iraqis are developing a virus which could destroy whole cities. Saddam Hussein replies: 'I am astonished . . . we are doing research but we are not producing anything.' He asks if the US is producing such weapons. One of the senators replies: 'No, but we too are doing research.' Saddam Hussein said:'Is it forbidden that Iraq should do research?' Senator Dole asks for a commitment that Iraq will stop biological, chemical and nuclear research, but Tariq Aziz replies: 'Senator, all right, we agree. We are ready to do this, but can you get such a pledge from Israel? If you can get it from Israel you can get it from Saddam Hussein.' Saddam Hussein adds that he has already proposed that the whole of the Middle East should become a zone free of nuclear and chemical weapons.

Turning to the seizure of the krytons in London, which had been extensively reported in the British media, Saddam Hussein says: 'What happened in London was a trap. That shipment which you arrested was not coming to us. It was a shipment made by the CIA in arrangement with British intelligence. It was clear to us that this was a conspiracy so that it could be the basis of a campaign.'

Saddam Hussein had other strong views about the media campaign which he did not mention to the senators. He believed that the three countries responsible, the US, Britain and Israel, had worked together to orchestrate it. He disliked Mrs Thatcher and suspected her of involvement, but regarded President Bush as a weak man and felt that real power in the United States lay with ultra-right elements who were virtually steering the administration's direction.

While the five senators were in the Middle East the US Senate passed a resolution accepting that Jerusalem was the historical capital of Israel. This caused outrage in the Arab world, but also surprised European governments, which had always made a point of keeping their embassies in Tel Aviv to show that they did not accept that Israel had the right to treat Jerusalem as its capital. Senator Dole pleased the Arabs by expressing his disagreement with the resolution.

18 April: Saddam Hussein warns Israel against trying to destroy sites where they suspect Iraqi missiles are based. Addressing the Association of Arab Labour Unions he says: 'Any Israeli attack will trigger a war which will not end until all the Occupied Territories have been liberated.'

19 April: The Elysée declares President Mitterrand's support for the proposed nuclear-free zone in the Middle East, and a few days later Washington also shows interest. (Later, in July 1991, all five permanent members of the UN Security Council will declare support for it, without explaining how this would affect the only nuclear power in the area – Israel).

21 April: Baghdad protests to Washington after detecting an AWACS surveillance plane flying over its territory, and gives details of the course the plane had followed. The incident had taken place three weeks earlier. If Baghdad had merely wished to express its anger it would have done so sooner, and the delay suggests an additional motive. A few days later the Iraqis announce that they are using a super-computer in their missile programme. It appears that Baghdad wants to show Washington and Tel Aviv that it has made progress in the use of high technology, perhaps hoping that this will have a psychological impact and might help deter an attack. The United States had sold a super-computer to Saudi Arabia, and press reports speculate that it might have been passed on to Iraq, but Riyadh issues a denial.

3 May: Kuwait enters the picture when Iraq says that the situation on oil prices is getting out of hand and implies that Kuwaiti overproduction is part of a conspiracy to hold prices down. Saddam Hussein says: 'In 1986 the price of oil went down to $7 a barrel, which in real terms was cheaper than in 1972. We are facing huge responsibilities following the war [with Iran] and we have nothing but oil to enable us to do so quickly.'

30 May: Sixteen heavily-armed Palestinian guerrillas attempt a raid on Israel from the sea. A ship lowers two boats which race to the shore but the guerrillas are intercepted and killed by Israeli forces. Responsibility for the raid is claimed by the Palestine Liberation Front, which is led by Abu El-Abbas, known in the West as Abu Abbas. Tel Aviv declares that the mother ship came from Libya. This alarms Muammar Gadaffi, who flies to Cairo to ask President Mubarak to talk to the Americans or Israelis. He points out that the headquarters of the PLF is not in Libya but in Baghdad. The US State Department, reluctantly and under pressure from Congress and the Israelis, freezes the US dialogue with the PLO and says it will not be resumed unless Yasser Arafat not only disassociates himself from the raid but dismisses Abu Abbas and the PLF from the PLO. It must have known that this was unthinkable. Contacts between the US and the PLO collapse, which is what Tel Aviv has always wanted, but the PLO feel little loss, as little has been achieved by this contact. In the words of Abu Iyad, second in command of the PLO: 'It was a monthly examination of us by the Americans. At every meeting the Americans would come to us with between three to six questions: What do you think of so and so? . . . How do you define this or that phrase or expression? . . . What do you intend to do here or there . . . ? At the beginning we took it seriously and went into a vast amount of paperwork. The questions were still flowing. We never received any replies or even comments. We were unable to know whether we passed their examinations or failed. At last we understood that it was only a *passe-temps* to interrupt the silence and entertain an audience which had already lost interest.'

The war of nerves was clearly coming to a head, but all assumed that any confrontation would involve Iraq and Israel. Another possibility would emerge at the Arab League's Baghdad summit at the end of the month, but a previous hint had passed unnoticed. A year earlier, during a visit by King Fahd to Baghdad, Saddam Hussein astonished the king by producing a draft non-aggression pact between the two countries, which Baghdad had prepared without consulting Riyadh. 'Do we really need that?' the king asked. 'I want you to sign it; it is better this way,' was the reply. Saddam Hussein said he had been approached by many people suggesting that Saudi Arabia was involved in a plot against Iraq, and he assumed that the king had heard rumours about Baghdad's intentions. 'It would be a blow to all of them if we signed a non-aggression pact,' he said.

King Fahd remained hesitant. 'We do not need to sign in ink what is assured by blood, being brothers,' he said. But signed it was, and the Iraqi leader confirmed his commitment to it during an unexpected return visit to Saudi Arabia at the height of the war of nerves. Knowing that the king was hunting at Hafr el-Baten, Saddam Hussein flew there with little advance warning and told King Fahd that he was convinced that the US was plotting against Iraq. The king replied that he knew President Bush very well and considered him a man of peace and a good friend of the Arabs. He did not think the US President was a 'man of conspiracies'. At a time when President Bush was enjoying the reflected glory of capitalism's victory over Communism, the king pointed out, it could not be in his interests to undertake an adventure in the Middle East. Washington would want international attention to remain focused on the changing face of Eastern Europe.

In retrospect, it appears that Baghdad was preparing the diplomatic ground for a crisis with Kuwait. It hoped at this stage to persuade Kuwait to make concessions by peaceful discussion, but knew it might have to threaten force. The pact was intended to make Riyadh realise that Baghdad's dispute lay solely with Kuwait, which was not offered a similar non-aggression treaty.

12

Why Kuwait?

The first signs that Iraq's annoyance with Kuwait was approaching a threshold of danger came in late May and early June 1990. Saddam Hussein's anger was clear to those who followed Middle East affairs, but initially attracted only moderate interest in the West. Even after months of tension and moments when a Middle East war seemed likely, the United States was still treating relations with Iraq as a secondary priority. The *Washington Post* later noted that not one meeting of the National Security Council was convened to discuss Iraq between October 1989, when President Bush set his Gulf policy, and 2 August 1990, the day of Iraq's occupation of Kuwait. As seen from Washington, Middle East problems were an annoying distraction from more important business – the US economy, German reunification, troop withdrawals from Europe, reform in the Soviet Union and fears that Nato might disintegrate for want of a new role.

At a lower level, some in the State Department were puzzled by what looked like a sudden change in Baghdad's priorities. It was as if Saddam Hussein had forgotten Israel and become furious with Kuwait in the space of a few days. This was an over-simplification. For eighteen months, from August 1988 to February 1990, Baghdad's top priority was to revive Iraq's post-war economy, which would require funds for reconstruction. This was not easy, as its debts to non-Arab countries exceeded $35 billion. Baghdad's best hope lay in increasing its oil revenue, but the price of crude oil remained stubbornly low. Efforts to talk the price up absorbed most of Iraq's diplomatic energy until early in 1990, when it began to fear an Israeli nuclear attack. The statements from Tel Aviv which Baghdad saw as nuclear threats were prompted by Israeli suspicions that Baghdad was trying to foment an Arab–Israeli war. It is now clear that neither side was in as aggressive a mood as the other believed. Saddam Hussein's Amman speech was certainly provocative but did not presage an imminent attack on Israel.

Tel Aviv, for its part, was thinking only of a limited conventional strike against Iraqi nuclear research facilities, not a nuclear attack on Iraqi cities. Saddam Hussein's televised speech about chemical weapons was mainly sabre-rattling to deter any Israeli aggression, and although he was unhappy with the way it was reported he thought it had succeeded in its aims. By late April, after Prince Bandar had carried his message to President Bush and Mrs Thatcher, and after seeing the US Senators, the Iraqi leader felt he had made his point. What was perceived in the West as a change in direction was in fact a return to former priorities.

The obstacles to higher oil prices were overproduction and lack of self-discipline within the oil producers' cartel. OPEC's ability to manipulate the oil market has always depended partly on psychological factors. The rise and fall of prices is not a perfect mirror of supply and demand; it also reflects the market's view as to whether the cartel is united or divided. If one member breaks ranks the price may drop sharply, even if the other twelve adhere to their quotas. The United Arab Emirates persistently produced more than the amount it was allocated, and Kuwait used the UAE's non-compliance as an excuse to exceed its own quota. Iraq was incensed that two rich sheikhdoms were preventing its own post-war recovery. By now Baghdad and Tehran were co-operating again and Riyadh, worried about its shrinking oil revenues, was ready to work with them, but their combined diplomatic pressure proved insufficient to bring the small states to heel. Oil prices at first remained stable and later dropped sharply, causing Iraq's revenue to slump by $7 billion, a sum equivalent to the deficit in its 1989 balance of payments. Baghdad was facing economic suffocation.

Kuwait, like Iraq, was in urgent need of greater revenue. The reasons were different but the result was the same – both countries were determined to make the most of their oil. Instead of giving them a shared interest in higher oil prices, this had the opposite effect, because of their economic differences. Kuwait had invested heavily in Western refining and marketing facilities, and its income came more from selling petrol and other products than from crude oil. As Kuwait's overseas companies were the initial buyers of Kuwaiti oil, anything gained initially from higher oil prices would be lost in lower profitability of the companies. What mattered to Kuwait was not the oil price so much as the volume sold. Its priorities were diametrically opposed to those of Iraq, which depended almost entirely on selling crude oil and needed the highest price that would not cause a collapse of demand. Each time the price dropped by one dollar, Baghdad's annual revenue declined by $1 billion.

A further economic difference was that Kuwait had also invested in a broad range of Western industries, giving it an interest in maintaining the general economic health of the countries concerned. When the price of crude dropped, these industries tended to make greater profits and Kuwait's investment income rose. By the second half of the 1980s there was a rough balance between Kuwait's two sources of income. Kuwait was now better protected against fluctuations in the market than any other Gulf producer, while Iraq was among the least protected.

There was also an important philosophical difference between Iraq and Kuwait. Iraq felt that countries which produced an important raw material should be properly rewarded, whereas Kuwait was dedicated to market economics. A drop in the price of oil would be seen in Baghdad as a blow to natural justice, and in Kuwait as a normal effect of changing demand and supply.

It might seem surprising, even selfish, that a wealthy Arab country should follow a policy damaging to the interests of an Arab neighbour. Seen from a Kuwaiti viewpoint, the need for greater income was so great that it had little choice. Part of this stemmed from feelings of insecurity. In the twenty years before the Iraqi invasion Kuwait spent $22 billion on its air force and on missile systems, buying equipment from the United States, France, Egypt, Britain and the Soviet Union. Its forces included eighteen Mirage FIs and three helicopter squadrons, as well as SAM and Sidewinder missiles. Far from reducing Kuwait's expenditure on defence, the Iran–Iraq ceasefire increased it. So long as Iran was the enemy, Kuwait could lean on Baghdad for protection, but with the war over its neighbour's benevolence could no longer be taken for granted. All Kuwait's military spending proved useless on 2 August 1990 because the country's leadership wrongly thought the Iraqi military build-up was a bluff. Kuwait's planes hardly fired a shot, though some escaped to Saudi Arabia.

Secondly, Kuwait was trying to catch up with revenue lost during the Iran–Iraq war, and faced heavy costs for repairs to oil installations after Iranian attacks, though the damage was small compared with what Iraq had suffered.

Thirdly, the Kuwaiti economy was still suffering the after-effects of a serious scandal. In the late 1970s and early eighties, when huge flows of oil money created a get-rich-quick mentality, an unofficial stock market grew up in Kuwait. It was called Souk el-Manakh (literally: 'the market where camels kneel'). Instead of trading in shares in industrial, commercial and financial companies, the Souk was a shaky structure built on speculation in promissory notes. Like a balloon keeping company with a pin, it was always likely to end in a bang. The explosion came in 1982, with losses estimated by the Kuwaiti Central Bank at $80 to $90 billion, affecting some 6000 traders and their creditors. A government rescue package used sums equivalent to 8 per cent of Kuwait's financial reserves to stabilise the situation in the first year after the crash, but the economy suffered the after-effects for years.[1]

For all these reasons Kuwait was philosophically and economically out of step with OPEC, and began to regard its aims as misconceived. Iraq, on the other hand, needed the organisation more than ever. The strength in unity which had given the producers so much power in 1973, 1974 and 1980 was now Baghdad's only hope of recovery. Kuwait's intransigence caused general outrage at an OPEC meeting in June 1989 . Ali Khalifa al-Sabah, Kuwait's oil minister, demanded a 30 per cent increase in his country's quota and resisted all pressure to back down. When the other countries came to an agreement he wrote on the final document: 'Kuwait neither accepts nor is bound by its assigned quota.'

Kuwait was previously allocated 1,037,000 barrels a day, but oil industry reports estimated its actual production at 1,700,000 barrels. The new quota was 1,093,000 barrels, but the minister said this was inadequate to supply Kuwait's overseas marketing and refining network and declared that it would produce 1,350,000 barrels a day, which was what it had demanded all along.

Iran and Iraq were allotted 2,783,000 barrels a day each, while Saudi Arabia's quota increased to 4,769,000. The total production of the thirteen countries, assuming they respected their quotas, was to rise by one million barrels a day to 19,500,000.

Baghdad was astonished by Kuwait's arrogance and tried repeatedly in the following months to persuade or bully it back into

---

[1] *The Cloud Over Kuwait* by Marwan Iskandar, a Lebanese economist, is a well-documented study of the collapse of the Souk el-Manakh.

line. When OPEC met in November 1989 Baghdad sought to impose discipline by issuing a strong warning. It was to no avail: the over-production continued and in the spring of 1990 the price of oil fell below $18 a barrel for the first time since the previous summer, and continued to head downwards. In February 1990 Saddam Hussein sent messages to Sheikh Jaber of Kuwait and King Fahd insisting on a price increase to at least $18 a barrel. Kuwait, however, was in a strong position. Halfway through the fiscal year that started in July 1989, its revenues were running 37.6 per cent higher than expected. The Kuwaiti oil minister cocked a snook at Baghdad by saying that OPEC quotas should be scrapped as soon as possible. Both the Iraqi leader and King Hussein of Jordan continued to lobby other leaders. Baghdad regarded Kuwait's policy as underlining its lack of appreciation for Iraq's service in protecting the Gulf Arab states from the Iranian revolution.

In the early stages of the Iran–Iraq war Kuwait contributed $5 billion to Iraq's war costs, part in the form of a loan and the rest as aid. Baghdad insisted that the whole amount should be regarded as a donation, and the dispute over this remained unresolved. It is estimated that the Gulf Arab states gave or loaned $30 to $40 billion to Baghdad during the war. As another contribution to Iraq's war effort, Kuwait acted as an intermediary to enable 125,000 barrels of oil a day to be exported on Iraq's behalf through Kuwait's outlets during the war. This was a risky policy, as Iranian missile attacks on Kuwait oil installations proved.

Another of Baghdad's grievances was Kuwait's refusal to allow it to build military installations on the Kuwaiti islands of Warba and Bubiyan, off the Faw peninsula. Had it agreed, Iraq might have recaptured the peninsula from Iran much earlier, but Kuwait feared that Iraq would find a reason to extend the war to Kuwaiti territory. Furthermore, Kuwait believed that if Baghdad were given access to the islands it would never leave, as Iraq's long-term aim was to dredge channels around the islands and build a new harbour on Iraqi territory behind them. This would provide the outlet to the Gulf which it had always wanted, independent of the exposed Shatt al Arab waterway. A civil engineering project on this scale would not be advisable without secure defences, which would be impossible without bases on the islands.

The rows over oil, debts and islands were secondary to a much deeper dispute, the fact that Iraq has always regarded Kuwait as part of its territory. Historically and politically, Iraq was divided into three administrative units, Mosul, Baghdad and Basra, with Kuwait an extension of Basra province. The entire area, indeed the whole of the Arab world, formed part of the Islamic Caliphate, the Ottoman Empire being the last of the Caliphates until its collapse in 1918. The empire had two main components – specific regions of historical importance, like Egypt, Syria, Hijaz and Iraq, and undefined desert areas. The Turkish governor general in Baghdad was responsible for a vast desert area stretching as far south as he could establish his authority. At the time Kuwait was no more than a small city of traders and fishermen.

This state of affairs was recognised by the British when they began to establish their authority in the Gulf. They were in regular contact with the Turkish governor general in Baghdad and treated him as a legitimate authority. British intentions were unclear towards the end of the nineteenth century because of a dispute between the (colonial) government of India and the British Foreign Office. The former was trying to bring the entire Gulf area under its influence, signing protectorate agreements with ruling families, while the latter feared that this might lead to complications with other European powers (France, Germany and Russia), and might cause a rift with the Ottoman Empire. As seen by the Foreign Office, Kuwait occupied an important position at the head of the Gulf and possessed a fine natural harbour, but there was no particular need for Britain to control it. The government of India disagreed, and on 23 January 1889 Lieutenant-Colonel Malcolm John Meade, Britain's political resident in the Gulf, reached an agreement with Kuwait's new ruler. Meade was not deterred by the ruthless way in which Sheikh Mubarak al-Sabah came to power, killing his two elder brothers after a row. According to Abdul Aziz el-Rashid, one of the Gulf's traditional historians, who wrote an account of the affair, the argument was over the paltry sum of nine Ottoman lire, plus the cost of mending a sword (a further seven lire). Under the agreement the sheikh signed away Kuwait's control of foreign policy, pledging not to receive an agent of any foreign power and not to 'cede, sell, lease, mortgage or give for occupation or any other purpose any portion of his territory . . . without the previous consent of Her Majesty's Government'. The British thought they had separated Kuwait from the Ottoman Empire, but the sheikh, although eager to assert his independence from Istanbul, was reluctant to make the break too explicit. Sir Percy Cox, the principal British intelligence official in the Gulf, asked the sheikh to abandon the Turkish flag, which at the time was flown by Kuwaiti ships. A memorandum from Sir Percy to the Secretary General of the government of India, dated 16 July 1905, records that he proposed three designs for an independent Kuwaiti flag. The sheikh demurred, saying that he did not want 'to provoke the Turks'. The most he would accept was the addition of the word 'Kuwait' in Arabic to the Turkish flag. Later, in the period immediately before the First World War, the government of India insisted on Kuwait being a separate entity, while the Foreign Office hesitated, not wanting an open break with the Ottoman Empire at that time. During the war Britain seized Iraq from the Ottoman Empire, which was allied with Germany. The Ottoman collapse after the war led to Iraq emerging as a new state under a League of Nations mandate administered by Britain.

The new Iraqi government believed that Kuwait was part of its territory, even if both countries were under British control. Disputes over this are recorded in exchanges between the British Resident General in Kuwait and the British High Commissioner in Baghdad. All Iraqi governments from 1921 to the end of the British mandate in 1932, during the rule of King Faisal I, King Ghazi and King Faisal II refused to accept the separation of Kuwait from Iraq. When the Hashemite Union was created in 1958, linking Iraq and Jordan, a plan was hatched to occupy Kuwait if it did not voluntarily join them in a Hashemite Federation. The Federation's plans were aborted by the revolution in Iraq in July 1958. In 1961, when Britain and Kuwait agreed to end their treaty, General Kassem's government in Baghdad refused to accept Kuwait's independence and accused the British of a conspiracy.

Baghdad's attitude and reports of a military build-up in Basra led to fears that Iraq was about to invade Kuwait. The Arab League (apart from Iraq) immediately united against this threat and sent forces to protect Kuwait. For a short period before they arrived this role was performed by British forces, who delayed the completion of their withdrawal until Egyptian and other units arrived. Iraq, however, denied that it had ever intended to use force. Kuwait complained to the UN Security Council, but Ambassador Adnan Pachacchi of Iraq, in a speech to the Council on 2 July 1961, rejected this on the ground that only a sovereign state could make such a complaint. 'Kuwait is not, and never has been, a sovereign and independent state. Historically as well as legally, Kuwait has always been considered an integral part of the Basra Province of Iraq, and therefore there can be no question of an international dispute arising between Iraq and Kuwait,' he said. This view would have been held by all in Iraq, regardless of their opinions on internal political matters.

Iraq managed to prevent Kuwait from becoming a member of the United Nations from 1961 to 1963, but it was eventually accepted. Kuwait borrowed the lobbying and public relations techniques of the United States to influence the decision, and Sheikh Jaber al-Ahmed al-Sabah, then finance minister but now emir, allocated $700,000 for the purpose.

Kuwait's view of the sovereignty dispute was conditioned by its years under British rule, which it thought gave it a special administrative status. After the First World War and the fall of the Ottoman Empire, it seemed to Kuwaitis that there was an opportunity to make a new start. As Britain held the League of Nations mandate, the Kuwaitis thought that London was entitled to decide their future. The al-Sabahs reached an understanding with the British on Kuwait's separateness long before independence. Despite the renewal of Iraq's claim when the British withdrew, the Kuwaitis felt by the mid-1960s that Baghdad was beginning to accept the situation. This was supported by the facts that Iraq did not carry out a threat to withdraw from the Arab League when Kuwait was accepted against its wishes (in 1961), and that Iraq remained in the UN after Kuwait became a member (in 1963). After that Iraq dealt with Kuwait as an independent state. Both countries had embassies in the other's capital, and there were exchanges of visits between leaders. When the Kuwaiti emir visited Iraq he was treated as a head of state.

One element was missing from this *de facto* acceptance of Kuwait's independence. Although Kuwait's borders were agreed with the British at the time of independence, the Iraqis never accepted the frontier. The Kuwaitis were keen to settle the issue because this would be a further implicit acceptance of their sovereignty. The Iraqis wanted to settle it too, but on different terms, believing they could use it to squeeze Kuwait to a smaller size. Iraq kept pressing for a 'political' meeting to discuss the border, while Kuwait tried to treat it as a 'technical' matter. Baghdad wanted a settlement within a wider framework, which it described as 'constant historical realities and the higher national Arab interest'. In other words, it wanted an important readjustment to both the land and sea borders.

For practical purposes, however, there was a tacit agreement that the border would be somewhere within a vague strip of territory. During the Iran–Iraq war, when Baghdad was too busy to pay attention to such matters, Kuwait began to encroach into the strip to drill for oil. The Rumaila oilfield, which straddles the area, transformed the dispute from one of territory into one of resources. Iraq claimed that Kuwait 'stole' oil from the field worth $2.4 billion over a ten-year period, though not all this oil came from the ground immediately under the part which Kuwait claimed; some was taken from the Iraqi side by drilling shafts at an angle instead of vertically. The Iraqis frequently raised these points with the Kuwaitis but never made much of a fuss. It was not one of the main reasons for the invasion of Kuwait, more a make-weight argument.

Before the colonial era there was little need for accurately defined borders, but when the British arrived they brought their European assumptions with them. Their efforts to impose borders were usually frustrating and often unsuccessful. It was a complicated business, as tribes and sand dunes were in constant motion. They tried to cover their failure by introducing trucial areas, neutral zones, mutual control and other verbal compromises. After the discovery of oil these compromises became diplomatic booby traps.

During the conference of El Akkir, held in 1922 to discuss the border between Saudi Arabia and Kuwait, Sir Percy Cox rode rough-shod over Abd Aziz al-Saud (then Sultan of Najd but later King of Saudi Arabia), creating a neutral zone of 5770 square kilometres in a disputed area on Kuwait's southern boundary. The British Public Records Office has this account by Cox's adjutant of the proceedings:

> After five days of fruitless haggling, he [Cox] summoned the Sultan . . . to his tent. I was astonished to see him being treated like a naughty schoolboy, and being told that he, Sir Percy Cox, would himself decide on the type and general line of the frontier. This ended .the impasse. The Saud almost broke down and pathetically remarked that Sir Percy was his father and mother who made him and raised him from nothing to the position he held and that he would surrender half his kingdom, nay the whole, if Sir Percy ordered. Cox took out a map and pencil and drew the line of the frontier with Saudi Arabia.

None of the participants could have known that the neutral zone contained important oilfields.

The Kuwaitis were adroit, tough negotiators on oil matters from the first. Sheikh Ahmad, who ruled from 1921 to 1950, played the British and Americans off against each other to get exploration started and secure favourable terms. At the beginning of the 1930s Standard Oil of California was exploring for oil in Bahrain, while King Ibn Saud was talking to both American and British companies about rights in Saudi Arabia. The British were becoming alarmed about US companies encroaching on their traditional area of interest and tried to insist that the Kuwaiti concession should go to the Anglo-Persian Oil Company, but the United States wanted the Gulf Oil Company to have it. Sheikh Ahmad spun out the talks and eventually gave a twenty-five-year concession to a joint venture involving both companies. He received an initial payment and annual fees while exploration was under way, followed by payments linked to production once oil was found. The Saudi concession went to the Americans, to the annoyance of the British Foreign Office. Both deals were completed in 1933, and five years later the first large oil strikes were made in both countries, within a few weeks of each other. The Second World War interrupted activities, but after 1945 large deposits were discovered in Kuwait and production began the next year. It was a period of immense growth in world oil consumption, from 8.7 million barrels a day in 1948 to 42 million in 1972. Oil revenues quickly transformed Kuwait City from a small port into a bustling hub of commerce, and living standards improved enormously. Sheikh Abdullah al-Salem al-Sabah, who succeeded Sheikh Ahmad in 1950, laid the basis of a comprehensive welfare system, spending oil royalties on education, health and infrastructure. He died in 1965 and was succeeded by his brother Sheikh Sabah al-Salem al-Sabah, who ruled until 1977 and was followed by his nephew Sheikh Jaber al-Ahmed al-Sabah, the current emir. The same social policies continued throughout this period, growing more comprehensive as Kuwait's wealth and status increased. By 1985 compulsory free education had reduced illiteracy to 25 per cent of the population, and three years later Kuwait University had 18,000 students. Free health care for all residents raised life expectancy to seventy-one for men and seventy-five for women, among the highest levels in the Arab world. Modern electricity, water and sewerage systems were built, the two commercial ports were expanded and the roads and airport greatly improved. All these benefits were funded by oil revenues and many public services were either free or inexpensive. As might be expected in a boom town, unemployment was barely measurable (0.3 per cent in the 1985 census).

One of the terms of the moral and political contract between the al-Sabahs and the families who arrived in Kuwait before them was that the al-Sabahs should stay out of commerce, raising money by taxation to run the state. The discovery of oil soon made most taxes unnecessary. The Kuwait Oil Company paid its first royalties to Sheikh Sabah in 1946, and four years later oil income was sufficient to pay for all state functions. The Kuwaitis' skill as traders helped them in investing their surplus oil revenue. High-quality personnel were hired to run the Kuwaiti Investment Fund, which gradually became a mainstay of the economy. The wisdom of this policy was clear by the early 1980s, when income from overseas investments was nearly half that from oil. When oil prices collapsed, the investments overtook oil as a source of income, and during the Iraqi occupation they enabled the government in exile to continue paying welfare benefits to Kuwaitis stranded outside their country. The al-Sabahs built themselves palaces and lived like a royal family, and after independence the salary of the ruler was fixed at one million Kuwaiti dinars a month. Kuwaiti citizens became among the richest in the Middle East, with a gross national product averaging $13,680 per head between 1986 and 1988.

Kuwait's economic success under the al-Sabahs gradually transformed the family's image of itself, allowing them to forget their origins as paid administrators. Before the discovery of oil other families tried to retain a balance of influence, and in the early 1920s an Advisory Council was set up against the al-Sabahs' wishes. It collapsed, but was succeeded in 1938 by a legislative assembly, which declared that the people were the legitimate source of authority. This too gave way to new arrangements at the end of the British era. The first election came six months after independence in 1961, producing a constituent assembly which drafted a new constitution. It invested executive power in the head of state, who took the title of emir after independence, and gave him power to appoint the prime minister and government. In practice (though not in the constitution) all important posts in all cabinets formed since independence have been reserved for members of the ruling family, especially the defence, finance, foreign affairs, petroleum and interior ministries. A single-house National Assembly was set up with fifty elected members, but political parties were banned and eligibility rules for voters were tightly restricted. Women, members of the armed forces, illiterates and all non-Kuwaiti residents were denied the vote. This left only 6.4 per cent of the population entitled to vote in the 1981 election, and of those only half turned out. By 1985, when a census was held, the electorate was still only 57,000 people, a tiny proportion of the population of 1.7 million. In 1990 it was estimated at 62,000 out of a population of just over two million.

Whenever the National Assembly tried to stand up to the al-Sabahs it was dissolved, often for long periods. Sheikh Sabah declared in 1976 that it was acting against the interests of the state, and it was not revived until 1981. The 1985 elections brought a number of more outspoken deputies into the assembly, including some Islamic fundamentalists. In the same year the assembly expressed opposition to legislation restricting the press and government proposals to increase prices for public services.

In June 1986 the assembly criticised certain ministers for their handling of the Souk el-Manakh stock market collapse, whose after-effects were still haunting the economy. The assembly was unhappy over the use of huge sums of government money to compensate creditors who had been left with liabilities of $92 billion. Half the money paid in settlements went to members of the royal family or others connected with it. The assembly also considered that those responsible should have been firmly punished. Its attacks over these and other issues led the Council of Ministers to submit its resignation to Sheikh Jaber, who dissolved the assembly and announced his intention to rule by decree.

From the earliest days of the Souk el-Manakh scandal there had been a row over what should happen to those responsible. Dr Abdul-Latif Al-Hamad, then minister of finance, was in favour of strong penalties, but the Cabinet took a milder line and decided to use government funds in a compensation scheme. Dr Al-Hamad implemented this policy but was apparently uncomfortable with it and resigned in August 1983. Two years later another minister resigned amid allegations that he had contributed to the collapse.

The government intervened on the pretext of safeguarding the interests of small investors, but its definition of 'small' caused many raised eyebrows. People who were owed anything up to two million Kuwaiti dinars (then nearly $7 million) by traders caught up in the scandal were compensated from a fund of 500 million Kuwait dinars taken from official reserves. Such people were indeed small investors compared with Sheikh Khalifa El-Abdullah Al-Sabah, who had liabilities of $3.4 billion and was only able to honour half that sum.

The government also bought huge numbers of shares on the

official stock exchange, hoping to stabilise share values and stimulate the economy, which by now was in recession. These and other schemes protected the banking sector from serious damage from bad debts, at the price of putting a strain on the treasury for years. The issue remained active in 1990, when there was speculation that a final compensation scheme might be announced. It was one of the causes of the Kuwait government's hunger for ready money, which brought it into conflict with Iraq over oil prices.

Other issues on which the assembly was beginning to agitate before its dissolution were freedom of the press and the limitations of Kuwait's democracy. The press, which had been relatively free, was brought under censorship, joining radio and television, which had always been controlled by the state. A campaign for democracy was begun by businessmen in 1989, and Sheikh Jaber announced elections for a consultative national council to change the constitution. These were held in June 1990 despite a boycott by the pro-democracy group. The last two months before the Iraqi invasion were marked by a strong sense of bitterness.

Sheikh Jaber's dissolution of the assembly was prompted not so much by sensitivity to criticism as by a fear of Kuwait's Shia minority, which formed about 30 per cent of the population. Throughout the Iran–Iraq war the al-Sabahs felt at constant risk of being overthrown by an uprising arranged by Tehran. The imprisonment of seventeen Shi'ites for terrorist activities had international implications. Pro-Iranian groups in Lebanon repeatedly demanded the release of the seventeen as a precondition for freeing Western hostages held in Beirut. Their release was also demanded by gunmen who hijacked a Kuwait Airways airliner in 1988. Two passengers were killed before the hijacking ended in Algeria. There was further tension when sixteen Kuwaiti Shi'ites were executed in Saudi Arabia in 1989 on charges of planning terrorist acts during the Haj.

Despite their drift towards authoritarianism, the al-Sabahs were not oppressive and in some ways their rule was fairly enlightened, spreading wealth more evenly than most countries and allowing more self-expression than might be expected. A number of other Gulf rulers would have moved more decisively to stifle the pro-democracy movement. Two demonstrations were broken up by police, but many large meetings were tolerated. The Kuwaitis had a tradition of holding weekly gatherings to discuss non-political matters, and this system became the forum of the pro-democracy movement.

In the eyes of many Arabs, Kuwait seemed in the 1970s and early eighties to be a unique phenomenon. Its experience with democracy, even if limited, its efficient, well-equipped university and its vigorous press set it apart from its less modern neighbours. By the end of the 1980s these institutions were shackled, but the attitudes of Kuwait's people were largely unchanged. It was still a thinking state, even if the freedom to express those thoughts had declined.

Another element of Kuwait's sense of being different was the relative freedom of its women, which stemmed from the huge responsibilities they carried before Kuwait became rich. Being seafarers, the men were away most of the time fishing or trading, while the women were left to take care of everything else, from children to property to family relations. Through these traditions Kuwaiti women have acquired an independence unparalleled in the Arab world. Between 1969 and 1983 more young women than young men graduated from Kuwait University, and the proportion of women in work grew from 9.6 per cent in 1980 to 13.8 per cent in 1985.

Kuwait's role in the Arab world was out of proportion to its size. It funded the education system in Yemen and, until the mid-1980s, gave lavishly to the PLO and other Arab causes, donating over 4 per cent of its gross national product to them. In 1982 its aid reached $1.6 billion, making it one of the world's top donors in terms of dollars per head of population. It cut back heavily from 1987 because of falling government revenue.

Among the sheikhdoms, the Kuwaitis had one of the better records for consistently supporting Arab causes. They assisted frontline states economically damaged in the 1967 war with Israel, sent troops to participate symbolically in the 1973 war, argued in favour of the use of the oil weapon against Israel's allies, and applied the OPEC ban vigorously. In 1978 Kuwait condemned the Camp David agreements and imposed sanctions against Egypt. It acted as a mediator between the two Yemens before their unification.

If its foreign policy seemed modern and vigorous, Kuwait's internal relationships were stuck in the past, with a rigid class system. Only descendants of less than thirty families which had arrived in Kuwait by 1920 were entitled to full citizenship, while a number of naturalised Kuwaitis (mainly people whose families arrived by 1936) were second class citizens. The rest were the 'bidoun', meaning without citizenship, and these included all the foreign workers. By 1990 there were 620,000 Kuwaiti citizens and 300,000 bedouins who were eligible for citizenship but did not apply for it, bringing the total number of Kuwaitis to 920,000, or just over 45 per cent of the population. The remaining 1,100,000 (just under 55 per cent of the population), including 300,000 Iranians and 46,000 Palestinians, were classified as *bidoun*. In the late 1970s the Kuwaiti government suspected the Shah of Iran of trying to change the demographic composition of Kuwait and the Gulf generally by sending his people to settle there. This and the Shia revolution led to the deportation of 11,000 Iranians in 1979. A general programme to reduce the proportion of non-Kuwaitis was begun, which cut their growth rate but not their numbers.

Overall, Kuwait was seen in the Gulf as a well ordered and intelligently managed sheikhdom with much to commend it. These positive views were somewhat clouded by a lack of modesty on the part of the Kuwaitis. Others in the Gulf became irritated by a sense of superiority, a tendency for Kuwait to see itself as a mini-superpower. It wanted to play a role on the world stage, forgetting that power is a whole concept, not something that comes automatically with wealth. It might seem obvious now that Kuwait was bound to be crushed if it was attacked by any of the regional giants, Iran, Iraq or Saudi Arabia, but the Kuwaitis had delusions of strength. Their defence plan was first to deter aggression and second to delay any invasion long enough for powerful friends to come to their aid. This concept went back to pre-independence times, when Britain had a small permanent military presence and could be counted on to reinforce it quickly if Kuwait were threatened. In 1965, four years after independence, a British Army sergeant, Percy Sidney Alan, handed the Egyptian and Iraqi military attachés in London contingency plans which had been prepared in case Kuwait should be invaded. The plans showed that the British would need forty-eight hours to move the first troops to Kuwait and three weeks to bring in a substantial force. The Kuwaitis could not expect help from Saudi Arabia, Qatar or Bahrain, and felt that only the West with its need for oil supplies and its strategic concerns would be prepared to defend them. Alan was court-martialled and sentenced to twelve years' imprisonment.

During the last two months before the war, Kuwait, already immensely rich by Iraqi standards, was looking forward to a boom caused by higher production. At the same time the government in

Baghdad realised that its attempts to revive the Iraqi economy had failed, and it was forced to introduce austerity measures. The reasons for its problems included expensive military programmes, falling oil prices and high internal consumption. In the two years since the Iran–Iraq war, the Iraqi government had created conditions in which the public felt able to spend money more freely than in the past.

Baghdad saw the oil price as the main source of its problems. The contrast with the Kuwaiti economy encouraged Iraq's suspicions that Kuwait was party to an American plot to ruin it economically. An Arab proverb holds that to stop a man's supply of *arzak*, the daily bread provided by Allah, is the same as beheading him. Saddam Hussein declared that Kuwait's policies were a war against Iraq's daily bread.

PART TWO
THE THIRD OIL WAR

'Our strategy for dealing with this
army is very simple. First we are going
to cut it off and then we are going to
kill it.'

GENERAL COLIN POWELL,
Chairman of the Joint Chiefs of Staff,
23 January 1991

1

Dust Before the Storm

It is said, not without irony, that every nation gets the leadership it deserves – an aphorism which may hold good for Western democracies, but tends to be harsh when applied to the Third World. The Arab nation deserved better than the leadership it was given in the middle of 1990, when effective politicians could have averted an inter-Arab conflict. For want of preventive political medicine, the dispute between Iraq and Kuwait ran out of control. During the early part of 1990 all the elements of conflict were assembled, but war was still avoidable. The lost opportunities which made it inevitable were spread over a period of twelve weeks, from early May to the third week of July. It was a time of provocation from one side and arrogance from the other, yet other Arab countries behaved more like spectators than partners. Not until late July did serious efforts by Saudi Arabia, Egypt and Jordan to avert a crisis get under way, and by then the situation was out of control.

This delay, and the weakness of the Arab world's principal political institution, the summit, ultimately made the difference between peace and war. Nothing proved more harmful than the habit of leaving major decisions to the summit, without consulting state presidential councils, ministerial committees or parliaments, or testing public opinion, even in countries which entertained illusions of democracy. It was the summit which had a chance to avert crisis, and the summit which failed to take it. A gathering of presidents, kings and sheikhs, none of them appointed by the will of their people, was not the right machine for the job. Like a political Trabant, it produced noise and hot air, but only the most lethargic motion. None of its members tried to harmonise the interests of his country with those of the Arab nation; none had the vision and influence to revive the sense of a shared Arab future which had been felt in the 1950s and sixties; none had the confidence in his own political legitimacy to govern without heavy-handedness; and each felt stronger than his neighbour. The sheikhs drew their strength from their bank accounts; the progressives from their arsenals. With everyone concentrating on his own small piece of the Arab puzzle, none saw the whole picture. Every leader had his own shackled media trumpeting his own limited message to his own captive audience; no attempt was made to turn this cacophony into a concert of Arab unity.

Lacking guidance, the masses swayed with every gust of opinion or fantasy which reached them. From a nation traditionally fond of story-telling, the Arabs have a tendency to embroider or over-simplify political rumours until something striking emerges. In the absence of reliable information, any good story becomes an accepted fact. Had there been a tradition of openness, or a free and trusted media with a pan-Arab perspective, the dispute between Baghdad and Kuwait might have been manageable. As it was, it got out of hand.

There were objective reasons for the ineffectiveness of the summit as a decision-making institution. The lack of a recognised Arab centre of leadership was a serious drawback. Cairo assumed that role from the beginning of the century until the early 1970s, but since then its authority as the economic and military base of Arab power had gradually declined. It was eroded first by the cost of successive Arab–Israeli wars, then by its economic policies in the late 1970s and early eighties, which contributed to the looting of the country by business interests, leaving an imbalance between an atrophied economy and a powerful military. The ostracism of Cairo by other Arab governments after the Camp David agreement knocked away what little remained of its influence.

Secondly, the key Arab regions and states were too absorbed in their own interests to pull together effectively. The Maghreb countries of North Africa were transfixed by the risks or opportunities presented by the integration of Europe and the single European market. Syria was mired in Lebanon, Iraq in its war with Iran, the Gulf sheikhdoms in suspicion of each other, and Yemen was far away.

Thirdly, the flowering of a great institution calls for inspirational concepts and people. In the Arab world progressive thought was stifled by the fact that wealth was concentrated in the hands of traditional Arab forces, encouraging anti-modernist and anti-democratic tendencies. Material wealth was matched by a poverty of leadership. No one had emerged who could equal the popular charisma of Nasser or the powerful traditionalism of King Faisal, both of whom possessed authority which transcended Arab borders.

Fourthly, the penetration of the Arab world by foreign influences weakened any cohesion it still retained. The collapse of the Soviet role in the region left the field open for Washington, and caused a more general shake-up of alignments. Britain and France were returning to their former zones of influence, in the Gulf and North Africa respectively, repeating in a smaller way the rush for empire of the late nineteenth century. The Soviet collapse was a double blow, not only because Moscow had been a loyal supporter of some Arab countries, but also because it left the United States reigning supreme. In the 1980s many in the Arab world felt adrift.

Any nation's sense of identity depends partly on being able to express itself with clarity and strength. In the fifties and sixties the Arab media had a sense of direction guided by the idea of Arab nationalism, which gave it the power to influence the masses. By the 1980s each Arab government was steering the media in its own country, creating a chaos of conflicting aims. Using the media to convey or defend pan-Arab values had never been easy, but a lack of united vision made it impossible. The audience drifted away, and became easy prey for Western predators, particularly the Voice of America, Radio Monte Carlo and the BBC World Service. Foreign stations were pumping out 412 hours of broadcasts in Arabic every twenty-four hours.

Another problem at summits was the wide difference in style between the main parties. Some countries tended to say too much, others too little. Summit meetings became a dialogue between the over-cautious and the over-bombastic, which made for one-way communication. The Saudis were always the introverts, trying not to step out of line, saying they would support an Arab consensus yet rarely lighting its path. Like the Sovietologists of the sixties and seventies, some people made a profession of trying to decode Saudi speeches. Some Western diplomats said this was like holding a mirror to a mirage, giving a reflected image of something that was not there. It was not that the Saudis had no opinions, more that they were reluctant to reveal them. Direct questions were futile: the Saudis would never say 'yes' or 'no', rarely even 'maybe'. It was always '*Inshalla*,' or 'We will see about it,' or 'It will be discussed in the future.' Their reticence came partly from a feeling that as custodians of the Two Holy Places, a certain code of conduct was expected. But it was also a form of defence against ideas they found threatening, especially Arab nationalism. They tended to use Islam as a shield, an excuse for not espousing bold concepts, and this in turn helped to create a wider belief that one could be either a committed Arab nationalist or a devout Muslim, but not both. This led to a meaningless debate over a supposed contradiction between Islam and Arabism, which wasted much intellectual energy.

In contrast to the Saudis, the Egyptians, Syrians and Iraqis tended to speak loudly but without much authority. President Saddam Hussein tried hardest to project himself to the Arab masses, with only partial success. He had been head of state for nearly eleven years, but for eight of them he had been preoccupied with the war against Iran. It was only from the beginning of 1989 that he started trying to reach out to a wider audience.

Egypt had a tradition of expressing itself forcefully which stemmed from the days when it had influence beyond its borders, although after its twelve years in the political wilderness following the Camp David accords Cairo carried less weight than previously. At the same time, its return to the fold changed a number of relationships between Arab leaders and contributed to the tension which exploded in 1990. Events at the Arab League summit in Casablanca in November 1989, the first attended by Cairo for a decade, were particularly significant, and brought noticeable signs of impatience from Saddam Hussein. It was on his initiative that President Mubarak was asked to attend from the start, without waiting for the summit to extend a formal invitation. 'We want to enliven the prospects of Egypt in the Arab nation, and the prospects of the nation in Egypt,' Saddam once said. This and the fact that Iraq and Cairo were now linked by the Arab Co-operation Council led Saddam to expect the Egyptian leader to behave as an ally during the summit. He was to be disappointed. The meeting also exacerbated the rift between rich and poor Arab countries.

The atmosphere was charged with tension from the start. King Hassan of Morocco insisted on giving full honours to every head of state as he entered the conference hall, with the result that the first two hours of each session were wasted. Observers had the feeling that the leaders were trying to reduce the time available for talk, which exposed their divisions. Cairo, for its part, was overcompensating, putting its name to resolutions that departed from its own policies, including condemnations of the United States and Israel.

The original purpose of the summit had been to discuss the

intifada and the policy changes announced by the PLO. When the foreign ministers met two days earlier, Jordan tried to add an item to the agenda supporting Arab countries in conflict with Israel. Since an August 1967 summit in Khartoum, Arab countries had been divided into two categories: confrontation states, which would inevitably be involved in any military clash with Israel, and support states, who provided financial assistance. The support countries, whose main contributors were the Gulf oil producers, paid a total of 250 million pounds sterling a year to Egypt, Syria, Jordan and the PLO (which at the time was led by Ahmed Al-Shukairi). This situation continued until after the Arab–Israeli war of 1973, but began to fall apart when President Sadat started trying to make a separate peace with Israel. A summit in Baghdad in 1979 (after the Camp David accords and the suspension of Egypt from the Arab League) produced a new agreement under which the remaining confrontation states (Syria, Jordan and the PLO) were promised $7 billion over a ten-year period, paid in annual instalments. In 1980 the oil revenues of all Arab countries reached a peak of between $350 and $400 billion, but many Arabs believed much of the money was being wasted because of a lack of co-ordination. It was felt that Arab countries should have complementary rather than competing development plans, and should avoid unnecessary duplication of projects. An 'Arab Development Plan' was launched at a summit in Amman in 1980, amid great hopes. It was estimated that it would cost $10 billion to create a co-ordinated Arab infrastructure over a five-year period. In the following years oil prices dropped, and the oil producing countries claimed that they could not afford to support both the confrontation states and the development plan. The total contribution for the two commitments was reduced to $5 billion over a ten-year period. In practice, however, the money was used for support, and the development proposals never materialised. Some Arab governments argued that a co-ordinated development plan was impossible while Egypt was absent from the Arab League.

As oil revenues were still low, the oil producers were in no mood to reconsider the subject at the Casablanca summit in 1989. The Kuwaiti and Saudi foreign ministers objected to the Jordanian proposal to add a new item to the agenda, not wanting to be asked to renew the original support commitments (undertaken in 1979 and by now expired). The Jordanian request was withdrawn, but the new item nevertheless appeared on the printed agenda drafted by the Secretariat of the Arab League. King Fahd summoned the secretary general to complain. 'Someone on your staff is cheating,' he said. 'I consider this bad faith.' The oil producers had their way, and the item was removed. The incident added to rich—poor tension.

Some weeks earlier Libya had threatened to break relations with Morocco and other North African countries if Egypt were readmitted to the Arab League. It relented before the summit, but remained unhappy. Muammar Gadaffi sent his foreign minister to tell the Secretary General of the Arab League that he did not want to sit next to Mubarak. The seating plan had been arranged so that the Arab Republic of Egypt and the Arab Republic of Libya were adjacent, as had been the practice before Camp David. Now Morocco and Mauritania were placed between them. As he entered the hall, Gadaffi spotted Mubarak, who waved to him. They went towards each other, embraced and kissed. The Secretary General of the Arab League looked on in bewilderment. When the second session opened, Mubarak and Gadaffi arrived together in the same car.

Syria's position changed just as swiftly. Before the summit it was against allowing Egypt to return, but inside the conference hall President Assad and President Mubarak got on well. Despite their policy differences over Israel and the ACC, the two leaders were sympathetic to each other. Both had been air force pilots and Mubarak had been stationed for a time in Syria. The original cause of the Egypt – Syria rift was Camp David, but the blame for that, in Assad's eyes, lay with President Sadat. Assad did not hold Camp David against Sadat's successor, who, he suspected, had never been wholeheartedly in favour of Egypt's separate peace with Israel, even if he continued Sadat's policies. From the moment of the Assad – Mubarak reunion, the former warmth between their countries began to return.

Given the enmity between Damascus and Baghdad, this blossoming friendship was a blow to Saddam Hussein. He had hoped that Mubarak would keep his distance from Assad, if only as a token of gratitude for Iraq's role in easing Egypt's return to the Arab League. Relations between Cairo and Baghdad had been exceptionally close over the previous months because of the Arab Co-operation Council. The warmth between Mubarak, Saddam Hussein and King Hussein was clear whenever they greeted each other. Their faces were usually hidden from view when they embraced, but the seams of their jackets looked about to split from the intensity of their affection. In part this was play-acting, but in part it was real, although none of the friendships was ever free of doubts and strains, especially that between Mubarak and Saddam Hussein.

The tension between the Iraqi and Syrian leaders led to an ugly scene which startled the summit. Conversation had turned to the Lebanese civil war, in which Iraq was supporting General Michel Aoun and his Christian militia against Syrian forces who were trying to restore the authority of the Lebanese government. Saddam Hussein and Assad began attacking each other, at first indirectly, then by name. Assad accused Saddam Hussein of using chemical weapons against the Kurds in 1988, and Saddam Hussein hit back by reminding the conference of a massacre in 1979, when Syrian government troops were fighting the Muslim Brotherhood, which was entrenched in the city of Hamaa, north of Damascus. Unable to flush them out, Assad ordered tanks to 'clear' the city. 'You killed 20,000 Muslims in Hamaa,' said Saddam Hussein. 'Your prisons are full of political prisoners and you gassed the Kurds, many thousands of them,' Assad replied. This was followed by an exchange of insults in unacceptable language. Soon afterwards Saddam Hussein left the summit in a huff. The last thing he said to Mubarak was: 'I am going back to Baghdad. I'll leave you with Assad and I hope you will discover for yourself what he and his clique are like, and when you have finished with them we will meet again.'

For all its tensions, the summit became a festival of Egypt's reacceptance, which meant that Iraq, for the first time in months, was not the centre of attention. All through 1989 Arab leaders had beaten a path to Baghdad to congratulate Saddam Hussein on his victory. Most had stayed away during the Iran–Iraq war, not wanting to endanger their fragile links with Tehran. In retrospect their caution was pointless, as Tehran was under no illusions about their allegiances, but Iraqi diplomats in some Gulf capitals found that no one would invite them to functions in case the gesture was noted and reported to Iran. Now a year had passed since the ceasefire, and Baghdad was once again a hub of diplomatic activity, especially after the creation of the Arab Co-operation Council.

Only one Arab neighbour abstained from the general homage paid to Saddam Hussein. The Emir of Kuwait was thinking of visiting Baghdad, but instead of offering thanks he expected to receive a reward. Kuwait felt it had contributed to Saddam's victory, and that Iraq was in its debt, both morally and financially. The total Kuwaiti contribution to the war effort was estimated at $14 billion, a huge sum considering that the country's gross national product in 1988 was $26 billion. The Kuwaiti government regarded at least part of that money as a loan, despite Iraqi objections, but knew that repayment was unlikely, or at best would be far in the future. It therefore felt that if Sheikh Jaber went to Baghdad, he should receive some other token of Iraq's appreciation. Iraq, however, felt that Kuwait had been a fickle ally. In August 1988, some days after the ceasefire, Iraqi intelligence had intercepted a telegram from Sheikh Sabah, the Kuwaiti foreign minister, instructing Kuwait's chargé d'affaires in Tehran to ask Ali Akbar Velayati, the Iranian foreign minister, whether there was anything Kuwait could do to help Iran after the war. Iran replied by requesting kerosene, and Kuwait soon began shipping supplies. Kuwait made no similar offer to Baghdad, presumably thinking it had already done enough for Iraq.

In late 1988 and early 1989 the Kuwaiti government was prepared to forget the war debts if Iraq agreed to recognise Kuwait's borders. Some officials thought this was psychologically the wrong moment for such an exchange. 'It would look like presenting the bill too soon,' they warned. But they were ignored, and the Kuwaiti ambassador in Baghdad, Ibrahim Gassim el-Bahu, was instructed early in 1989 to raise the matter. It was therefore Kuwait, not Iraq, which reopened the oldest dispute between the two countries.

By this time the Emir of Kuwait was being advised to go to Baghdad as quickly as possible. King Fahd, President Mubarak, Muammar Gadaffi, President Chadli of Algeria, Sheikh Khalifa of Qatar, Sheikh Zayed of the UAE and President Saleh of Yemen had already paid visits to congratulate Saddam Hussein, and it would look odd if the emir stayed away, especially as Kuwait had been more at risk from the Iranian threat than Iraq's other neighbours.

Iraq sent a sharp reply to Kuwait's request to reopen the border question, saying it would be happy to discuss the matter because Kuwait had appropriated certain areas of Iraqi territory during the Iran–Iraq war. It was clear that Kuwait had touched a nerve, and that the time was not right for a visit at head of state level. The Kuwaiti government decided that the crown prince and prime minister, Sheikh Saad al-Abdullah al-Salim al-Sabah should go to Baghdad first.

The crown prince's visit from 6 to 9 February 1989 was preceded by a campaign in Kuwaiti newspapers about the need to settle the border question. Iraq assumed that this was officially inspired, and replied with a press campaign of its own, attacking the Kuwaitis for encroaching on its territory. Then an armoured Iraqi gunboat violated Kuwait's territorial waters and was involved in a skirmish with a Kuwaiti patrol. The Iraqi newspaper *Kadisseya* published an article stating that Iraq was not just seeking the islands of Bubiyan and Warba, as it was a foregone conclusion that these belonged to Iraq, but wanted the return of Iraqi territory which Kuwait had occupied during the Iran–Iraq war. Observers felt the article was written in the style of Saddam Hussein.

Sheikh Saad's visit, intended to prepare the way for better relations, took place in inauspicious circumstances. In his first meeting with the Iraqi defence and foreign ministers the prince said that in view of the hostile atmosphere he was thinking of cutting short his visit, but they persuaded him to stay until the following day. He then had a meeting with Ezzat Ibrahim, a vice president, and Abdullah El-Douri, Deputy Chairman of the Ba'ath Party, who left him in no doubt that the Iraqis would be tough on the border issue.

After these unpromising beginnings, the prince's meeting with Saddam Hussein came as a surprise. The Iraqi leader said he was annoyed with the Iraqi press and felt the issue should be solved quietly. Someone in the Iraqi delegation observed: 'You [Kuwaitis] started it and we just replied to you.' Saddam Hussein appeared weary of the whole matter. 'This subject is just an additional burden on me,' he said, and asked the prince to settle it with Tariq Aziz, the foreign minister. Seemingly wanting to put the prince at ease, Saddam Hussein referred to Aziz in a way which would only be used between friends. 'Here you have Abu Ziad [literally 'Father of Ziad', Aziz's eldest son]. Solve everything with him. He is delegated from me to settle it.' Saddam Hussein turned to Aziz and said: 'Tariq, solve this problem . . . set up a committee at the highest level and let us finish with it.'

Aziz suggested that the committee should consist of the prince, the president and the two foreign ministers, but Saddam Hussein was reluctant to be drawn in. 'Please, do whatever you want. This is a problem I do not want to get involved in,' he said.

Saddam Hussein remarked that Iraq's aims were not confined to settling the border. It had a navy which was dispersed off Jordan, Egypt and Italy for lack of a deep-water port on the Gulf. It urgently needed to deploy it in the Gulf, not just for Iraq's security but for all Arabs. The solution Iraq envisaged would require the co-operation of eleven GCC countries and a change in the status of the islands of

Warba and Bubiyan. 'We would be ready to consider giving you facilities if the border problem were solved,' the sheikh said, but Saddam Hussein would not continue the conversation. .

In practice, Dr Sa'adoun Hammadi, the Iraqi deputy prime minister, and Sheikh Sabah, the Kuwaiti foreign minister, proved to be the main figures in the border committee. As the discussions progressed, questions of money and territory became entwined. The Kuwaitis mentioned the war loan, but Sa'adoun Hammadi replied: 'It is not a matter of repaying a debt. Iraq needs substantial cash to meet its vital needs.'

The emir made his delayed visit to Baghdad from 23 to 26 September. By this time the issues were fully out in the open, though the border committee was making no headway.

In January 1990 Baghdad requested an emergency loan of $10 billion and asked for its $14 billion debt to Kuwait to be written off. The Kuwaiti response was not clear, but it hinted that it might give $500 million in aid. It was not inclined to write off its earlier loans, but said it would not seek repayment of them. Despite this, there were times during the talks when the Iraqis felt that Kuwait wanted the entire sum repaid.

In February Sheikh Sabah made another attempt to deal with the border question separately, writing a letter to Sa'adoun Hammadi about a proposed agreement on the borders which had been discussed in 1963. After recalling that the draft was not finally approved, he said: 'We had agreed that the Iraqi Republic recognises the independence of Kuwait and sovereignty within the preliminary map which was sent by the Prime Minister of Iraq on 21 July 1932 and which the Governor of Kuwait had agreed to in the letter dated 10 August 1932.' The exchange of letters in 1932 took place while Iraq and Kuwait were under British rule; in effect, both sides of the correspondence were dictated by London. On the map the border was marked by dots. Realising that it would have to be marked somehow on the ground, no easy task in a desert with no fixed features, Sheikh Sabah proposed that a committee of technicians and experts be set up to discuss the border.

Sa'adoun Hammadi replied: 'I have studied very carefully your letter concerning the frontiers . . . I think you know more than anyone else, because of your experience as minister of foreign affairs, that the frontiers between us were never a matter for technicians and experts. It was always a political issue. You mentioned that tentative [1963] agreement, but that so-called agreement has no existence, neither legal nor practical. Its pages were closed long ago.' Hammadi reminded Sheikh Sabah of 'the great sacrifices offered by Iraq in stopping that [Iranian] aggression', and said it had acted in the interests of all Arabs.

On 18 February 1990, during a further visit to Baghdad, Sheikh Sabah pointed out that Iraq had signed a non-aggression pact with Saudi Arabia and asked why Baghdad was unwilling to have a similar agreement with Kuwait. There was no response, which in itself was an answer. The contacts continued, and at the beginning of May 1990 Sa'adoun Hammadi went to Kuwait with a clear request for $10 billion immediately.

During this period details were coming to light in the West of Iraq's so-called 'super-gun' and its research into nuclear weapons. Western criticisms of these programmes was strongly resented in Iraq, which felt that it had a right to carry out any research it wished, and that it was the victim of a Western campaign. The idea that Kuwait might somehow be linked to this campaign took root in Saddam Hussein's mind. He remembered an incautious remark made by a Kuwaiti diplomat in 1989 when Sheikh Saad visited Washington to buy F-18 aircraft. His delegation was asked by a Congressional committee whether Kuwait intended to use the planes against Israel. The reply, given at a public meeting, was that the planes were not for the Arab – Israel conflict; Kuwait needed them for protection against its neighbours. Baghdad felt that a finger had been pointed in its direction.

Trying to regain the diplomatic initiative, Saddam Hussein invited the Arab leadership to a summit in Baghdad, not to discuss the dispute with Kuwait but the anti-Iraqi campaign in Israel and the West. The title of the summit was to be 'Threats to Arab National Security'. The invitation reached the other capitals at an inauspicious time. While Iraq saw itself as the victim of a war of nerves, others felt that Saddam Hussein was himself partly to blame. Most Arab capitals were in no hurry to take sides, preferring to stay out of the row. Secondly, there was a general weariness with summits; a feeling that the institution had been devalued by over-use. Summitry had become a substitute for solutions, a way of expressing frustration when leaders had run out of ideas.

Yasser Arafat, chairman of the PLO, was the first to give Saddam Hussein a positive answer, arguing that Iraq was facing psychological warfare and that the rest of the Arab world should rally round him.

Syria, as expected, immediately said it would not attend. Egypt and Saudi Arabia, fearing a summit might make matters worse, played for time. Crown Prince Abdullah Ibn Abd al-Aziz of Saudi Arabia and President Mubarak agreed to ask for a postponement on the pretext of preparing the summit carefully, but after visiting Cairo Prince Abdullah went to Damascus, where he received instructions from King Fahd to accept the invitation. It was not clear why Saudi Arabia changed its mind so abruptly, but some Arab diplomats believe it followed a telephone call from Saddam Hussein to King Fahd. By 11 May eighteen of the twenty-one members of the Arab League had agreed to attend.

Baghdad suggested that the theme should be the challenges facing Arab security from Israel. There were four items on the agenda: the threats Iraq was facing from the United States and Israel; Western restrictions on the transfer of technology to the Arab world; the revival of an Arab mutual development plan which had been agreed in 1980 but virtually shelved; and any other business.

A taste of the friction to come was given at a preparatory meeting held by the foreign ministers on 22 May. Prince Saud al-Faisal, the Saudi foreign minister, objected to the first item on the agenda, saying that no state should be named unless there was clear evidence against it. He was supported by the Egyptian foreign minister. Tariq Aziz, who was chairing the meeting as the host country's representative, went to the podium and began attacking plots, conspiracies, imperialism and Zionism. He recalled Iraq's sufferings in the eight-year war against Iran and implied that other Arab countries had not done enough to help. He was clearly angry, and his tone disconcerted other delegations. Dr Esmat Abdel-Meguid, the Egyptian foreign minister, said: 'I am astonished that the word "imperialism" is being used . . . this is yesterday's terminology. We did not come here to take lessons about nationalism, and if anybody is talking about sacrifices in the Iraq–Iran war I must remind you of Egypt's sacrifices in the Arab–Israeli wars, and if you say that nobody stood by Iraq, it is not true.' The tension was now out in the open.

The summit, held between 28 and 30 May, was to be a crucial stage in the development of the crisis. It was held in an atmosphere charged with anger following the US Congress's resolution recognising Jerusalem as the capital of Israel. At the same time the US government was trying to persuade the UN General Assembly to repeal a resolution which defined Zionism as a form of racism. Thirdly, the Israelis had announced earlier in the year that Jews arriving from the Soviet Union would be allowed to settle in the Occupied Territories. By now they were making their presence felt. Pictures of Soviet Jews moving into homes on the West Bank were shown on television, and several hundred of them staged a demonstration against living conditions in the temporary camps which had been set up for them.

Fourthly, the plight of Palestinian children affected by Israel's reaction to the intifada had been the subject of fourteen reports issued between January and May 1990 by the International Red Cross, Amnesty International and the Arab Human Rights Committee. The Red Cross said that 362 children had been killed by plastic bullets or gas. The UN Security Council discussed the matter three days before the Baghdad summit and considered a draft resolution calling for a UN mission to investigate the situation. Israel declared that it would not give permission for such a committee to visit the area, and the Security Council did not pursue the issue.

Then, on the second day of the summit, Israeli forces intercepted an attempt by the Palestine Liberation Front to land sixteen guerrillas on the coast of Israel, killing twelve of them.

In that atmosphere, speeches attacking the United States and Israel were sure of a receptive audience, but Saddam Hussein went further than anyone had expected. Months of anger and bitterness poured out in a torrent of fury. He spoke of a clear conspiracy against Iraq, of a campaign of economic, psychological and military encirclement. In an obvious reference to the Gulf sheikhdoms he said that those who had forgotten themselves and their own struggle should remember that Arab security was not divided on a state-by-state basis, and that Washington was the enemy. The United States was thinking of using its new monopoly as a superpower to humiliate the Arabs. 'We are all on the mouth of a volcano and those who think that the lava will differentiate between one Arab and another are mistaken.' Some of his guests shuffled uneasily, but the US State Department's attention was attracted more by another comment: Washington and Kuwait, Saddam said, were waging 'economic warfare' against Iraq. The *Washington Post* later reported that this gave the Bush administration its first clear indication that Saddam Hussein's target might be an Arab state rather than Israel.

During the summit the PLO asked for a further $150 million to finance the intifada, but there was silence from potential donors. Saddam Hussein spoke of the need to help all the Arabs and mentioned that Iraq was asking Kuwait for money and that the Kuwaitis were stalling. 'Maybe we can be patient, but the Palestinians in the Occupied Territories cannot be asked for patience. They are facing difficulties,' he said. There was still little response from the rich countries. Jordan returned to the question which it had tried unsuccessfully to add to the agenda of the Casablanca summit in 1989, asking the oil-producing states to repeat the pledge they had made in 1979 to support the confrontation states for ten years. That commitment had now expired. The Sheikh of Qatar and others took the view that the circumstances of the 1979 summit were different, and that there was no need to repeat the pledge. They were still willing to give aid, but felt it should be agreed between countries bilaterally, not collectively. King Hussein of Jordan said his country could not manage on such a year-to-year basis, because it needed to plan ahead, but this fell on deaf ears.

Not only were the rich countries unwilling to make long-term commitments, but the potential recipients of aid lacked unanimity. Egypt preferred bilateral deals and Syria adopted the same attitude, which weakened the case made by the PLO and Jordan.

Later, King Fahd and Saddam Hussein held a private meeting. 'I noticed that you were angry,' the king said. 'As a matter of fact, my brother king, fire was coming out of my nose and I restrained myself,' Saddam Hussein replied. 'Yasser Arafat described the plight of the people in the Occupied Territories and yet all those rich, fat people with all the money they have refused to budge.' He brought up his complaints against Kuwait, both on the frontier issue and on Kuwait's refusal to respect OPEC oil quotas. 'Even the way they deal with us is humiliating,' he said, accusing Kuwaiti tourists of buying up Iraqi art works, speculating against the dinar, and treating Iraqi women with disrespect. 'I was furious when I heard that a Kuwaiti man went to a cabaret and tried to get a lady from the cast.' He added that a Kuwaiti diplomat had boasted that a Kuwaiti could get any of the '*el-magidat*', meaning 'pure and unapproachable virgins', for ten dinars.

But Saddam's deepest anger was reserved for the oil quotas issue. 'This is an effort to ruin us,' he said, recalling his suspicion that Kuwait was involved with the United States in a conspiracy. King Fahd replied: 'We had better try to find a solution.' Saddam asked for a restricted summit between himself, King Fahd and the sheikhs of

Kuwait and the UAE, with King Fahd acting as mediator. The king agreed to arrange it.

King Hussein's speech to the summit struck a more subdued note. 'Our dear brothers, about a quarter of a century has passed since we first started to energise the institution of the summit,' he said. In fact it was President Nasser who originally proposed the institution, in late 1963, at a time when the Israelis were diverting the Jordan River. After that it became a habit. 'I hope you agree with me that this is the most important and dangerous summit,' the king continued. 'What we decide here will not only determine the future of the summit institution but the whole Arab world.' He went on to speak of the dangers the Arab world faced and made a call for unity. 'We have 65 per cent of the world's proven oil reserves, 40 per cent of oil trade passes through the Gulf; we have all the possibilities; what we lack are joint visions.'

The summit ended with a communiqué full of critical references to the United States, holding it mainly responsible for the regional situation. Afterwards President Mubarak went to Damascus to brief President Assad, who had boycotted the summit. It was a move certain to displease Saddam Hussein.

As the heads of state dispersed Saddam and Sheikh Jaber of Kuwait travelled to Baghdad airport together in an official Mercedes. The sheikh, clearly nervous, said: 'You know, all problems can be solved.' The president reminded him of Iraq's request for $10 billion and Kuwait's reply. 'When we ask for more aid, you remind us of the debts.' Sheikh Jaber pointed out that Kuwait had not asked for the debts to be repaid, it had only mentioned them. Saddam Hussein asked why Kuwait did not cancel the debts. Sheikh Jaber said: 'Did anyone from our side ask you to pay anything? Let me explain why we are not cancelling them on paper. Some of our experts think it is not in our interest to do so because our other debtors would ask for the same treatment. The experts also think it is against your interests, because it would mean that Iraq's general debt as recorded by the IMF would be reduced, and others would think that Iraq's ability to repay its remaining debts had increased. So it would be better to retain it on the books, to keep other creditors off your back.' Saddam Hussein was not convinced by this argument. They started to talk about the border, and the sheikh, in a muted way, said that the committee discussing it needed some new life.

Two of the governments involved in the crisis changed composition in June. Yitzhak Shamir formed a government in Israel on the ninth, his Likud Party depending on support from small religious groups. On the tenth elections were held in Kuwait, in an atmosphere of strong disagreement between the opposition and the emir. The elections followed a long campaign by parliamentarians and businessmen for the restoration of the National Assembly, which had been suppressed since 1986. Instead of reinstating the Assembly in its previous form, the emir decided to set up an elected National Council to change the constitution, including the rules governing elections and the composition of the National Assembly. One of the most controversial proposals was that half of the Assembly's members should be appointed by the emir. The opposition boycotted the elections, but a number of leading Kuwaiti personalities put themselves forward as candidates. In the last few days before the election 40 per cent of these candidates withdrew, citing government interference in the election campaign as the reason. The turnout of voters was hard to gauge, but the Western press estimated that not more than 25,000 out of an electorate of 60,000 participated. There were reports of demonstrations against the emir's plans and clashes with security forces. These events left much bitterness, but the opposition nevertheless refused to co-operate with the Iraqis after the invasion seven weeks later. After the election, the emir reappointed Sheikh Saad at the head of a new cabinet.

The UAE responded to King Hussein's plea at the Baghdad summit by sending Jordan a cheque for $40 million, but Kuwait showed no signs of paying the $10 billion which Baghdad had requested. Saddam Hussein sent Sa'adoun Hammadi back to Kuwait on 25 June to ask for the money again.

Baghdad also pursued its complaints against Kuwait and the UAE at successive meetings of OPEC. The falling oil price had prompted an emergency meeting in Vienna on 17 March 1990 at which a reduction of production quotas was agreed. This was followed by allegations that some countries were exceeding their quotas, and on 10 April the oil ministers of Saudi Arabia, Kuwait and the UAE met to pledge their commitment to the quotas agreed in March.

A further full OPEC meeting was held in Jeddah on 10 July, at which the ministers announced their determination to keep the price at $18 a barrel, but the Kuwaitis hinted that their willingness to respect production quotas depended on other oil producers not exceeding theirs. 'If we believe that the agreement is not being taken seriously, then obviously we will act to protect our national interests,' their minister said. This was a reference to the UAE, which had usually been the first to break ranks. Iran was in full accord with Iraq and Saudi Arabia, and the Iranian oil minister, Reda Agha Zadeh, carried a message from President Ali Akbar Hashemi Rafsanjani to Sheikh Zayed of Abu Dhabi urging him to keep the Emirates in line with OPEC policy. After the meeting there was a temporary cut in Kuwaiti production but not in overall OPEC output. The price now sank below $14 a barrel.

Facing economic disaster, Baghdad demanded a reference price of $25 a barrel, which would have been a huge jump. Sa'adoun Hammadi, the deputy prime minister, delivered urgent messages to Saudi Arabia, Kuwait, the UAE and Qatar blaming Kuwait and the UAE for Iraq's predicament. He warned: 'Iraq cannot tolerate this situation. Our financial and economic situation motivates us to speak loudly.'

By mid-July Baghdad felt it had almost exhausted diplomatic methods of resolving the dispute. Its remaining hopes of making Kuwait toe the line without resorting to force depended on the mini-summit which King Fahd had promised to arrange. Saddam Hussein was therefore furious when he heard that after the Jeddah meeting of OPEC, the Saudi oil minister had called together his counterparts from Iraq, Kuwait, the UAE and Qatar. A meeting at this level fell far short of the king's promise.

The meeting was set for 11 July, but two days earlier Iraqi intelligence intercepted a phone call from King Fahd to the Sheikh of Qatar, Sheikh Khalifa Ben Hamad Al-Thawi. According to the Iraqis, the king discussed the need to placate Saddam Hussein by holding a meeting at oil ministers' level. The Iraqis recorded the conversation, and later broadcast parts of it, including this extract:

'I don't know what Saddam Hussein is aiming at. He is going into a confrontation with the Israelis. He forgets that it was published that the Israelis have got 200 atom bombs. It seems to me that he has forgotten what happened to Nasser when he challenged the West. Instead of defying America to that extent, he should take a lesson from what is happening to Moscow. The Soviet Union defied the United States for decades and now it is disintegrating. By God, I am afraid he is going to get himself and all of us into a catastrophe.'

The Iraqis felt that the conversation demonstrated bad faith, by making it appear that Saudi Arabia's only reason for convening the meeting was to keep Baghdad quiet. The Saudi government confirmed that King Fahd had talked to Sheikh Khalifa by telephone, but reports in Saudi newspapers claimed that the recording had been tampered with to suit Iraq's purposes.

A further OPEC meeting on 26 July produced an agreement on a new reference price of $21 a barrel, but this was too little and too late to avert a violent confrontation.

2

American Connection

The most surprising aspect of Iraq's occupation of Kuwait was that it came as a surprise. Saddam Hussein had hinted at his intentions and explained his reasons well in advance, yet found no one willing to believe him. Until the tanks began to roll, the West and the Arab world remained convinced that he was bluffing. The United States recorded every detail of the military build-up with satellite photographs, yet came to the wrong conclusions. Its eyes in the sky were supplemented not only by substantial embassies in Baghdad and Kuwait, but also by a CIA unit working directly with the Kuwait government, whose duty was to foresee and avert any threat to the Sabah family.

The evidence of this unit's presence came to light after the invasion when the Iraqis gained access to the files of the Kuwaiti government. The most telling document was a report marked 'Top Secret', written at the end of November or early December 1989 by a member of the Kuwaiti royal family, Brigadier Saad Ahmed al-Fahd al-Sabah. It bore the number S540 and was addressed to the interior minister, Sheikh Salem al-Salem al-Sabah. The report recorded that on 22 October 1989 the minister ordered two officials to undertake a secret mission to the United States. One was the report's author, the other Colonel Ishak Abdul Hadi Shaddad, director of security of Ahmadi, the most sensitive area of Kuwait, where many of its oil installations are located.

The document read: 'We went on a visit to the headquarters of the CIA, a visit which the American party wanted to be top secret so that it would not raise the sensitivities of our brothers in the Gulf Co-operation Council, and also the Iranians and Iraqis. That visit took place in the period between 12 and 18 November 1989. I want to inform Your Highness about what we agreed upon with Judge William Webster, the Director General of the CIA, through a private meeting I had with him on Tuesday 14 November 1989.' The first point agreed was that the Americans would take care of the training of a Kuwaiti protection squad of 128 men to guard the emir and the crown prince. An attempt to assassinate the emir had been made on 25 May 1985, and the report noted that the Americans were 'not happy at all' with the way the emir's guards reacted.

It continued: 'We agreed with the Americans that there should be visits and exchanges of information between the administration of the security of state and the CIA and also we should exchange information about Iran and Iraq, especially in the fields of armaments, political and social conditions.'

The next points were that the CIA would help reorganise Kuwait's internal security, including a better computer system, and that there would be exchanges of information about the activities of Shi'ite fundamentalist groups in the country and in the nations of the Gulf Co-operation Council. Then came the heart of the evidence:

'Number five: We agreed with the American side on the necessity to exploit the deteriorating economic situation in Iraq so that we can press its government to accept the designation of our frontiers with them . . . the CIA gave us its ideas about how we can conduct the suitable means of pressure and how to co-ordinate our co-operation with them, but they ask that that should be on the highest level.'

The CIA thought that Kuwait should 're-programme' its relations with Iran and 'reinforce our alliance' with Syria. Kuwait should avoid expressing negative views of Iran, and if it needed to exert pressure on Tehran this should be done 'in a very subtle way'.

Finally, the report recorded an agreement to co-operate on drugs control and spoke of evidence that the Kuwaiti capital was being used 'on a very large scale' by traffickers. It concluded by giving a secure telephone number in Washington for exchanges of information, and ended with the words: 'I am waiting for instructions. God bless you.'

When they discovered this report the Iraqis linked it with America's secret deliveries of missiles to Tehran during the Iran–Iraq war, the damaging effects of Kuwait's policy on oil prices (which they felt had been encouraged by Washington), the continuation of a large US naval presence in the Gulf after the Iran–Iraq war had ended, and US criticisms (before the invasion of Kuwait) of Iraq's policies on human rights and chemical weapons. Putting all these elements together, the Iraqis saw the report as further confirmation of their suspicions that the Americans had been trying to encircle Baghdad politically and economically.

The Iraqis found the letter after the occupation of Kuwait, but as early as April or May 1990 Saddam Hussein received information from a friendly head of state that a decision had been taken at the highest levels in the West to treat Iraq as a new danger in the region. The West was waiting for an opportunity to remove Saddam from power, according to the same source. Baghdad had also been told of a private discussion after the Iran–Iraq ceasefire involving King Fahd, who had said: 'If the Iraqis behave well, things will be all right, but if they behave like victors and create havoc in the region, by God they are going to get it.'

It took the Iraqis some time to decide what to do once they realised that the pressure they had exerted at the Baghdad summit had produced no results. The entire Arab world was now exasperated with the institution of the summit. President Mubarak commented: 'Summits are now only a forum for exchanging insults. All we do is tear each other's clothes apart.' The Revolutionary Command Council in Baghdad held a series of discussions to consider alternatives, and reached a decision on 8 July. Normally communiqués at the end of such meetings merely record that the RCC met, but on 8 July it was announced that they had talked about moves towards democracy in Iraq. No one believed this. Arab observers assumed that the announcement was a cover for something Iraq wanted to keep secret. What in fact happened was that the RCC decided to change tactics, greatly increasing the pressure on Kuwait and continuing to show readiness to hit back hard if attacked by Israel. The RCC believed at the time that the economic pressure Iraq was suffering was a prelude to such an attack. They had taken note of an ambiguous statement on 4 July by the new Israeli chief of staff, General Ehud Barak, who had said: 'Those who talk of an imminent war in the area are alarmists. The red lights are not yet lit, but the green lights have gone off. I would say that the orange lights are on.'

The Iraqis felt that the longer they allowed the situation to continue, the greater their diplomatic encirclement by hostile powers would become. On 9 July Ali Akbar Velayati, the Iranian foreign minister, made his first visit to Kuwait, bringing a message from

President Rafsanjani, and soon afterwards the two countries resumed diplomatic relations, Iran appointing one of their most able diplomats, Hussein Sadikki, as ambassador.

Saddam Hussein chose 17 July, the anniversary of the Ba'ath Party's return to power in 1968, to come into the open. In a speech at a public meeting he threatened to use force against 'some' Arab countries if they did not cease their overproduction of oil. 'Oh God almighty, be witness that we have warned them,' he continued. The West and much of the Arab world assumed that this was mere rhetoric, but it was widely reported. The *International Herald Tribune* said that the reference to 'some' Arab countries was 'an obvious allusion to Kuwait and the United Arab Emirates'.

The attention given to this point eclipsed other elements in the speech. Saddam Hussein developed his conspiracy theory, arguing that the United States was trying to dictate the terms on which Iraq sold its oil, while imposing civil and other wars on it. 'They will never forgive us our victory . . . our technological achievements,' he said. 'What we are facing now is a loss of $14 billion a year in oil prices. This is a conspiracy to make us live in famine . . . this is an American policy and there are Arabs who are mobilised in the service of that policy. I feel sorry to talk about those Arabs, I feel tormented . . . but we have to stand up to those who have come with a poisoned dagger and thrust it into our backs. Iraq is not going to accept that.'

Saddam Hussein avoided naming names, but the following day Tariq Aziz was more explicit in an open letter to Chedli El-Klibi, Secretary General of the Arab League, which he submitted at a foreign ministers' meeting in Tunis. The ministers were discussing a proposal to boycott countries which facilitated the passage of Soviet immigrants to Israel, but the press found Tariq Aziz's letter more newsworthy. It accused Kuwait of exploiting Iraq's involvement in the war with Iran to seize Iraqi territory in the Rumaila oilfield, of stealing oil, and of involvement in a conspiracy to force the oil price down. The letter reiterated Iraq's arguments and its sense of being betrayed by those it had protected against Iran. 'Those who should have hailed our victory are waiting for us with poisoned daggers,' said Aziz. Iraq regarded Kuwait's moves as 'acts of aggression'.

The ministers discussed the letter in rather muted terms, not wanting to give a view until they had reported back to their governments. Tariq Aziz showed his irritation on the second day: 'I am astonished that you are dealing with my memorandum in a routine way, distributing it and studying it. I am talking to you about a state of war, and you are not moving.' His remark should have brought the meeting to life, but none of his colleagues had authority to deal with such issues, and some probably dismissed Aziz's words as more Iraqi rhetoric.

Even if the ministers seemed slow to react, within forty-eight hours the remarks had caused a sensation in the Arab world. King Fahd phoned Saddam Hussein the following day and later issued a statement saying that the Iraqi leader had assured him that all Arab differences would be dealt with in a brotherly way. The king despatched Prince Saud al-Faisal, the foreign minister, to Baghdad, while the Emir of Kuwait sent his minister of Emiri affairs to see Mubarak, and most of the Arab leaders consulted each other by telephone. In Egypt the impact of Aziz's attack on Kuwait was blunted by other remarks in his speech which Cairo newspapers saw as an insult to Egypt. Aziz said that some Arab countries had forgotten their past and were now accommodating imperialism, a criticism which could have been directed at half a dozen countries, but was not aimed at Egypt. It was a trivial matter, but it caused a disproportionate fuss, and Saddam Hussein was clearly worried that it might divert attention from his complaints against Kuwait. In a phone call to President Mubarak a few days later he said: 'Brother, I was astonished when I saw in the Egyptian papers that you thought for a second that there was an attack against Egypt. I have ordered Tariq Aziz to come to you to explain what he meant. He is also carrying a tape recording of what he actually said. If you find anything that could be an insult to Egypt, I give you the authority to try him and put him in prison.' Aziz arrived in Alexandria the following day, 22 July, carrying a bag packed, he said, with his prison clothes. He told Mubarak that he was ready to go to Tora maximum security prison, in a suburb south of Cairo. The gesture might seem exaggerated, but given the sensitivity of inter-Arab relations at the time something extraordinary was needed to make amends.

While Tariq Aziz was in Alexandria seeing Mubarak, King Hussein arrived from Jordan and the three men had a joint meeting at which they discussed arranging a high-level meeting between Iraq and Kuwait.

By now the Kuwaiti government was receiving daily reports of Iraqi troop movements from Ibrahim Gassim el-Bahu, its ambassador in Baghdad. 'I don't want to raise too much alarm, because these movements can always be explained,' he said in a report shortly after Tariq Aziz's speech. 'If I ask the Iraqis they will say that it is to do with Iran, because not all Iraqi – Iranian problems are settled. But I have to report heavy troop movements, including tanks.'

Soon afterwards el-Bahu decided to stop using coded radio signals to make his reports, preferring trusted messengers, who were told to keep their eyes open for further signs of military activity. He also contacted April Glaspie, the American ambassador, and urged her to seek a meeting with Saddam Hussein. She replied: 'We have tried in the past, but it's hopeless. He never receives ambassadors.'

Henrik Amneus, the Swedish ambassador in Baghdad, held a meeting with Ezzat Ibrahim, the Iraqi vice president, who told him: 'Iraq is not prepared to die in silence. Even if we lose sixteen million of our population, we are prepared to do whatever is necessary to ensure the dignity of Iraq and its remaining one million people.'

The *Washington Post* later reported that on 20 July a foreign military attaché driving along the six-lane highway from Kuwait to Baghdad had seen hundreds of army trucks filled with troops and weapons moving south. He counted more than 2,000 vehicles on the road, transporting two divisions of the Republican Guard. The *Post* said that this prompted Washington to use its satellites to observe the border area more closely.

Kuwait had placed its armed forces on alert on 20 July, but still thought an invasion unlikely. It regarded Saddam Hussein's threats as mere rhetoric, and calculated that the reflagging episode during the Iran–Iraq war had secured it unconditional American support. In Middle East terms, that was the ultimate deterrent.

The following day, 21 July, Saddam Hussein gave an assurance to Prince Saud al-Faisal. 'Yes, there are troop movements, but they are not for aggression,' he said. The United Arab Emirates asked Washington to find some discreet way of showing that it would support them in the event of attack. The Americans complied by arranging a small joint exercise by the US and UAE air forces and by moving six warships to positions closer to Kuwait and the UAE, but these moves were disclosed to the American press, which upset the UAE. The US administration considered a larger show of force, possibly moving the aircraft carrier *Independence* to the area, but decided against it.

Prince Saud al-Faisal returned to Saudi Arabia with news of apparent progress. The Iraqi leader had accepted an offer by King

Fahd and President Mubarak to arrange a high-level meeting between the Iraqis and Kuwaitis at a place to be chosen by the Kuwaitis. After discussions with Kuwait it was fixed for 1 August in Jeddah, between Sheikh Saad al-Sabah, the Kuwaiti crown prince, and Ezzat Ibrahim, the Iraqi vice president. Saddam Hussein had told Prince Saud al-Faisal that the troops moving south were heading for the Faw peninsula, an area where there was a continuing risk of conflict between Iranian and Iraqi forces. The prince learned from other sources that the divisions moving south were not at a high state of readiness. The king passed this on to President Mubarak, but he was clearly in two minds. 'We do not believe there is anything alarming, but you know it is dangerous,' he said. Mubarak, in the meantime, had talked to Saddam Hussein on the telephone and to King Hussein in person. The Egyptian leader felt he should go to Baghdad and Kuwait to encourage a diplomatic solution, and King Fahd backed the idea: 'By Allah, may it do some good,' he said.

Mubarak and Saddam Hussein held a private meeting in a closed room in Baghdad, leaving their assistants outside. Mubarak understood Saddam Hussein to say that he was only trying to scare Kuwait and would not use force. Baghdad's version was that Saddam Hussein said there would be no use of force before Iraq and Kuwait held their high-level meeting. If the meeting produced an agreement, there would be no problem; if not, Iraq would defend its interests. Mubarak came away convinced that there was no danger, while Saddam Hussein thought he had given a clear warning. As no note-takers were present it is impossible to tell how the confusion arose.

The meeting ended with a ten-minute open talk in the presence of others, during which Saddam Hussein said that Sheikh Jaber had $17 billion in his personal bank account, enough to pay off half Egypt's debts.

Mubarak flew to Kuwait and Saudi Arabia and passed on what he thought he had been told. 'Rest assured, he is not going to use military force,' he said. His aim was to calm all concerned, as he felt that reassurance was needed at this time of high tension, but after the invasion some Arabs argued that his move weakened Iraq's chances of frightening Kuwait into submission without using force. Saddam Hussein later said: 'Supposing I told him that I only wanted to scare them, why did he pass it on to the Kuwaitis? It was bound to spoil my manoeuvre.'

The Egyptian leader also phoned President Bush and Margaret

Thatcher and told them the situation was only a war of nerves. President Bush later made much of Mubarak's version, arguing that the Iraqi leader had lied even to his friends, but the facts were not clear enough to support such a judgement. Two explanations seem possible: either Mubarak misunderstood what was said, or Saddam Hussein used the Egyptian leader as an unwitting party to a double bluff. Knowing that anything he said would be passed on to Kuwait, the Iraqi leader may have wanted them to think that his forces on the border were merely part of a hoax.

As the Jeddah encounter approached, Kuwait came under stronger pressure from Saudi Arabia and others to be more accommodating towards Iraq. Riyadh shared Baghdad's annoyance with Kuwait and the UAE over the oil quotas issue, and also felt that the Iraqi wish for an outlet to the Gulf was reasonable. It proposed that Kuwait should consider leasing the islands of Warba and Bubiyan to Iraq for a long period, an idea supported by the Egyptians. At this point, a week before Iraq's occupation of Kuwait, relations between King Fahd and Saddam Hussein were still close, despite their mutual dislike of each other's regimes. Most other Arab countries supported parts of the Iraqi argument, especially as regards Kuwait's encroachment into the Rumaila oilfield, which was seen as unnecessary provocation. King Hussein, realising that the crisis had taken a dangerous turn, visited Sheikh Jaber and conveyed a general Arab desire for a compromise settlement. He also added his support to the Saudi and Egyptian proposal on leasing the two islands. The sheikh said: 'This is Kuwaiti soil, and the Kuwaiti constitution does not permit me to give up one inch of Kuwaiti territory.' King Hussein replied: 'I understand the Kuwaiti constitution, but is your territory more sacred than Jerusalem, which has been occupied by Israel for more than twenty-five years?'

In the last days of July many in the Arab world thought the row was moving towards a peaceful resolution, with the Kuwaitis facing overwhelming peer pressure. But things were not what they seemed. A handwritten note by Sheikh Jaber, discovered by the Iraqis after the occupation, showed that the Kuwaitis had not had the slightest intention of compromising. King Fahd had sent a telegram to the sheikh asking him, in the most tactful and indirect way, to ensure that the crown prince showed some flexibility at the 1 August meeting. The sheikh passed it on to the crown prince, adding his own comments underneath.

The letter is headed: 'Kingdom of Saudi Arabia, the Office of the Prime Minister' (King Fahd is also prime minister).

> Your Highness, dear brother, Sheikh Jaber al-Ahmad al-Sabah, the Emir of the State of Kuwait.
>
> God bless you and give you his care. I pray for good health and prosperity for His Highness. My brother, I want to mention the brotherly contacts which went on between Your Highness and His Excellency, our brother President Saddam Hussein, the President of the Iraqi Republic. It was agreed that there should be a meeting between His Highness, brother Sheikh Saad Abdullah al-Sabah and His Excellency, brother Ezzat Ibrahim in your second home, the Kingdom of Saudi Arabia. It is my pleasure to welcome His Highness, brother Sheikh Saad al-Sabah in the City of Jeddah on the day of Tuesday, 9th of Moharram, 14/11 Higri, which coincides with 31 July 1990 . . . I look forward to this brotherly meeting and I am sure to the depths of my heart that your wisdom and your penetrating look will be able to achieve all that we desire in the Arab world, softening all difficulties and transcending all obstacles and assuring brotherly feelings and peace of soul and mind between the two brotherly countries. I take this opportunity . . . friendship and respect . . . best brotherly wishes for His Highness, the brother, with good health and happiness for the Kuwaiti people . . . God give you long life and take care of you. Your brother, the Servant of the Two Holy Places, Fahd Ibn Abd al-Aziz al-Saud.

At the bottom, Sheikh Jaber added a clear note to the crown prince to stand firm:

> We attend this meeting under the same conditions we agreed on . . . Whatever you may hear from the Saudis or the Iraqis about brotherhood and Arab solidarity, forget it. Every one of us has his own interests. The Saudis want to weaken us . . . so that they can press us in the future to give them concessions in the neutral zones. The Iraqis want to compensate for their losses in the war at our expense. Neither of these should happen. That is the view of our friends in Egypt, Washington and London. Insist on your discussions. We are more powerful than they imagine. With all my wishes for success, Jaber.

The instructions given to Ezzat Ibrahim by Saddam Hussein were just as tough. The Iraqi vice president was ordered to take a hard line if the Kuwaiti crown prince proved unco-operative on the border dispute. 'Tell him that we have pictures of Kuwait when it was a walled city, and the only borders we recognise are those walls,' he said. Parts of the old wall still exist, but most of Kuwait City now lies beyond them. If Kuwait were reduced to this extent, it would cease to have any meaning as a separate state.

3

A Crossroads of Confusion

In the last days before the invasion six capitals assessed the situation and came by parallel routes to wrong conclusions. The Kuwaiti government had thought all along that Baghdad was bluffing, and remained confident until the final hours that no military move was imminent. King Fahd and King Hussein were satisfied that Saddam Hussein would honour his assurance that all Arab differences would be settled in a 'brotherly' manner. President Mubarak continued to think that Saddam Hussein was only trying to frighten Kuwait. A dialogue of misunderstandings or deception between Washington and Baghdad left both capitals with distorted impressions of the other's intentions. Saddam Hussein began to think that American commitment to Kuwait was not as strong as the Kuwaitis believed. The US State Department did not expect a full invasion of Kuwait, believing the main risk was of a limited operation to seize the islands of Warba and Bubiyan and the Rumaila oilfield. This was indeed Iraq's preferred option at first, and might have been its course of action but for a last-minute change of plan.

Nothing contributed more to the confusion than a meeting between Saddam Hussein and April Glaspie, the US ambassador in Baghdad, eight days before the invasion of Kuwait. It left the Iraqi leader with an impression of American uninterest and pliability, and reinforced Washington's misconception of Iraq's intentions. The misunderstandings arose partly from a stark contrast in personalities. Miss Glaspie had been promoted through the ranks of the State Department on the strength of her knowledge and experience of Arab affairs, but did not have the strong presence expected of a superpower ambassador. She seemed overawed by the Iraqi leader's forceful personality, and was later judged by the American press to have behaved in an unduly deferential manner.

Attacks on US policy in speeches by Saddam Hussein on 17 July and by Tariq Aziz on the eighteenth prompted Washington to ask Miss Glaspie to seek clarification. US satellite photographs were showing that an Iraqi armoured division with 300 tanks had moved close to the border with Kuwait, and that a rapid military build-up was under way. Miss Glaspie obtained an appointment on 24 July with Nizar Hamdoun, Iraq's undersecretary of state for foreign affairs, who was Tariq Aziz's second deputy. Hamdoun, one of Iraq's most talented diplomats, was the principal point of contact for senior ambassadors based in Baghdad. Meetings with Tariq Aziz were rare, and with Saddam Hussein almost non-existent. So far as anyone could recall, he had never phoned any of the American ambassadors who had served in Baghdad during his eleven years in power. Hamdoun took a conciliatory attitude with Miss Glaspie, and at about 6 p.m. the meeting ended and she returned to her embassy. On arrival she was told that Hamdoun had phoned asking her to return to his office immediately. She found him waiting in a car parked outside the embassy, and they set off at once without explanation. Miss Glaspie assumed that she was being taken to see someone senior, probably Tariq Aziz. They entered a guest house and she found herself in Saddam Hussein's presence. This put her at a disadvantage, as she was unprepared and had no note-taker with her, but it was immediately obvious that the Iraqi leader had something urgent to say. He underlined this in his opening remark: 'This is a message to President Bush.' When a Third World leader indicates his intentions to the ambassador of a great power, he assumes that he is addressing a person of importance, not just a cog in its bureaucracy. This misconception is a legacy from colonial times, when an ambassador's reactions to a leader's remarks were carefully observed and noted: a lack of disapproval would be taken to mean that the leader's intentions could be implemented without interference from the ambassador's government.

Miss Glaspie must have realised that this was a crucial meeting, yet she seems to have missed the significance of Saddam Hussein's remarks. The meeting was recorded, and a transcript released by the Iraqis was acknowledged by the US State Department to be substantially accurate, although Miss Glaspie later said that they omitted some of her own remarks and warnings.

After a long account of US–Iraqi relations Saddam Hussein complained about a 'planned and deliberate' policy to force the price of oil down, and said this amounted to a war against Iraq. He accused Kuwait and the UAE of being at the forefront of the policy, and said its aim was to weaken Iraq's position and deny its people higher economic standards. He then stated his feeling that Iraq had performed a service through the Iran–Iraq war. 'You [the Americans] are not the ones who protected your friends [the Gulf sheikhdoms],' he said. 'Had the Iranians overrun the region, American troops could not have stopped them except by the use of nuclear weapons. I do not belittle you, but I hold that . . . yours is a society which cannot accept 10,000 dead in one battle.' This was a clear hint that Saddam Hussein thought Washington would have no stomach for a ground war in the Middle East. It is not known whether Miss Glaspie observed this in her report.

Other remarks by Saddam Hussein showed that the possibility of a military clash between Iraq and the US was in his mind. He gave a clear warning that if Washington used military force, Baghdad would reply with terrorist attacks on US targets. 'If you use pressure, we will deploy pressure and force. We know that you can harm us, although we do not threaten you, but we too can harm you. We cannot come all the way to you in the United States, but individual Arabs may reach you.'

In another comment he appeared to predict Washington's use of air and missile power, which was to come six months later. 'You can come to Iraq with aircraft and missiles, but do not push us to the point where we cease to care. When we feel that you want to injure our pride and take away the Iraqis' chance of a higher standard of living, then we will cease to care and death would be the choice for us. We would not care if you fired a hundred missiles for each one we fired, because without pride life would have no value.'

Saddam appeared to assume that if there was a clash between Washington and Baghdad it would come about as a result of an Israeli – Iraqi conflict, and treated Iraq's dispute with Kuwait as a separate matter. His next remark hinted that the use of force against Kuwait had not been ruled out, but he later gave a more forceful warning:

> We are hurt and upset that such disagreement is taking place between us and Kuwait and the UAE. The solution must be found in an Arab framework and through direct bilateral relations. I do not put all these states on the same level. Israel stole Arab land, supported by the United States, but the UAE and Kuwait do not support Israel. Anyway, they are Arabs. But when they try to weaken Iraq they are helping the enemy, and then Iraq has the right to defend itself . . . I

hope the president [Bush] will read this himself and will not leave it in the hands of a gang in the State Department.

Miss Glaspie's reply was more than conciliatory. 'I thank you, Mr President. It is a great pleasure for a diplomat to meet and talk directly with the president. I clearly understand your message. We studied history at school. They taught us to say "Freedom or Death".' She said she had direct instructions from President Bush to seek better relations with Baghdad.

Saddam Hussein interjected: 'But how? We too have this desire, but matters are running contrary to it.'

Miss Glaspie's tone remained gentle, without a hint of warning. She encouraged Saddam Hussein to appear on American television, and seemed to support his attacks on the Western media. 'I am pleased that you add your voice to the diplomats who stand up to the media, because your appearance in the media, even for five minutes, would help us to make the Americans understand Iraq. This would increase mutual understanding. If the American president had control of the media, his job would be much easier.'

Miss Glaspie said that Washington had 'no opinion' on conflicts between Arabs such as the Iraqi–Kuwaiti border dispute. She used exceptionally mild language when raising Washington's concern about the threats Baghdad had made to Kuwait in the 17 and 18 July speeches. The United States could see that Iraq had deployed massive forces in the south, she said, and this would not be its concern but for the speeches and Baghdad's argument that policies followed by the UAE and Kuwait were 'parallel to military aggression': 'Then it would be reasonable for me to be concerned and, for this reason, I received an instruction to ask you, in the spirit of friendship, not in the spirit of confrontation, regarding your intentions.'

Her reference to 'massive forces' implied that she was aware of the latest intelligence from the Pentagon. Satellite photographs showed that Iraq had moved eight divisions to the border in eleven days and now had 100,000 men facing Kuwait. Each division had moved between 450 and 600 kilometres.[1]

Saddam Hussein replied: 'What we ask is [that you should not] express your concern in a way which would make an aggressor believe

[1] Bob Woodward, *The Commanders*

that he is getting support for his aggression. We want to find a just solution which will give us our rights but not deprive others of their rights. But at the same time, we want others to know that our patience is running out.'

During the two-hour meeting Saddam Hussein was called to the next room to receive a telephone call from President Mubarak. It was this call which settled arrangements for the Kuwaiti crown prince and the Iraqi vice president to meet in Jeddah on 1 August.

The Iraqi account of the meeting between Saddam Hussein and the American ambassador conflicts with the testimony Miss Glaspie gave to the Senate Foreign Relations Committee in March 1991. She said she warned Saddam Hussein several times that Washington would not allow military aggression against Kuwait and made it clear that the US regarded Kuwait as a vital interest. While acknowledging her comment that the US had 'no opinion' about the border dispute, she said that the Iraqi version included only part of her remarks. The part omitted was: 'But we insist that you settle your disputes with Kuwait non-violently.'

She was asked: 'Did you ever tell Saddam Hussein: "Mr President, if you go across that line into Kuwait, we are going to fight"?' She replied: 'No, I did not,' but added that it was not US policy at the time to make such a threat.

Four months after her testimony, the State Department allowed the Senate Foreign Relations Committee to see the report which Miss Glaspie cabled to Washington after the meeting. Her account of the way she put the question about Iraq's military build-up tallied almost exactly with the Iraqi version. She said that she posed the question gently, 'in the spirit of friendship, not confrontation'. Her warning against military action was neither direct nor explicit. She said: 'We can never excuse settlement of disputes by any but peaceful means.'[2] Her account was described in *Newsweek* as portraying her as 'embarrassingly deferential'.

The cables also suggest that Miss Glaspie thought her role was to defuse US–Iraqi tensions. She reported that she had stressed repeatedly that President Bush wanted to improve relations with Iraq and not to confront Saddam Hussein. She came away from the meeting believing that there would be no invasion: 'His emphasis that he wants

---

[2] *Washington Post*, republished in *International Herald Tribune*, 13/14 July 1991

peaceful settlement is surely sincere.' She said the Iraqi leader was alarmed by the small joint exercise conducted by the US Air Force and the UAE which was carried out at the UAE's request after the 17 and 18 July speeches. She reported: 'We have fully caught his attention,' and added: 'I believe we would now be well-advised to ease off on public relations criticism of Iraq until we see how the negotiations develop' (referring to the 1 August meeting). General Colin Powell, Chairman of the Joint Chiefs of Staff, was relieved when he saw Miss Glaspie's report, as it implied that there was still room for Iraqi–Kuwaiti negotiations.[3] A report in the *International Herald Tribune* on 15 September, six weeks after the occupation, said that Saddam Hussein received such kind and gentle handling from the ambassador that he could only have concluded that he could invade and annex Kuwait without facing American retaliation.

According to the Iraqi transcript, Saddam Hussein repeated to Miss Glaspie the two-edged assurance he gave President Mubarak. It quotes him as follows:

> Brother President Mubarak told me they [the Kuwaitis] were scared. They said troops were only twenty kilometres north of the Arab League line [the Iraq–Kuwait border]. I said to him that regardless of what is there, whether they are police, border guards or army . . . give them [the Kuwaitis] our word, that we are not going to do anything until we meet with them. When we meet and when we see that there is hope, then nothing will happen. But if we are unable to find a solution, then it will be natural that Iraq will not accept death, even though wisdom is above everything else.

It is hard to understand why Miss Glaspie gave the State Department such an optimistic assessment, as Saddam Hussein's message was clear. Kuwait would have to make concessions at the 1 August meeting if it wanted to avert an invasion. It appears that she simply missed the point. One possibility is that language difficulties contributed to the misunderstanding. The conversation was mostly in Arabic, though Nizar Hamdoun, who speaks good English, acted as an interpreter at certain points. Miss Glaspie was regarded as one of the best Arabic speakers among European diplomats based in Baghdad, and kept up

[3] Woodward, *The Commanders*

her knowledge of colloquial phrases by chatting to ordinary people in markets.

She had previously been Director of the Office of Jordan, Syria and Lebanon at the State Department, and before that had served at the US embassy in Cairo. American reports said she was highly regarded by her colleagues. During her nomination hearings in 1987 she faced opposition from Senator Jesse Helms of North Carolina, who appeared to think her unduly sympathetic towards the Arab world. One of the questions he asked was: 'Does Iraq pose any threat to Saudi Arabia or Kuwait?' She replied: 'No, not at present,' and recalled that in 1973, during the radical phase of Ba'ath Party rule, Iraq made territorial claims on two Kuwaiti islands and its troops briefly occupied a Kuwaiti border post. Pressure from Saudi Arabia and the Arab League forced them to withdraw. Until the beginning of Saddam Hussein's presidency relations with both countries were tense. Since then Kuwait and Saudi Arabia had emerged as Iraq's main financial backers against Iran. As a relatively large and rich state with a powerful army, Iraq would always play a role in Gulf politics.

'We presume this poses some concern for Kuwait and Saudi Arabia in the long run, but at present Iraq poses no threat to those countries,' she said. She was then asked: 'Does the Saudi or Kuwaiti leadership share this assessment?' Her reply was classified by the State Department.

Miss Glaspie was the first American woman to become ambassador to an Arab country. When she took up her post in 1988 she was impressed by Saddam Hussein's popularity, and US–Iraqi relations were improving. Saddam seemed in complete control, despite the high human cost of the war and financial losses which the US estimated at $500 billion. Iraq had a policy of giving the best reconstruction contracts to American firms, including a $1.2 billion deal with Bechtel for oil installations, dams, ports and other facilities. At the time the United States was selling wheat worth $1 billion a year to Iraq and buying 400,000 barrels of Iraqi oil a day. The following year, 1989, the United States took 19.2 per cent of Iraq's exports, a figure equalled only by West Germany, and supplied 12.5 per cent of Iraq's imports.

Glaspie's second and third years in Baghdad were marked by a steady worsening of Iraqi–US relations, which the West attributed to Saddam Hussein's post-war mood. A report in March 1991 said that for two years there was a 'mind set' at the State Department which refused to acknowledge growing signs that Saddam Hussein was planning a conquest,[4] although James Baker, the US Secretary of State, dismissed such criticisms as 'twenty-twenty hindsight'.

It is a rule of diplomatic life that ambassadors remain at their posts at times of crisis, however personally inconvenient that may be. Every flight out of Baghdad was full of foreign workers and diplomats going home on holiday, and Miss Glaspie, like most people, was looking forward to a break. Her misplaced euphoria at the end of her meeting with Saddam Hussein led her to think that she could safely go ahead with her plans. 'I thought to postpone my trip because of the difficulties we're facing, but now I will fly on Monday [30 July],' she told him. Some diplomats were astonished by her decision, and at least one Arab ambassador begged her to stay, but she was convinced that nothing unexpected would happen.

Harold Walker, the British ambassador, also left Iraq just before the occupation of Kuwait. A high-level meeting at the US State Department came to the conclusion on 27 July that Iraq was unlikely to invade. Prince Bandar, the Saudi ambassador in Washington, thought that Saddam Hussein was sabre-rattling.[5] King Hussein of Jordan phoned President Bush on 28 and 30 July, and was 'extremely reassuring that the quarrel would be solved peacefully'.[6]

Miss Glaspie was not seen again in public for months. The following spring, testifying to the Senate Foreign Relations Committee, she said that during that time she had been extremely busy working at the State Department.

Her failure to understand Saddam Hussein's warning had two immediate effects. On the day of their meeting, the Kuwaiti military attaché in Basra, Colonel Said Mater, told his government that an Iraqi military operation would be launched on 2 August. He said this was confirmed by informants in the Iraqi Revolutionary Guards. If Miss Glaspie had told the State Department that military action was on the cards, Washington would have briefed Kuwait and Colonel Mater's information might have been heeded. In the absence of supporting sources, it was ignored.

Secondly, Kuwait made its preparations for the Jeddah meeting on the basis of wrong assumptions. Its self-confidence was underlined three days before the occupation when Sheikh Jaber, the emir, declined

---

[4] *Wall Street Journal*, 22 March 1991
[5] Woodward, *The Commanders*
[6] *Washington Post Magazine*, 17 March 1991

to discuss the crisis with Yasser Arafat, turning the conversation to Arab–Israeli issues. Sheikh Saad, the crown prince, went to the Jeddah meeting thinking that there was no urgency and that any concessions could be left until subsequent meetings, while Ezzat Ibrahim, the Iraqi vice president, assumed that the Kuwaitis realised that this was their last chance.

The crown prince arrived at 10 a.m. and was met by Prince Abdullah, his Saudi counterpart, who took him to a royal rest house. Ezzat Ibrahim was given similar honours, and soon afterwards a reception was held to bring them together. King Fahd was pleased to see that they greeted each other like Arab brothers, with the traditional kisses on both cheeks. He suggested that they should rest before their talks in the afternoon. The two men were left alone during the meeting, and separate cars were arranged to pick them up from their rest houses for dinner with King Fahd at 9.30 p.m. Instead, Ezzat Ibrahim called the director of ceremonies to say they would travel together in the same car, with a Kuwaiti flag on one side and an Iraqi flag on the other. 'This was a very good omen,' King Fahd said later. 'I was so happy . . . we went together for dinner. I did not ask what they did in their first meeting because I thought they should keep it to themselves.' He confined himself to a general query: 'How is it going?' and was met with smiles from both sides. 'I told them: "I'm glad that you are both happy."'

'Over dinner we talked about the doubts between Arabs and observed that Arabs should adopt a different way of dealing with each other. Then, after dinner, they had a further meeting and I was told, all of a sudden, that the Iraqi vice president said they had had enough talks here and had agreed to hold a second meeting in Baghdad. I said I would give my blessing for that.'

Ezzat Ibrahim left at 11 p.m. for Baghdad, but Sheikh Saad stayed a little longer for a private meeting with King Fahd before setting off for Kuwait. The king was not surprised by the outcome, because the Iraqis had originally wanted the meeting to be in Baghdad, but had accepted the Saudi argument that this would give the impression that the Kuwaiti crown prince was going there to surrender. Having helped the Kuwaitis to save face, the king saw nothing wrong in holding the next meeting in Baghdad.

What happened between Sheikh Saad and Ezzat Ibrahim is still a matter of controversy. The Saudis say they do not know, although it would have been unusual for the meeting not to have been bugged.

The Iraqis say the Kuwaitis showed no readiness to make concessions. There were hints that they might do so at a subsequent meeting, but Baghdad's patience was exhausted. The concessions Kuwait had in mind were military facilities on Warba and Bubiyan, and arbitration over Rumaila, but that would have taken years. Kuwait continued to resist the Iraqi demand for $10 billion, and showed no flexibility on the border issue.

The Kuwaiti account was that Ezzat Ibrahim merely reiterated Iraq's known positions and was not ready to negotiate. The talks lasted only an hour and a half in the afternoon and an hour after dinner, and drifted into details without addressing the real issues. This did not worry the Kuwaitis, as they assumed the Iraqis wanted to wait until the Baghdad meeting. The crown prince remained in a confident mood, warning the Iraqi vice president not to threaten Kuwait, because it had 'powerful friends'. By the time Ezzat Ibrahim left Jeddah, Iraqi troops were on the move.

Plans for the invasion to go ahead that night had been settled forty-eight hours earlier, but were arranged so that they could be halted if the crown prince made serious concessions at the talks. The original intention had been to seize only the islands and the oilfield, but Saddam Hussein had had second thoughts at the end of July. The change of plan came at a meeting of the Revolutionary Command Council two days before the occupation. Saddam argued that a limited operation would leave the al-Sabah family in power in Kuwait, and they would undoubtedly mobilise world opinion and use their relationship with Washington to ensure a US military response. Kuwait would then become a US base threatening Iraq. It seemed better to move decisively so that the al-Sabahs would not have time to call in the Americans. The Iraqis thought that once they were in occupation no other Arab country would dare summon US help, for fear of being accused of giving Washington the bases the Arab world had struggled to avoid.

Washington had followed the Iraqi build-up closely but felt little alarm because of the State Department's belief that Saddam Hussein was bluffing. This belief was supported by the fact that certain vital elements of an offensive force were not in place, including communications networks and large artillery stocks. These omissions were made good on 30 July, and the whole picture changed. Satellite photographs on 1 August showed that hundreds of tanks were on the border, spaced fifty to seventy-five metres apart, with artillery behind them.[7] Dick Cheney, the US Defense Secretary, and some of the military still thought it might be an elaborate bluff, but the CIA correctly forecast that Saddam Hussein would invade that night or the following morning.

The CIA station in Kuwait was in close contact with the ministries of interior and defence over arrangements to safeguard the emir and other key members of the ruling family. The liaison went back to the Iran–Iraq war, which could have affected Kuwait at any turn during its fluctuating course. When the Iranians started a counter-offensive in 1984, and the Iraqis were in retreat, both the CIA and its Kuwaiti contacts feared that Tehran might seize the opportunity to occupy Kuwait, reinforcing its hold on the Gulf and encircling Basra. A rapid pincer movement could have cut off the whole of southern Iraq from Baghdad and the central reserve of the Iraqi army.

It appears that the high command of the Iranian popular army toyed with such a plan. The Kuwait part of it was based on two assumptions. The disappearance of the emir and those members of the family qualified to replace him would create a vacuum of legitimacy. In a tribal society of this type, a loss of recognised leadership would leave the people adrift, ready to surrender to a new conqueror. No one would have the authority to ask other tribes for help, nor would other tribes seriously consider such pleas. Secondly, if the disappearance of the emir and his relatives coincided with an uprising by Shia elements inside Kuwait, the emirate could fall in a matter of hours.

The Americans and Kuwaitis prepared a contingency plan for the evacuation of the emir and his family, while at the same time intensifying surveillance of the Shia community in Kuwait. Despite these precautions there was an attempt on the emir's life the following year, 1985, for which a group calling itself Islamic Jihad claimed responsibility.

Five years later, when the head of Kuwaiti intelligence met CIA director William Webster in Washington, the safety of the ruling family remained the top priority. A co-ordinating group was formed between the two intelligence services to revise and galvanise the 1984 contingency plan. The group was reinforced on 1 August 1990 with

[7] Woodward, *The Commanders*

two American officers who had arrived only twenty-four hours earlier, and the situation was re-evaluated. Some believed that the Iraqis might be thinking along the same lines as the tentative Iranian plan of 1984. The emir and his family would remain the first target, but Iraqi divisions amassed on the border would play the role assigned to Shia masses in the Iranian plot.

During the morning of 1 August the Kuwaiti minister of defence Sheikh Salem al-Sabah received the following message: 'We do not want to alarm you unnecessarily, but we think the contingency plan should be put into effect.'

An immediate report was ordered on the whereabouts of the emir and his close relatives. As it was a Wednesday, the security group knew that some would be preparing to leave the city for the weekend (Thursday and Friday in the Arab world). Kuwait has no 'countryside', but people like to relax at second homes in open areas known as the 'Barr', especially in the vicinity of Al-Ahmadi, south of Kuwait City, where luxurious villas and moored yachts line the shore. The emir's usual custom was to spend the weekend at one of his rest houses in the Barr, but he wanted to remain in close touch in case news came through from Sheikh Saad in Jeddah. He therefore decided to spend Wednesday night in the city, either at Seif Palace, where he works, or at Dassman Palace, his principal residence.

Early in the afternoon the special security group advised the defence minister that 'Under no circumstances must the emir be allowed to spend the night anywhere in Kuwait City.' It was essential, they urged, that he be moved as soon as possible to any rest house in the south, close to the Saudi borders.

By sunset, all other key members of the family who could be contacted had been advised to implement the contingency plan and leave the city within two hours. A few minutes before midnight word came that the emir, by now in the Barr, should cross into Saudi Arabia and go to Khafji, twenty kilometres south of the border. The royal procession was to be made to look like ordinary traffic, avoiding long motorcades with glaring headlights.

Sheikh Saad arrived from Jeddah after midnight and was met at the airport and briefed on the crisis. He managed to contact the American ambassador, who gave him a brief summary of Iraqi military moves inside Kuwait and advised him to leave as soon as possible because the sky was packed with Iraqi helicopters. Sheikh Saad told him that Kuwait's hour of need for real and powerful friends had arrived. The ambassador asked if this was 'an official request for military assistance'. 'Yes, yes,' was the sheikh's reply.

As he travelled south, the crown prince felt that his request needed official confirmation. After trying to contact the emir, who was already in Khafji, he phoned the ambassador from his car to say: 'I am now speaking officially in the name of the emir and the government. We are formally requesting the assistance of the US to defend Kuwait. We depend on you. We depend on the friendship of the US and the resolve of President Bush.'

The evacuation plan came close to complete success, enabling some twenty-five members of the ruling family, including wives and children, to escape. The only casualty was Fahd al-Ahmad al-Sabah, a cousin of the emir and head of the Kuwaiti Olympic Committee, who missed the warning because he was out at the time. Returning late at night he found soldiers inside his palace, drew his revolver, and was shot dead.

Small Iraqi units arrived a few hours later to round up members of the family in villas up to forty-five kilometres south of the city, which led to reports that Iraq was advancing towards the neutral zone between Kuwait and Saudi Arabia. The troops found no one at home.

By dawn Baghdad had achieved a military success, but the political aim of capturing the Kuwaiti leadership had failed. Tacticians would argue later that Baghdad should have held its forces well back from the border to avoid alerting Washington, while infiltrating guerrilla forces into Kuwait. The guerrillas would have been used in conjunction with helicopter-borne forces to attack the family at numerous locations simultaneously, before the alarm could be raised, delaying the main invasion by several hours. As it was, in failing to prevent the al-Sabahs from summoning American help, Baghdad lost the gamble before it had thrown the dice.

4

Opportunity Lost

King Fahd awoke with a start at 5 a.m. on 2 August. The phone by his bedside in Jeddah never normally disturbed his sleep, but now it was jangling. The news that Iraqi troops had entered Kuwait was scarcely believable, coming only six hours after he had wished Ezzat Ibrahim farewell. Summoning an aide, he ordered a call to the Saudi ambassador in Kuwait, musing as he waited that the Iraqi operation was probably confined to the islands and the oilfield. The ambassador did not yet have the whole picture, but he knew it was more serious than that. 'It hit me like an earthquake . . . I was unable to think about it,' the king said later. His next order was: 'Get me President Saddam Hussein on the telephone,' but in his haste he took the line before the operator had got through. A presidential aide at the other end was astonished to find the king speaking in person. 'I want to talk to the president,' he said. Saddam Hussein was not there, but the aide, Ahmed Hussein Khodeir, who later became minister of foreign affairs, promised he would call back.

In Amman King Hussein was woken at 5.15 a.m. by a call from King Fahd. 'Have you heard?' Fahd asked. 'Heard what?' Hussein's first reaction was disbelief and astonishment. 'I tried to contact brother Saddam in Baghdad but I couldn't get him,' Fahd said. 'Perhaps you could try?'

'Maybe it's a limited operation and can be remedied right away. I'll phone you back in a few minutes,' King Hussein said. But before his staff could get through to Baghdad, Fahd was on the phone again: 'No, it's not limited. They're inside Jaber's palace.' The news had just come through from his ambassador in Kuwait, Sheikh Abdullah Abdul-Aziz Al-Sudairi, who is related to King Fahd. In the Arabian peninsula it is the tradition that when ruling families exchange ambassadors they must be relatives, not bureaucrats.

A few minutes later King Hussein got through to Tariq Aziz in

Baghdad. 'I'm sorry, I'm taking the call in President Saddam's place. He's not near a telephone.' The king pressed him for information but the foreign minister hedged.

Egypt is an hour behind Jordan and the Gulf countries. It was 4 a.m. when Dr Mustapha el-Fekky, head of the president's secretariat for information, was woken by a call from Said Rifat, Egyptian ambassador in Kuwait. Iraqi forces had occupied Rumaila oilfield and were heading for Kuwait City, but their aims were still unclear. As Egypt's foreign ministry had half expected some sort of limited action, Dr el-Fekky delayed disturbing President Mubarak, who was spending the night at a presidential rest house in Borg el-Arab, a suburb of Alexandria. Half an hour later the phone rang again; this time it was the Kuwaiti ambassador in Cairo, Abdul Razzak el-Kandari. 'Please wake the president,' he said. 'They are now in Kuwait City.'

Mubarak felt numb with disbelief. 'What do you mean? Operations on the borders?' 'No, an operation in depth. There are reports that the Iraqis are in the emir's and crown prince's palaces and the defence and foreign ministries,' Dr el-Fekky said.

Ibrahim Gassim el-Bahu, Kuwait's ambassador in Baghdad, was awakened by guards with the news that Iraqi troops had surrounded the embassy. He ordered all documents to be burned, then settled down to wait for the unknown. Later in the day Iraqi officials arrived and took away the embassy's cars. The ambassador assumed they had been confiscated, but to his surprise they were returned the following morning, with new Iraqi numberplates, reflecting Baghdad's declaration that Kuwait was Iraq's nineteenth province.

Everyone who mattered in the Arab world was awake by dawn. Washington, with the benefit of an eight-hour time difference, did not have the problem of leaders losing sleep. Dick Cheney, the Defense Secretary, was informed by 9 p.m., East Coast time, and President Bush soon afterwards. Two and a half hours later the White House issued a statement condemning the invasion and demanding Iraq's immediate and unconditional withdrawal. Orders were given for all Iraqi and Kuwaiti assets in the United States to be frozen.

For ten months American policy towards Iraq had baffled all who tried to follow it; now it clarified in a matter of hours. The speed of Washington's response could only mean that President Bush was acting on impulse, feeling that his hour of decision had come. A third scenario had been added to Washington's two main Middle Eastern worries, a Soviet threat to oil supplies or a further Arab–Israeli war.

Saddam Hussein's recent speeches had prompted a suspicion that the Iraqi leader was seeking regional leadership, and the invasion seemed to remove any remaining doubt. If the tanks kept rolling south the Arabian peninsula could fall under his control in days or weeks, creating an Arab giant. The 'domino theory', invented to describe Cold War nightmares, now gained a new lease of life in a non-Communist context. Bahrain, the United Arab Emirates, Saudi Arabia, Qatar and Oman could be toppled in quick succession, and the United States had nothing in place to stop the pieces tumbling. Bush knew he could not let this happen, but how was he to prevent it? As the hours passed Americans sensed a hardening of his views. Comments snatched from him by waiting journalists showed a transition of thought from uncertainty to determination. Saddam Hussein had stepped inside a forbidden circle of American influence; the invasion was an attack on US interests and a blow to its standing; the Iraqi leader must not be allowed to escape with his prestige and military power intact.

The situation presented opportunities as well as risks. If Baghdad could be taught a lesson, dangers to oil supplies and Israel might recede for many years. Bush realised that Moscow, his newest diplomatic ally, could be useful. The Nato allies were fairly sure to follow Washington's political lead, but their stomach for a fight was open to question. The Russians could be counted on not to exploit the situation and might be prepared to put pressure on their friends in Baghdad. The Bush – Gorbachev summit in Washington a few weeks earlier had underlined the Soviet Union's economic dependence on American co-operation. Here was an opportunity to test what sacrifices Moscow would make to pay for it.

Saddam Hussein returned King Fahd's call at about 8 a.m., Gulf time. 'I am sending you a special messenger to explain what is happening,' he said. 'He is already on his way.' The messenger, a deputy prime minister, arrived by mid-morning and was taken straight to the king. 'What happened?' Fahd asked. 'Nothing happened,' the messenger replied. 'This is just part of Iraq returning to Iraq.' He reiterated Baghdad's territorial claim as if the Saudi monarch had never heard it.

The lack of clarity this showed infuriated Fahd. 'That sort of talk is out of order here. If it were really part of Iraq returning to Iraq, what were we talking about yesterday and before yesterday?' He pointed out that Iraq had treated Kuwait's leaders as representatives of a sovereign country. 'Haven't you anything better to tell me?'

The king now had a clear picture of the situation, but had not yet decided how to react. When his nephew Prince Bandar, ambassador to the US, phoned before 11 a.m. (Gulf time) asking for instructions, the king wanted to wait until he saw what attitude others were taking. He added: 'People at your end [meaning in the West] must be firm.' Prince Bandar replied that from all he saw and heard the Americans appeared to be very firm, and asked if there was anything he could convey to the Americans. The king said he would reply when he knew the outcome of a meeting which the Arab League foreign ministers were planning to hold in Cairo.

By this time Kuwaitis were streaming across the border in their cars, fleeing from the advancing Iraqis. Sheikh Jaber, who had spent a few hours at Kafji, travelled to Hafr El-Baten and then phoned King Fahd in a state of agitation, describing the Iraqi action as that of 'infidels'. The sheikh said repeatedly that the Iraqis should be expelled from Kuwait that very day, and that if they were allowed to stay until sunset they would never leave. The king tried unsuccessfully to put the sheikh into a calmer state of mind, and then asked Prince Abdullah, the crown prince and Commander of the National Guard, to send a plane to take the Emiri family to Taif.

Prince Bandar called again to say that he had been to a meeting at the White House where he was told that an armoured Iraqi unit was moving towards the neutral zone, and that Kuwait had made an official request for help. Bandar said he felt that if Riyadh was ready to make a similar request, it should do so immediately. He also wanted to know whether Saudi Arabia was prepared to offer the Americans the military facilities they would need to confront the Iraqis in Kuwait. This was not yet a formal American request, he added, but the National Security Council was preparing an option paper for the president, and needed to know what might be available. The king was not ready to be specific. He wanted to wait and see.

King Fahd then received a phone call from Prince Saud al-Faisal, the foreign minister, who was about to attend the meeting of Arab foreign ministers and wanted to know what position to take. Before replying, the king asked him about the mood of the ministers. The prince replied that they were all in shock. The king commented: 'Khair inshallah' ('That is for the good, God willing'). What lay behind this remark was his concern that Egypt, Jordan and Yemen might have had prior knowledge of the invasion, because of their membership with Iraq in the Arab Co-operation Council. By this time the king had established, by talking to President Mubarak on the phone, that Egypt had had no fore-warning.

The king's instructions were as follows: 'All our brothers should know that the situation is very grave, and that this is going to open the gates of Hell.' He told the prince to co-operate closely with the Egyptians and Syrians. When the prince remarked that events were moving quickly, the king replied: 'The terrain is full of thorns and we should not rush.'

Prince Turki bin-Faisal, director of Saudi intelligence, phoned Prince Bandar, who is his brother-in-law, to ask what attitude Washington was taking. Bandar repeated what he had told the king and added his own view that the Iraqi action would not be confined to Kuwait. 'He who eats Kuwait for breakfast is likely to ask for something else for lunch,' he said. Turki wondered whether the Iraqi action had been co-ordinated with Iran, reasoning that Baghdad would not have undertaken such an action if there had been a risk that the Iranians would exploit the situation. An American AWACS aircraft had been concentrating since midnight on monitoring signals from Iran. Turki expressed a fear that any such co-operation between Iran and Iraq would imply that the two countries had agreed to divide the loot, and also that the Iranians might attack Bahrain.

A discussion between the king and some of his brothers had been going on all morning between telephone calls. Only senior brothers of the king's generation, such as Prince Abdullah bin-Abdul-Aziz and Prince Salman bin Abd-el-Aziz were involved. They thought an Iraqi attack on Saudi Arabia unlikely but not impossible, and knew that the kingdom would be incapable of defending itself unaided against the full weight of Baghdad's armour. But the instinct to refuse non-Arab assistance remained strong. Most argued that accepting US military help would be an open acknowledgement of Riyadh's dependence on Washington, which would negate the policies of the last thirty years. The king's role as Servant of the Two Holy Shrines would be meaningless if Saudi Arabia needed protection by a Christian country. Inviting foreigners to trespass on holy territory could rekindle the Islamic revolution, turning its full force against the Saud family, a prospect little better than bowing to Iraqi sovereignty. After two hours of talks the consensus of the senior members of the royal family was that the risks of accepting foreign help at that time outweighed the benefits. Instead, Saudi Arabia would seek political support through the Arab League and the Islamic Congress.

While these talks were going on, younger brothers and nephews, men in their twenties, thirties and forties, had been meeting informally, and most felt American help should be summoned immediately. Some of King Fahd's sons, including Mohamed bin-Fahd, went to see the king, who listened to their views. The essence of their argument was: 'We should not wait until the Americans tell us what to do. It is above all our problem, our security and our future, and if we show enough determination we will encourage others.' One of the ideas they put forward was to close the pipeline that carried Iraq's oil across Saudi Arabia to the Red Sea. They argued that to allow the oil to continue to flow would be tantamount to rewarding Iraq for its aggression. The king was still in a pensive mood, and did not give a definite reply.

By this time the US had offered Saudi Arabia a squadron of F-15s, which the sons assumed was no more than an opening bid. Washington, however, was not yet ready to say whether it wanted any greater involvement. 'We are not ruling any options in, but we are not ruling any options out,' President Bush said at a press conference later. Although he had not yet decided how to react, he was beginning to see the political possibilities of the situation and wanted a free hand. Less than fifteen hours had elapsed since the invasion and already the American media was in full cry, attacking Saddam Hussein as a tyrant; within a few days he would be seen as an enemy of the United States. Whether it occurred to Bush at the time or not, the situation offered a solution to a long-standing problem. His presidential campaign two years earlier had been handicapped by the 'wimp factor', an impression he gave of weakness. It had faded away as Washington emerged triumphant from the Cold War, but this was his first chance to eliminate it permanently. A Third World leader had thrown down a challenge to a president who needed to prove himself.

When President Mubarak came down to his desk at the rest house in Borg el-Arab a long memorandum with a full analysis was already waiting for him. The invasion might have been expected, it suggested, by anyone who looked beneath the surface of regional politics and watched Baghdad's efforts to assert itself after the Iran–Iraq war. The report, prepared by presidential staff and the foreign ministry, saw Iraq's enthusiastic involvement in the Arab Co-operation Council (linking it with Egypt, Jordan and Yemen) as camouflage for a plan 'to isolate Syria and neutralise Egypt'. The absorption of Kuwait had always been one of its aims. The invasion was viewed as 'a blow to Egyptian policy and interests' on many levels. It was contrary to the central theme of Egyptian policy, the need for general Arab co-operation. It would force Cairo to choose between friendship with Baghdad and relations with other Gulf countries which were 'very profitable and very important'. It would be 'a final blow, a knockout, to the Arab Co-operation Council' and would 'definitely lead to foreign intervention'. The invasion would also give the impression that 'the Iraqi leadership was able to dupe the Egyptian leadership'.

The report predicted that Baghdad would try hard to keep links with Cairo during the critical period, so as to maintain indirect lines to Washington and Tel Aviv. Cairo, it recommended, should insist on unconditional withdrawal, try to contain the crisis, prevent it from spreading, and maintain contacts so that Egypt could give diplomatic cover for a withdrawal. This called for three measures: Cairo should issue a declaration condemning the invasion; it should contact the Iraqis and be firm with them; and Egypt should use Arab channels to increase the pressure on Iraq, including a meeting of foreign ministers, who had just arrived in Cairo for a conference on 'Foreign Relations in the Islamic World'.

Any American involvement should come about gradually, without undue fanfare, to avoid playing into Iraq's hands, the report recommended. 'We should send a clear message to the Israelis that they should not interfere,' it added (that morning, to the amazement of its listeners, Radio Israel had referred to 'the brotherly state of Kuwait'). A suspicion that Iraq might be working in co-ordination with Iran, as they had co-operated on the oil quotas issue, was also reflected in the Egyptian report. Finally it said that everything possible should be done to prevent Libya from siding with Iraq. It was an incisive and far-sighted analysis, but only parts of it were to be implemented.

As President Mubarak read the memorandum, the Arab world was preparing its first tentative steps towards a collective response to the invasion. Syria contacted the Secretary General of the Arab League, Chedli El-Klibi, and called for an emergency meeting of foreign ministers. 'Thank God they are all in Cairo,' the secretary general said. Around 10.30 a.m. they gathered in the InterContinental (Semiramis) Hotel on the Nile to consider what to do. There was a fog of indecision. Egypt sounded a cautious and conciliatory note, not wanting to give a view until President Mubarak made up his mind (he told colleagues several times that morning that he felt mentally blocked). Prince Saud al-Faisal had not been given a clear policy line by Riyadh and felt torn between moderation and condemnation. He later received instructions, but the indecision in Saudi Arabia was reflected in a twenty-four-hour delay before news of the invasion was mentioned in its newspapers. The UAE showed even greater hesitation, delaying the announcement by forty-eight hours. This may have been because its ruler, Sheikh Zayed bin-Sultan Al-Nahayyan, was in Alexandria at the time, though he cut short his visit and flew back on the morning of 2 August.

Syria was pressing for immediate condemnation, but others at the meeting felt it was using the situation to pursue its quarrel with Baghdad. The PLO urged moderation and felt the conflict could be contained. All delegates were startled by the speed and trenchancy of Washington's condemnation and felt under pressure to react. King Hussein had decided that something could be done and instructed his delegates to take a moderate line which would not cut across the initiative he planned to attempt. His friendship with Saddam Hussein and his traditional links with the Gulf sheikhdoms offered a hope of mediation. This obliged the Arab world, with the exception of Syria and Lebanon, to take a cautious initial line to avoid upsetting his efforts. Iraq was represented by an undersecretary of foreign affairs and its ambassador in Cairo, Nabil Nejm el-Takriti, a relative of Saddam Hussein. They told the ministers that they did not yet have instructions but understood that a high-level delegation would arrive in the afternoon and urged them not to make a statement before hearing Iraq's explanation. A further complication was that some countries assumed that Iraq, as a member of the Arab Co-operation Council, would have consulted Egypt, Jordan and Yemen before invading Kuwait.

While President Mubarak was taking Sheikh Zayed bin-Sultan of the UAE to Alexandria airport he missed a phone call from King Hussein, who was anxious to discuss his initiative. The two made contact at 3.20 p.m. and King Hussein suggested he himself should come to Alexandria to talk it over. Meanwhile Dr Sa'adoun Hammadi, the Iraqi deputy prime minister, was on his way from Baghdad to address the foreign ministers. He landed at Cairo at 6 p.m., just as King Hussein was arriving in Alexandria, and went straight to the meeting. A crowd of Kuwaitis had besieged the InterContinental Hotel all day, waving portraits of Sheikh Jaber which had been distributed by the Kuwaiti embassy. They shouted a single slogan over and over again: 'It is written on our hearts that Sheikh Jaber is our beloved.'

Within an hour the ministers realised that Sa'adoun Hammadi had nothing new to say, but they were not yet free to pass a resolution. The Egyptian and Saudi ministers still had no clear instructions, and King Hussein's visit reinforced the need to wait.

President Mubarak met King Hussein at Alexandria airport. In their haste both men dropped all formalities, the president standing alone on the tarmac waiting for the king, who had flown his own plane. They climbed into Mubarak's black Mercedes, the president at the wheel, and set off for Ras El-Teen Palace, overlooking the sea, one of the finest former royal palaces in Egypt and summer seat of every ruler for 170 years before the revolution. On the way Mubarak complained that Saddam Hussein had made him the laughing stock of the Western world by giving him assurances that there would be no military action against Kuwait.

Both Mubarak and King Hussein felt that the Kuwait conflict should be contained within an Arab context, with an Arab solution. They agreed that King Hussein should go to see Saddam Hussein, and Mubarak suggested a mini-summit in Saudi Arabia between Saddam Hussein, Sheikh Jaber, King Fahd, King Hussein and himself. King Hussein said it was a good idea, but at this point the two men diverge on what was agreed. Mubarak says he stipulated that there should be two preconditions for a summit: an Iraqi withdrawal and the return of the legitimate Kuwaiti government. King Hussein acknowledges that Mubarak mentioned these points, but says that they were to be the aims of the summit, not preconditions for convening it.

In his anger and embarrassment Mubarak had refrained from phoning Saddam Hussein, but now he accepted King Hussein's suggestion that he should do so. Contact was established at 6.28 p.m. Mubarak says he told Saddam Hussein: 'I have agreed with King Hussein that he will come and see you. We are thinking of a mini-summit and there are some points which he will explain to you when he arrives.'

King Hussein's version is as follows:

> It was not like that. It was not a matter of my carrying two conditions to President Saddam Hussein for convening a mini-summit and getting him to accept them. If it were that easy, and he was going to accept those two points, then there was no necessity for a summit,

whether mini or full-dress. As I saw it, my mission was to convince him of the idea of a mini-summit so that we could discuss a dangerous situation which surprised us all, and to ensure that the Emir of Kuwait could take part. If he had agreed to Sheikh Jaber's participation, then clearly the Iraqis would have been prepared to discuss the crisis with him. That would mean that they recognised the emir as the relevant party in the crisis. With all of us present, this would have been the best way to reach our agreed aims: Iraq's withdrawal and the return of the legitimate Kuwaiti government.

President Bush had already phoned Mubarak, and tried to call King Hussein but missed him, as he was on his way to Alexandria. Mubarak suggested that they should speak to Bush together. Bush told them: 'The Iraqi action is a clear act of aggression which cannot be accepted.' He continued that Washington's statement condemning the invasion and calling for unconditional withdrawal would not be the end of the matter; he was going to accept Saddam Hussein's challenge. The invasion was a direct threat to US interests, and Congress, government departments, public opinion and the media were urging him to act.

Bush added that he had not yet noticed any clear Arab condemnation, although the issues concerned the Arab world even more than the United States. He had expected King Fahd to ask for assistance, but there had been no such request. He had telephoned the king himself and was shocked by his reluctance to ask for US help.

He said he told King Fahd that the US was capable of protecting its interests, but unless the Arabs were ready to look after theirs, or call on their friends to do so, no one would care for them any more. If they did not stand up to aggression now they would have nobody to blame but themselves and their own inhibitions. He warned that the United States would be entitled to act alone if the Arab states concerned declined to co-ordinate any action with it, and pointed out that he had received an official request for aid from Kuwait, but that the crisis was of larger dimensions.

King Hussein urged Bush to delay any US action and to give him forty-eight hours to find an Arab solution, explaining his planned trip to Baghdad. The American president was irritated. 'All right, have your forty-eight hours, but if you Arabs don't make up your mind I don't know who will make it up for you.'

After the call Mubarak pointed out that the Arab League meeting was under pressure to issue a statement condemning the invasion. Syria and Lebanon had already made separate statements, and other countries were anxious to follow suit. Mubarak said that Egypt planned to call for Iraq's withdrawal from Kuwait and the return of the legitimate government, in a way which would not embarrass Iraq. He says that this upset King Hussein, who replied: 'Please postpone any statement, otherwise it will torpedo my efforts in Baghdad.'

Esmat Abdel-Meguid, the Egyptian foreign minister, phoned Mubarak to tell him that there was nothing new in Sa'adoun Hammadi's speech. There was a growing feeling among the Arab foreign ministers that their meeting should produce a strong condemnation of Iraq's action. It was argued that the Americans and British appeared to be in the forefront of opposition to Iraq's action, while the Arabs were still talking. The Soviet Union had already condemned Iraq and the news wires were full of similar declarations from West European countries. By this time Prince Saud al-Faisal had received instructions from Saudi Arabia to press for such a statement. The Egyptian foreign minister told Mubarak: 'My Saudi colleague [who was with him] is really pressing and others are backing him. It is a very difficult situation.' Mubarak, in the presence of King Hussein, spoke to Prince Saud al-Faisal directly. 'Wait until tomorrow. Give King Hussein's mission a chance,' he said. The foreign ministers agreed, adjourned their meeting, and arranged to meet the following evening at six o'clock.

King Hussein was unable to fly directly from Alexandria to Baghdad because Iraqi airspace was closed to non-Iraqi flights. He went to Amman and made an arrangement with the Iraqi authorities for the next morning. He would fly his own plane to a Jordanian airbase on the Iraqi–Jordanian border, and an Iraqi plane would pick him up and take him to Baghdad. President Mubarak phoned him in Amman at 10.20 a.m., as he was setting off. 'Why aren't you in Baghdad?' he asked. 'I'm going right away,' the king replied, explaining the arrangements.

He arrived in the Iraqi capital to find Saddam Hussein in a confident mood, surprised but not taken aback by the torrent of condemnation from outside the Arab world. 'It was no use talking to those people [the Kuwaitis],' he said. 'They wouldn't understand reason. I had to do what I did.' He explained why he had not forewarned Jordan or Egypt, despite their alliance in the Arab Co-operation Council. 'I did not want to put you in an embarrassing situation with the Kuwaitis, the Americans and the West generally. We wanted to take this on our own responsibility.'

King Hussein explained the dangers of the situation. 'I know the West better than many others, and I can tell you that the West will intervene. I plead with you to withdraw.' Saddam Hussein replied: 'Abu Abdullah [the father of Abdullah], don't let them scare us.' Then he added: 'And anyhow, we are going to withdraw. It was announced in the communiqué we issued this morning.'

The Iraqi Revolutionary Command Council's statement was expressed in rhetorical language and sought to set the invasion in a religious context:

> In the name of God the merciful . . . we hurl good at evil, and the good will destroy the evil [a quotation from the Koran] . . . Oh great Iraqi people, beautiful jewel in the Arab crown and symbol of their pride and ability . . . Oh Arabs who believe in one nation, strong and powerful, pure and free of any evil and betrayal. Oh people of justice . . .

It went on to compare the Kuwaiti royal family with King Karun, a legendary monarch who amassed all the world's gold in his caves, only to be swallowed up by an earthquake, then continued:

> God helped the free people from the pure ranks in Kuwait. They have swept away the old order and brought about a new order and have asked for the brotherly help of the great Iraqi people . . . [which], represented by the Revolutionary Council, has agreed to help the Kuwaiti Interim Government. It will only take a few days or weeks.

King Hussein asked Saddam Hussein: 'But when are you going to withdraw?' The Iraqi leader replied: 'As it says in the statement, days or weeks.' The king looked doubtful. 'I don't think we have weeks.' He stayed with Saddam Hussein until he felt he had seen the gravity of the situation and agreed to begin withdrawing in a few days.

After some discussion with King Hussein, the Iraqi leader accepted the summit proposal but objected to the Emir of Kuwait taking part. The king says that Mubarak had asked him not to mention the emir's presence, as it was bound to put Saddam Hussein off, but he was tired and said more than he intended. Mubarak's fears were borne out: the Iraqi leader talked of sending one of his deputies rather than going himself. 'Maybe if I went personally it would be embarrassing to some. Apart from that I have so many tasks to attend to here,' he said. The king insisted that there should be 'practical evidence' of Iraq's intention to withdraw before the summit took place. 'That evidence is not only essential to your credibility and mine, but also to satisfy the rest of the world.'

Saddam Hussein asked for time to consult with colleagues, and the king departed for Amman. During the journey the Iraqi leader sent him a radio message to say that the Revolutionary Command Council accepted his point of view and would make an announcement that day, Friday 3 August, that the withdrawal was beginning. A symbolic withdrawal of one brigade would take place soon afterwards.

A few hours later the official Iraqi news agency carried a statement attributed to a spokesman of the Revolutionary Command Council saying: 'If there are no threats against Iraq or Kuwait, Iraqi forces will start to withdraw tomorrow [Saturday 4 August]. A plan to withdraw from Kuwait has already been approved.'

Baghdad's apparent willingness to withdraw implied that it realised its position was untenable. The escape of the emir's family had knocked away the pivot of Iraq's plan, and the family's appeal to Washington to assist Kuwait was now common knowledge. Iraq's priority was to find a formula for withdrawal which would give an appearance of having achieved limited aims. If the Arab world could be persuaded that there was indeed an anti-Emiri uprising and that Baghdad had supported the Kuwaiti masses, it could depart with good grace. But no one believed the Iraqi communiqué.

King Hussein felt he had made a breakthrough, and was eager to tell Mubarak. On the journey back from Baghdad he contacted the control tower in Amman, issued several orders and received a message that President Bush was trying to contact him. The king told his minister of court to tell the Jordanian ambassador in Cairo to let President Mubarak know that he would soon receive an important message. Time was running out, as the Arab League foreign ministers were due to reconvene their meeting in Cairo. Algeria and Morocco had issued separate statements demanding Iraq's withdrawal from Kuwait, following Syria and Lebanon the night before. The lack of a collective Arab League view was becoming embarrassing; the king knew that the ministers' patience was at its limit. He ordered another message to be faxed to the Jordanian foreign minister, who was in

Cairo for the meeting. 'Hold everything,' it said. It was too late. Although the scheduled meeting was still about two hours away, Egypt issued a separate statement condemning the invasion, albeit mildly worded. The exact timing of the statement is a matter of controversy.

King Hussein phoned President Mubarak as soon as he landed in Amman. There are two versions of what was said and the sequence of events. The points of agreement are that the call took place at 4.30 p.m. Cairo time and that the king explained what had happened in Baghdad. President Mubarak's version is that he asked the king whether Saddam Hussein had accepted the two points (the withdrawal of Iraqi forces and the restoration of the legitimate government of Kuwait). The king replied that that was what was supposed to be discussed at the summit. Mubarak felt this was not good enough and, according to his version, it was at this point that he ordered an Egyptian statement condemning the invasion to be released. 'I did not issue the statement until King Hussein called me and told me that he and Saddam Hussein did not discuss the two points, which were my conditions for convening the mini-summit,' he said.

King Hussein's version is that the Egyptian statement was issued before his call to Mubarak. 'I phoned President Mubarak and told him about my breakthrough, but by that time there was already an Egyptian statement. I was furious,' he said. In his talks with Saddam Hussein he had put all the emphasis on withdrawal from Kuwait, feeling that allowing the legitimate government to return would be a logical outcome of the mini-summit, as Sheikh Jaber would be present.

As further evidence that the statement was issued before he phoned President Mubarak, the king says that he asked Mubarak why he had rushed into making a statement.

'I was under pressure,' replied Mubarak.

'Pressure from whom?'

'Newspaper men in Cairo and public opinion.'

The king felt this explanation was unconvincing, as Egyptian newspapermen are not noted for pushiness when questioning their president. Egyptian public opinion, however, was clearly against the invasion.

Mubarak was still overwhelmed by the developing crisis. 'I feel my mind is blocked,' he said.

'All right. When you reach a decision, please contact me,' the king snapped. The two leaders had met fifty-one times at bilateral or multilateral summits, yet this first crisis showed that they did not understand each other.

The timing of the Egyptian statement astonished the foreign ministers, coming as it did only a short time before a meeting scheduled at Egypt's request, and seeming to cut across everything Mubarak had done to help King Hussein's mission. President Bush had been conducting personal telephone diplomacy all day, and President Mubarak was among those he contacted. The American leader's impatience for Arab moderates to make their voices heard was evidently too overwhelming to resist.

When the foreign ministers gathered all were opposed to the invasion but there was disagreement on how to react. Apart from Iraq, the entire Arab world agreed that Baghdad should be asked to withdraw immediately, that a summit should be called, and that the use of force as a means of settling disputes should be condemned. It was widely reported at the time that they were divided over the principle of condemning Iraq by name, but in fact the split was over the choice of words. Some wanted an outright condemnation of aggression and a statement that it should be resisted, while others preferred a more guarded wording, to avoid giving foreign powers a legal or moral basis for military intervention, at a time when American naval manoeuvres and air movements had already begun. In the final communiqué a majority, including Egypt, Saudi Arabia, the other Gulf Arab states, and Syria took the hard line, while Jordan, the PLO, Yemen and others were more reserved.

King Hussein phoned King Fahd that night (3 August) and told him about Saddam Hussein's agreement to a summit.

'What summit? What's the point of a summit now?' Fahd asked. He did not entirely reject the idea, but was unenthusiastic, feeling that it was too late for such a meeting. Riyadh had just issued its own statement condemning the invasion.

Word reached Cairo that Fahd was refusing to accept US assistance despite huge American pressure and a now open revolt by the younger Saud brothers and sons. Although Washington's initial offer was confined to a squadron of F-15s, Prince Bandar, the Saudi ambassador, had been told that 200,000 American troops would be needed to ensure the kingdom's defence. At this stage no one mentioned an offensive capability, which would require a much bigger force. Bandar saw Brent Scowcroft, the National Security Advisor, on

3 August and pointed out that Saudi confidence in American help had been damaged by an incident a decade earlier. After the fall of the Shah of Iran, President Carter had offered Saudi Arabia two squadrons of F-15s, which Riyadh accepted. Before they reached Saudi Arabia Carter announced that they were unarmed, which destroyed the credibility of the whole operation. While Bandar and Scowcroft were talking President Bush came into the room and Bandar mentioned these unarmed F-15s. 'I give my word of honour I will see this through with you,' Bush said.[1]

Bush's hard line was strongly supported by the British prime minister Margaret Thatcher, who was in Aspen with Bush and discussed the crisis with him. Many observers felt that she played an important role, and Bush later acknowledged her influence. Although Britain was a junior partner to the United States in terms of Middle East influence, its financial interests there were considerable, not least because London was one of the main centres used by the Kuwaiti Investment Fund. Britain's historical and political ties with the Gulf sheikhdoms were second only to those of the United States, although it was being challenged by France's greater economic dynamism. Thatcher had begun criticising Saddam Hussein before the invasion, and was now in a clear position of enmity with him. The strain of her weakened position at home, irreparably damaged by the imposition of the Community Charge, or 'poll tax', on the entire adult population, may have been another factor, reminding her that Conservative fortunes had been at an equally low ebb just before the Falklands War of 1982. It was too soon to tell how the British public would respond to Iraq's invasion of Kuwait, but at this early stage a revival of the 'Falklands factor' seemed possible.

By now Prince Bandar was satisfied that Washington was serious, and agreed to urge Fahd to accept American forces. The king was surprised when his nephew phoned requesting permission to fly from Washington to Saudi Arabia to see him. Bandar said he had important news which he wanted to present in person. King Fahd was reluctant to allow the ambassador to leave his post at such a crucial time and suggested that an assistant could carry his message. Bandar persisted, prompting King Fahd to remark: 'The most important thing is that they [the Americans] should be sure of what they want to do before

[1] Woodward, *The Commanders*

they ask us about anything.' The king was worried that Saudi Arabia might be affected by fluctuations in American policy. At this point Prince Bandar told his uncle that he had talked to 'the Big Man' – meaning President Bush.

'Your Majesty knows George Bush very well and you know that he is a man who always keeps his word,' he said.

On the way to Riyadh Bandar stopped in Morocco to pick up his father, Prince Sultan, the defence minister, who was convalescing at Rabat after an operation in Switzerland. Before continuing the journey they talked to King Hassan, who noticed a generation gap in attitudes. While the father remained hesitant about American involvement, the son felt there was no time to be lost. They arrived in Riyadh early on 5 August, and the ambassador told the king that he had seen American satellite photographs of Iraqi forces which supported the US argument that the Saudi kingdom was threatened. But Fahd still suspected a US ploy to gain bases for its troops without regard for Saudi sensitivities, and continued to resist American offers to send a senior official to see him.

As the week ended, American policy was evolving rapidly. In the first twenty-four hours Washington had appeared to confine its aims to the defence of Saudi Arabia, but within two days it was talking of reversing the invasion of Kuwait. This huge change in objectives, with its vast consequences for the Middle East, the United States and Europe, slipped out in response to a reporter's question. The decision was taken by Bush alone without consulting the National Security Council.[2] By the time the president went off to Camp David for the weekend, America was on a course which would lead to war.

[2] Woodward, *The Commanders*

5

In Search of a Cover

The loneliness of power weighed heavily on the King of Saudi Arabia in the week after the invasion of Kuwait. Never in his eight years on the throne had King Fahd faced a decision as difficult as the one Washington now demanded. Saudi instincts rebelled against pressure to accept American help, yet George Bush's threat to leave the Arabs to their fate if they refused to stand up to Iraq's aggression could not lightly be dismissed. It has been said that the first responsibility of a Saudi monarch is to keep intimate relations with Washington, and the second is to do all he can to hide it. If Fahd opened the gates to American troops, he might be accused of breaking the unwritten rules of Saudi Arabia's survival and credibility. Every Saudi monarch since Ibn Saud had understood that his rich, vulnerable, underpopulated country needed a powerful protector, but that the protection must always be implicit, never overt. Quite apart from the risk that a visible American presence might stir up religious or revolutionary elements, the Saud family themselves hated the idea of being Washington's pet. King Fahd reminded President Bush: 'We have faced countless problems in the past without asking for your help. There was a time in the 1960s, during the civil war in Yemen, when Nasser of Egypt started threatening us, and even then we did not accept American forces.'

The king's initial decision to remain faithful to this policy, taken with the support of his senior brothers on 2 August, became harder to sustain with every hour that passed. President Bush refused to take no for an answer, phoning him repeatedly, his voice brimming with urgency, pressing him to believe that Saddam Hussein had ambitions beyond Kuwait's borders. Fahd's wisdom and experience told him to play for time, but the Americans knew his ways and kept up the pressure.

Like all his predecessors, Fahd sought consensus in everything he did, first within the family, then in pan-Arab forums. Maintaining equilibrium had never been easy; someone was always rocking the boat. As Riyadh saw it, Saudi Arabia's steadying influence in the Arab League was constantly challenged by hotheads stirring up the masses, fomenting wars or plotting revolutions. Time after time Riyadh used its financial muscle to keep poorer neighbours and critics quiet, while within the Saudi royal family the potential for jealousies, rivalries and palace revolts was almost limitless, as the murder of King Faisal by a disaffected nephew in 1975 had shown. Maintaining peace among 6,000 princes depended on the skilful distribution of oil income, another of the king's responsibilities.

It was second nature to King Fahd to seek a solution to the Kuwait crisis through compromise. But it became clear within twenty-four hours that something more than the usual pouring of oil on troubled waters would be needed. The arrival of Prince Bandar from Washington added a powerful voice to those who were calling for a different approach.

Bandar had seen American satellite pictures of the Iraqi forces, but interpreting such photographs was not easy: to the layman they simply looked like a pattern of dots on a blank background. The ambassador had to rely on the Pentagon's experts, which increased the king's scepticism. If Iraqi tanks were taking up positions close enough to threaten the Saudi border, why had the kingdom's military scouts found no trace of them? During the weekend President Bush phoned the king from Camp David and again pressed him to accept troops. Fahd replied that all he needed was some aircraft, but he agreed to see an American technical team which would discuss Saudi Arabia's requirements. The king said it should be a low-level mission, but Bush wanted Brent Scowcroft, his National Security Advisor, to lead it.[1]

By now pressures were growing on King Fahd to be more accommodating towards the Americans, not only from his sons, his younger brothers and Prince Bandar, but also from rulers of other sheikhdoms, most of whom were related to him. The United Arab Emirates, which had angered Baghdad just as much as Kuwait, and Bahrain, a few minutes' flying time from Kuwait, were in states of alarm. Fahd relented slightly and agreed that the American delegation could be

[1] Woodward, *The Commanders*

led by Dick Cheney, the Defense Secretary.

There was a period of forty-eight hours between 3 and 5 August when the king's mind was changing, but not yet made up. Some of the younger princes noticed that he appeared to think the Kuwaitis had brought the invasion upon themselves by being too inflexible with Baghdad, but at the same time Washington was steadily eroding his resistance. President Bush told him that the latest satellite pictures showed Iraqi forces advancing in the neutral zone towards Saudi Arabia. The US chargé d'affaires reinforced this by saying he had seen the pictures from Washington. On the morning of 4 August King Fahd phoned King Hussein, who had returned from Baghdad the previous day, and passed on this information. 'I can't believe it, but anyhow I will contact President Saddam Hussein,' the Jordanian monarch replied.

He phoned the Iraqi leader, who seemed surprised. 'I issued no such orders and our position is clear. We are tied with Saudi Arabia by a non-aggression pact, which I proposed. It can't be true, but let me check. I have some of the senior military staff with me now.' While still on the phone he spoke to his staff, who said that the only troops in the area were those who had been sent to look for members of the Kuwaiti royal family. Saddam Hussein told King Hussein: 'Our nearest forces are about thirty to forty kilometres from the neutral area, but anyhow I have given orders now that they should keep a distance of at least fifty kilometres. So you can assure King Fahd that there is nothing advancing towards him.'

At this stage Saddam Hussein still assumed that the mini-summit that had been discussed with King Hussein the previous day would take place on Sunday 5 August, and was not aware that President Mubarak had lost interest after his differences with King Hussein over the preconditions he had wanted to set. Baghdad published pictures which it said showed 10,000 soldiers withdrawing from Kuwait, a move intended to set the right atmosphere for the meeting.

King Hussein called King Fahd to pass on Saddam Hussein's assurances, and used the opportunity to press for a bilateral meeting. 'Things are becoming more complicated than necessary. Would you allow me to come and see you, because I think I need to talk to you.'

Fahd clearly did not want the meeting. King Hussein continued trying to persuade him, but Fahd put him off, promising to send Prince Saud al-Faisal to Amman to hear his views. The prince had been attending the Arab League foreign ministers' meeting which finished late on 3 August, but the following day the Gulf Co-operation Council foreign ministers decided to hold a meeting, as they were all in Cairo. This prevented the prince from leaving, so King Fahd sent Abd al-Aziz al-Khuwaiter, the minister of higher education, to Amman in his place. He arrived on 5 August with news that the American chargé d'affaires in Saudi Arabia had given King Fahd a photograph which appeared to show Iraqi troops advancing.

King Hussein referred to the assurances Saddam Hussein had given him, and to the fact that Iraq had officially notified the United Nations of its intention to withdraw from Kuwait. To show his confidence in the assurances he offered to send half the Jordanian army to patrol the border area between Saudi Arabia and Kuwait, so that his men would be the first to face any Iraqi troops who might be there. He had thought of making the same suggestion on the phone the previous day, but held back for fear that King Fahd might think he was working in co-ordination with Saddam Hussein. 'I tried to impress on the minister the fact that things were bound to deteriorate,' said King Hussein.

A foreign news agency had discussed the possibility that Saudi Arabia might close the pipeline which carries Iraqi oil to Yanbu, on the Red Sea. This worried King Hussein, but the Saudi minister thought it unlikely. 'I was with King Fahd in a meeting yesterday when the closure of the pipeline was raised as a means of retaliation, and the king assured everybody that he did want an escalation of the situation and that it would continue working in spite of everything.'

The minister was close to King Fahd, but the meeting with him fell short of the personal diplomacy King Hussein had wanted to exercise. The assurances from Saddam Hussein which King Hussein passed on were not believed in Riyadh, while the minister's assessment of the likelihood of the closure of the pipeline was soon overtaken by events. Saudi Arabia did not respond to King Hussein's offer to send Jordanian troops to patrol the border, which was not surprising because of historical tensions between the Hashemites and the Saud family. Many felt it would be unthinkable for Hashemite troops to be permitted to enter the Saudi kingdom. In short, all these diplomatic moves ran into the sand.

A few hours after the invasion it had been announced that the Emir of Kuwait, the crown prince and most of the royal family were safe in Hafr El-Baten in Saudi Arabia. On 5 August Sheikh Jaber said in a broadcast speech that Kuwait would resist and would never surrender, adding a further element to the pressures on King Fahd.

By that evening the king was clearly wavering, but still only to the extent of being willing to accept American aircraft, not troops. The following morning, 6 August, Dick Cheney arrived in Riyadh with General Norman Schwarzkopf, Commander of the US Central Command. A US presentation had been carefully prepared to convince Fahd of the dangers Washington thought he faced. The king delayed the meeting by some hours, as he needed to check with religious leaders to see whether they would accept an American presence.[2] That, however, was not the only reason. The previous day Washington had thought of a way of conquering King Fahd's principal objection to the presence of American troops.

The idea arose from President Bush's efforts to overcome the Saudi monarch's reluctance by conducting telephone diplomacy at large. In conversation with some Arab heads of state Bush noticed their bewilderment at Fahd's hesitation to ask for assistance, 'even though his kingdom is dangerously vulnerable to Iraqi aggression', as one of them put it. A few expressed readiness to respond to a Saudi call for help, an offer which the president mentioned to his advisers. It was his Chief of Staff John Sununu who sensed the Saudi king's dilemma and said: 'By God, the man needs a cover, an Arab or Islamic cover.'

As it happened, a crisis committee appointed by the National Security Council had reached the same conclusion. According to a well-connected Arab diplomat in Washington, their recommendation was that 'Any American troops sent to Saudi Arabia could be dispersed in a call for assistance directed to all friends of Saudi Arabia.'

President Bush phoned King Hassan of Morocco and asked him to respond positively if Saudi Arabia requested help. The king willingly promised to send a battalion, and President Mubarak was ready to send a much larger force, although he made no definite commitment at this stage. It was at this point that President Bush phoned King Fahd and asked whether, if the American troops were merely part of a more broadly-based force, their presence might be less objectionable. Fahd was by now almost ready to give way, and the prospect of an Islamic cover was enough to make the difference. His decision to accept American troops apparently coincided with Dick Cheney's visit,

[2] Woodward, *The Commanders*

giving an impression that the defense secretary had been remarkably persuasive. In fact, however, the king had changed his mind before he saw Cheney. It appears that the long delay in holding the meeting was caused by this process. The decisive element was not the American satellite evidence but a change of heart among Fahd's brothers once they realised there would be an Islamic cover. Prince Sultan, the defence minister and father of Prince Bandar, had been among the most hesitant, but he came round to the idea, followed by Prince Abdullah, Prince Salman and others.

Prince Abdullah suggested that Syria be invited to send troops, as this would make a favourable impression in the Arab world. President Assad has a reputation for toughness because of his refusal to make compromises in the Arab – Israel dispute. Unlike Egypt, Syria did not sign a peace treaty with Israel. Unlike Rabat, Damascus did not receive a visit by an Israeli prime minister. Although the Kuwait crisis was a different issue, Prince Abdullah felt that Syrian involvement would strengthen Saudi Arabia's political position, aside from its military contribution. King Fahd phoned President Assad, who immediately accepted the request.

The phone call gave rise to a story which circulated in Arab chancelleries for weeks afterwards, though whether it had any basis in truth was never clear. Fahd was said to have asked Assad whether he needed funds to prepare Syrian forces to be sent to Saudi Arabia. Assad replied: 'No, nothing at all. We are ready and our troops will arrive in the Kingdom in a few days.' Mahmoud El-Zoghbi, the Syrian prime minister, whispered to his president: 'Sir, ask him for some assistance. We have our economic needs, and sending troops will only add to our burdens.' Assad waved at him to be silent. After finishing the call he told El-Zoghbi: 'You must realise that the time to ask for money is not when they ask us for troops – it is when they ask our troops to leave.' In addition to Syria, Saudi Arabia asked other Muslim countries to contribute forces. Pakistan and Malaysia accepted, but Indonesia seemed reluctant.

The decision to ask for American troops left its mark on King Fahd for months afterwards. When he attended a Gulf Co-operation Council summit in Qatar on 22 December 1990, the Bahrainis asked him about the days of hesitation. He was moved to explain himself. 'Many people think that I was weak at the time. I was not weak. Many people think I was hesitating. I was not hesitating. The decision was a heavy burden and I did not want to utter a word until the right moment. I wanted to keep the reins in my own hands.' From this point of view, King Fahd's behaviour was consistent with Bedouin traditions. It is not their way to take quick decisions; they prefer to give themselves time for reflection, speaking in vague terms until they feel sure how to proceed.

Cheney conveyed an assurance from Bush that American troops would stay in Saudi Arabia no longer than necessary and would leave when Riyadh asked them to go. He also said that Washington was not seeking bases, but it is unlikely that the king took this assurance at face value. The history of US–Saudi relations since the Second World War had been dominated by this issue. Cheney and Schwarzkopf were already saying that they would need to occupy the Eastern oilfield, which brought to Arab minds a plan Washington had pressed the UAE to accept in 1974, which also involved protecting oilfields. In 1980 Washington had urged Riyadh to allow the US to create a rapid deployment force based in Dhahran. Saudi Arabia refused to accept the presence of the troops, but agreed to allow infrastructure and storage facilities to be built at Dhahran as a precaution.

Cheney phoned Bush at the White House to tell him of Fahd's decision, and found that the American president was talking to Margaret Thatcher at the time.[3] She was about to fly back to London to organise Britain's participation in a multinational force.

On his way back to Washington, Cheney stopped in Alexandria and held a meeting on 7 August with President Mubarak. During their talks the Egyptian leader agreed to allow the American aircraft carrier USS *Eisenhower* to pass through the Suez Canal, a departure from Egypt's policy of banning vessels carrying nuclear weapons, or powered by nuclear propulsion, from the canal. Until then the policy had been firmly enforced, despite the close links between Cairo and Washington. Later the same day, in the course of a phone call from Bush, President Mubarak agreed to send troops to Saudi Arabia.

King Hussein's heart sank when he heard of the decisions by King Fahd, President Mubarak and King Hassan. He felt that there had been a rush to create conditions which would legitimise American intervention. The pressures Washington was bringing to bear had been obvious to Arabs since 3 August, when American diplomats appeared to lead the UN Security Council to its condemnation of the

[3] Woodward, *The Commanders*

invasion. With the Arab world still unaccustomed to the recent changes in Soviet foreign policy, it was disheartening to King Hussein that Moscow had allowed Washington to call the tune. The complicity of much of the Arab world in letting the Americans take over what was essentially an Arab affair seemed even worse, and he was convinced that it would greatly increase the danger.

Meanwhile, President Mubarak was still trying to avoid a polaris-ation of the Arab world, and did not think matters were out of control. By nature he resents being pushed into decisions and likes to take his time, but he agreed quickly to Bush's request to send troops to Saudi Arabia because he felt it was in Egypt's interests. To Mubarak's mind, being responsive to Washington did not mean he had to abandon his own efforts to find a solution. On 7 August, the day he saw Cheney and spoke to Bush, Mubarak was in the midst of another initiative. The previous day he had met Yasser Arafat and his lieutenant Abu Iyad, both of whom agreed with him that it was not too late to find an Arab solution. By this time Syria was calling for a full Arab summit, and Arafat was ready to oil the wheels. The PLO leader felt he could persuade Saddam Hussein not to reject the idea: 'I will try to convince him to come personally. If he cannot, then he should send a high-powered Iraqi delegation with full authority to take decisions.'

Mubarak gave Arafat and Abu Iyad a message to take to Saddam Hussein, but he did not want to leave matters at that. He phoned the Iraqi ambassador in Cairo, Nabil Nejm el-Takriti, and said: 'I want you to go to Baghdad right away and take a message to President Saddam Hussein. All I ask of him is that he should declare openly that Iraq is ready to withdraw from Kuwait unconditionally, and then we will see how we can arrange matters.' Mubarak said he had in mind a scenario for Iraqi withdrawal which would 'come out in a nice way and not embarrass President Saddam Hussein'. The ambassador was provided with an Egyptian plane, and as he was about to set off Mubarak told him: 'Please tell Saddam Hussein that I don't want the Arab family to appear impotent in a crisis like this.'

The following day, 7 August, the ambassador returned with Ezzat Ibrahim, the Iraqi vice president, with Saddam Hussein's reply. The Iraqi plane was parked not far from the aircraft which had brought Dick Cheney to Alexandria. As President Mubarak recalls it, Ibrahim said that the situation did not allow Iraq to take any steps because Arab countries had co-operated in raising the tension, making it impossible for Saddam Hussein to consider withdrawing. He now regarded the occupation of Kuwait as a final decision, and any talk of withdrawal would be a surrender. President Mubarak took this as a sharp rebuff.

Ibrahim's recollection of Saddam Hussein's reply is different. Its main theme, he says, was not the principle of withdrawal, but of timing. Saddam was under the impression that his intention to withdraw was by now common knowledge. He thought President Mubarak's main demand was that Iraq should announce a timetable for complete and unconditional withdrawal before any summit was held. Saddam Hussein had considered Cairo's request but felt the circumstances made it difficult to set a timetable before rather than during a summit. This reply did not affect Iraq's earlier announcement that it would withdraw. The Iraqi version implies that the differences between Baghdad and Cairo were over a relatively minor detail — whether a timetable should be announced before or during a summit.

The most likely reasons for the disparity between the two interpretations of Saddam Hussein's reply are: either the Iraqi message was hastily worded or presented; or President Mubarak's understanding of it was affected by his growing suspicion of the Iraqi leadership; or the Iraqis altered their version after the event to present themselves in a better light.

Whatever the explanation, allowance has to be made for Saddam Hussein's tendency to dramatise his statements, appearing to take irrevocable decisions even when he might still be open to persuasion. It may well be that President Mubarak's version is broadly accurate, but that Saddam Hussein's reply reflected his state of mind at that particular moment, rather than a considered view. It was unfortunate that Ibrahim delivered it on the same day as Cheney's visit and Bush's pressing phone call.

The first American forces, including F-15 jets and paratroops, arrived in Saudi Arabia the next day, 8 August, while an Egyptian advance unit was already on the ground preparing a report on what facilities would be needed for Egyptian troops which would arrive later. News agencies carried reports that 300,000 troops would be required for any intervention and that the build-up would take at least forty-five days.

A dramatic televised speech by President Mubarak at 3 p.m. Cairo time the same day made millions of Arabs realise that the situation was close to the point of no return. Looking unusually agitated, Mubarak said: 'Unless we change course now, war is inevitable

. . . Nobody knows the consequences of war more than myself, having lived through and watched similar experiences. I speak as an ex-officer: I know what war is.' He invited all Arab leaders to a summit in Cairo, to be held the following day, 9 August, probably in the hope that this new initiative would prompt Saddam Hussein to reconsider the message delivered by Ezzat Ibrahim the previous day. He concluded by stating: 'Oh God, I have given my message. Please be my witness.'

The first leader to arrive in Cairo after the announcement was Muammar Gadaffi of Libya, and a procession of kings, sheikhs and presidents followed over the next twenty-four hours. In Tunis, the Secretariat of the Arab League commented on the use of radio broadcasts for such important announcements, which was a gentle way of complaining that it had not been consulted. The League was supposed to organise the meeting, but could not send a team to Cairo immediately because no flights were available. At eleven o'clock that night a Libyan plane flew to Tunis, picked up the secretary general and his staff, and flew them to Cairo. The following morning they began setting up the meeting.

It was now a race against time. With American forces and an Egyptian advance unit already in Saudi Arabia, and Moroccan troops on their way, the obstacles to a purely Arab diplomatic solution were increasing by the hour.

Early on 9 August the Egyptian leader again phoned the Iraqi ambassador in Cairo and told him to send a message to Saddam Hussein. 'Tell him that I have issued an invitation for a summit. If he cannot attend himself, please ask him to send a delegation.' Mubarak pointed out that he had already received many acceptances from other leaders. 'If Saddam Hussein came, I think all the dangers could be contained,' he said. Two hours later the ambassador called back to say that Baghdad was sending a high-level delegation. No one knew who was on the plane until it landed at Cairo airport at 6 p.m., but the delegation proved as senior as Baghdad had promised. It was headed by Taha Yassin Ramadan, first vice president, second in the hierarchy after Saddam Hussein and Commander of the National Guard, a position of importance in its own right. Also in the delegation was Tariq Aziz, deputy prime minister and foreign minister.

The atmosphere was strained, as might be expected in the circumstances. Before leaving Baghdad the delegation had been told that they would be staying in hotels like the other delegations, but on arrival they were assigned to a hospitality house. Tariq Aziz immediately objected. 'Why in a hospitality house? Where are the other delegations?' The Iraqis were told that they were scattered in hotels all over Cairo, but Tariq Aziz was not satisfied. 'Do you mean that we are confined? Are you putting restrictions on us?' Egyptian officials explained that they were worried about the large number of Kuwaitis in Cairo and the fact that many Egyptians were upset by the invasion. 'We can face that. Leave us to our fate,' Tariq Aziz said, but the Egyptians insisted: 'No, this is a matter of security, and the state is responsible for your safety.' They were taken to Andalus hospitality house, an undistinguished building in comparison to the palaces used for visiting heads of state. Some previous guests had been far from impressed by its accommodation and service.

The Iraqis were beginning to feel under siege. This impression was reinforced when they discovered that only Taha Yassin Ramadan had been invited to see President Mubarak, rather than the whole delegation, as they had assumed. Tariq Aziz was now even more upset. 'I am a member of the delegation and a deputy prime minister. We came here as one delegation: there is no need to differentiate between us. And anyhow, I consider myself a friend of President Mubarak and I want to attend.' But the Egyptians were immovable.

Ramadan told Mubarak that Iraq felt several Arab countries had crossed a safety line (a clear reference to Saudi Arabia, Egypt and Morocco), and that the situation looked like a trap to ensnare Iraq. They had decided to attend the summit because they still had confidence in Mubarak, but they had lost faith in many others.

President Mubarak said it was too late for such talk, and only an immediate change of heart by Baghdad could save the situation. The summit could not start unless Iraq gave not just a renewed pledge to withdraw from Iraq but a fixed timetable, to be supervised by the Arab League. The Iraqi vice president said he was not authorised to discuss a timetable.

The Egyptian president had hoped that by now Baghdad would have realised that it had stirred up a hornets' nest by invading Kuwait, and would be glad of an opportunity to withdraw with dignity. Baghdad, however, saw the situation in a different light. After announcing its intention to withdraw and publishing pictures supposedly showing a brigade leaving, it set about forming a 'revolutionary government', which it named on 8 August, with an army officer, Colonel Al'a Hussein Ali, as prime minister. Baghdad argued that these moves demonstrated the sincerity of its intention to withdraw completely, but that it was unable to proceed as planned because of subsequent events. When Saddam Hussein heard of Cairo's decision to allow the USS *Eisenhower* through the Suez Canal, he called a meeting of the High Command, which came to the conclusion that an American attack on Kuwait was inevitable. The Iraqis felt they could not withdraw and leave the government they had just formed in an impossible position, and they would therefore have to stay and face the Americans. This thought process was largely self-deception: nobody outside Iraq was ready to believe it.

As the infighting continued on the eve of the summit, Washington was forging ahead with its own preparations. President Bush made a nationwide television broadcast from the Oval Office on 8 August asking Americans to support his decision to send US forces to Saudi Arabia. Meanwhile American diplomats in Europe and the Arab world were beginning to construct what would later be called the 'coalition'.

6

'Whose Dagger is in Whose Back?'

Dawn broke over the Nile on 9 August to find the largest city in the Arab world in a state of agitation which grew by the hour. Sirens wailed up and down Cairo's congested streets as police on BMW motorcycles shepherded black Mercedes limousines with tinted windows through a teeming mass of humanity. Hospitality palaces and five-star hotels were packed with heads of state or their deputies from all over the Arab world, each with a retinue of advisers. Thousands paused on their way to work to watch a spectacle not seen in Cairo for years, because of Egypt's long isolation after the Camp David accords. The announcement on the radio the previous evening of an extraordinary summit, called without notice, had given Egyptians a sense of being restored to their former place at the hub of Middle East diplomacy. The Arab world's chance to prove itself in a real crisis had arrived, and Cairo was in the thick of it. The foreign media, always avidly followed by Egyptians, were preparing to give the event intensive coverage. Some of the journalists arriving from Europe and America reduced the issues to three words: 'Peace or war?' It was not that simple.

In other Arab capitals public opinion was beginning to waver. For the first few days after the invasion most Arabs were opposed to Iraq's action, but now many were beginning to feel uncomfortable with the dominant Western role in the crisis. The speed of America's military preparations, the feeling that Britain was generating war fever, and France's decision to join the coalition, aroused defensive feelings which worked to Iraq's advantage. They contributed to the division in the Arab world which followed Arab League foreign ministers' meeting in Cairo, a division which was particularly evident in North Africa.

Arab public opinion outside Egypt started to tilt against what was seen as an American war, and against Arab governments following pro-American policies. Dr Abed El-Jabri, a prominent Moroccan intellectual, says: 'There were two contradictions at the same time: an Arab – Arab contradiction resulting from the occupation of Kuwait by Iraq on the one hand, and an Arab–American contradiction resulting from imminent American moves against Iraq on the other. The first was a minor matter; the second was the major issue.' Dr El-Jabri felt that the Arab world should stand up to to what he saw as a risk of American hegemony and the destruction of an important Arab power. Similar views were gaining strength throughout the world, forcing some pro-Western Arab leaders to adjust their positions to avoid loss of support.

The mood was also growing restive in air-conditioned hotel lobbies around Cairo, though for a different reason. Ministers and officials began to realise that the summit could not possibly take place that day. The Arab League Secretariat had not yet set up shop; there was no agenda, no draft resolutions, not even a programme. President Zine el Abidine Ben Ali of Tunisia sent a message from Tunis appealing for a delay of two days to allow time for preparation. King Hassan of Morocco said he would not attend because he did not think the summit would achieve anything, but would show his good will by sending a high-level delegation. Normally, in the Arab world, this would imply sending one of his sons, but he chose the prime minister.

The suspense became even harder to bear when radio reports carried an official announcement by Baghdad that it had annexed Kuwait. Until then most Arab capitals had hoped that Iraq intended to occupy Kuwait for only a short period. Saddam Hussein later explained the timing of the announcement to King Hussein: 'I realised that the Americans were determined to go to war.' He felt it was one thing to ask the Iraqi army to defend their country unto death, and another to expect them to die for the defence of Kuwait. If Kuwait were officially part of Iraq, it would be a different matter. 'That's why I did it at that time,' he said.

While the Arab summit was trying to collect itself on 9 August, the UN Security Council passed its third resolution since the crisis began. The first had been a week earlier, on the day of Iraq's action, condemning the invasion, demanding the immediate withdrawal of Iraqi forces, and calling on Iraq and Kuwait to begin negotiations to resolve their differences, thereby supporting the Arab League's search for a solution. This resolution was passed on 2 August, with fourteen countries in favour and none against.

Another resolution was passed on 6 August imposing mandatory sanctions against Iraq and establishing a standing committee to supervise their implementation. The vote was thirteen in favour, none against, with two abstentions (Yemen and Cuba). This resolution made no mention of the Arab League or of any possible Arab solution through negotiation.

The third resolution, passed on the day the Arab summit was originally meant to start, declared the non-validity of the Iraqi annexation, and was passed unanimously.

President Bush, in a press conference held the same day, used his famous phrase: 'I have drawn a line in the sand.' Meanwhile Turkey drew a line in the mountains by putting its air force on alert, a move which took Baghdad by surprise. It had felt so confident that Ankara would stay out of any confrontation that few forces had been left in the north of Iraq. Turkey's announcement coincided with a visit by James Baker, the US Secretary of State.

The battlefield was taking shape even as the Arab world was trying to set its summit in motion. By late morning some delegates were thinking about lunch or grumbling that this was the most disorganised summit they had ever attended. This was perhaps a little harsh: even at the best of times Arab summits tended to be short on planning and long on improvisation. A programme eventually emerged, stating that the summit would not start until the following day, 10 August. As this was a Friday, there would be an interruption of two hours for prayers. It was only at this stage that delegates realised the summit would have no second day, and began to wonder why they had been asked to come so far for such a short meeting. A suspicion arose that the aim of the summit was not to find an Arab solution but to legitimise decisions which had already been taken. The Saudis, some suggested, wanted not just a cover of Muslim troops but an Arab League stamp of approval for King Fahd's decision to call in the Americans.

Andalus hospitality house, a white villa standing back from the main road from the wealthy suburb of Heliopolis to Cairo's principal airport, with a fountain playing in its front garden, looked a picture of tranquillity. But the mood of its occupants, the Iraqi delegation, was far from tranquil. Tariq Aziz called the Egyptian delegation to ask if the foreign ministers would be holding a preparatory meeting. The reply came back that in such a complicated situation it would be better if foreign ministers left the matter in the hands of the heads of state. Aziz protested that it was unheard of to hold a summit without the foreign ministers tabling and discussing draft resolutions and settling the agenda. Egyptian officials pointed out that extraordinary situations sometimes called for extraordinary measures.

This remark acquired an unintended double meaning the following morning, when it became clear that Saudi Arabia and others had indeed taken extraordinary measures during the night. A draft resolution had been prepared in complete secrecy, with very few delegations seeing the text. Someone from outside this group managed to obtain it, and soon there was an unplanned proliferation of photocopies. Before the summit opened the Saudi delegation delivered an official copy to Chedli El-Klibi, the Arab League secretary general, who did not have time to read it, but sent it to be printed and officially distributed as a summit document. An aide then drew his attention to the wording of Item 6, which called on the Arab world 'to comply with the request of the Kingdom of Saudi Arabia and other Arab states of the Gulf that Arab forces should be deployed to assist the armed forces already there in Saudi Arabia'. Realising that the words 'armed forces already there' were dynamite, the secretary general went to see Prince Saud al-Faisal, the Saudi foreign minister. 'This can only mean that we are asking Arab states to go and assist American troops, because they are the only forces already there,' he said. Saud al-Faisal took the point immediately. 'You are completely right,' he said, and crossed out the offending words by hand. A new version was ordered, making it clear that the other Arab forces would be assisting Saudi troops.

King Hussein had already seen one of the unofficial photocopies and felt sure the text could not have been written in Arabic originally. The language was contorted and awkward, like a second-rate translation from a foreign tongue. Others had the same impression, and a rumour spread that the original had been written in English. Soon the International Conference Centre was in uproar, with the Jordanians, Libyans and Iraqis suggesting that the resolution had been prepared by Washington and then translated into Arabic. Muammar Gadaffi took the resolution to Sheikh Zayed, ruler of the UAE, and said: 'Why are you hiding behind the Americans? Wouldn't it have been easier to get the Israelis to protect you? They are nearer.' Then he approached a group of other Gulf foreign ministers, including Sheikh Saad of Kuwait, and said: 'Why don't you ask the Israelis to come and defend you?'

Tariq Aziz demanded: 'Who did this? I want an investigation. I asked if there was going to be a meeting of foreign ministers and I was told there was not, and yet now we find this has been prepared in advance.' The meeting was supposed to start at 10 a.m., but because of the row over the resolution no one went into the Grand Hall, remaining outside in the lobby. The reprinting of the resolution caused a further delay, and the meeting did not begin until about 11.30 a.m.

President Mubarak delivered a speech about the gravity of the situation and the need for Arabs to make a stand and not to condone aggression. 'If we do not find solutions, others are going to do so,' he said, referring to the Americans. 'In spite of all the suspicions I don't think it is too late.' But many in the hall felt that the hour of the Arabs had already passed. The meeting adjourned for Friday prayers, but some delegates stayed in the lobby.

King Hussein felt unable to move, and sat with his hand on his cheek, in a cloud of gloom. 'I felt right away, after the first instant, that this was going to be the most tragic summit in the history of the Arab nation,' he said to the secretary general half an hour later. The delegates came back from prayers at 2 p.m., but the meeting did not resume then, as had been planned. Instead it was postponed to 4 p.m. to give delegations more time for consultations. Four o'clock came and passed, but delegates were hanging about talking in the lobby, mixing with journalists and others. Again, everyone seemed reluctant to go into the Grand Hall to start the meeting.

The atmosphere in the corridors was electrified by a rumour of an outbreak of physical violence between Tariq Aziz and his Kuwaiti counterpart Sheikh Sabah al-Ahmed al-Sabah, who was said to have stormed out with blood on his white *abaya* after an incident which supposedly took place before all the Arab foreign ministers. One version was that Tariq Aziz had hurled a plate at the sheikh's face while they were waiting for a side meeting between some of the heads of state to begin.

What actually happened was that while the two foreign ministers were waiting with their colleagues for the meeting to start, Prince Saud al-Faisal of Saudi Arabia, sitting next to Tariq Aziz, remarked that some of the statements coming from Baghdad Radio were abusive and insulting. Before Aziz could reply Sheikh Sabah interjected: 'Brother Tariq, am I to be called an agent of imperialism?' Aziz replied: 'I am sorry, we did not say that, but the documents we found when we took over your office say that.' Sheikh Sabah was furious. He stood up abruptly and stormed out of the room, failed to notice a heavy glass door, and walked into it in full stride. The blow knocked him flat, leaving him with a bleeding nose, which accounted for the stained *abaya*. Aides took him to receive medical attention.

The delegates eventually took their seats more than five hours later than originally planned, at 7.15 p.m., in a mood hardly conducive to dialogue.

President Chadli of Algeria stood up and said: 'We have fought all our lives to get rid of imperialism and imperialist forces, but now we see that our endeavours are wasted and the Arab nation – and I am not nominating anyone specifically – is inviting foreigners to intervene. We were not given a chance to solve this problem in an Arab way or an Arab context.'

President Mubarak replied that the Arabs had had every chance to find a solution, but Muammar Gadaffi raised his hand and said: 'Only forty-eight hours.' Everyone understood he was referring to the delay before America moved which President Bush had reluctantly accepted at King Hussein's request on the day of the invasion.

The resolution was still on the table, but many delegates felt they were being asked simply to give it a '*basma*', the traditional thumbprint formerly used in the Arab world as a stamp of approval. At this point the Egyptian delegation confessed that there had been a foreign ministers' meeting after all, but late at night, involving only the foreign ministers of the Gulf countries, Egypt, Syria and Lebanon, and that they had drafted the resolution. 'We did not want to disturb our brothers so late,' they said, in explanation of why the other delegations had not been invited. No one believed anyone.

The Emir of Kuwait made an unprovocative speech, clearly seeking to avoid making matters any worse, but when he sat down Taha Yassin Ramadan of Iraq commented: 'I don't know on what basis the sheikh is addressing us. Kuwait does not exist any more.' He spent the next twenty-five minutes rehashing Iraq's differences with Kuwait and the efforts it had made to reach a settlement. As he spoke the emir left the hall in anger, went straight to the airport and flew back to Taif in Saudi Arabia, where the government-in-exile had made its base in a hilltop hotel.

When Ramadan sat down, Sheikh Saad, the Kuwaiti crown prince, reminded the summit that Iraq had accused Kuwait of stabbing it in the back because of its policy on oil prices. 'They are talking about a dagger in the back. After what has happened we have to ask: "Whose dagger is in whose back?"'

He continued: 'We told the Iraqis on several occasions that we are not asking them to repay the debts, and that the reason we have not cancelled them is that it would be in neither their interests nor ours. From Iraq's point of view it would encourage other creditors to ask for more money or guarantees from Iraq. From Kuwait's point of view, every debtor on earth (and we are creditors of so many countries) would ask us to forgive their debts. We tried to explain this but they would not understand.' On the border issue, he said that after the 1 August meeting in Jeddah, Kuwait had expected further discussions to take place in Baghdad on 4 August. 'We were ready. We know they have needs and we were ready to find a way of accommodating them without infringing Kuwait's sovereignty.'

He defended the emir against Ramadan's attack. 'I am astonished that Taha Yassin Ramadan talks about the emir in this way. When the emir visited Iraq a few months ago President Saddam Hussein gave him the highest Iraqi decoration and the chief of his cabinet read out an elaborate citation.'

He said that Saddam Hussein, referring to the Iran–Iraq war, had stated: 'We will never forget that in the time of crisis the Kuwaitis were ready to share their bread with us.'

Yasser Arafat, realising that there was no point in going over old ground, got up and said: 'I have a practical suggestion, which many people were discussing in the corridors outside.' He proposed that the summit should appoint a delegation of three of its members, one from the Arab Co-operation Council, one from the Maghreb countries and one from the Gulf Co-operation Council, to go to Baghdad with a message asking Saddam Hussein to withdraw Iraqi troops from Kuwait. He said he was sure this would succeed, and it later became clear that Baghdad had encouraged the idea. Arafat thought such an approach would appeal to Saddam Hussein's sense of dignity and encourage him to be more accommodating.

As this was being discussed Prince Saud al-Faisal, the Saudi foreign minister, brought a note to King Fahd, who was seated at the table, and whispered something in his ear. Fahd read the note and passed it to President Mubarak. Neither of them commented on it, but it was clear that a serious additional complication had arisen, and the whole tone of the meeting changed abruptly. The idea of sending a delegation to Saddam Hussein had been gaining ground, but President Mubarak began to show impatience with it.

Most delegates did not find out what had happened until later, when they learned that during the meeting Baghdad Radio had broadcast an appeal by Saddam Hussein addressed 'to the people of Egypt and the people of Najd and Hejaz'. The Egyptian people (not the government) were asked to close the Suez Canal to stop the USS *Eisenhower*, which was passing through it. The people of the two Saudi regions were asked to 'cleanse the two holy shrines of the usurpers who took it without any right'. The text clearly shocked King Fahd and President Mubarak, who saw it as an incitement to their peoples to rebel. The reference to Najd and Hejaz was considered provocative, as these had been the names of the two largest territories of the Arabian peninsula before Ibn Saud unified them and created Saudi Arabia. King Fahd probably felt this was an implicit attack by Saddam Hussein on his family.

Arafat was still pressing his proposal, unaware of this turn of events. He suggested that President Mubarak should lead the delegation of three representatives of different elements of the Arab world, plus the secretary general. Mubarak brushed the idea aside: 'I have been several times and have done all I can; I am not ready to go. Think of someone else.' Arafat tried to plead with him but Mubarak said: 'There's no time for all this nonsense.' The PLO leader turned to King Hussein. 'Your Majesty, would you . . . ?' but the king interrupted him: 'The problem is that I too have been several times. Some of our colleagues here think that I am taking sides. I am not taking sides. I am trying to make the Arab nation avoid a catastrophe.' Arafat then tried Sheikh Zayed of the UAE, but he too refused.

The President of Sudan, General Omar Hassan al-Bashir, stood up and said: 'We should not give any excuse for a foreign presence on our soil,' but President Hafez al-Assad of Syria replied that it was those who occupied Kuwait who were responsible for the foreign presence.

King Fahd interjected: 'Our brother from Sudan is mixing issues. I was not going to comment on what he said, but I feel obliged to do so. The forces present now in Saudi Arabia will never be used in an offensive act and will not go out of Saudi Arabia unless it is provoked to defend itself.' The king had appeared on Saudi television the previous day to announce the involvement of foreign troops. 'These forces from brotherly [Muslim] and friendly [American] powers are here temporarily. They are to help defend the kingdom, participate in joint exercises, and will leave here as soon as the kingdom so demands,' he said. The king hardly looked up from his prepared script as he made the announcement.[1]

Muammar Gadaffi proposed a secret meeting restricted to kings and presidents, because there were too many outsiders following the discussions. At this point President Mubarak's patience appeared to snap. 'I do not want it to drag on any longer. I am putting the resolution to the vote,' he said. Immediately other heads of state protested that the discussion should be allowed to continue, but Mubarak insisted: 'I am going to ask for the votes. Who is for the resolution and who is against it?'

The Iraqis, feeling they had been encircled, stood up and walked out of the room in protest, leaving behind only the Iraqi ambassador to the Arab League, who stayed to the end. They phoned for their bags and went straight from the conference hall to the airport. Gadaffi, surrounded as usual by the group of girl soldiers who act as his bodyguards, sat stunned by Mubarak's move. Arafat called out: 'President Mubarak, please wait, please delay the voting,' but it was already starting.

According to the Arab League Charter, resolutions are valid only if passed unanimously. This rule tended to cause paralysis, because it took only a single dissenter to block a resolution. Over the years the charter was gradually modified, and a convention arose that in the case of a majority vote, only those who voted for a resolution would be bound by it. The convention applied only to resolutions on routine matters, such as non-controversial economic issues or cultural affairs. It did not apply to resolutions concerning collective measures relative to national security, for which the unanimity rule remained in effect.

The vote was narrowly in favour of the resolution, but some delegates protested that the issue fell into the category of collective action on national security, thereby necessitating a unanimous vote. This argument was not accepted by the Egyptian delegation. Never before had the Arab nation used a majority vote to take an important decision when it was deeply divided.

Afterwards there was confusion over the exact voting figures. Sudan, Palestine and Mauritania expressed reservations about the resol-

[1] Michael Sherridan of the *Independent*, London, 10 August 1990

ution, Iraq and Libya opposed it, Tunisia was not present, and Algeria and Yemen abstained. Jordan's vote was so unclear that the Secretary General of the Arab League was unsure whether to count it as a rejection, an abstention or an expression of reservations. As the delegates left the hall he ran after King Hussein and caught him as he was about to step into his car.

'Your Majesty, what exactly is your vote?'

'Ask the foreign minister,' the king replied, and the car sped away.

Yasser Arafat, still in the hall, shouted at the top of his voice: 'It is unconstitutional! The decision we have taken is unconstitutional!'

He was met by an answering voice from Egypt's ranks. 'No, it is constitutional and legal,' said Dr Mufid Shehab, chief legal consultant of the Egyptian delegation.

Arafat, by now furious, bellowed: 'You are all agents!'

Dr Shehab replied: 'If you are looking for agents, look behind you in your own ranks.'

President Mubarak went in search of Muammar Gadaffi, who had left the hall. 'Where is Muammar? Where is brother Muammar?' he asked. Gadaffi came up to him and said in front of a crowd of delegates, journalists and guards: 'You were not democratic in the way you directed this session.'

Mubarak replied: 'I won't allow you to say such a thing to me.'

Then, noticing that others were listening, they went into a corner and started whispering.

The time was 9.10 p.m. It had taken just under two hours to create the deepest divisions the Arab world had ever seen. The last slender chance for an Arab solution had been lost.

When the final document was sent to the United Nations, Jordan's vote was recorded as an abstention. The vote was not summarised clearly, but there appeared to be ten countries in favour and nine with various other views. The Arab world was split down the middle.

The most important points were as follows:

Paragraph Three condemned the aggression against Kuwait, withheld recognition of the annexation and called on Iraqi forces to withdraw immediately to their pre-1 August positions.

Paragraph Four reaffirmed the sovereignty, independence and territorial integrity of Kuwait as a member of the Arab League and the United Nations, and insisted on the restoration of the legitimate government which existed before the invasion. It supported all measures Kuwait might adopt to liberate its territory and exercise sovereignty.

Paragraph Five condemned threats made by Iraq against the Arab Gulf states, censured its concentration of forces along the border with Saudi Arabia, and supported Saudi Arabia and other Gulf states in exercising their right to self defence. It cited Article 2 of the Arab League's Joint Defence and Economic Co-operation Treaty, Article 51 of the UN Charter, and UN Security Council Resolution 661, passed on 6 August 1990. It also reiterated the understanding that measures against Iraq would cease immediately when Iraq withdrew and the legitimate government was restored.

In Paragraph Six, which had aroused much of the controversy, the delegates resolved to 'comply with the request of the Kingdom of Saudi Arabia and the other Arab states of the Gulf that Arab forces should be deployed to assist its armed forces in defending its soil and territorial integrity against external aggression'.

As the curtain fell in Cairo the Iraqi delegation was flying back to Baghdad in a bitterly resentful mood, feeling that Mubarak had set them up. The real trap, however, was not the summit but the invasion itself. The Iraqis had ensnared themselves in Kuwait through a series of miscalculations. They had underestimated the outrage which the invasion would cause. They had undervalued the importance of Arab oil to the US in the twenty-first century. They had ignored the restraints and deterrents which limit the use of force in the modern world. They had disregarded the shifting balance of East–West power and its impact on Soviet foreign policy, and had failed to realise that Moscow would not stand by them. They had deluded themselves with outworn assumptions that Gulf sheikhs would not dare summon foreign troops and that the anger of the Arab masses would sweep away the West's collaborators.

The mood in the Arab world by the evening of 10 August was one of foreboding, as the sense grew that a third oil war was becoming likely. Although concern about the dominant Western role in the crisis was growing, it was not yet sufficient to provoke demonstrations. Palestinians would later show their opposition to the US role, but at this stage they were quiet. Virtually the only Arabs clearly in favour of a fight were the thousands of Kuwaitis outside their own country. As they saw it, their chances of returning home depended on persuading the Americans to fight for the restoration of Kuwaiti sovereignty, and that could not be taken for granted. All the precautions implemented so far were designed to defend Saudi Arabia, and opinion in Washington was divided, with many questioning whether the US should go to war to defend the privileges of a wealthy sheikh. Additionally, some in the Arab world felt that the invasion had its roots in tribal culture. It had been a tradition for centuries that one tribe would punish another by raiding its territory, seizing its possessions, and departing immediately. This was known as a *khatat* and was practised in Yemen even in fairly recent times. In such a culture it might be inappropriate to apply the principle of inviolable state frontiers too rigidly. However, this comparison would have been credible only if Iraq had withdrawn within a few days.

Some weeks later a Kuwaiti minister approached an Arab observer and asked: 'Do you think the Americans are serious?'

'I am sure it is going to end in war,' was the reply.

'God bless you, you've reassured me,' the minister said.

In the American and British press the main reaction to the Cairo summit was relief. There was a feeling that the Arab League resolution improved the chances that an economic and military blockade of Iraq might work without a need to resort to force. The Americans and British had begun to fear that their troops in the Gulf would lack support from the Arab world and Europe, but now a truly multi-national force with broad-based support seemed in prospect.[2]

Many Arabs claimed afterwards that the Cairo summit was planned and steered by Washington, and that the Arab League vote marked the completion of a four-stage American plan, the aim of which was to surround Iraq with diplomatic, economic and military pressures. The earlier stages consisted of securing Moscow's co-operation, which James Baker achieved with Eduard Shevardnadze in Vladivostock on 2 August; harnessing the United Nations Security Council; and persuading King Fahd to drop his objections to US forces. All four elements were needed before the coalition could be built.

The Security Council's unprecedented near-unanimity was seen in Washington as evidence that a new world order was asserting itself. American politicians allowed themselves to believe that an era of peace was dawning, based on a rejection of the use of force by all the main powers. Many in the Arab world doubted this analysis, feeling that

[2] Simon O'Dwyer-Russell, *Sunday Telegraph*, London, 12 August 1990

what had changed was not the world order but the style of the existing Pax Americana. The emphasis was less on a monopoly of power and more on determined management. The United States was the general manager of the crisis, delegating responsibilities to other capitals according to their usefulness or effectiveness in a particular field. Moscow had its role to play, and the Group of Seven, made up of the richest industrialised countries, was assigned specific tasks, as were the fifteen members of the UN Security Council and the thirty-five coalition countries. The results took everyone by surprise, including those who formulated the management policies.

There were clear reasons for Washington's unprecedented ability to steer the Security Council's decisions. All four other permanent members – the Soviet Union, China, Britain and France – were under its influence in one way or another. Gorbachev's new foreign policy and the Soviet Union's growing economic dependence on Washington had given Moscow a strong interest in co-operating with the United States. Peking, equally, was in no position to use its veto, as its main priority was to recover Western favour after the public relations disaster of the Tiananmen Square killings of June 1989. The United States was the first Western nation to throw Peking a diplomatic lifeline, quickly followed by Britain. By coincidence, these overtures were made in the weeks before the invasion, but the question of when Western economic sanctions against China would be lifted was still a controversial matter. Peking had everything to gain by taking a passive line in Security Council decisions, and consistently supported the majority view. Britain could be counted on to support US resolutions, as its foreign policy was based on shadowing Washington. France had reservations about Washington's hard line, but lacked the diplomatic weight to modify it.

Javier Pérez de Cuéllar, Secretary General of the UN, was surprised by the high degree of co-operation between the US and the Soviet Union, even allowing for the recent transformation of their relationship. The rapid succession of resolutions on the crisis underlined a further improvement in the United Nations' standing in Western capitals. When Pérez de Cuéllar first took office the UN was practically ignored by the developed world, which felt that Cold War confrontation made it worthless as a forum. The deadlock left the Third World free to dominate the General Assembly, using it as their principal outlet of opinion. All this was changing between 1986 and 1990, and the Kuwait crisis completed the transition.

The secretary general was even more surprised by the change in Washington's attitude when it realised how useful the UN was proving in the Kuwait crisis. After having withheld part of its contributions since 1977, Washington suddenly paid up $50 million of the $146 million it owed. The cheque was handed over on Friday 3 August. This may have looked like an attempt to keep the Secretariat sweet, but it was probably more a long-overdue recognition by Washington that its former misgivings about the UN were now out of date. Many had expected Bush to adopt a more positive policy towards the UN much earlier, but he was held back by right-wing elements in the US administration. He and Pérez de Cuéllar knew each other well from earlier days when both represented their countries at the UN.

As the crisis wore on, the secretary general became worried that an impression was being created that the coalition was a United Nations force, and later that the war was a UN war. The UN resolutions provided the political mandate on which the coalition was based, but did not order its creation. It was for this reason that coalition troops did not wear blue berets or fly UN flags. Pérez de Cuéllar did his best to keep a distinction between UN resolutions and a UN force, but he was battling against hopeless odds, because media reports tended to reinforce the wrong impression. As everyone knew that the economic sanctions had been passed by the Security Council, it was difficult for them to understand that the coalition was under different management.

A Second Channel

A week after the invasion of Kuwait, the unease of much of the Arab world outside the Gulf states over America's role in the crisis was growing. The misgivings of millions of people in Egypt, Jordan, Syria, Algeria, Tunisia, Libya and Morocco did not pass unnoticed in the West, but the reasons for their attitude were misunderstood. It was widely assumed in the US and Britain that those Arabs who did not welcome US protection of Saudi Arabia must be supporters of Saddam Hussein. Those Arabs who tried to explain the dispute between Iraq and Kuwait tended to be seen in the West as apologists for Baghdad. Neither of these generalisations was fair or accurate. Virtually all Arabs outside Iraq were opposed to the invasion and wanted Iraq to withdraw. Contrary to many reports, the Palestinians took the same view as the rest of the Arab world, despite their links with Baghdad.

The increasing resentment of the US role was a separate matter, stemming partly from a feeling that Arabs themselves should be given time to resolve an Arab crisis, and partly from historical sensitivities. The first of these points was widely reported in the West, and not without sympathy; the second was almost entirely overlooked. The influence of history in creating what the West saw as an over-suspicious Arab attitude to Western involvement was much stronger than most people in the West realised. The causes of these suspicions can only be understood if the Arab world is seen as an interface between Europe and Asia, a region of perpetual struggle between civilisations.

The crusader, the colonist, the mercenary and the spy have all made their mark on Arab attitudes. But the history of a fifth category, the secret messenger, perhaps offers the best insight into the bitter experiences which shaped Arab suspicions. Unlike the other four, whose intentions were unmistakable, the role of the messenger was shrouded in ambiguity.

The messenger had many guises, but was usually not a diplomat. As the region was an arena of rivalry between European empires, vying to displace each other more by infiltration than conquest, conventional diplomacy had limited uses. The empires used a wide variety of people to carry offers of protection, help or friendship to rulers or tribal leaders. In time some rulers became skilled at using secret contacts with European powers to their own advantage.

The Mamelukes were military slaves of uncertain origins who gradually became soldiers of fortune and later rulers of large areas of the Middle East. Egypt was under their control for two centuries before the Ottoman conquest of 1517. After the conquest, the Turkish Caliph, Sultan Selim, returned to Istanbul (then Constantinople), leaving Mameluke rulers to run affairs in his name, acting as administrators and tax collectors and paying the sultan an annual sum called the '*jizyah*'. Mameluke rulers in different areas were in constant competition with one another, leading to quarrels, conspiracies and assassinations. Having no known roots, no loyalty to each other, and no real attachment to any area, except as a source of riches, they were unable to establish a dynasty.

It was this situation which gave an opening to European powers and their trading companies in the seventeenth and eighteenth centuries. Their aim was to gain access to two land routes vital for trade with India; one between Alexandria and the port of Suez, linking the Mediterranean with the Red Sea, and the other from Syria to Iraq and on to India. Contacts with local Mameluke rulers could not be made openly because external relations were the prerogative of the Caliph in Constantinople. Apart from this, it would have been disastrous for the Mamelukes if their subjects had known that they were in touch with infidels. The outcome was a tradition of secret diplomacy which continues to this day.

Messages carried by traders, missionaries, explorers and private travellers led to trading arrangements which enriched both the Europeans and the Mamelukes, while weakening Constantinople's hold on the region. Camel caravans carrying silk and spices across the desert were used to convey messages to remote tribal chieftains. When the Caliph heard of these contacts his main fear was that the Europeans were encouraging the Mameluke rulers to secede from the empire. These fears were borne out in 1769 when Aly Bay El-Kebir, a Mameluke ruler in contact with Britain and Russia through secret envoys, declared the independence of Egypt. He was killed four years later by another Mameluke who became ruler of Egypt after declaring his loyalty to the Sultan of Turkey.

As its military power waned, the Ottoman Empire increasingly used Islam as a shield against foreign encroachment. The British, French, Russians and later the Germans knew that any direct attack on Ottoman possessions would entitle the Caliph to declare an Islamic Jihad, or Holy War, in which all Muslims would be obliged to take part. Not wanting to replay the crusades, the new powers tried more subtle approaches.

When Napoleon arrived in Egypt in 1798 with an army he was careful not to say that he had come to end Ottoman rule. Instead, when his forces landed at Abu Qir he issued a proclamation to the Egyptian people saying that he had become a Muslim. As a declared convert to Islam he was able to claim that his army would protect the Ottoman Caliph against the attempts by the Mamelukes to take Egypt out of the empire. None of this was true: Napoleon had not converted to Islam in anything more than a token sense. He was no friend of the Caliph, and the French were secretly in contact with certain Mameluke and Bedouin chiefs through unofficial messengers. At the same time the British were in touch with two other famous Mamelukes, El-Alfy and El-Bardisi, both of whom resisted Napoleon. The effect of these contacts was to turn Egypt into a proxy battlefield in the struggle between Britain and France. The British won the friendship of the Caliph and joined forces with the Ottomans to expel the French at the beginning of the nineteenth century. Britain maintained the pretence that Egypt was still part of the Ottoman Empire even when British forces occupied Egypt in 1882.

Throughout the nineteenth century competing empires were looking for secret links with tribal, ethnic and religious sects in Ottoman territories. The French established their influence with the Maronites in Lebanon, while the British made inroads with the Druze. The Russians tried their luck with the Orthodox Coptic Church in Egypt but were less successful.

When the Turks sided with Germany in the First World War, the British and French felt free to try to seize Ottoman territories, and in 1914 Egypt was declared a British protectorate. Tribal chiefs who had been in secret contact with the two powers for decades now became their allies against the Ottoman sultan. This put them in a strong position, when the Ottoman empire collapsed in 1918, to ask for more formal links with London and Paris. Men like General

Allenby, Sir Percy Cox and T.E. Lawrence ('Lawrence of Arabia') played roles in securing written pledges and draft treaties with the chiefs.

After the Second World War, when the Americans began focusing their interest on the Middle East and drawing up plans to take over British and French areas of influence, back-door diplomacy had its heyday. Undercover contacts were established through businessmen, journalists, bankers and others, to avoid arousing the suspicions of the older powers. At a later stage, after establishing their supremacy, the Americans used unofficial envoys of great influence, including David Rockefeller, John McLoy, Robert Anderson and Eugene Black.

After the Suez crisis and the loss of Britain's position in Egypt, London sometimes sent unofficial envoys to Cairo. When Field Marshal Montgomery (by then Viscount Montgomery of Alamein) visited Egypt in 1967 to celebrate the twenty-fifth anniversary of the battle of El Alamein, he carried a message from Lord Shackleton, a minister in the British Labour government, concerning southern Arabia and Aden.

After the colonial period the newly independent Arab countries began building their own diplomatic services, but at the same time used the experience of secret diplomacy they had gained over the centuries. The Lebanese businessman Emile Bustani, a renowned figure in the Arab world, took messages from President Nasser to many of his contacts in the West. In the 1970s and eighties, when increasing oil wealth created a new stratum of Arab businessmen, the 'Second Channel', as Henry Kissinger described secret diplomacy, became almost routine in the Arab world. Its exponents included a group of Palestinian businessmen who acted as unofficial ambassadors in promoting the cause of their people through contacts in the United States and Europe.

It was this long historical background which lay behind the suspicion which millions of Arabs felt about American intentions. Secret diplomacy was, of course, only one of many factors, but it was an important one.

The use of secret diplomacy came naturally to Baghdad in August 1990. In the first days after the invasion Baghdad thought it might be able to soften the furious American reaction if it could speak directly to the White House, without passing through the State Department. A search began for a messenger with established contacts among White House aides. It was Yasser Arafat who suggested that Baghdad's contacts with the Palestinian community could be helpful in this respect.

Six days after the invasion, a prominent Palestinian businessman, who must remain anonymous for his own safety but who has high connections in the Bush administration, sent a message to a fax number at the White House. It read as follows

On Sunday 5 August, between 4 p.m. and 7 p.m. London time, I received two telephone calls from my good friend Nizar Hamdoun, Assistant Secretary of State for Foreign Affairs in Iraq . . . who asked me, in the name of the Foreign Minister, Tariq Aziz, to go to Baghdad . . . I apologised for safety and family reasons. Meanwhile, almost at the same time, Chairman Arafat on a mediation mission between Kuwait and Iraq, called me from Baghdad and repeated the same request. Again I declined, suggesting that I meet him somewhere else at a place nearer to London. He agreed. On Monday morning, Nizar Hamdoun again called twice to convince me to go to Baghdad but I stuck to my position. At the same time I sought the advice of Richard Murphy [former US Assistant Secretary of State for the Middle East] who came back after contacting the State Department [saying] that I should not go to Washington and that any contacts should be confined to either the American Embassy in Baghdad or the Iraqi Embassy in Washington. That is why I chose to send this message by fax. On Monday evening, Chairman Arafat called me from Jeddah and suggested that we meet the next day in Vienna, where he was due for the funeral of the late Bruno Kreisky [former Federal Chancellor of Austria].

On Tuesday 7 August I arrived in Vienna and met the Chairman, who later departed for Jeddah. The Chairman informed me that during his meeting with President Saddam Hussein they both agreed that there should be a channel between Baghdad and Washington. My name came up as a possible go-between, hence the phone calls I received from Baghdad. The Chairman said that he was extremely worried and that the rapid deterioration in the situation should be contained immediately. He added that he abstained from taking sides at the Arab League meetings in Cairo in order to keep open his chances for mediation. [This was before the Cairo summit, at which Arafat used Palestine's vote to express reservations on the Saudi resolution.]

The businessman said that Arafat asked him to convey the following set of proposals from Baghdad:

1) Iraqi troops shall withdraw from Kuwait.
2) The Sabah family shall be reinstated.
3) Pending negotiations and final settlement, there shall be an Iraqi military presence on Bubiyan island and the disputed border areas in the north of Kuwait.
4) The two questions of Iraq – the debts and compensation to Iraq – shall be settled in a way satisfactory to Iraq.
5) The Iraqi President is willing to reach an agreement with the American administration on all matters pertaining to oil.

The businessman also said that Arafat saw dangers in an Iraqi withdrawal without an interim alternative.

He is particularly alert to the possibility of the Iranian Muslim Fundamentalists fomenting trouble. He believes that an Arab League interim force should be stationed in Kuwait, similar to the one of 1961 when General Kassim [then leader of Iraq] threatened Kuwait . . .

The situation is so delicate, explosive and fraught with dangers that I am in no position to venture an opinion. However, I feel I should mention that the Chairman is one of the very few people who have direct access to the Iraqi President at any time. He is therefore capable, under the current gloomy circumstances, [of making] a small opening that might put Washington and Baghdad on a talking course instead of a head-on clash. If the need arises I am prepared to come to Washington. Regards

Nothing came of this approach because Washington did not respond, but its timing was significant. The calls from Hamdoun and Arafat came on Sunday 5 August, the day that Iraq realised that the mini-summit which King Hussein and Saddam Hussein had discussed would not, after all, take place, and immediately before the arrival of Dick Cheney and General Norman Schwarzkopf in Riyadh. Baghdad had announced its intention to withdraw and had published pictures supposedly showing the start of the pull-out. The circumstances suggest that Saddam Hussein, alarmed by Washington's moves and realising that the US was taking all the elements of the crisis in its own hands, was ready to reach a settlement directly with President Bush. The terms which Baghdad offered amounted to a step backwards from the limited occupation it had originally envisaged, before the decision to occupy the whole of Kuwait. In President Carter's day this would probably have been seen as an opening bid, leading to secret talks, but Bush had decided there was nothing to discuss.

Further evidence that Saddam Hussein was ready to negotiate came at noon the following day, 6 August, when he asked to see Joseph Wilson, the American chargé d'affaires in Baghdad during Miss Glaspie's absence. The meeting began two hours later and was recorded by the Iraqis. The transcript (which is not challenged by the State Department) shows that Saddam Hussein offered assurances about Iraq's intentions, asked what he needed to do to settle US doubts, and made it clear that Baghdad did not want a confrontation with the United States. He did not mention the proposed package deal, probably preferring to leave that to the indirect contacts Baghdad thought it was establishing with the White House.

Saddam Hussein said he realised that the United States took positions on events everywhere in the world. 'So we are not astonished that the United States is taking a position condemning what we did. But I want to tell you that I hope that the United States will not rush under bad advice to things which can jeopardise the present and the future.'

The Iraqi leader made an implicit comparison between the situation in Kuwait and his dealings with Iran a decade earlier, just before the start of the Iran–Iraq war. 'We tried to give them [the Iranians] a free consultation, [but] because I talked to them very frankly, they thought I was playing tactics . . . You know what happened. I wish the Iranians had taken my free consultation seriously, and what happened need not have happened.'

Returning to the Kuwait crisis, Saddam Hussein said he wanted to make three points. Dealing first with the border dispute, he described Kuwait as 'a state without any borders' and said that until 1961 not everyone regarded it as a state at all. Secondly, he said that since 1975 Iraq and Saudi Arabia had enjoyed good relations and trust at all levels, and argued that these links were not harmful to American interests.

'Good relations between us and Saudi Arabia is one of the pivots of stability in the area and anybody shaking it would inflict huge harm . . . We don't understand the sudden talk about the Americans fearing [the use of] Iraqi power [against] Saudi Arabia. I do not understand it because there is no danger to Saudi Arabia. If you want to push Saudi Arabia to do something against our interests, that is another thing. Kuwait is a different problem. Kuwait was always part of Iraq and instead of acting in a proper way, they acted in a very wrong way. But Saudi Arabia is a completely sovereign state.'

Saddam Hussein reminded Mr Wilson that the non-aggression pact between Iraq and Saudi Arabia was an Iraqi initiative and added: 'We were ready to offer the same thing to Kuwait, provided the frontiers with Kuwait were arranged.'

Speaking warmly of 'our friends in Saudi Arabia', Saddam Hussein recalled their help during the war with Iran and the fact that the pipeline carrying Iraqi oil across Saudi Arabia to the Red Sea was built at Riyadh's suggestion.

'Now I see that you are trying to sabotage the relations between us and them. If you were really worried about Saudi Arabia, I am telling you that this is unrealistic. But if you are pretending to be worried, to push Saudi Arabia into something else, then that is another thing.'

Saddam Hussein's third point dealt with the assurance he was said to have given President Mubarak that he would not invade Kuwait. 'Many people are . . . telling you that Saddam Hussein gave a pledge not to use force . . . I never gave that pledge to anybody.' He reiterated Iraq's version: that he had said there would be no use of force before the Iraqi–Kuwaiti meeting of 1 August. 'That happened. We did not make any military move before that meeting, because we were waiting for a serious result . . . what happened was that our vice president returned from Jeddah to tell us that the Kuwaiti position was as it had always been.'

Explaining the decision to invade, Saddam Hussein said: 'We are Arabs and obviously, when we find somebody trying to hurt us, we try to hurt him. We felt our vital interests were in danger and we tried all means before using force. Now I want a reply from the American president and all the Americans responsible: where is the danger to American interests? . . . What is the danger for which you are preparing military action? Who are you trying to defeat and how are you going to defeat them?

'You are a great power and we know that you can hurt us, but you are going to lose the area after that and you will not be able to make us go on our knees, even if you use all your might. You can destroy all our military and technical and economic and oil installations, but the more you destroy, the more it will be a burden to you, and then we will not keep quiet against your interests in the area . . . Why do you want to be our enemy? You made horrible mistakes [in the past], when you weakened your friends . . . I want to urge you to give yourself and your friendships a chance.'

The Iraqi leader raised his grievances about an interview he had given to ABC Television in which he tried to correct earlier reports which suggested that he had threatened a chemical weapons attack against Israel, whereas in fact he had said that they would be used in defence if Israel attacked with nuclear weapons. When the interview was broadcast this point was omitted. The Iraqis had made their own video recording of the interview, and Baghdad television screened the two versions together to show what ABC had done.

Dealing with the risk of war with Israel, Saddam Hussein said: 'Baghdad can take so many rockets, but the cities of Israel cannot take that. We are happy that we have not reached that situation. Who should be happy? The party which is seeking peace or the party which wants to strike? In conclusion, if what the American president wants is what is declared [about safeguarding American interests], we think honestly that this degree of escalation is against those interests. If it is something else, all right . . . we need stability and we need peace, but we hate submission and slavery and we are not going to accept that. We also hate hunger, because our people have been hungry for a thousand years, and we are not going back to it. This is my new message which I want sent to President Bush.'

Wilson thanked him and said he would relay the message immediately, giving an initial summary by telephone and then a report. In a discussion which followed, Wilson adopted a fairly conciliatory tone, but was firmer than Miss Glaspie had been two weeks earlier, and seemed more astute. He sought and received specific assurances and clarifications, and backed out of an argument with the Iraqi leader over Kuwait's oil-price policy when it became clear that the discussion was leading nowhere.

'These are very dangerous times, not only for American–Iraqi relations but because of the stability of the area and the world,' he said.

'Why the world? Why is it so dangerous for the world?' Saddam Hussein asked.

'Because as you may notice, Mr President, even the financial markets are seeing some very volatile changes.'

'You did that,' Saddam Hussein said. 'You were playing havoc with oil. We have accepted twenty-five [a reference to Iraq's proposal shortly before the invasion that the oil reference price should be $25 a barrel]. You have pushed others to have an economic conspiracy which is almost as fatal as a conspiracy by arms.'

Wilson said: 'I am sorry, Mr President, I feel as if I have touched a nerve in this. Anyhow, I want everybody, you and us, all of us, to get out of that emotional situation and to base our calculations on factual thinking.'

He asked whether he had clearly understood that Saddam Hussein was asserting that Kuwait was part of Iraq. Saddam Hussein said: 'Historically that is correct,' and added that the links 'ought to be built on feelings of brotherhood and mutual respect'. Wilson observed: 'But that was not there in the Kuwait–Iraq relations in the past several weeks.' Saddam Hussein said: 'Yes, correct, especially in the last week.'

Turning to Saudi Arabia, Wilson said: 'I want you to give me an assurance that in the circumstances as they are, you are not . . . intending to do anything military against Saudi Arabia.'

Saddam Hussein replied: 'You can take that assurance to your president and to the Saudis and to everybody in the Middle East. Those who do not attack, we are not going to attack. Those who do not hurt us, we are not going to hurt. Those who seek our friendship, we will rush after them and beg for their friendship.'

Saddam Hussein said he understood Saudi Arabia's reasons for giving sanctuary to the Sabah family, and would only be annoyed if they were given a chance to work against Iraq. 'Give my regards to President Bush and tell him to consider [Sheikh] Jaber and the people who are with him as a spent force.'

Mr Wilson mentioned a breach of diplomatic immunity in Kuwait, where the grounds of the home of a senior US diplomat had been entered by Iraqi soldiers. Saddam Hussein said Iraqi forces had been told to behave well in Kuwait, and anyone disobeying orders would be tried. Wilson also raised concerns about American citizens in Iraq and Kuwait and said that any taking of hostages would be 'looked on with doubt and anger in America'. Saddam Hussein replied: 'Please be assured about them.'

On Iraq's declared intention to withdraw, Wilson said he had seen three convoys leaving Kuwait and asked when the withdrawal would be completed. Saddam Hussein replied: 'It took us three days for our forces to go into Kuwait, and we cannot withdraw in one day. Our withdrawal from Kuwait depends on the world atmosphere and we are not going to leave Kuwait to its fate, an easy loaf of bread to be swallowed by anybody.' He implied that the withdrawal would be reversed if the Americans intervened.

'If there is a threat against Kuwait, we are going to reinforce our forces there, and if that threat is in volume, we are going to meet the threat in the same volume.'

Wilson said he had been worried about Iraqi intentions but felt the Iraqi leader had given him 'a generally assuring picture'. Saddam Hussein replied: 'Tell me what . . . would remove your anxiety, and I will give it.'

The meeting ended with compliments and a joke. Wilson said: 'I must congratulate you on the high professional standard with which your Ministry of Foreign Affairs is acting.'

Saddam Hussein, laughing, said: 'Ah yes. You diplomats are passing compliments to each other, but you did not compliment me [over the fact that] I called you to convey a message to President Bush.'

Wilson said: 'As a matter of fact, I paid my respects to you and if you revise the minutes . . . you will find that . . .I thanked you very much. Now, thank you, Mr President.' And he left.

In the space of four days (3–6 August) Saddam Hussein had agreed to a mini-summit, accepted the need for a faster pace of withdrawal, pulled back a token portion of his forces, sent Washington a secret message proposing a package deal, and conveyed assurances to President Bush on his intentions. Whatever Washington's suspicions that the Iraqi leader's offers were purely tactical, it is an oversimplification to say that Saddam Hussein was a man incapable of second thoughts.

Baghdad's case, in this respect, is not helped by the timing of its announcement that it was annexing Kuwait and its appeal to the people of Egypt and those of Najd and Hejaz, on 9 and 10 August. Had these statements come after the Cairo summit rather than before and during it, Baghdad could not have been accused of wrecking the last hopes of an Arab settlement.

The waters were further muddied on 12 August when Baghdad tried to link the Kuwait dispute with the Arab–Israeli conflict. A presidential statement, announced by a spokesman, called for the lifting of the United Nations economic blockade of Iraq, coupled with an international acceptance of the historic links between Iraq and Kuwait, and a resolution of all problems in the Middle East where one country was occupied by another, including the Israeli occupation of Palestinian territories and the Syrian occupation of Lebanon. It implied that if these other problems were solved, arrangements would be made for Iraqi forces to withdraw from Iraq. Saddam Hussein expected a serious reply, but the West dismissed the statement out of hand on the grounds that it was not clearly worded and contained no explicit promise to leave Kuwait. Many saw it as a ploy to divide the Arab and Western elements of the coalition, but that was probably only part of the motive. Baghdad was pushing at every diplomatic door that might offer a dignified exit; if the West had agreed to discuss the two issues in the same context, Baghdad's honour would have been satisfied. But that was not what the West wanted. Washington and London had decided that Iraq should be dealt with firmly, as an example to others. It was now preferable, from their point of view, that Iraqi troops should stay in Kuwait and take the consequences, even if this made life difficult for the Kuwaitis. Saddam Hussein had stepped into a trap and would have to stay there until the West was ready to finish with him. The Iraqi leader, on the other hand, did not yet see himself as cornered. He was willing to withdraw, but not unconditionally: as a minimum he wanted the islands and the Rumaila oilfield. The money was by now less of an issue, because the booty seized from the Central Bank of Kuwait alone approached $2 billion. This was made up of $1.2 billion in gold, $600 million in other metals, and the balance in various currencies. In an earlier era it would have been seen as an outstanding *khatat*. Huge quantities of equipment were seized from Kuwait University and other institutions.

A Kuwaiti official asked an Iraqi army commander at the time: 'If you are saying that this is part of Iraq, why are you taking everything away?'

The commander's reply was: 'Because no province can be better than the capital.'

Baghdad's proposal of 12 August coincided with the start of a tour of Western capitals by King Hussein, amid rumours that he was carrying messages from Saddam Hussein. The king insisted that he had no message, but he was clearly trying to serve as an intermediary. He had known George Bush for some time and they got on quite well, so it was not difficult for him to phone and ask for a meeting. 'I read a statement several days ago in which you said you were astonished at the position I am taking, and that you feel I am taking sides. I want to explain the situation,' he said. The president was at Kennebunkport, his summer resort in Maine, playing golf and clearly determined to show that Saddam Hussein could not make him a 'prisoner of the White House' like Jimmy Carter, who hardly left Washington during the Tehran hostages crisis of 1979 and 1980. Bush agreed to see the king, but was not immediately able to fix a date. He phoned back at 1 a.m. on 10 August to suggest an appointment on the twelfth. This presented a problem, because it would be normal diplomatic practice for the US ambassador in Amman to accompany the king on such a trip. The US had changed its ambassador a few weeks earlier, but the king had been so busy that he had not had time to receive him and accept his credentials. The unfortunate envoy, Roger Harrison, was summoned from his bed in the middle of the night, made to present his credentials while half asleep, sent back to his embassy to pack a bag, and whisked off to the airport to join the king on a thirteen-hour journey to the United States. They had time for only a few hours' sleep before Bush called in person to pick them up for the talks.

The king told the president that American actions were raising tension in the Middle East, but Bush replied: 'It's not us who raised the tension.' The Jordanian monarch sensed that the American leader's attitude towards him had hardened considerably since their last meeting. Bush said he realised that King Hussein was worried about Jordan's economic position, and suggested that other Arab countries (meaning Saudi Arabia and other Gulf sheikhdoms) could help.

King Hussein replied: 'I didn't come to raise that subject. I came because of something bigger: the subject of peace.'

Bush said: 'Hussein, oil to us is a way of life. I'm not going to allow that man [Saddam Hussein] to control two thirds of the oil of the Gulf [in fact, the proportion was two fifths]. This is a man who is hostile to the United States and his hands are on our lifeline.' Bush described Saddam Hussein as a dictator.

Bush continued: 'You [Arabs] are all living on a powderkeg and this man is threatening you. He is threatening you, not me; we are far away from him, but we have our vital interests there and we are going to protect them.'

In his talks at Kennebunkport the king also raised Saddam Hussein's willingness to withdraw. President Bush replied: 'Conditional withdrawal, and I'm not going to accept that. If he wants to withdraw he should declare it to be unconditional and immediate.' The American president argued that Saddam Hussein had put himself in confrontation not just with the United States but with a new order which was prevailing in the world. King Hussein tried to talk to him but there was no real communication.

In his briefing for members of the Council of Dignitaries, an upper house of the Jordanian parliament without any legislative powers, the king said that his meeting with the American leader was interrupted by a phone call from President Mubarak to President Bush. Afterwards Bush told the king: 'One of your colleagues was urging me to act quickly by force, otherwise Arab streets would explode.'

King Hussein left the United States with a sense of hopelessness, and went to London, where he saw Prime Minister Margaret Thatcher. They had held countless discussions in the past on the Arab–Israel conflict, and were on close terms. The meeting started amicably and Mrs Thatcher asked the king why he was backing Saddam Hussein, who she described as 'an evil man'.

'I am not backing anybody. I am trying to save peace in our area,' the king said.

'Who is responsible?' she asked.

The king is usually as tactful as the most polished diplomat, but on this occasion he stumbled. 'Margaret, I want to talk to you frankly. Gunboat diplomacy belongs to the nineteenth century,' he said.

The famous Thatcher eyes blazed with anger. 'You are backing a loser and I want you to know that before it is too late.' Her voice full of disdain, the British prime minister dismissed the Iraqi leader as 'a third-class dictator'. Her friendship with the king came to an end with that conversation, and subsequent letters exchanged between them were less than civil. 'We were insulting each other,' the king said later, describing her as a lady whose tongue was taller than her body.

King Hussein went on to Paris, where met President Mitterrand on 3 September. The French leader, showing a more sympathetic attitude, said that the Americans and British were clearly working together on a plan, and were mainly worried about oil supplies. He advised that it would be best for Saddam Hussein to withdraw immediately, because that would be the only way of aborting the military action which was in preparation. Mitterrand spoke of the importance of an 'Arab factor', but said that as usual the Arabs were held back by their internal divisions.

'We joined the coalition because we wanted to put the brakes on from inside, but all our Arab friends must give us a clear position, and then maybe we will be able to move. Before that it is very difficult,' Mitterrand said.

The king made other calls, including Rome, but Washington, London and Paris were the important ones. He returned to Amman in a gloomy and bitter mood, wondering what more he could do. The West continued to feel that he was defending Saddam Hussein, as did some in the Saudi leadership. After King Hussein's visit to the United States an open letter written by Prince Bandar, the Saudi ambassador to Washington, and distributed to the media by a public relations company, was published in the *Washington Post*, the *New York Times* and the *Los Angeles Times*. The letter challenged the king's argument, expressed in a speech during the tour, that the Iraq–Kuwait border was disputed and was based on a historical situation created by the British. Prince Bandar stated: 'Your Majesty, you should be the last one to say that. Not only all your borders, but your whole country was created by the colonial British.' The letter also took King Hussein to task for comparing the situation to 1914, when the world was sliding into a war it did not want but could not stop. Prince Bandar suggested a different parallel: 'Your Majesty, we are today in a period like the 1930s when a madman decided to annex his neighbours and the world did nothing. That led to World War II.'

King Hussein followed up ideas which had emerged from the least discouraging part of his tour, the visit to Paris. He proposed a solution based on an Iraqi withdrawal and the deployment of an Arab League peace-keeping force. The departure of the Iraqis would be staged to coincide with a withdrawal of foreign forces from the Gulf and a gradual lifting of the UN blockade against Iraq. A symbolic Iraqi force would be allowed to stay on Bubiyan and Warba islands and in the Rumaila oilfield until negotiations started on a permanent settlement. A plebiscite would be held in Kuwait to decide what sort of government they wanted. Mitterrand had argued that nobody in Kuwait cared for the al-Sabah family, as they had deserted the country.

This proposal, which was mainly inspired by France although put forward by Jordan, was immediately rejected by Egypt and Saudi Arabia, and then by the rest of the Arab world, apart from Iraq. Meanwhile Jordan was falling still further from Washington's favour, following allegations that the port of Aqaba had remained open to merchandise bound to and from Iraq, despite the UN blockade.

Saddam Hussein tried to appeal directly to the American people by making a long broadcast on American television. It lasted for an hour and ten minutes, while President Bush's reply took just seven minutes. The disparity was a further illustration of the Iraqi leader's anxiety to find a solution and Bush's increasing confidence.

By early September it was becoming clear that Saddam Hussein's 12 August proposal, linking all the main Arab causes – Palestine, Kuwait, Lebanon and the need for a just distribution of wealth – was proving popular with many Arabs. The Iraqi leader's aim in making the proposal had been to broaden his appeal to the Arab masses by reviving old slogans of Arab nationalism, awakening dormant aspirations and suppressed hopes. To that extent the proposal partly achieved its aim, but there was an unforeseen side-effect. At the time Saddam Hussein was divided between his wish to avoid a loss of prestige, on the one hand, and the need to avert an American attack, on the other. Prestige became the stronger priority once he realised that a section of opinion in most Arab countries was on his side. The wider his constituency, the more difficult it became for him to leave Kuwait unconditionally.

8

Towards the Abyss

If leadership is the art of making choices between unacceptable alternatives, September 1990 was a particularly difficult month for Saddam Hussein. Four weeks after the invasion of Kuwait, the Iraqi president was torn between incompatible aims and realities on a number of important questions.

There was a conflict between his readiness to withdraw from Kuwait and his fear that withdrawal would not resolve the crisis. He was beginning to think that any sign of weakness on his part might make Iraq more rather than less vulnerable to American pressure. This led him to look for some sort of international guarantee of Iraq's security in exchange for withdrawal.

Secondly, his wish to mobilise Arab public opinion in his favour tended to cut across his wish to resolve the crisis. His proposal of 12 August that the Kuwait issue should be linked to the Arab–Israel dispute and other matters had increased his support in the Arab world, but that support came from those who wanted a strong Arab leader to stand up to Washington. If Saddam Hussein chose to play that role, he could not leave Kuwait without obtaining some important concession in return.

Thirdly, there was a conflict between withdrawal from Kuwait and the survival of his own regime. Saddam Hussein believed that if he ordered the troops to return home, his future as leader of Iraq would be in question.

A further inconsistency was that Saddam Hussein tended to present himself in different ways, depending on his audience. When seeking support from the Arab and Muslim masses, his tone was forceful. When talking to Arab leaders, his voice was muted. When meeting European elder statesmen, Saddam Hussein gave the impression of being quiet and thoughtful. His aim, presumably, was to communicate with each group on an appropriate level, but the effect was to cause confusion. Arab leaders became increasingly perplexed, and Western statesmen returning home after talks with Saddam Hussein tended to be ignored, because what they said conflicted with other reports.

There was also some disagreement within the Iraqi leadership as to how the crisis was likely to develop. In late August and early September, some members of the Revolutionary Command Council thought that President Bush's mandate from US public opinion was confined to the defence of Saudi Arabia, and were encouraged by King Fahd's statement at the Cairo summit that foreign forces would not move beyond Saudi Arabia's borders unless attacked. Other members were convinced that the US would attack Iraqi forces in Kuwait. That view gained ground after 11 September when President Bush, in an address to a joint session of Congress, said that he would not allow Iraq's annexation of Kuwait to stand.

Saddam Hussein had been convinced since the Cairo summit that the crisis was out of Arab hands. That opinion was strengthened on 4 September when King Hussein visited Baghdad and reported on his meeting with President Mitterrand the day before and his earlier discussions with President Bush and Mrs Thatcher. The king urged Saddam Hussein to abandon hopes that an Iraqi – Saudi summit could produce a solution, and said that the Americans were certain to advise King Fahd against such a meeting.

'It is no longer a question of the future of Kuwait, it's a matter of saving Iraq,' King Hussein said. 'We, your friends, are also in a tight spot. Remember the Falklands war: we in Jordan backed the British, not because we cared about the Falklands or were worried about the British, but because we had to declare our position, as Argentina had occupied the Falklands by force. We stood by the British on principle. Now we are in a difficult position as regards Iraq and Kuwait.'

Saddam Hussein called a senior staff officer to his side and asked him: 'What would be the feeling of the army if I gave the order to withdraw?' The general replied: 'Oh, God forbid, sir, please don't utter those words.' The king did not press the matter any further.

The Iraqi leadership had been hoping that a split would emerge in the Western camp, with France, Germany or Japan refusing to follow the American lead. King Hussein advised Saddam Hussein to forget that idea. Mitterrand had made it clear, he said, that unless Iraq showed flexibility on withdrawal and on releasing foreign hostages, war was inevitable and France would fight alongside the other coalition countries. Thousands of Westerners had been trapped in Iraq and Kuwait since 9 August, when Iraq declared the borders closed. A week later the 4000 Britons and 2500 Americans in Kuwait were ordered to report to registration points. Many went into hiding, but those who complied or were caught were detained in hotels in Kuwait and later transferred to Baghdad, where most spent a further period in hotels as government 'guests'. Iraq declared that they were to be a shield against attack by coalition forces, and transferred some of them to factories and military installations, hoping that this would deter Western bombing raids.

The French community in Kuwait and Iraq was estimated on 17 August to be 530. Any doubts about the French government's attitude were removed on 15 September when Paris announced that its forces in Saudi Arabia would be reinforced by a mechanised armoured brigade. On the same day the Iraqi military attaché in Paris and his fourteen staff were ordered to leave Paris within forty-eight hours.

Baghdad was beginning to realise that diplomatic doors were closing on all sides. One of the Revolutionary Command Council's hopes had been that the United Nations would play a role which Iraq could regard as constructive. When Tariq Aziz met Javier Pérez de Cuéllar in Amman on 31 August, that hope was already much weaker because of the Security Council's resolutions on the invasion. Aziz reminded the UN secretary general that during the Suez crisis in 1956 the United Nations was the political instrument through which the world brought pressure on Britain, France and Israel to end their aggression against Egypt. As permanent members of the Security Council, Britain and France were able to veto Security Council resolutions on the crisis, but John Foster Dulles, the US Secretary of State, took the case to the General Assembly, where there was no veto power. Dag Hammarskjöld, then secretary general, submitted his resignation, on the grounds that two founder members of the UN had violated the UN Charter. His resignation was not accepted, but it served to increase pressure on Britain and France, and the General Assembly then imposed a ceasefire. Tariq Aziz hoped that the UN might be of similar service to Iraq, but Pérez de Cuéllar pointed out that both the nature of the crisis and the world situation were different. A new world order was emerging with the UN at its centre, but the secretary general's role was more limited than Hammarskjöld's in 1956, being confined to ensuring that the Iraqi government understood the meaning of the resolutions passed by the Security Council.

Iraq's remaining hopes of avoiding diplomatic isolation depended on the Soviet Union. A meeting of the Revolutionary Command Council on 5 September, the day after Saddam Hussein's meeting with King Hussein, decided that Tariq Aziz should visit Moscow, but when Aziz saw Eduard Shevardnadze two days later the mood was icy. The Soviet foreign minister insisted that Iraq should withdraw from Kuwait and made no offer of political support. Taken aback by Shevardnadze's attitude, Aziz said that the Soviet Union was throwing away a political investment in the Arab world which it had built up over forty years. Shevardnadze replied that the Soviet Union now had a new foreign policy based on following its own interests. The two men parted on poor terms.

A number of Soviet army officers protested that Shevardnadze's policy amounted to abandoning the Soviet Union's strategic interests in the Middle East, as Iraq had been its strongest ally in the Arab world. They were also concerned that a lack of Soviet support for Iraq might provoke unrest in the Soviet Muslim republics. When President Gorbachev heard of these views he decided to transfer responsibility for contacts with the Iraqis to Yevgeni Primakov, a close aide and former journalist. Primakov had worked as a *Pravda* correspondent in the Middle East and first met Saddam Hussein in 1969, soon after the Ba'ath Party came to power in Baghdad.

Two events in the next two weeks further hardened Iraqi views. On 15 September General Michael Dugan, the US Air Force Chief of Staff, said that in the event of war the US would attempt to 'decapitate' the Iraqi leadership by targeting Saddam Hussein, his family, and senior advisers and commanders. The Joint Chiefs of Staff had concluded that the most effective way to drive Iraqi troops out of Kuwait was not with a ground attack but by the use of air power on a massive scale. Apart from military and industrial sites the air force would also attack the centre of Baghdad. 'If push came to shove, the cutting edge would be in downtown Baghdad,' Dugan said. Richard Cheney, the Defense Secretary, discussed these remarks with President Bush and dismissed Dugan the following day. 'I simply thought [Dugan's comments] were inappropriate,' Cheney said. No member of the Joint Chiefs of Staff had been dismissed since 1949. The Iraqi government assumed that Dugan was punished not because what he said was untrue but because the US had wanted to keep its options secret.

Secondly, the Iraqis noted that the West objected to certain remarks made by the Saudi defence minister Prince Sultan at a press conference in Riyadh on 22 September, in the presence of twenty-six Arab and foreign correspondents. 'We see no insult in any Arab country giving its sister Arab country any land or money or outlet to the sea. If Iraq has got claims against Kuwait they are entitled to their rights, but not through the use of force,' the prince said. James Baker phoned Riyadh to point out that the prince's conciliatory tone was likely to demoralise the troops, and Prince Sultan issued a statement saying that he had been misunderstood.

In Baghdad the Revolutionary Command Council held a series of meetings from 23 September to discuss tactics, and decided that in the event of war Iraq's interests would be best served by widening the conflict. Iraq's reply to any attack by coalition forces would be to launch a missile strike against Israel, with the aim of forcing Tel Aviv to retaliate. This would create an Arab – Israel conflict, enabling Iraq to call on other Arab countries for support. Secondly, Saudi Arabian oilfields and terminals would be attacked with missiles in the hope of precipitating a world oil crisis. An outline of this plan was made public in a statement saying that, as the US was resorting to the law of the jungle, Iraq would turn any conflict into an all-out confrontation.

On 26 September Yitzhak Shamir, the Israeli prime minister, wrote to President Bush saying that, in the light of the Iraqi statement, Israel felt obliged to take preventive measures of self-defence at any appropriate time. He hinted that pre-emptive attacks against Iraqi missile sites would be launched unless the Americans promptly eliminated the source of danger.

In reply President Bush asked Shamir for restraint, and assured him of America's determination to deal with the threat. Bush requested the Israelis not to take actions which could create strains in the Arab – Western coalition, and added that Israel would be depriving itself of a historic opportunity to get rid of an enemy without making sacrifices if it acted unilaterally. The same letter invited Shamir for talks in Washington.

Fearing that an Israeli action could wreck the coalition, Saudi Arabia initiated secret meetings with influential American Jews. Nine months later, in July 1991, Henry Siegman, executive director of the American Jewish Congress, disclosed that he and other Jewish leaders held meetings with Prince Bandar, the Saudi ambassador to Washington, after the invasion of Kuwait. Siegman recalled their conversation: 'I asked him: "Mr Ambassador, will your country – after this crisis is over – say unconditionally that Israel's right to exist is not challenged by the Arab world and Saudi Arabia? Are you also willing to say that your country will fully normalise ties with Israel once the Palestinian issue is resolved?"'

According to Siegman, Bandar replied: 'Yes, this is exactly what I am saying. I am telling you not just Saudi Arabia but Syria will also say this.' Siegman said that after the war he saw Bandar again and raised these assurances. 'Give us time. We are working on it,' he quoted the prince as saying.[1]

Israel came under renewed international pressure over the Palestinian issue after a clash at Temple Mount in Jerusalem on 8 October, in which more than twenty Palestinians were killed and 150 injured. The clash stemmed from a long-standing dispute between Jews and Muslims over part of the site. Jewish fundamentalists carrying out an annual ceremony to mark Jewish claims said that they were attacked by Palestinians throwing stones. What might have remained a minor incident was exacerbated by a delay in the arrival of Israeli security forces, allowing the ensuing fight to develop into a near-riot, which police quelled by firing into the crowd with live ammunition. On 12 October the Security Council passed Resolution 672, which expressed alarm and condemned 'the acts of violence committed by the Israeli security forces'. The secretary general announced a mission of inquiry to establish the facts, but the Israeli authorities did not allow the UN representatives to carry out this task.

The United States, which might have been expected to veto a resolution so critical of Israel, voted in favour of it. President Bush, addressing journalists at the White House press centre on 12 October, described the events at Temple Mount as 'very grave', called on the Israeli government to give access to the UN investigating mission, and said that if Tel Aviv did not allow the mission to undertake its task, the Israeli government would be taking responsibility for the events upon itself. Washington was well aware that its attitude to the Temple Mount killings could affect – for better or for worse – the unity of the coalition, and that a refusal to condemn Israel would have played into Iraq's hands. The White House hoped that by supporting the resolution it would clear the air and allow the main focus of

---

[1] *Jerusalem Post*, 8 July 1991

attention in the Middle East to return to the Kuwait issue.

King Hussein followed up his visit to Baghdad at the beginning of the month by holding a meeting with King Hassan of Morocco and President Chadli of Algeria. The prospects of an Arab solution now looked minimal, but they agreed that a further effort should be made. On 22 September King Hussein sent Saddam Hussein a letter reflecting their views.

'I do not want to find myself obliged to tell the rest of the world that there is no Arab solution,' he said. 'I am authorised to ask you one question: what is it that you want?' The king requested the Iraqi leader to put forward 'moderate and acceptable conditions for a settlement', and added: 'Please specify what exactly you want concerning the borders, the debts, the compensation and the facilities to reach the sea. We three promise that we will adopt your position if it is clear to us, and we will take it to [the rest of] the world, but we want you to understand clearly that the world is not going to accept the annexation of territory by force.' King Hussein pointed out that the Arab world would undermine its main argument against Israel over the occupation of the Palestinian territories if it condoned the seizure of one country's territory by another.

The reply came in the form of a visit to Amman by Tariq Aziz on 29 September. 'President Saddam Hussein appreciates your effort and wants you to continue,' Aziz said. King Hussein replied: 'I am ready to do whatever I can, but you must give us a clear position.' Baghdad did not respond.

The lack of clarity in the Iraqi position prompted the three leaders to approach President Mitterrand, who announced an initiative on 10 October. He proposed that Saddam Hussein should set a timetable for withdrawal, and that the full UN Security Council or its five permanent members should declare their commitment to an international conference to discuss all Middle East problems. This would give an implicit linkage between the Kuwait and Palestinian issues, providing Saddam Hussein with a diplomatic cover for withdrawal. The initiative was rejected by both Washington and Baghdad.

The mood in Baghdad was sombre by late September. The Ba'ath Party issued a *'ta'amim'* (a brief) to its members saying that they 'should not indulge in discussions on whether or not to withdraw. Such discussions are divisive and will only weaken the resolve of the Iraqi people. More than that, they will be taken by Iraq's enemies as a sign of weakness, and could affect the wide support for Iraq in the Arab and Third worlds.' Talk of withdrawal, it said, 'would now amount to treason'.

The economic blockade imposed by the Security Council was beginning to make itself felt. Street lights in Baghdad were dimmed to save energy, and fuel restrictions were imposed, including petrol rationing. Iraq had no shortage of oil, but there was uncertainty as to how long its stocks of imported additives needed in the refining process would last. Baghdad, like many cities around the world, was also quieter than usual because millions of people chose to stay at home watching events develop on television or listening to radio news broadcasts.

Despite the party warning against 'treason', the Iraqi leadership tried to assess how the people would react to a decision to withdraw. Six Iraqi intellectuals were invited to see Sabawi El-Takriti, the director of Iraqi intelligence and brother of Saddam Hussein. They were asked to be frank and given assurances that they would not be harassed if they differed with official views. After a hesitant start they began to speak their minds, and for three days they formed a discussion group with some of the president's advisers. Four of them said that Iraq was facing overwhelming dangers and should withdraw. On the last day they were asked to consider how Iraq could withdraw without embarrassment. The intellectuals devised a scenario in which King Hussein would be asked to propose that withdrawal should take place on the basis that Iraq's security would be guaranteed.

Not everyone in the Ba'ath Party was convinced of the inevitability of war. Some developed a theory that there would be no shooting because it would upset both the actual world order and the promised new one. A party delegation which visited Yemen in mid-October returned home with a story about a supposed meeting between a Yemeni minister and a brother of President Bush who worked for an American company which had interests in Yemen. The minister asked Bush's brother whether there would be war, and he replied: 'No war for sure.' If the story is true, the minister must have assumed that the brother of an American president must know what was in the president's mind – an idea which might hold good in a tribal society, but not necessarily in America.

President Gorbachev sent Yevgeni Primakov to Baghdad in early October to resume the search for a diplomatic solution. The Soviet leader asked Primakov to convey a strongly-worded message calling on

Iraq to withdraw its forces and restore Kuwait's sovereignty. Saddam Hussein saw Primakov on 5 October, and at first he seemed to reject Gorbachev's demands out of hand. 'You are asking me to declare Iraq's withdrawal, but I will never utter that word,' he said. 'Even if I withdrew, the Americans would not be satisfied. You have no guarantees to offer us against an American attack.'

He then made a remark which seemed to Primakov, at the time, to be little more than a repetition of his previous comment. 'Suppose we do consider "withdrawing", which everybody thinks is the magic word. What guarantees could you give?' It was later argued that these words were more significant than they seemed.

Saddam Hussein gave Primakov three questions to take back to Gorbachev: What guarantees could he offer for the security of the region? What guarantees could he offer for the security of Iraq, its people and the regime? And what guarantees could he offer for the security of the Palestinians in the Occupied Territories?

Primakov replied he had no guarantees, and that any such talk might be interpreted in the West as a trick to draw the Americans into negotiations.

When Saddam Hussein reiterated his belief that the Americans were determined to destroy Iraq, Primakov pointed out that an Iraqi withdrawal would tie President Bush's hands, leaving the US without a motive for military intervention. This drew a sceptical response from the Iraqi leader, who doubted that anyone could tie Bush's hands.

A further Soviet objective was to secure the release of the 7830 Soviet military and industrial personnel working in Iraq. Although not hostages in the sense of being held by the Iraqi authorities, they were not being granted exit visas to return home. Saddam Hussein agreed to allow them to leave at the rate of 1500 a month.

Late that night (5 October) Primakov held a meeting with Yasser Arafat, who had travelled to Baghdad at the Soviet envoy's request. Realising that Primakov was discouraged, Arafat tried to persuade him that Saddam Hussein's words 'Suppose we do consider withdrawing' were a hint of flexibility.

'That is it,' Arafat said. 'He could not have made it clearer than that.'

'Yes, but he tied it to other conditions,' Primakov replied.

'I know what he told you,' Arafat retorted. 'I am ready to waive anything he said about the security of the Palestinians.' Then he added: 'I am asking you to forget about what you were told by President Saddam Hussein on that point. The Palestinian people will not buy their security at the expense of Iraq's destruction.'

Primakov returned to Moscow the next day and submitted proposals to President Gorbachev two days later. The envoy's main idea was that Saddam Hussein should withdraw from Iraq on the basis that once his forces had left a process would begin which would resolve the Arab – Israel conflict. Primakov's attempt to find a middle line was not successful. President Bush, who held a two-hour meeting with the Soviet envoy on 19 October, said that Saddam Hussein's remarks to Primakov did not amount to a change in the Iraqi position. Bush showed little interest in the Soviet envoy's proposals, but asked him for an assessment of Saddam Hussein's personality.

Primakov subsequently described the impression Saddam Hussein made on him when they first met in 1969. 'He possessed a firmness that often turned into cruelty. A strong will, bordering on implacable stubbornness, a readiness to go charging towards his goal, regardless of obstacles, and an overblown understanding of such concepts as honour and dignity.'[2]

Bush was also briefed on the Iraqi leader's characteristics by at least five American academics of Arab origin who were considered specialists on Iraq. One of them, a professor at one of the Ivy League universities, advised the American leader to refer to the Iraqi president as 'Saddam', without adding 'Hussein'. The effect, he said, would be to belittle Saddam Hussein in the eyes of Iraqis. The same professor briefed Bush on how to anticipate Saddam Hussein's reactions to American initiatives. Bush made frequent references to 'Saddam', especially when appearing on CNN television, which was watched by millions in the Arab world. On 1 October, after delivering a speech at the United Nations, the American president told journalists that he was giving 'Saddam' every opportunity to 'save face' and to 'save his skin', comments which the academics had advised would give offence. He made similar remarks on 27 October, and on other occasions referred to Saddam Hussein as a 'horrible man', a 'liar', a 'thug' and a 'killer'. The use of offensive phrases was calculated to make it difficult for Baghdad to respond positively, and the White House got the reaction it wanted.

On his way back to Moscow, Yevgeni Primakov stopped in

[2] *Time*, 4 March 1991

London to brief Prime Minister Margaret Thatcher. She gave him a hearing and then spoke for an hour about the need to deliver a devastating blow to Iraq and destroy its entire military and perhaps industrial potential.

Primakov's own account of the conversation was as follows: 'Mrs Thatcher did not mince any words. "No one should interfere with that objective," she declared. "So you see no other option but war?" I managed to get in, with difficulty. "No," she replied.'[3]

President Gorbachev, however, was still determined to find a diplomatic solution, and sent Primakov back to the Middle East. The Soviet envoy's second meeting with Saddam Hussein, on 24 October, was attended by most of the Revolutionary Command Council. The Iraqi leader said that there were 'hawks' and 'doves' among them, but Primakov felt that all the decisions were taken by Saddam Hussein.

Primakov warned that the coalition would attack Iraqi forces unless Saddam Hussein announced a withdrawal and promptly implemented it. Saddam Hussein said such a move would be 'suicidal' for him, and continued to link any withdrawal to the departure of US forces from Saudi Arabia, the lifting of UN sanctions, an agreement to give Iraq an outlet to the sea, and a solution to the Palestinian problem.

Primakov also visited Damascus, Riyadh and Cairo and told President Mubarak that Saddam Hussein appeared to have forgotten the most important lesson of the Iran–Iraq war. During the early part of the war the United States leaned towards Baghdad because it was afraid that the Islamic revolution in Iran might pose a threat to oil supplies. A decade later, Saddam Hussein had placed himself in the same position that Iran was in then, by arousing American fears that a powerful Iraqi regime might be a threat to oil supplies.

After receiving Primakov's report of his second mission, Gorbachev declared, at a press conference on 29 October during a visit to Paris, that 'The time has come for the Arab factor to play a role.' He proposed that the Arab world should hold a further summit to seek a solution. Washington was clearly not in favour of such a move. A State Department spokesman said on 30 October that the US government had asked Moscow to explain Gorbachev's remarks.

Primakov's two meetings with Saddam Hussein in October 1990

3 *Time*, 4 March 1991

formed part of a procession of influential foreign visitors to Baghdad. Kurt Waldheim, the Austrian president, who visited the Iraqi capital on 26 August, was well-regarded in the Arab world but lacked credibility in Europe and America because of his Second World War service with German intelligence units. Former British prime minister Edward Heath, who held talks with Saddam Hussein on 21 October, appeared to favour a suggestion that Iraq should withdraw its forces to a small area of northern Kuwait, but the Americans regarded this as a 'nightmare scenario'. On 20 December Heath gave an account of his talks with Saddam Hussein to the Senate Armed Services Committee. 'For the three hours in which we talked,' the former prime minister said, 'he never once raised his voice. He spoke to me quite frankly and I talked to him very bluntly.' Heath pointed out that the international community seemed to have forgotten that the first of the UN resolutions after the invasion, number 660, included a call for Iraq and Kuwait immediately to begin intensive negotiations to resolve all their differences. Despite this, he said, no attempt had been made to bring the two sides together for discussions.

Saddam Hussein agreed to release hostages whose cases were raised by Mr Heath, including fifty-nine British workers who were constructing a building described in the British press as Saddam Hussein's presidential palace. 'This was the only occasion on which he referred to his foreign minister,' Heath said, quoting Saddam Hussein as saying to Tariq Aziz: 'I have not got a presidential palace. What is Prime Minister Heath referring to?'

Tariq Aziz replied: 'We have a guest house in the compound and there are fifty-nine workers.'

Saddam Hussein said: 'If it is in this compound where I have my offices, it is my personal responsibility that they go back,' and promised that the men would be home in four weeks. Heath told the committee that Saddam Hussein kept his promise on the hostages. 'In all the situations in which he gave his word, it has been carried out,' he said.

Heath urged Saddam Hussein to release all other hostages and said the policy of keeping them at strategic sites would achieve nothing.

Saddam Hussein: 'They are [there] to help defend my country from the Americans and the British.'

Heath told the Armed Services Committee that his reply to this remark was: 'I must tell you that as far as Mrs Thatcher is concerned, having put her citizens there would in no way stop her from bombing strategic points. She is quite as prepared to bomb the British as she is the strategic points . . . You are not helping your cause, but you are causing grave offence not only to the outside world but to your Arab friends.' He pointed out that part of the Arab tradition of hospitality was that guests were free to depart.

When Heath urged Saddam Hussein to withdraw from Kuwait, the Iraqi leader replied: 'But what guarantee will you give me that if I pull out of Kuwait, the Americans and the British won't come in with forces and be in a better position to bomb me and my country than they are at the moment; to attack us from Kuwait instead of Saudi Arabia?'

Heath suggested that the Arab League should create a buffer force along Iraq's borders with Saudi Arabia and Kuwait, and he reminded the Armed Services Committee that the Arab League had acted in a somewhat similar capacity in 1961. Heath recalled that in 1960, as a junior minister, he was responsible for the negotiations which led to Kuwait's independence. 'At the time we suspected that Iraq might then have designs on Kuwait. So we had a private arrangement with the Emir of Kuwait that if there was any sign of this, then the British would put their forces back,' he said. In July 1961 British intelligence reported that Iraqi forces were moving into Basra, and the emir requested British military help. The following month, the British withdrew and were replaced by Arab League forces.

One of Saddam Hussein's first diplomatic moves after the invasion of Kuwait was to settle Iraq's remaining differences with Iran, by making a number of concessions, including granting Iran an equal right of passage in the Shatt al-Arab waterway. This surprised the West, as the dispute over the waterway was one of the main causes of the Iran–Iraq war. The West assumed that Saddam Hussein's aim was to eliminate the need to retain substantial forces on the border with Iran, so that he could move them to Kuwait. The West also thought that the concessions to Iran would anger those in Iraq who had lost relatives in the war. Far from causing uproar, however, the move seemed to be popular. The conclusion drawn by most Western diplomats was that Saddam Hussein's hold on Iraqi public opinion was so strong that he could do as he wished. Having shown himself capable of making sudden and extraordinary policy changes when it suited him, Saddam Hussein was not believed by Western governments when he said it would be difficult for his forces to leave Kuwait.

These thoughts were clearly in Edward Heath's mind during his meeting with Saddam Hussein. After reminding the Iraqi leader of the concessions on the waterway, Heath said: 'You were applauded by your people and your military supported you. If you can do that after eight years of war against Iran, surely you can manage a situation in which you decide, with certain arrangements with Kuwait, to leave Kuwait?'

Saddam Hussein: 'Well, I still think it will be difficult.'

After Edward Heath, Saddam Hussein's next two important visitors were Yashuhiro Nakasone, the former Japanese prime minister, who was in Baghdad from 3–8 November, and Willy Brandt, former chancellor of West Germany, who was there from 7–9 November. Brandt was well placed to speak frankly because he was respected as a champion of Third World causes. After explaining the capabilities of US forces in Saudi Arabia, he said: 'The whole maxim behind the Iran–Contra affair was that the Americans were not going to allow you to get on top of Iran. Do you really think they will allow you to get on top of Middle Eastern oil, two thirds of the world's reserves?' (In fact, Arab states possess 62 per cent of the world's known reserves.)

In the early stages of the crisis, when Saddam Hussein's speeches were broadcast in the United States and Europe, questions were frequently asked about his sanity. To the secular north European mind his tendency to mix religion and politics seemed to belong to another era. The British, with their love of understatement, disliked his rhetorical style. As the home of Arab poetry, Iraq has always tended to flavour its statements with imagery and triumphalism, making it difficult to convey the meaning in English without seeming pompous.

These cultural differences tended to divert attention away from more important matters. The real issue was not Saddam Hussein's state of mind, nor his manner of self-expression, but his persistent miscalculations.

One of many Iraqi beliefs which proved incorrect was that it was in a position to manipulate the oil markets. Baghdad reasoned that Washington would hesitate to take action which might jeopardise so large a proportion of Western supplies, forgetting that the West had learned the lesson of the 1973/4 crisis. President Bush ordered that some of America's huge strategic reserves of oil should be sold, at the rate of five million barrels a day from 14 August. Saudi Arabia raised its production from 2.5 million barrels a day to 9.2 million barrels, and Venezuela went up from 2 million to 5.5 million. Instead of being able to manipulate the markets, Baghdad discovered that its oil was not needed.

Edward Heath was among many in the West who believed in Iraq's ability to cause an oil crisis. He had been advised that if Iraq's forces detonated the mines they had attached to Kuwaiti oilwells, the temperature of the entire area would rise to 60 degrees centigrade or more. The heat and smoke would create impossible working conditions in Saudi Arabia's eastern oilfields, about 160 kilometres away. In his evidence to the Armed Services Committee, Heath estimated that 40 to 50 per cent of the world's oil supplies could be stopped. 'You can imagine what that will do to the price of oil,' he said, adding that much of the West's industrial production would come to a halt.

Iraq also attached undue importance to the experience its forces had gained in the war against Iran, and underestimated the battle-readiness of US forces, which had been inactive since the fall of Saigon, apart from sideshows in Lebanon, Grenada and Panama. Iraq overlooked the fact that Western forces had been under constant training in readiness for war with the Soviet Union. The illusion that Iraq was the world's fourth-largest military power, an American invention which Baghdad accepted as a compliment, further enhanced its confidence.

Desert conditions were assumed by Baghdad and most of the Western media to give the Iraqis an advantage, as the Americans and British had had no experience of fighting in the desert since the Second World War. The reality was very different: conditions in Vietnam, with frequent cloud and rain and dense jungle, limited the effectiveness of air power, whereas desert conditions enhanced it, making most targets visible unless they were hidden underground. The Vietnamese were able to conduct their war through hit-and-run guerrilla tactics, whereas desert terrain forced the Iraqis to confront the full military strength of the Americans. The Vietnamese had the benefit of military supplies from the Soviet Union and China, while Iraq was encircled and isolated.

Iraq was not alone in overestimating its military capabilities, as the following passage from Edward Heath's evidence to the Armed Services Committee shows:

'What I would emphasise is that not only is he [Saddam Hussein] very determined, but he has made detailed and extensive preparations for a long war. He has a very large force, [much of which fought] in the eight-year war against Iran. They are used to the climate. They are used to desert warfare . . . I don't think any expert can say there will be a quiet single strike [by coalition forces] and the whole thing is over.'

The Iraqi plan was to sit tight while the Americans carried out initial bombing raids, absorb an American first strike, and then draw US forces into a war of attrition, the aim being to cause enough casualties to influence public opinion in the United States. Saddam Hussein believed strongly in the 'body bag factor', as his remarks to April Glaspie and Joseph Wilson about the American inability to accept heavy casualties showed. The Iraqis assumed that the bombing would be similar to Israeli attacks during the 1967 war, which destroyed the Egyptian air force in three hours while its planes were on the ground. Iraq took precautions by building fortified hangars, but it was not prepared for a month of sustained bombing. The weakness of the Iraqi theory about the 'body bag factor' was that it assumed that the Americans had learned nothing from the Vietnam war. President Bush, however, knew that the key was to use overwhelming force, securing victory before public opinion had time to turn sour.

9

Fatalism and Miscalculation

By early November two great armies were facing each other across the sands of Kuwait's border with Saudi Arabia, both preparing for a conflict which looked less avoidable with every day that passed.

In the first five weeks after the invasion the Americans moved 75,000 people and 65,000 tons of equipment to Saudi Arabia by air, and a further 180,000 tons by sea. General Colin Powell, Chairman of the Joint Chiefs of Staff, told the Senate Armed Services Committee that it had been the largest and most complex rapid deployment of US forces since the Second World War, equivalent to moving a city the size of Chatanooga, Tennessee some 12,000 kilometres. The initial rush was over by mid-September and the Americans felt capable of containing any Iraqi attack against Saudi Arabia, but the build-up continued at a brisk pace throughout the next two months.

A flurry of small developments in the first two weeks of November made it clear that the Americans were nearly ready for action. Officers briefing the press began to argue that keeping the troops waiting too long could be bad for morale. At a press conference on 2 November, President Bush said that even if Saddam Hussein withdrew from Kuwait arrangements would be needed to ensure the future peace and security of the region. American diplomats at the UN began sounding out other members of the Security Council to see if they would support a resolution authorising the use of force against Iraq. On 8 November President Bush announced a further increase in US deployments, including an army corps and a marine expeditionary force with an additional brigade. In a letter to Congress on 16 November he said that the coalition was deploying sufficient forces for 'an adequate offensive military option, should that be necessary'.

Baghdad realised that the US was moving from a defensive to an offensive mode. The warnings about American capabilities and intentions given to Saddam Hussein in October by foreign dignitaries had not yet brought about any policy changes; on the contrary, the Iraqi leadership was psychologically preparing itself for war rather than trying to avert it. A member of the Revolutionary Command Council said later: 'A mood of fatalism was beginning to dawn on us all.'

Yevgeni Primakov foresaw this shift of attitude several weeks earlier during his talks with Saddam Hussein. 'Doesn't it seem to you that, just like the Israelis, you have a Masada complex?' Primakov asked. Saddam Hussein nodded. 'But then your actions will, to a great extent, be determined by the logic of a doomed man?' There was no reply from the Iraqi leader.[1]

Primakov's parallel with the siege of the Jewish fortress of Masada in A.D.73, whose inhabitants committed mass suicide rather than surrender, was not entirely appropriate. One of the themes of Iraqi history and culture is the glory of martyrdom, the most recent manifestation of which was the stoicism shown by thousands of Iraqi families after the loss of their menfolk in the Iran–Iraq war. By its nature, Iraqi culture precludes an admiration of mass-suicide.

Saddam Hussein was by now fully convinced that withdrawal from Kuwait would make Iraq more rather than less vulnerable to an American attack. He disagreed with moderate Western politicians who thought that withdrawal would resolve the crisis. He reasoned that the Americans had already changed their objective once (from defending Saudi Arabia to liberating Kuwait), and were capable of changing it again. Any sign of weakness, he thought, would encourage Washington to make more demands. If he brought his troops home the Americans might insist on the destruction of Iraq's missiles, chemical weapons, and nuclear and biological research facilities.

King Hussein wrote to Saddam Hussein on 1 November asking whether there was anything the Iraqi president wanted him to do. Tariq Aziz arrived in Amman two days later with his leader's answer, but it contained no change of position: Baghdad still wanted security guarantees in exchange for withdrawal from Kuwait. As Yevgeni Primakov had already conveyed these demands to President Bush, who had dismissed them, there was little room for negotiation. King Hussein used the opportunity to urge the Iraqis to reconsider their policy of holding hostages. The Iraqis had rewarded foreign dignitaries who

---

[1] Yevgeni Primakov, in *Time* magazine, 4 March 1991

had visited Saddam Hussein by releasing some of their countries' hostages, and thought that this was having a favourable effect on Western public opinion. The numbers released after each visit varied widely. The Rev Jesse Jackson, who visited Baghdad in October, secured the release of eighty Americans. Kurt Waldheim's visit resulted in seventy-six hostages being set free; Edward Heath, thirty-three; Yashuhiro Nakasone, seventy-four; and Willy Brandt 174. However, thousands of Westerners remained in hotels or at strategic sites as Iraq's 'guests', and Baghdad's theory that their presence made bombing raids less likely failed to take account of the West's anger over the hostages' plight. Public opinion in Britain, which had more of its nationals in Iraq and Kuwait than any other Western country, appeared to favour military action against Iraq, even though this might have resulted in the deaths of many hostages.

The importance of the hostage issue was emphasised by President Mitterrand in a meeting with King Hussein on 15 November in Paris. The French president offered his analysis of the crisis: As matters stood, the Americans were not prepared to negotiate with Iraq. The US government had two declared reasons for military intervention against Iraqi forces: the annexation of Kuwait and the holding of hostages. There was a need, Mitterrand felt, to alter the framework of the crisis to make negotiations possible. That could be achieved if Iraq released all the hostages. Such a move would be regarded as the first phase of a two-stage plan to resolve the crisis. Phase two, dealing with the annexation issue, could then begin in a less emotional atmosphere.

King Hussein said he believed Baghdad would release all hostages in return for assurances from France, the Soviet Union, China, Germany and Japan that force would not be used against Iraq. After a long discussion the king modified the request, asking only that two permanent members of the Security Council (France and either the Soviet Union or China) give such an assurance.

Mitterrand replied that the United States was certain to regard any request for guarantees as setting a precondition for releasing the hostages. Washington had always insisted that they should be freed unconditionally.

On 10 November the Revolutionary Command Council in Baghdad discussed the Paris meeting and found itself divided. Some members wanted to accept Mitterrand's suggestion that the hostages be released unconditionally; others thought that such a move would deprive Iraq of its protection against air and missile attacks. The Council decided to leave the question in the president's hands. Saddam Hussein gave a statement to the Iraqi News Agency on 17 November that Iraq would be ready to release all hostages immediately in return for guarantees that it would not be attacked. Secondly, Iraq was considering the release of all hostages over a three-month period. The statement implied that the second proposal was not conditional on guarantees being given. Iraqi diplomats told British reporters that the three-month period would start on Christmas Day and end on 25 March, but made it clear that the releases would stop if Iraq were attacked.

Between mid-October and mid-November many of the coalition countries were involved in an argument over the legal basis for any action to liberate Kuwait. During the first few months of the crisis the Americans and British argued that they already had authority to act as necessary, because the Emir of Kuwait had invoked Article 51 of the United Nations Charter. The article gives any UN member the right to defend itself if attacked, and to receive help from other members, but implies that this right should be exercised only on a temporary basis until the Security Council has had time to take charge of the situation. The key words are: 'Nothing in the present charter shall impair the inherent right of individual or collective self-defence, if an armed attack occurs against a member of the United Nations, until the Security Council has taken measures necessary to maintain international peace and security.' The article would have given the Americans a legal basis for the use of force during the first few days after the invasion, had that been possible, but probably ceased to have legal validity once the Security Council began to exercise its authority. When this was pointed out by UN lawyers the Americans and British decided that a further resolution was needed to remove any doubt about the legality of an attack on Iraqi forces in Kuwait. James Baker began a tour of the Middle East on 4 November to discuss a draft resolution with coalition countries. One of his aims was to ensure that moderate Arab states were still prepared to participate in a coalition attack, following reports in Washington that some were having doubts. Syria and Morocco had declared that the role of their forces serving with the coalition was limited to the defence of Saudi Arabia. Baker discovered, however, that the moderates were not only willing to take part but anxious that the action should begin as soon as possible.

President Bush had arranged to visit Europe and the Middle East and spend the Thanksgiving holiday with the troops in Saudi Arabia. King Hussein asked the American leader to see him during the European part of the tour, and suggested a meeting in Paris. Bush initially accepted and made an appointment for 17 November, then changed his mind. The American leader felt that the king was behaving like a negotiator on behalf of Saddam Hussein, and feared that such a meeting could give a confusing impression of US intentions. On 16 November Bush sent the king a message of apology.

In the Gulf the American leader came under pressure from King Fahd and Sheikh Jaber to begin the offensive without delay. The two Arab leaders argued that time was running short, because two holy days, followed by a holy month, were approaching. They feared that Muslim concerns over the presence of US forces would be greatly increased if there were any fighting during that period. The first sensitive date was the 27th of Rajab in the Hijree calendar, the night the Prophet was raised to Heaven, corresponding with the beginning of February. The second was a month later, the 15th of Shaa'ben, a night for atonement and forgiveness. March would be taken up by Ramadan, and after that there would be preparations for the Haj. At the same time, US commanders were aware of a risk that Saudi imams would disclose the fact that US troops were secretly carrying out Christian religious ceremonies in their camps. The Thanksgiving service attended by President Bush had to be held on a ship offshore. There was also a ticklish moment in Saudi – US relations when officials monitoring the unloading of American stores at Dhahran discovered a shipment of Bibles. The officials impounded them in a warehouse, but after communications with the US embassy in Riyadh the shipment was released on condition that the Bibles were confined strictly to US forces.

On 22 November, during his Thanksgiving visit to Saudi Arabia, President Bush asked the Emir of Kuwait: 'When do you want us to go to war?' The emir replied: 'This minute, before this hour.' The US leader did not tell King Fahd or the emir the date he had in mind, but replied in vague terms. 'Rest assured, Your Majesty, we are going to fight, and we are going to fight quite soon.' He said that Saddam Hussein had made the conflict 'a question of him or me', and added: 'The future of my presidency and my place in history depends on the outcome.'

King Fahd told him: 'People are uneasy. There is talk that

America will not fight in the end and will rely on economic sanctions.' Bush replied: 'Sanctions alone will not make him obey the Security Council resolutions, and would allow him to keep his military power. We are going to use force.'

Another leader who was keen to press ahead was President Assad of Syria, who had sent two infantry brigades and one armoured brigade, totalling between 15 and 17,000 men, to join the coalition forces in Saudi Arabia. Unlike other Arab members of the coalition, Syria felt no need of a United Nations mandate, having its own quarrel with Baghdad to pursue. Assad made two visits to Saudi Arabia and told King Fahd: 'Our [Arab] alliance is stronger than you might imagine. Don't forget that it was the same alliance which won the 1973 war against Israel.' Assad felt that this gave the alliance credibility with the Arab masses, although in reality the two situations were not comparable.

On 29 November the United Nations Security Council passed Resolution 678 authorising the use of force, which settled arguments within the coalition over the validity of any action. A number of Iraqi and other Arab experts argued, however, that Resolution 678 was itself contrary to the UN Charter. After the war Adnan Pachacchi, a former Iraqi foreign minister who was Iraq's ambassador to the UN in the 1960s, wrote a paper asserting that the basis of Resolution 678 was unsound. He recalled that the Security Council's first move had been Resolution 660, which declared that the invasion of Kuwait was a breach of international peace and security within the meaning of articles 39 and 40 of the charter, and called on Iraq to withdraw immediately and unconditionally its forces to the positions they had held on 1 August 1990. Four days later, on 6 August, the Security Council, acting under Article 41 of the charter, decided in Resolution 661 to impose economic sanctions on Iraq. These sanctions were further extended and reinforced in resolutions 665 and 670, passed on 25 August and 13 September, imposing a maritime and air blockade.

Pachacchi continued:

> The next phase of United Nations action envisaged in the charter would have been the use of force, in accordance with Article 42, which states clearly that if the Security Council considers that the measures taken in accordance with Article 41 proved to be inadequate, then the Security Council may take whatever measures are necessary, including the use of force. In other words . . . force may be used only after the

Security Council had determined that the sanctions . . . were inadequate to achieve its purpose. Such a determination had never taken place, neither explicitly nor implicitly. Resolution 678 mentions nothing about the inadequacy of sanctions; it refers merely to Iraq's refusal to withdraw.

Pachacchi's view was supported by many Arab lawyers, including Dr Aisha Rateb, an Egyptian expert on the United Nations and a former cabinet minister under presidents Sadat and Mubarak. The paper was not submitted to the Iraqi government, because Pachacchi is an opponent of the regime and lives in the United Arab Emirates.

The fact that UN rules were not followed to the letter was also pointed out by Señor Pérez de Cuéllar, the UN Secretary General. In a report on the work of the UN written after the war, he said:

> Another important aspect is that the enforcement action was not carried out exactly in the form foreseen by articles 42 et sequentia of Chapter VII. Instead, the [Security] Council authorised the use of force on a national and coalition basis. In the circumstances and given the costs imposed and capabilities demanded by modern warfare, the arrangement seemed unavoidable. However, the experience of operations in the Gulf suggests the need for a collective reflection on questions relating to the future use of the powers vested in the Security Council under Chapter VII.

Many experts in international law saw this as another way of saying that the legal basis for 'Desert Storm' was unsound, but that in practical terms the Security Council arrangement was unavoidable.

In Baghdad the Revolutionary Command Council spent two days discussing Resolution 678, and invited legal experts to give their views. Saddam Hussein urged them to speak freely and declared the discussion to be '*adlieh*', meaning that no one would be taken to task for expressing views contrary to RCC policies. Dr Sa'adoun Hammadi, deputy prime minister, urged that Iraq should take its objections to Resolution 678 to the International Court of Justice, but this was rejected on the grounds that there was no chance of success. Some of the invited experts pointed out that in 1985 Nicaragua began an action at the International Court of Justice over America's support for the Contra rebels, but the United States refused to acknowledge the court's jurisdiction over such matters.

Resolution 678 gave the Iraqis six weeks to comply with all previous resolutions from 660 onwards. The period was a compromise between American demands for a one-month deadline and the Soviet view that two months should be allowed. Roland Dumas, the French foreign minister, felt that full use should be made of this period to find a solution. 'The world cannot just keep silent for six weeks waiting for the explosion,' he said. After the resolution had been passed, on the night of 29 November, Dumas attended a dinner in New York at the home of Pierre-Louis Blanc, the French ambassador to the UN. The discussion centred on a French idea that the European Community should try to promote a solution, with help from Señor Pérez de Cuéllar. During the dinner the secretary general phoned Dumas and told him that this idea had already been overtaken by events: President Bush had proposed that Tariq Aziz should travel to Washington for talks at the White House, while James Baker went to Baghdad to see Saddam Hussein. Dumas was furious, claiming that the Americans were determined to monopolise the management of the crisis and did not want other countries to use their good offices.

The Iraqis were unsure what to make of Bush's proposal. Some members of the RCC suspected a trap, believing that Bush was determined to crush Iraq's military power. That belief had been reinforced by a statement made by Henry Kissinger to the Senate Armed Services Committee on 28 November, in which he said: 'Any solution to the crisis must provide for a reduction of Iraq's offensive capability which now overshadows its neighbours. Without addressing this fundamental imbalance, a solution will only postpone, and probably exacerbate, an eventual resolution of Gulf instability.' Although Kissinger was not a member of the Bush administration, his views were seen as a guide to American thinking. It was assumed that the opinions of Bush and Baker would be somewhat harder than those of Kissinger.

A mini-summit was held in Baghdad on 4 December, attended by King Hussein, Yasser Arafat, Salem El-Bid (vice president of Yemen) and Saddam Hussein. The following day it was announced that Iraq had accepted Bush's offer of talks and would respond by releasing all hostages in time to return home for Christmas. The Iraqi announcement began with a verse from the Koran which President Sadat had used in 1977 when preparing Egyptian public opinion for his visit to Jerusalem: 'And if they lean to peace, go with it and depend on Allah.'

A message was sent to President Mitterrand that the first phase of his plan for defusing the crisis had been implemented. The Elysée Palace replied that Mitterrand's Concorde was ready to fly him to Iraq as soon as he saw a chance of implementing the second phase (talks on Iraq's withdrawal from Kuwait).

Saddam Hussein accepted a suggestion from other members of the RCC for a way of creating a better atmosphere for the second phase. The Iraqis knew that Saddam Hussein's proposal of 12 August that the Kuwait issue should be linked to other Middle East problems was certain to be an obstacle to any negotiations. It was agreed that Iraq would say that this was a political rather than a chronological link. In other words, it did not mean that the various issues had to be settled at the same time. The Iraqis would be satisfied with an understanding that after an Iraqi withdrawal from Kuwait the other matters would be discussed at an international conference.

King Hussein's role throughout this period was the subject of much comment in the West. Those who favoured military action against Iraq tended to see the king as at best a nuisance and at worst a collaborator with Saddam Hussein. Those who wanted to avert a fight thought he was the only Arab head of state still working effectively to find a solution. Overall, there was a feeling of disappointment in Washington and London that an Arab leader who had been regarded as a friend of the West now appeared to be closer to Saddam Hussein. In the past the king's political profile had been much higher than that of his country, but a series of events had weakened his position.

For several years before the mid-1970s King Hussein was probably the Arab world's most active contact with American, British and French leaders. The position changed some time after the 1973 Arab – Israel war, because of President Sadat's decision to move clearly into the Western camp. Sadat and later President Mubarak established links with Western countries comparable with those of King Hussein.

Another of King Hussein's roles was weakened by the rapprochement between Cairo and Tel Aviv. Until 1977 the king was the only Arab leader who kept in regular touch with the Israelis, although his talks had to be carried out secretly. After Sadat's visit to Jerusalem in 1977 and the Camp David accords in 1978, the Egyptian and Israeli leaderships were in constant and relatively open contact.

In the early 1970s the king had been regarded as an important figure in any discussion of the Palestinian problem, but the Palestinians – both east and west of the Jordan River – gradually turned their backs on him. His position was further weakened by Ariel Sharon's proposal that all Palestinians living in Israel should be moved into Jordan. The influx of Jews from the Soviet Union into Israel added a further dimension to his problems by arousing fears that many of the newcomers would be settled in the Occupied Territories.

Another source of anxiety was that King Hussein had put much time and effort into campaigning for Egypt to be accepted back into the Arab fold, which had not helped his own position or that of his country. He had hoped that the Arab Co-operation Council, of which he was the original proponent, would bring some political benefits, but the Kuwait crisis put paid to that prospect.

From the mid-1980s onwards Jordan was beset by economic difficulties. The slump in oil prices cut the remittances sent home by Jordanian workers in Gulf states, and Saudi Arabia and the Gulf states ignored Jordan's requests for assistance. Jordan's water shortage was aggravated by Israel's use of a large proportion of the existing supply. The United Nations sanctions against Iraq aggravated Jordan's economic problems, because of its heavy dependence on trade with Iraq.

All these matters impelled the king to attempt to recover lost ground by playing an important role in the Kuwait crisis, but hard as he tried, success always eluded him.

Apart from the king and Yasser Arafat, most Arab leaders had by now reduced their peacemaking efforts. President Chadli of Algeria tried to arrange a meeting between Saddam Hussein and King Fahd, but he was persuaded by Saudi Arabia to postpone the plan, on the grounds that the time was 'not appropriate'.

President Mubarak and Saddam Hussein exchanged thirty-eight verbal messages and typed or handwritten letters between August and the end of December. The deteriorating tone of the correspondence reflected the progression of the crisis.

On 19 August, nine days after the Cairo summit, Mubarak called Nabil Nejm el-Takriti, the Iraqi ambassador, and asked him to convey three points to Saddam Hussein. The points were dictated over the telephone to the ambassador, who personally took them to Baghdad.

One: The president [Mubarak] wants him to reconsider, to find a way out of the crisis. Two: The president is ready to undertake any contacts or initiatives which might find a way out for Iraq. Three: The president is ready to do anything which would avoid spilling Arab blood.

Saddam Hussein replied on 23 August with a message accusing President Mubarak of being the cause of the situation, in that he had agreed to work closely with the Americans. He added that the Egyptian leader should bear responsibility for any bloodshed.

The same day Mubarak again called the Iraqi ambassador and told him to take a further message to Baghdad. After seeing Saddam Hussein's remarks he had decided to drop oral messages and reply in writing. Mubarak said that Egyptian forces were sent to Saudi Arabia at the request of Riyadh and no other party, and Cairo did not bow to pressure from anybody. 'I want you to declare right now that you are ready to withdraw and that will change everything,' he said.

The correspondence paused for several weeks, then resumed on 22 November with a further appeal by Mubarak, making five points:

a) Please try to withdraw and then we will find something to save your face; b) Don't depend on opposition to Bush inside the United States which you see in the newspapers; c) The dangers are huge and you must take responsibility; d) We notice that Radio Baghdad is insulting us in all its broadcasts. All right, go ahead, but please listen to the voice of reason; e) I think you are not seeing the complete picture and that those around you are not giving you enough information about the gravity of the situation.

Mubarak appeared not to realise that his reference to 'saving face' would offend Saddam Hussein, making the offer futile.

Saddam Hussein replied with an oral message repeating his argument that responsibility would fall on Mubarak.

On 26 November, after seeing President Bush in Cairo, Mubarak wrote to Saddam Hussein again, telling him that Bush had insisted more than ever on the need for an Iraqi withdrawal and the return of the legitimate Kuwaiti government. 'Talking to President Bush, I know that they are determined on military action, and with the volume and size of American forces there, the firepower is more than we can imagine,' he said, predicting that any confrontation would result in a massacre. 'Please try to think realistically and try to re-evaluate the facts.'

There was no answer from Baghdad until 19 December, when Saddam Hussein made further allegations. 'You have sacrificed the Arab nation and you do not mind if we are all slaughtered. I don't know what you are gaining from it; only a few dollars.' He said that the Americans would not have dared to land in Saudi Arabia if Riyadh had not been encouraged by other states to accept them. 'You are allowing yourself to be sold to the imperialist powers.' The Iraqi leader expressed anger over Mubarak's move in telling the Kuwaitis, Americans and others that Baghdad was bluffing, after the Saddam Hussein – Mubarak meeting in Baghdad on 24 July. 'I did not authorise you to do that and, even if you felt from me that I was only bluffing, it was not your right to assure the others. Anyhow, you misunderstood . . . everybody in the world understood me correctly except you. I wonder why? Was it lack of intellect or bad faith?' After returning from the Baghdad meeting, Mubarak had described the situation as a summer cloud which would pass. Saddam Hussein said he was astonished at this, because it was clear at the time that the crisis was leading to war. He accused Mubarak of minimising and devaluing the issues, and concluded by saying: 'Don't write to me any more. I don't want any contact with you.'

Mubarak replied on 29 December that he was astonished that Saddam Hussein wanted to end the correspondence. 'But still I insist that I will write . . . I wish your letter had confined itself to the rules of a real dialogue based on frankness . . . I notice that you are trying to score points.' Dealing with the row over the 24 July meeting, he rejected Saddam Hussein's version of what was said and pointed out that he would not have reassured Kuwait about Iraq's intentions if he had known that Iraq was thinking of an invasion. Mubarak also denied using the word 'bluffing' with the Kuwaitis. As for the row over his phrase 'a summer cloud', he said: 'What did you expect me to say? Did you expect me to beat the drums of war? I was trying to be a mediator.'

Saddam Hussein's letter of 19 December had accused Mubarak of blocking efforts at the Cairo summit to find an Arab solution. Mubarak replied: 'I am astonished that you say that, because I did all I could to persuade you [the Iraqis] to take a reasonable position.'

Mubarak said he thought Saddam Hussein was aiming for negotiations with the United States. 'This is what you want, and you are not ready to negotiate with anybody else. With us you are harsh and insulting and with them you are nice and soft. You told them that you are ready to agree with them on the production of oil, the prices and everything. And you accuse me of being a lackey for the Americans?'

The Iraqi leader had been hoping for a meeting with King Fahd, believing that they could still settle the dispute together, but Washington advised Riyadh against it. Saddam Hussein mentioned this in his 19 December letter, prompting Mubarak to reply: 'We would welcome such a dialogue, but don't you think that we should have the right atmosphere? More than that, you must remember that Saudi Arabia cannot talk on behalf of Kuwait.'

Saddam Hussein had accused Mubarak in the same letter of being two-faced, to which Mubarak replied: 'I know that you are facing a very difficult situation, but I wonder how you can allow yourself to direct unfair accusations against me, turning facts upside down. This is not the language of dialogue, and for my part I don't think I am going to have any dialogue with you.'

A reply came back from Baghdad on 1 January 1991: 'In spite of all the differences . . . I cannot imagine a sincere Arab nationalist standing in the same line as the Americans and Israelis. That is the end of it.' And the correspondence ended.

10

The Last Hour

After months of tension the mood in many capitals lightened in early December, reflecting hopes that President Bush's offer of talks and the Iraqi decision to release the hostages might lead to a peaceful solution. The Iraqis refused permission for Western aircraft to land in Baghdad, but allowed Western governments to charter Iraqi planes. As a result it was Iraqi airliners which took the hostages home, helping to create a less negative impression of the Iraqi government. Scenes of rejoicing at Western airports as returning hostages greeted their families after months of separation provided television stations with an alternative to reports about the military build-up.

The original cause of the crisis was no nearer to resolution, but, for a time, it received less attention. The West turned a blind eye to what some lawyers saw as a breach of the UN ban against air links with Iraq. The Kuwaiti people, with the possible exception of the estimated 100,000 citizens still living in Kuwait, did not share the increased optimism. They feared that any negotiated solution would result in something less than an unconditional Iraqi withdrawal from their country. When Sheikh Jaber was first told of President Bush's offer of talks with Baghdad, he is said to have wept. The Saudis did not hide their concern that, having given the coalition their full backing, they were in danger of being let down at the last moment. From the Saudi government's viewpoint, a peaceful compromise would leave the kingdom in a difficult and embarrassing muddle. The sequence of international events – Gorbachev's search for a diplomatic solution, Primakov's two visits to Baghdad in October, Bush's offer of talks and Baghdad's response on the hostages – put the Riyadh leadership into a state of nerves. Their worries were shared by Cairo, though not as strongly.

When President Bush announced his proposal that James Baker should visit Saddam Hussein and that Tariq Aziz should go to Washington, there appeared to be no problem over timing. Bush said at a press conference on 29 November: 'Secretary Baker will be ready to go to Baghdad any time from 15 December till 15 January.' Through diplomatic channels, the Americans then proposed a series of dates, the last of which was in the first week of January. Whenever the Iraqis rejected a date, the Americans proposed another. In all, seventeen dates were proposed.

The Iraqis were not worried about the timing of Tariq Aziz's trip to Washington, as they assumed it would be merely a formality, with no real negotiations. Baker's visit was more sensitive from their point of view. There was a fear that the secretary of state would arrive in Baghdad to deliver an ultimatum. Baghdad decided to arrange the Aziz–Bush meeting first and to delay Baker's visit until 12 January, three days before the deadline set by Resolution 678.

The Americans were not prepared to accept this arrangement. The rejection of all their seventeen dates and the Iraqi counter-proposal of 12 January was seen by the US as evidence of bad faith. It seemed likely to the Americans that if Baker went to Baghdad so close to the deadline, the Iraqis would offer him substantial concessions, designed to open a negotiating process which might last for weeks. The Americans suspected that the Iraqis would try to spin out any talks until the holy season started. By then Iraq would be in a stronger position, because Arab members of the coalition would be seriously embarrassed by any fighting during Ramadan, and the hotter weather would put US troops at a disadvantage. Three weeks later (at a press conference on 9 January), James Baker described the Iraqi insistence on a 12 January meeting as 'an obvious effort to avoid the deadline of 15 January'.

The Americans insisted that the two visits should be co-ordinated and that the Iraqis should accept one of the dates they had been offered. When Baghdad refused, the negotiations reached a stalemate. Angered by Iraq's apparent intransigence, the Americans adopted a tougher tone and increased their demands. Apart from Iraq's unconditional withdrawal from Kuwait, the US now also called for the elimination of Iraq's missile and nuclear facilities and said that Kuwait should be compensated for losses and damage. On 21 December President Bush issued a statement saying that the release of the hostages had relieved him of a heavy moral burden and gave him a free hand to act as necessary.

Elements of the Iraqi leadership began to suspect that the French proposal that Iraq should release the hostages had been a ruse to persuade Baghdad to give up its human shield. Some Arab capitals had been receiving reports from Morocco of a shift in French policy. The royal court in Rabat was well placed to understand the French mind, because close links with Paris had continued after the colonial era. Up to this point France had been better disposed towards Iraq than any other Western member of the coalition, but this started to change after 18 November when George Bush visited President Mitterrand in Paris. It appeared after that meeting that Paris had decided to adopt an unambiguous position at the centre of the coalition, instead of trying to keep a foot in both camps.

In early January 1991 Moroccan sources gave further details of the French position. Divisions between Mitterrand's civilian and military advisers had been resolved in favour of the military. Until then, civilian advisers had wanted Paris to keep a certain distance from Washington, for commercial reasons, while the generals preferred full co-operation with the United States. The French president had accepted the advice of the military advisers for two main reasons. He was now certain that war was imminent, and believed that France's role in Middle East affairs after the war would be strengthened if it played an important role in the fighting. Secondly, countries which helped in the liberation of Kuwait could expect contracts for reconstruction and rearmament after the war. American and British companies were already receiving large contracts from the Kuwaiti government-in-exile before the fighting had even begun, while France was having less success (although the largest deal secured by French companies at this stage, the renovation of Kuwaiti television, was worth 150 million French francs).

Moroccan sources quoted instructions given to Admiral Jacques Lanscade, Chef de l'Etat-Major du President. The admiral was to tell his American liaison officer that 'the position of France in the imminent Gulf confrontation should be considered exactly as that of England'. Jean-Louis Bianco, minister of social affairs and a close confidant of Mitterrand, used the same phrase when speaking to an Asian ambassador.

Little of this information was available to Baghdad when the Revolutionary Command Council discussed Mitterrand's role in persuading Iraq to release the hostages. The Council came to no conclusion as to whether the French president had been a party to a plot to deceive Iraq over the hostages or had acted in good faith. One member of the RCC thought that King Hussein might have been a conspirator in the supposed plot, but Saddam Hussein defended him. If there had been any deception, he declared, the king was as much a victim as the Iraqis.

The Iraqi leader said he did not regret releasing the hostages, because they had proved an additional burden and a lever for Western political pressure. He felt the gesture had demonstrated Iraq's good intentions to world public opinion, and did not significantly increase the risk of an American attack. He reasoned that as Bush would have to risk the lives of thousands of US soldiers on the battlefield, the danger that hostages might be killed by US bombing raids would make little difference to his course of action.

In late December, with no solution in sight to the stalemate between Washington and Baghdad over dates, President Gorbachev decided to intervene. Igor Belousov, Deputy Chairman of the Council of Ministers, was sent to Baghdad to try to persuade Saddam Hussein to agree to a meeting between American and Iraqi representatives in Geneva. As a result of this preparation, the Iraqis accepted immediately when the Americans proposed such a meeting.

Before announcing this proposal the Americans, aware of the nervous Arab reaction to the earlier Bush initiative, contacted governments participating in the coalition. In some cases, however, this was done only fifteen to thirty minutes before the announcement. The Egyptian government was told that the meeting would probably not last more than half an hour and that the aim was to show that the Americans had done everything possible to find a solution.

On Wednesday 9 January Baker and Aziz faced each other across a table, each supported by five or six officials and experts. The American Secretary of State handed over a letter from President Bush to President Saddam Hussein. Tariq Aziz asked if he could read it and Baker said: 'By all means.' It was addressed to 'His Excellency Saddam Hussein, President of the Republic of Iraq', and began:

Mr President,
    We stand today at the brink of a war between Iraq and the world. This is a war that began with your invasion of Kuwait; this is a war that can be ended only by Iraq's full and unconditional compliance with UN Security Council Resolution 678.

The letter went on to say that if Baghdad complied with the resolution,

Iraq could rejoin the international community and the Iraqi military establishment would escape destruction:

> But unless you withdraw completely and without condition, you will lose more than Kuwait. What is at issue here is not the future of Kuwait – it will be free; its government will be restored – but rather the future of Iraq. This choice is yours to make.

The US president pointed out that the UN Security Council had passed twelve resolutions on the invasion, twenty-eight countries were taking part in the coalition, and more than 100 governments were complying with UN sanctions against Iraq. 'All [these] highlight the fact that it is not Iraq against the United States, but Iraq against the world.'

The letter ran to ten paragraphs, and concluded:

> I write this letter not to threaten but to inform. I do so with no sense of satisfaction, for the people of the United States have no quarrel with the people of Iraq. Mr President, UN Security Council Resolution 678 establishes the period before January 15 of this year as a 'pause of good will' so that this crisis may end without further violence. Whether this pause is used as intended or merely becomes a prelude to further violence is in your hands, and yours alone. I hope you weigh your choice carefully and choose wisely, for much will depend on it.
>
> George Bush

Tariq Aziz read the letter slowly and carefully, put it back in its envelope, and passed it back across the table. 'I can't deliver to my president a letter written in a way which is not fit to be directed to heads of state,' he said.

Baker made some preliminary remarks. 'I want to make several points clear. I am not here to negotiate the Security Council resolutions . . . it is not in my authority to discuss or negotiate them.' He asked Tariq Aziz whether he wanted to reply but the Iraqi foreign minister declined: 'No, I prefer to listen to you to the end.'

Baker said that Bush's initiative of 30 November was prompted by a wish to allow all concerned to think about the gravity of the situation. 'Unfortunately you were not able to take that chance. I must confess this looks very strange to us. We gave you seventeen days to choose from and . . . no date was good for your president to see me. Had you been really busy in that period I would have understood it.' Baker said he was astonished that Saddam Hussein had found time to see figures from the past and not the American Secretary of State. 'I want you to know that there is a great Arab and international alliance against you and that you should take it seriously.'

Tariq Aziz interjected: 'Don't talk about an Arab alliance, because you know how that Arab alliance was formed.'

Baker replied that Iraq had set itself against its brother Arabs, adding 'if you call them your brothers'.

Aziz: 'We are sure of our real brothers.'

Baker said Iraq had invaded and lied to its brothers. He said his main aim was to tell Tariq Aziz what Iraq was facing. After setting out an inventory of the coalition's units and weapons he said that Iraq had 'no idea' of the level of technology which would be used. The firepower and the swiftness of the battle would be on a scale that no army had ever experienced. He added: 'We know that you have a vast stock of chemical weapons either in missiles or as artillery shells. Our sincere advice to you is not to even think of using them. If you do, or if we feel that you did, then our reply will be unrestrained. I hope I am understood well.'

Aziz replied: 'I hope we did not come here to exchange threats.' He understood that Baker was hinting at the use of tactical nuclear weapons.

Baker turned to another point: 'I am sorry to tell you that if . . . the battle I am trying to describe happens . . . your government will not be the government which will decide the future of Iraq.'

The Iraqi delegation, which included Barzan El-Takriti, a younger half-brother of Saddam Hussein, was startled by this prediction. Some of the group expected Aziz to walk out, but instead he said: 'I prefer to remember the secretary of state who I used to know.' Baker and Aziz had met several times before the crisis, and their discussions had been amicable.

Aziz said that the military picture which Baker had set out was similar to assessments made by Iraq. 'We see it and we understand it,' he added. This appeared to surprise some of the Americans, who probably assumed that the Iraqis did not know what they were facing. The Iraqi foreign minister then spoke at length, recalling Iraq's defence of the Arab world against the Iranian revolution, and its historical claims to Kuwait. 'Kuwait was always part of Iraq, and never, in all the history of Iraq, has any Iraqi government agreed to surrender it,' he said.

Replying to Baker's remark that after the war the existing government in Baghdad would not decide Iraq's future, Aziz said: 'Let me tell you that your friends in the Arab world will be the ones with no future. Their people will rise up against them; you will be practically killing your friends, not killing us.'

Baker said: 'Those people were your friends,' and repeated the claim that Saddam Hussein had lied to President Mubarak when the Iraqi and Egyptian leaders met on 24 July, by saying that the purpose of Iraqi forces on the Iraq–Kuwait frontier was only to frighten Kuwait. Aziz replied: 'Let me put the record straight,' and expressed the Iraqi version that Saddam Hussein had said there would be no use of force against Kuwait before a meeting between the Kuwaiti crown prince and the Iraqi vice president. He continued: 'We can fight a battle with you and we can come out politically victorious, as Nasser did in 1956.'

Baker invited a member of his delegation, Dennis Ross, an expert on the Suez crisis, to reply to Aziz's remark. When Ross had finished Aziz said: 'I don't think it is the right of anybody to scare us with [threats of] war,' and added: 'We have given our lives to a cause and we have not changed our minds.'

Baker said: 'You have not changed your mind, but is it your right to threaten others?' reminding Aziz of Saddam Hussein's remark about 'burning half of Israel' with chemical weapons.

'That was said in self-defence,' Aziz said.

'No, I don't think so,' Baker replied.

Aziz realised with surprise that Baker was not aware of Iraq's explanation that Saddam Hussein's speech had been a reply to an implied Israeli threat to attack Iraq with nuclear weapons. He pointed out that Saddam Hussein had proposed that the Middle East should be free of nuclear and biological weapons.

These remarks represent only a small fraction of the discussions, which lasted the whole day, apart from a break of one hour in the morning and another recess at about 4 p.m. Most of the rest was repetition. Neither side went to the meeting with fresh proposals or ideas.

American reports said that Baker phoned President Bush three times during the day. According to the management of the InterContinental Hotel in Geneva, Aziz made no international phone calls, and other sources confirm that the foreign minister did not once call Saddam Hussein. The Iraqi view was that nothing new had emerged; they suspected that the whole event had been staged to strengthen international public support for US action by showing that no diplomatic stone had been left unturned.

The unexpectedly long time the talks were taking aroused speculation in the West that there might be a breakthrough, while tension rose in Gulf capitals, especially when it was announced, at about 7.30 p.m. Geneva time, that a joint press conference would be held. This proved to be a misunderstanding; instead of appearing together the two men spoke separately, Baker taking the stand first while Aziz sat in his hotel suite watching him on CNN. It was not until Baker's opening remarks, which included the words 'I am sorry to say . . .' that the world knew the meeting had been a failure.

Baker said he had heard nothing that suggested any Iraqi flexibility on complying with the UN resolutions, and spoke of 'devastating consequences for Iraq' if there was no withdrawal from Kuwait.

Asked if there had been a failure of diplomacy, he replied: 'There has been more diplomacy exercised in this crisis than in almost any other I can think of. I would ask you not to equate diplomacy and appeasement. We made that mistake in the 1930s. At least for our part, we don't intend to make it again.'

Baker said he had requested and received assurances that Joseph Wilson, the American chargé d'affaires in Baghdad, and the four other American diplomats, would be allowed to leave Baghdad that Saturday, 12 January. The Secretary of State left the press conference, and Tariq Aziz took the stand after a short interval.

Aziz said that if the American administration changed its position and worked with Iraq and others in the region to bring about a 'comprehensive, lasting, just peace', Iraq would be glad to participate. Discussing the 'new world order', Aziz said that Iraq 'would love to be partners in that order, but that order has to be implemented justly and . . . not in a selective manner'.

The Iraqi foreign minister was asked why he refused to accept Bush's letter. 'The reason is that the language in this letter is not compatible with the language that should be used in correspondence between heads of state,' he said. 'Politeness does not contradict with substance.'

Some of the journalists' questions dealt with Saddam Hussein's proposal of 12 August that an international conference should be held on all Middle East problems. The main reasons for the West's rejection of the proposal had been that it was not clearly worded and that it was seen as a ploy to divide the coalition. A further point was that the proposal contained no explicit offer to leave Kuwait even if such a conference were accepted. Tariq Aziz was asked whether Iraq would make such an offer. He said: 'I did not put it in that way. I told the secretary [of state] that if you [the Americans] are ready to respect and implement international legality [and] the principles of justice and fairness as far as all the issues in the region are concerned, you will find us very co-operative.'

Another question was: 'Mr Foreign Minister, if the war starts, will you attack Israel?' Aziz replied: 'Yes, absolutely yes.'

The two press conferences lasted three hours. Tariq Aziz had originally planned to stay the night in Geneva, but instead he asked Barzan el-Takriti to accompany him to Baghdad, in the hope that they could report to Saddam Hussein without delay. They arrived to find that the Iraqi president had gone to the front. Saddam Hussein spent much of the next day (10 January) acting as host to Kenneth Kaunda, President of Zambia, who was visiting Iraq. The two presidents were personal friends, and it was Kaunda who had persuaded Saddam Hussein to release Daphne Parish, an English nurse who had been imprisoned in March 1990 for assisting Farzad Bazoft, the *Observer* journalist who was executed on spying charges. Aziz and el-Takriti did not have an opportunity to make their report until the next day. Saddam Hussein took it quietly. 'It is what I expected,' he said.

The following day, Saturday 12 January, President Bush asked Señor Pérez de Cuéllar to accompany him to Camp David. Later the president asked the UN Secretary General to undertake an immediate mission to Baghdad. Pérez de Cuéllar said it was too late, but Bush pressed him to go. The secretary general arrived in Baghdad the next day, and spoke with Saddam Hussein, but had to leave later the same day for Europe. He said that he was not carrying a message or acting as an envoy, but had come to see if there was any way he could help avert a confrontation.

According to the Iraqi transcript of the meeting, Pérez de Cuéllar said that Saddam Hussein had performed 'a great service to the Palestine issue', by putting the future of the Palestinians on the international agenda. 'Even Mr Bush, when I saw him on Saturday, admitted the urgent need for tackling the crisis of Palestine.' He continued in a highly conciliatory tone: 'The scope of UN action has substantially expanded through the benefits reaped from Your Excellency's initiative,' he said, apparently referring to Saddam Hussein's proposal of 12 August. 'I want to be in a position to go back with something that we could build upon in order to reduce tension and deny the warmongers their opportunity.'

Concerning the 12 August proposal, Saddam Hussein said: 'We did not think it would be accepted in full. However, we never thought it would be turned down without being looked into. The president of the US turned down the initiative while he was on a plane two hours after it was announced, and without looking into it.'

Saddam Hussein used a map to explain Iraq's claim that Kuwait had expanded its territory at Iraq's expense. He pointed out that Mitllah (now a town inside Kuwait) had been a border crossing point before Kuwait expanded. Yasser Arafat worked in Kuwait as an engineer in the 1950s, and his passport contained a stamp showing that he had crossed the border at Mitllah. Saddam Hussein added that at the beginning of the twentieth century, when Kuwait was a new British protectorate but the rest of the region was still under the Ottoman empire, the Ottoman Parliament defined the protectorate as being the area within Kuwait's city walls.

'We have documents to prove all we are saying, so when someone says, "Let Iraq withdraw," the question is: "Where to?"' Pérez de Cuéllar replied: 'If you have such a good case, you can go to the International Court of Justice.'

Pérez de Cuéllar disclaimed personal responsibility for the UN resolutions on the invasion: 'These were not my decisions but the resolutions of the Security Council.' Saddam Hussein replied: 'These are American resolutions; this is an American age.'

As the conversation wound up, the secretary general said he needed something to take back to give a prospect of peace. Saddam Hussein replied: 'In each point we have discussed, you are getting something.' Pérez de Cuéllar said he would think about it carefully, but added: 'I am afraid that what I will take back with me might not be considered tangible enough to curb the threat imposed on us, like a sword brandished, not only at my head, but at the head of the world.' In reality, he was leaving Baghdad empty-handed.

The 15 January deadline passed without incident. That night, Mudar Badran, prime minister of Jordan, offered a bet of US$100 that no fighting would take place. Yasser Arafat was in contact with

Giulio Andreotti, the Italian prime minister, trying to persuade him to go to Baghdad and promising to join him there the following morning. Italy, of all the Western countries with forces in Saudi Arabia, was showing the strongest misgivings about military action. The PLO leader supposed that what might be called a 'Christian miracle' could be achieved if respected figures from Christian countries, perhaps including the Pope, became directly involved.

At 1.20 a.m. Riyadh time on 17 January, President Bush phoned King Fahd to tell him, in a carefully coded way, that the action was about to start. The same message was given to President Mubarak at 2.30 a.m. Cairo time. James Baker then phoned Aleksandr Bessmertnykh, who had taken over as Soviet foreign minister in December following the resignation of Eduard Shevardnadze. Bessmertnykh informed Mikhail Gorbachev, who phoned Yevgeni Primakov at 2.45 a.m. Moscow time and summoned him to a meeting at the Kremlin with other aides. Gorbachev decided to ask for a postponement to allow time for a further attempt to persuade Iraq to withdraw. The foreign minister passed the request to Baker, but it was too late. The war had already begun.

11

The Apotheosis of Air Power

The idea that a Third World country could absorb and withstand an intensive aerial bombardment by a superpower and its allies began to fall apart in the first minutes of Operation Desert Storm. The Iraqis had made thorough preparations, with a well-co-ordinated system of close-range defences, consisting of fighter planes, surface-to-air missiles and some 10,000 anti-aircraft guns. Despite this, the attacks caused massive damage. One of the first targets was the Iraqi air force headquarters, at Habbaneys, about 60 kilometres from Baghdad, which was partly destroyed by a 2000-pound laser-guided bomb dropped from an American Stealth fighter, a state-of-the-art aircraft invisible to radar systems and therefore almost immune from Iraqi defences. A Tomahawk Cruise missile, never before used in combat and carrying a conventional warhead weighing nearly half a tonne, was fired from the US warship *Bunker Hill* in the Gulf. During the night of 16–17 January a wide range of coalition aircraft, including F-15Es, F-11s, F-117As, A6s, F-4Gs and Tornado GR-1s, demonstrated the huge technological advances of recent years. The use of 'smart' bomb techniques, highly accurate navigational systems and improved methods of evading anti-aircraft missiles greatly improved the chances of hitting a designated target. In the forty-three days of the air campaign, allied air forces dropped some 88,000 tons of bombs with an accuracy which steadily increased as Iraqi defences were destroyed. Towards the end of the war some US squadrons were achieving a confirmed direct hit in eight out of ten attacks.

Briefings given by coalition military spokesmen suggested that the campaign's main aim was to weaken Iraq's offensive military capabilities, and particularly its air force and Scud missile launchers. While this was probably true during the initial attacks, the choice of targets widened after a few days. The United States intended to break the fighting spirit of the Iraqi forces, demoralise the population, destroy

Iraq's military and civilian infrastructures, and cripple its industrial capacity. Dr Sa'adoun Hammadi, then deputy prime minister, said after the war that 22,000 civilians were killed in air raids on Baghdad.

The objectives included the destruction of most of Iraq's electrical, water and telephone networks and its petrol refining capacity, its main bridges, and many of its principal roads. While this did weaken Iraq's fighting capabilities, the suffering it caused the civilian population was out of all proportion to the military impact. American officials argued that hardships caused by the destruction of these facilities would increase the psychological impact of UN sanctions against Iraq. Putting this another way, the Americans were suggesting that the use of force would make peaceful methods of persuasion more effective. Many Arabs felt that the real reason for destroying the Iraqi infrastructure was to ensure that Iraq would take many years to recover from the war, and would be unable to do so without Western loans, technology and expert assistance.

Before the war Iraq's infrastructure was beginning to approach the standards of a modern industrialised country. Two months later it had been bombed back to the lowest rungs of the Third World. The key element, on which most other parts of the infrastructure depended, was a network of twenty main electricity generating stations with a capacity of 9000 megawatts, linked by a modern grid system. Coalition air forces attacked twenty-eight transformer stations, switching systems and generating plants in 215 sorties, bringing the whole system to a halt a week after the bombing started. Sections of the network were later restarted, but on a small scale. Many of the systems destroyed will take between one and five years to rebuild, requiring imported equipment and experts from industrialised countries, and an investment which will be possible only if Iraq again becomes a large oil exporter. Prince Sadruddin Aga Khan, Executive Delegate to the UN Secretary General and leader of a team appointed by Señor Pérez de Cuéllar after the war to study Iraq's humanitarian needs, reported that Iraq's electrical capacity was 'negligible' by the end of February 1991. The Iraqis later managed to restore about a quarter of the pre-war output, but seemed unlikely to be able to sustain this level.

'This restoration process has been accomplished through such methods as cannibalising parts from damaged units, making risky makeshift repairs, and operating the remaining plants without the normal breaks for maintenance and repairs . . . little more can be done to increase power generation further unless major imports of new parts are allowed. Barring this, power output can be expected to decline from now on,' the report said.

Iraq's oil facilities were pounded with 1200 tons of bombs, causing serious damage to twenty-eight main targets. The Sadruddin Aga Khan report found that what remained was sufficient for Iraq to supply its own fuel needs, but its oil export capacity, even if it were permitted to export oil, had been reduced by two thirds.

The telephone, water and sewerage networks were also badly affected. Four hundred thousand of the original 900,000 phone lines were damaged beyond repair. Before the war most Iraqis could count on plentiful supplies of clean drinking water. In June 1991, three months after the war ended, supplies to 14.5 million people (out of a total population of 17 million) were running at only a quarter of pre-war levels, and much of the water was of doubtful quality. The remaining 2.5 million people were still cut off from the public water supply. The national sewerage system had suffered serious damage owing to the loss of electrical power during the war, and raw sewage was flowing in the streets of Basra and into rivers. The incidence of diarrhoea was four times greater than a year earlier, and there were outbreaks of typhoid and cholera.

The Sadruddin Aga Khan report also noted that before the crisis Iraq imported about 70 per cent of its food and about US$360 million worth of drugs a year. The combined effects of economic sanctions imposed by the UN and the hazards of poor drinking water and untreated sewage posed a challenge to public health. This was exacerbated by the inability of hospitals and clinics to maintain normal standards because of the shortages. The country had virtually exhausted its food stocks, and cereal production in 1991 was expected to be only one third that of 1990. The report said that the Iraqi food rationing system was 'basically equitable in its distribution' but provided only one third of a typical family's food needs, resulting in a 'strikingly low' level of food intake and posing a danger of 'massive starvation throughout the country'.

Another report carried out after the war, by the Harvard Study Group team, said that damage to infrastructure facilities had caused epidemics and acute malnutrition to much of Iraq's civilian population and estimated that this would lead to the deaths of at least 170,000 children over the following twelve months.

In January and February 1991 few people in the world outside the American, British and Iraqi leaderships could have foreseen that the consequences of the air campaign would be as serious as this. At the time international attention was focused on Iraq's military power, and particularly its chemical weapons. Anything which might reduce that threat was seen as justified. Public opinion in the US and Britain, and to some extent in France, Belgium, Holland, Germany, Italy and Canada, generally supported the air campaign and viewed it as an international (rather than mainly American) response to Saddam Hussein's intransigence. That view was shared by most Arab governments, but not by a majority of their people. Millions of Muslims, even in countries which supported the coalition, regarded the Americans rather than the Iraqis as the originators of the conflict. Without condoning the invasion, Arabs felt that the attack had little to do with American sympathy for the Kuwaiti people, and everything to do with demonstrating Washington's determination to protect oil supplies. Their suspicions, which might seem exaggerated to non-Arabs, cannot be properly understood without recalling the historical context.

The US willingness to use force to protect Middle East oil supplies has never wavered since the Second World War. The permanent presence in the Mediterranean of the Sixth Fleet, with its 27,000 men, two aircraft carriers, two nuclear submarines, twelve major warships and eleven support ships, created a feeling in the Arab world that powerful forces just over the horizon were constantly ready to intervene in its affairs. The presence of 3800 American servicemen at two bases in Turkey reinforced that belief. The construction of the huge military base at Dhahran under US supervision during the Second World War, followed by the building of naval bases at Yanbu and Damman in the 1950s, protecting oil terminals on the Red Sea and the Gulf, further underlined US policy. Although under Saudi control and ownership, the bases were constructed by the US Navy Department in the hope that they would be made available to US forces if needed.

The American presence was felt even more strongly after a shift of US policy, caused by the occupation of the American embassy in Tehran in November 1979 and the taking of fifty-four members of staff as hostages. When US economic sanctions proved ineffective without international support, President Carter sought backing for sanctions from the UN Security Council, but was blocked by Moscow. (The Soviet invasion of Afghanistan in December 1979, followed by the imposition of US sanctions against Moscow, precluded any super-power co-operation on the hostage crisis.) Carter then considered air strikes against Iran, but neither Turkey nor Saudi Arabia would allow their bases to be used for action against a fellow Muslim country. They also objected to any rescue attempt being mounted from their territory.

President Sadat, who happened to be in the US in April 1980 when Carter was considering such an operation, agreed to allow the Wadi Kena air base in Egypt to be used. This was not ideal for the Americans, who would have preferred to operate from a base nearer Iran, but it was the best option available. Supplies and fuel for the attempt were flown to a rendezvous point in the Iranian desert on 24 April 1980 by C-130 transport planes operating from the Egyptian base via Masirah Island off the coast of Oman. The transports were due to meet a Delta Force contingent flown to the same point on board six helicopters, with a seventh as a back-up. To avoid detection the helicopters flew at low altitude at night without lights and in radio silence, depending solely on their instruments and moonlight.

The helicopters were only 150 kilometres inside Iran when one of the pilots noticed a warning light in his cockpit. The Americans had failed to realise that the operation would involve flying for hours through clouds of fine white dust, which is commonly found above desert areas. The engines were not adequately adapted for desert conditions and the dust overwhelmed their filters. One helicopter had to be abandoned on a dry lake bed, though its crew and Delta Force members were picked up by another machine. A second helicopter had to turn back, and a third was found, on arrival at the rendezvous point, to have burned out one of its hydraulic systems. An accident while the other helicopters were being refuelled resulted in the deaths of eight Americans and caused so much damage that only one helicopter remained serviceable. The commanders decided that the original plan, involving the use of Delta Force men carried by helicopters to storm the embassy and rescue the hostages, was now unworkable. The mission was abandoned and no subsequent attempt was possible because the element of surprise had been lost.

The fact that the US had been unable to obtain the use of suitable bases in the Gulf for the rescue attempt drove the Americans to try harder to secure permanent bases in the region whose availability would be assured. Washington had been aware of such a need for decades, especially after the Arab oil embargo against the US and other Western nations in 1973.

Washington hoped in 1979 that Gulf Arab states might regard

a US presence as a guarantee against invasion by Iran, and was disappointed by the rejection of its proposal that a Rapid Deployment Force should be stationed in the region. Another opportunity to gain a foothold had arisen a year earlier, in 1978, when Carter, Sadat and Begin signed the Camp David accords. The US suggested that an international force under US leadership should be based in the Sinai desert, as a listening post covering the region. The idea was accepted and the international force is still functioning in Sinai. In 1987 the United States reached agreements with Oman, Bahrain and Saudi Arabia to allow limited pre-positioning of certain supplies which would be essential if American military assistance were needed in the region. This enabled the US to build up stocks of munitions, fuel and equipment.

The US spent $170 million on infrastructure and buildings at Masirah Island because of the staging facilities made available to it and Britain by the Omani government. A small Omani airbase near the Straits of Hormuz was available on a contingency basis to US maritime patrol aircraft.

By the late 1980s all major Saudi airbases were equipped with certain facilities which would be essential in an emergency requiring US assistance. Bahrain accepted the presence of a small American support unit, allowed the US to build various military facilities, and provided the US and British navies with regular access, but like Saudi Arabia it refused to grant permanent bases. Egypt allowed a small continuous US presence, apart from the International Force in the Sinai. About 100 US servicemen were stationed in Egypt and assisted in joint US–Egyptian operations involving F-15 aircraft and AWACS surveillance planes.

Despite all these arrangements the US remained worried about its dependence on having to persuade Saudi Arabia to accept US deployment on a case-by-case basis. American military reports constantly stressed the risk that, in the event of a Gulf crisis, the US might have to rely on facilities at Diego Garcia (a British island in the Indian Ocean leased to the US), Djibouti (the former French colony in the Horn of Africa), or on the co-operation of Turkey and Egypt. All these options were too far from the Gulf for efficient military operations.

A further American aim was that the Middle East should become accustomed to the US intervening to protect its interests in the region. There were several stages of this process, beginning in June 1983, when the Second World War battleship *New Jersey* used its heavy guns against Syrian positions around Shuweifat, overlooking Beirut. In April 1986 US aircraft operating from bases in Britain bombed the Libyan capital Tripoli. Two years later, in April 1988, the US Navy sank half of the Iranian fleet in the Gulf, in a rout which lasted less than six hours. Operation Desert Storm took the process a stage further, in that American force was used without restraint against an Arab country, yet with the consent of more than half of the governments in the Arab world.

American planning for Desert Storm began just before the invasion of Kuwait when General Colin Powell, Chairman of the Joint Chiefs of Staff, asked General Norman Schwarzkopf, Commander of the US Central Command, to report on what military response the US could make if Iraqi troops crossed the border. The first squadron of F-15s was largely symbolic, but it was quickly followed by other American aircraft, including F-16s and A10s, as well as British Tornados and Jaguars. Even this had little military significance, but it demonstrated political intent. Schwarzkopf thought he would need seventeen weeks to deploy sufficient forces to defend Saudi Arabia, while an offensive capability would take eight to twelve months to assemble. This proved to be a pessimistic estimate: Desert Storm took less than seven months to prepare, and its most important elements, the allied air forces of the US, Britain, France, Canada, Italy and Arab members of the coalition, were in place by late September.

In October, when an offensive plan was considered in more detail, Schwarzkopf asked for two heavy tank divisions and one mechanised division to be transferred from West Germany to Saudi Arabia. George Bush approved the request, but no US president would have been able to do so if the crisis had arisen a few years earlier. The divisions Schwarzkopf wanted were the kernel of US forces in Europe. Their transfer would have been unthinkable but for the relaxation of tensions between Nato and the Warsaw Pact.

The Arab world, which had expected the fighting to last months rather than days, felt after the war that Schwarzkopf had used ground forces disproportionate to the requirements of the situation. The American argument was that by insisting on heavy forces and a long preparation time for the ground offensive, Schwarzkopf ensured that the coalition achieved its aims quickly and with few coalition casualties. The flaw in this argument was that ground forces were not the main instrument of attack: their role was to finish a task which was almost entirely achieved by coalition air power. Powell described the ground offensive as essentially 'a mopping-up operation'.

At the outset of the crisis Iraqi air power included over 1100 aircraft, huge airfields, large numbers of bomb-protected aircraft shelters, substantial close-range defences and an early-warning system. Yet it was not as formidable as it appeared. Firstly, only a small proportion of the planes, four squadrons of MiG-29s (i.e. just over fifty planes), could be regarded as advanced. Most of the others were fifteen to twenty years old. Such a force was no rival to six US aircraft carriers armed with Cruise missiles and 1100 coalition aircraft. Secondly, by observation of Iraqi training flights the coalition was able to assess the capabilities of the Iraqi Air Force, and concluded that the potential of Iraqi pilots and aircraft was being underused. One of many important areas neglected in the training flights was attacking by night. The lack of this capability, and many others, put the Iraqi Air Force at a serious disadvantage.

In a paper written after the war Air Vice Marshal W.J. Wratten, Deputy Commander British Forces, Middle East from November 1990 to March 1991, said: 'Normally [before the war] fewer than 200 sorties were flown every twenty-four hours of all types. In the period immediately before 15 January, the [Iraqi] air force hardly flew at all.' Some saw this as a husbanding of resources, but others realised that Saddam Hussein could not possibly be sustaining a capability of any significance, as he was not pursuing the training essential to do so. Wratten described the training as 'exceptionally basic', which led coalition observers to realise that the Iraqi air force could not be used in an offensive role.' By contrast, in the weeks before the deadline expired the coalition air forces spent most of their time training.

'Iraq appeared to have learned nothing from its experiences against Iran but had continued in its largely defensive, unaggressive and mechanical attitude towards modern air warfare. It could not possibly pose an opposition which would begin to equal the awesome coalition air assets which were formed up against it by 15 January 1991,' said Wratten.

Although the Iraqi Air Force was not used to any significant extent in an aggressive role, it formed part of a defensive system which caused a number of coalition losses, mainly during the early and middle parts of the air campaign. The US Air Force, which flew 64,826 sorties during the war (59 per cent of total sorties), lost fourteen aircraft in combat. The US Navy and Marines, which flew 16 and 9 per cent of sorties, lost seven and eight aircraft respectively. The remaining coalition air forces accounted for 17,580 sorties (16 per cent of the total) and lost nine aircraft. Britain's Royal Air Force lost four Tornado aircraft in the first week, while the French Air Force suffered serious damage to four Jaguar planes in the first twenty-four hours.

The three American services dominated the air campaign not only in terms of numbers but also in firepower and technology. The US Air Force unleashed almost 6000 tons of precision-guided weapons, including 'smart' bombs and guided missiles. While the British and French were equipped with comparable weapons, the quantities were small by American standards. RAF Tornado pilots carried out many attacks with laser-guided weapons, but needed the assistance of another British plane, a Buccaneer, to mark the targets with a laser beam. The technology of some American aircraft was a step ahead, dispensing with the need for the support plane.

The RAF was extensively used in anti-airfield attacks because some of its Tornado aircraft were adapted to carry a specialised weapon for breaking up runways. The weapon was designed for use in high-speed bombing runs, reducing the vulnerability of the aircraft to Iraqi defences. Some Iraqi airfields were three times the size of large European airports, which made it impractical to destroy all their runways, but the RAF caused considerable inconvenience by cratering the areas around hardened aircraft shelters. The same weapon also scattered small bomblets over a wide area to hamper repair work. It was thought that the attacks would have to be repeated frequently to frustrate the efforts of Iraqi airfield repair crews, but after a few days the Iraqi Air Force largely withdrew from the battle. The coalition assumed that the Iraqi pilots were demoralised, but in fact their withdrawal was ordered by the Revolutionary Command Council. Iraq was losing an average of seven or eight aircraft a day, a rate it could not sustain. The losses were mainly caused by a type of American bomb unfamiliar to Iraqi forces, designed to twist like a screw to drive through hardened concrete shelters and explode inside. The Iraqis took to painting shelters to look as if they had already been hit by these weapons, which confused the coalition pilots but did not solve the problem. Baghdad decided that there was no point in losing its aircraft, as it was unlikely to be able to use them in battle; the question was how to evacuate the planes to safety. Before the war started nearly all civilian planes and most of the heavy military transports had been sent abroad for storage in Jordan, Sudan and Yemen, keeping only the fighters and bombers in Iraq. The ideal haven for these planes would have been Jordan, but that would have exposed Amman to the risk of being treated as an ally of Iraq. The only other neighbouring country not involved in the coalition was Iran, but sending the planes there would be a last resort. The RCC decided at a meeting a week after the outbreak of the air campaign to take a chance and send the planes to Iran. Pilots were ordered to escape if they could, but few managed to take off from airfields which had been attacked with the cratering weapon. Airfields in northern Iraq had been bombarded less intensively and many planes got away, though some were shot down before reaching the border with Iran. Iraq estimated that 135 planes got out safely over a period of about three weeks. Instead of asking for Tehran's permission, Baghdad sent a note saying that the planes were on their way and requesting that they should be given sanctuary. After the war a dispute arose between Iran and Iraq as to how many planes had reached Iranian territory. Tehran acknowledged receiving only twenty-three aircraft.

The exodus encouraged speculation in the West that the Iraqi Air Force was in rebellion against the leadership, and this strengthened when a senior air force commander was dismissed. The reports were untrue. Although Iraq's internal divisions exploded as soon as the war ended, the armed services were relatively united, and during the air campaign the whole country was engaged by a feeling of standing alone against a hostile world.

The withdrawal of the Iraqi Air Force removed one of the dangers faced by coalition bombers and fighters. The RAF no longer needed to carry out its airfield attacks at low level, as there was no risk of being intercepted by Iraqi fighters. By switching to medium levels the RAF was able to avoid anti-aircraft fire, but not always SAM missiles, one of which destroyed a fifth RAF Tornado. Towards the end of the air campaign Iraq's efficiency in operating anti-aircraft missiles began to fall off, partly because many of their radars had been destroyed by specialised American air-to-surface missiles. During the earlier stages of the air campaign US Air Force ground-attack aircraft flew to their missions at altitudes of 25,000 to 30,000 feet to allow time for detecting and evading Iraqi SAMs, but as the missile threat declined they were able to drop down to 10,000 feet. Below this altitude anti-aircraft guns remained a substantial threat.

Air Vice Marshal R.A. Mason, of the Foundation for International Security, said in a paper written after the war that in the first ten days of the campaign forty-two Iraqi bridges were destroyed and 70 per cent of major roads disrupted. By 5 February, a third of all main bridges in Iraq had been destroyed. By mid-February, supplies to Iraqi forces in Kuwait had been reduced by 90 per cent, while fuel, ammunition and maintenance stores were being steadily located and destroyed. The Iraqis made good some of the damage by building pontoon bridges during the night, but they were impeded by the night-attack capabilities of coalition aircraft. By 20 February coalition air attacks were destroying 100 Iraqi tanks a day, and by the time the ground offensive began there was little that the air campaign could do to weaken Iraqi ground forces any further. Mason concluded: 'The success of the air campaign may be measured by the statistics: 103,000 sorties; sixty allied aircraft lost; 141 Iraqi aircraft destroyed, and 138 departed.' (Mason's figure of 103,000 sorties was somewhat less than the figure given by the Pentagon: 109,876. His figure of 138 Iraqi planes was three more than the tally provided by Arab sources).

Once air superiority was established, public opinion in the US and Britain began to assume that the coalition's air power was almost unlimited. The real picture was rather different. Far from finding the campaign straightforward, coalition air forces were under considerable strain. One problem was that the distance from bases in Saudi Arabia to Baghdad (about 900 kilometres) was much greater than the relatively short-range combat in Germany for which Western forces were trained. A typical bombing mission would last six, seven or even eight hours, far longer than training missions in Europe. The need for regular in-flight refuelling created situations where several fighters would be circling above tanker planes waiting their turn to approach the fuel nozzles.

Secondly, the huge number of missions flown and a shortage of suitable ground facilities put great pressure on maintenance crews. Although some Saudi airbases were well equipped, others lacked hardstanding, overhead cover and workshops, which were virtually essential for maintenance work. The Americans overcame these problems by flying in some of the missing facilities, including aluminium matting to lay on the sand and prefabricated aircraft shelters, but these could not fully compensate for the shortage of workshops. The huge number of sorties flown meant that aircraft typically put in as many flying hours during the campaign as they would in more than a year of peacetime exercises, greatly increasing the amount of servicing needed. Depending on the type of aircraft, an engine might need a complete service, taking two days, for every 200 hours of flying time. Despite these problems, about 80 per cent of aircraft were available for use at any time.

Memories of the effects of suspended sand on the helicopters involved in the 1979 attempt to rescue hostages from Tehran prompted fears that desert conditions would prove extremely damaging to coalition aircraft. A combination of intensive servicing and improved technology generally overcame this problem for fixed-wing aircraft, but helicopters continued to present special difficulties because of the huge amounts of sand thrown up by their rotors. Pilots tried to avoid hovering close to the ground, but they could not prevent sand being ingested by the engines, which could often manage only half their usual 'life' between services and also delivered less power. Apart from sand, another enemy of the maintenance crews was condensation, caused by variations of as much as 40° centigrade between daytime and night-time temperatures. Some types of helicopter needed three hours of cleaning and drying for every day of use, apart from other forms of servicing.

While the air campaign was under way, helicopters from the US Navy, the British Royal Navy and from the Saudi forces destroyed Iraq's fast guided-missile patrol boats and mine-laying craft in operations around the islands of Bubiyan and Warba and several other areas. The boats were sunk without difficulty because none of them had defensive systems against attack by air-launched missiles, other than machine guns. Meanwhile American and British minesweepers carried out a search for more than 1000 mines laid by the Iraqis in the relatively shallow waters around Iraq. Although many mines of various types were found and destroyed, three US warships were damaged. On 18 February the commanding officer of the USS *Princeton* was addressing his crew on the dangers of mines when a ground mine blew up under the ship's stern. A few seconds later a second mine exploded near the bow. The two explosions caused serious damage and some injuries.

Shortly before the ground offensive began, General Colin Powell told the Senate Armed Services Committee: 'Air power has been the decisive arm so far, and I expect it to be the decisive arm throughout the end of the campaign, even if ground forces and amphibious forces are added to the equation. If anything, I expect air power to be even more decisive in the days and weeks ahead.' This prediction was partly confounded by the weather. Normally the Gulf would be ideal terrain for an air campaign, with cloudless skies and no trees to hide targets, but in January and February the Gulf experienced the most unusual weather in living memory. The coalition's ground offensive coincided with one of the worst periods of rain and low cloud, limiting the operations of aircraft other than helicopters, which played an important role in anti-tank operations.

Before the air campaign it was widely thought that Iraq's Scud missiles would prove a significant factor, because of their ability to deliver chemical warheads to Israeli and Saudi cities. Baghdad believed that a Scud attack on Israel would change the whole picture of the war by winning the support of millions of Arabs and diverting attention away from the Kuwait issue. When the first Scud missiles hit Israel on the night of 18 January there was elation in every Arab country, not excluding those involved in the coalition. It was the first time in forty years of Arab – Israel tension that an Arab country had succeeded with an attack of this type. As Baghdad had hoped, the attack caused immense strains within Arab governments in the coalition. Presidents Mubarak and Assad conferred on how to respond and agreed that any retaliation by Israel would make their position extremely difficult. For several days it seemed inevitable that Tel Aviv would hit back, and Arab governments would come under irresistible public pressure to assist Baghdad. On 24 January, after Iraq had fired three Scuds at Israel, Mubarak said that any country which was attacked had a right to defend itself, a view which was generally unpopular in the Arab world. The Syrian government did not make a similar statement, but repeatedly quoted Mubarak's remark, which suggested that it was in agreement with the Egyptian president.

The Israeli government came under strong internal pressure to retaliate, especially from Ariel Sharon, the leading Likud hardliner with ministerial responsibility for settlements, who, in the eyes of many Israelis, remained the hero of the 1973 war. Tel Aviv said that Israel would reply to the attacks, but that the form and timing of the response would be chosen by the Israeli government. Yitzhak Shamir, the Israeli prime minister, had reached a secret understanding with President Bush at a meeting in Washington on 11 December that Israel would not retaliate against Iraqi attacks without US approval, in return for assurances of US protection and a promise that the Americans would deal with the Iraqis without any sacrifice on Israel's part. The Israelis also hoped that the agreement would help to reduce US pressure on the Palestinian issue after the war. Shamir would probably have been unable to keep this agreement if a Scud with a chemical warhead had hit a heavily-populated area of Israel. Around 25 January the Iraqi military command recommended to the Revolutionary Command Council that chemical warheads should be used, but Saddam Hussein refused. After James Baker's warning to Tariq Aziz at their meeting in Geneva on 10 January it was clear that any use of chemical weapons would bring an American nuclear response. Iraq subsequently disclosed to the UN that it had 375 warheads filled with chemicals.

These diplomatic pressures (Bush – Shamir and Baker – Aziz) were the main factors in neutralising the Scud factor. A further element, which received much greater publicity, was the success of the US Patriot missile in intercepting many of the Scuds. The missile was originally developed as part of Ronald Reagan's 'Star Wars' programme and was also in service with Nato forces in Europe. The Kuwait crisis coincided with the delivery of supplies of an enhanced version of the missile called PAC-2, which was substantially more effective than the original missile. Two Patriot batteries were delivered to the Israeli Defence Force in December and after the 18 January attack two more were transferred from Germany. A further sixty Patriot launchers were deployed in Saudi Arabia. Iraq fired thirty-nine Scuds against Israel and thirty-six against Saudi Arabia, of which about forty-five were intercepted by Patriots. Most of the interceptions were achieved at low altitudes directly above the cities attacked, and debris from both Scuds and Patriots caused extensive damage. Millions of people throughout the world watched live television pictures of incoming Scud missiles streaking over Riyadh and Dhahran and Patriots intercepting them. The television coverage increased the psychological and political impact of this form of warfare, but General Schwarzkopf said later that it was not significant from a military point of view. Even if chemical warheads had been used, the casualties would have been limited, he believed, because the Scuds lacked a mechanism to make them blow up in mid-air. Without this, any contamination would have been confined to the area of impact.

Whether Schwarzkopf was right about this or not, the Americans generally underestimated the scale of the Scud threat. At the beginning of the war US intelligence believed that Iraq had between eighteen and forty-eight Scuds. After sixteen had been destroyed

Schwarzkopf felt confident that the threat was virtually eliminated. After the war Iraq was reported to have had fifteen battalions with fifteen Scud launchers each at the outset of hostilities, and an unknown number of missiles. Sites in western Iraq prepared for launching Scuds were among the first targets of the allied air campaign, but the missiles were mounted on trailers, and could be moved to safer locations. The US Air Force's constant searching forced the Iraqis to fire the missiles from sites which were not always suitable. This accounts for the fact that some of the missiles not intercepted by Patriots fell on uninhabited areas of Israel or into the sea. However, a Scud attack on Saudi Arabia on 26 February landed on a barracks at Dhahran, killing twenty-seven American servicemen and wounding ninety-eight.

By mid-February it was clear that a ground offensive would begin some time in the next two weeks. President Gorbachev sent Yevgeni Primakov on a third mission to Baghdad to try to persuade Saddam Hussein to withdraw unconditionally from Kuwait. Primakov met the entire Iraqi leadership at a guesthouse in the centre of Baghdad on 11 February, and proposed that Iraq should announce its withdrawal with the least possible delay. Saddam Hussein asked a number of questions but made no decision. Two days later, on 13 February, Tariq Aziz travelled to Moscow carrying a statement saying that Iraq was considering the Soviet proposal and would reply soon. On 15 February the Revolutionary Command Council said it was ready to comply with Resolution 660 (which called for unconditional withdrawal from Kuwait), but attached a number of conditions. This apparent inconsistency was taken up by Gorbachev on 18 February at a meeting with Aziz in Moscow. The Soviet leader suggested that Iraq should announce a total withdrawal from Kuwait, mentioning Kuwait by name (which it had not done in its statement), and should say when this would be implemented. Under the Gorbachev plan Iraq would receive a guarantee that departing forces would not be attacked, but otherwise the withdrawal would be unconditional. The United States again made it clear that it would accept nothing less than a completely unconditional withdrawal. When the talks between Aziz and Gorbachev resumed on 20 February it was clear that there was little time left.

At 3.30 a.m. Moscow time on 21 February Vitali Ignatenko, Gorbachev's spokesman, announced that certain points had been agreed. Iraq would accept Resolution 660 and withdraw from Kuwait, but there was no agreement on the timing of withdrawal. Gorbachev conferred by telephone with Bush, who expressed his appreciation of the Soviet efforts but restated his previous demands. Later the same day, 21 February, Bush announced that he was giving Baghdad a deadline of forty-eight hours to begin withdrawing, expiring at noon New York time on Saturday 23 February.

In a speech on 22 February Saddam Hussein said: 'They [the Soviet leadership] told us that if Iraq agreed to withdraw then the war will end and negotiations will start. Iraq said it would withdraw, but what did Bush say? He said it was a trick and the war would continue. They [the Americans] never considered what we said, never studied it carefully.'

Washington's view that Baghdad had not dropped its conditions for withdrawal caused some surprise in the Arab world. King Hassan of Morocco called the US ambassador in Rabat and said he felt that Iraq's statements had been misunderstood and that Baghdad was saying it would accept Washington's terms.

Gorbachev continued to press Aziz to move further towards the American demands, and the Iraqi foreign minister contacted Baghdad to pass on the Soviet leader's views. At 6 p.m. on 22 February, New York time (2 a.m. on 23 February Moscow time), Baghdad sent what Moscow regarded as a positive reply. Tariq Aziz said later that Baghdad had agreed to the immediate and unconditional withdrawal of all its armed forces from Kuwait. However, he also reiterated many of the earlier issues, including Baghdad's demand that all UN resolutions on the Kuwait crisis should be declared invalid. The Soviet leadership knew that Washington would regard this as setting conditions, but Gorbachev phoned Bush and suggested convening the UN Security Council. The United States continued to insist that unless the Iraqis began their withdrawal by the time the deadline expired, the ground offensive would go ahead.

General Schwarzkopf's plan for the ground offensive was completed by 10 November and never changed. The plan, code-named 'Hail Mary' (which was bad taste from a Muslim point of view), depended on the fact that Iraqi forces were concentrated in Kuwait, leaving an unprotected flank on Iraq's border with Saudi Arabia. The original intention was to achieve air superiority first, so that Iraq would be unable to carry out reconnaissance flights, and then to transfer huge forces some 250 kilometres into north-western Saudi Arabia. After a month of air attacks the ground forces would sweep through a wide arc around Kuwait, attacking Iraqi positions from the rear.

For some time coalition commanders felt that the unguarded flank was too good to be true, and that there must be some hidden catch. Could it be, they wondered, that the Iraqi army was aware of some reason why such an attack could not succeed, such as a wide belt of soft sand which tanks and lorries would be unable to cross? The Egyptian and British armies had conducted patrols in the area in previous decades and believed that the ground would carry tanks without difficulty. Scouts were sent to examine the terrain and discovered nothing which would impede the operation.

The reason for Iraq's failure to protect its flank was later explained by a captured Iraqi officer. The Iraqis assumed, he said, that the coalition would not attempt to operate in a featureless desert, because of the risks of losing their way. The Iraqis were unaware that American, British and French forces carried electronic equipment which gave a constant reading of their exact position, using signals beamed from satellites.

Throughout the last two months before the deadline expired General Schwarzkopf was constantly concerned that Baghdad would try to plug the gap in Iraq's defences, but US monitoring showed that every wave of reinforcements was deployed in Kuwait itself. The Iraqis were expecting a frontal attack and had built protective sand barriers around their positions to hamper any coalition advance. Some of these barriers were surrounded by oil-filled ditches, which could be set alight to create a screen of smoke and fire. The coalition encouraged the Iraqis to expect a combined land and sea assault on their positions in Kuwait by staging a large-scale amphibious exercise on the Saudi coast near the border with Kuwait. Substantial forces stormed the beaches from landing craft, watched by Arab and Western journalists, whose reports were sure to be seen by Baghdad.

Schwarzkopf's plan involved a huge logistical operation which would take five weeks to complete. In view of the coalition's confidence that it could achieve air superiority in a short time, the plan was altered slightly, and the transfer of forces to north-western Saudi Arabia began earlier than originally intended, on 17 January, taking a risk that it would be spotted by Iraqi aircraft.

At a press conference on 23 January General Colin Powell said: 'Our strategy for dealing with this [Iraqi] army is very simple. First we are going to cut it off and then we are going to kill it.'

On 30 January Iraqi forces crossed the border into Saudi Arabia and seized Khafji, a town in the north-west which had been virtually evacuated. They held it for two days before being overpowered by coalition forces. The aim of the Iraqi operation in Khafji was primarily to inflict American casualties. At this stage Saddam Hussein thought that ground combat would work to Iraq's advantage. If Iraq could sustain the fight for at least a month and cause perhaps 1000 American casualties, the 'body-bag factor' would turn US public opinion against the war and Iraq would be victorious. This idea was based on the fact that the deaths of sixty-seven Americans in the bombing of the US embassy in Beirut on 18 April 1983, followed by the suicide-bomb attack against a US barracks in Beirut on 23 October 1983, which killed 241 marines, had been sufficient to persuade President Reagan to withdraw all US forces from Lebanon. Thirteen Americans died at Khafji.

A further Iraqi hope was that black American soldiers, who made up about 30 per cent of the US forces, would feel that whites had sent them to die in Iraq, and would turn against their commanders. An Iraqi radio station broadcast pop songs specifically aimed at the black troops. At the same time the Americans, Israelis and Turks had eleven stations broadcasting to the Iraqi army and people. The Arabic services of the Voice of America, Radio Monte Carlo and the BBC stayed on the air for eighteen hours a day and were widely followed in Iraq and throughout the Arab world. Another important factor was CNN Television, which was viewed in most parts of the region, as well as in the West. Broadcasts from Baghdad by its correspondent Peter Arnett showed the effects of the coalition bombing and proved that the targets were not confined to military facilities. The bombing of an underground air raid shelter in Baghdad on 13 February, killing women and children taking cover inside it, caused shock and anger in the Arab world.

The Western military resented Arnett's reports, but the psychological effects of CNN's broadcasts were not one-sided. Arabs sympathetic to Iraq were disheartened by CNN pictures demonstrating the ability of American 'smart' bombs and missiles to home in on targets such as bridges, which are hard to destroy with conventional free-fall bombs because of the need for a direct hit. Such pictures contributed to a feeling that it was useless to struggle against an enemy armed with science-fiction weapons.

In the days before the beginning of the ground offensive, coalition leaders were still unsure about the extent of the air campaign's impact on the Iraqi forces. The effects on infrastructure and the civilian population were obvious, but there were wide differences of opinion as to how much it had impaired the fighting ability of the 500,000 Iraqi troops estimated to be in Kuwait. Deserters captured by coalition forces said Iraqi soldiers were living on a handful of rice and a piece of bread a day, but this was not necessarily a reliable guide to the overall picture.

Air Vice Marshal Mason said later that when the ground offensive started, Schwarzkopf believed that the Iraqi forces had lost somewhere between 25 and 75 per cent of their fighting strength. Indian and Pakistani diplomats, who were particularly well-informed, put the loss at 20 to 25 per cent. After the war it emerged that some units of the Republican Guard came through the air campaign with almost negligible casualties.

The significance of the bombing lay less in the casualties it caused than in the damage done to communications systems linking Baghdad with the troops in the field. Originally there were three independent communications systems. Two of them, both German-made, were damaged in the first week of the war, but the third, a relatively old-fashioned system using ordinary telephone wires, continued working until the beginning of the ground offensive. It was at this point that Baghdad realised that the fight was hopeless and sent messengers to tell the men to get out of Kuwait. This was not easy, because units were spread over a huge area. Not all received the message, some being attacked by coalition forces before the messengers could reach them.

At dawn on Sunday 24 February coalition forces began a rapid advance through undefended desert towards a point in Iraq which had been selected as a refuelling base. It was seized by aerial assault and secured by troops carried on the fastest lorries. As coalition tanks swept around the huge arc of territory they encountered Iraqi tanks and troops moving north, trying to escape the aerial bombardment, which was now joined by a heavy artillery assault.

One American commander made a radio call to General Schwarz-kopf from the Euphrates valley to say that he and his men had captured 3200 prisoners and that the only coalition casualty was one American wounded in action. Over the next two days long columns of Iraqi prisoners were seen trekking across the desert to Saudi Arabia, often escorted only by a handful of coalition troops.

The ease of the advance caused euphoria in the West, which assumed that the morale of the Iraqi army had been broken by the air campaign. Many in the Arab world saw the situation in a different light, feeling that the troops had simply decided that there was no point in getting killed in a hopeless battle.

Substantial numbers of Iraqis fled Kuwait when they received the message from Baghdad, but others were delayed by the damage the coalition air campaign had caused to roads and bridges. Units which received the message too late were caught from the rear by Operation 'Hail Mary' and either killed or taken prisoner. Most of the Iraqi tanks destroyed by the coalition were trying to flee, and if they put up a fight it was usually because they were cornered. American, French and British tanks, assisted by anti-tank helicopter gunships and missiles, left a trail of burned-out Soviet-built tanks across the desert. Six months after the war it was disclosed in the United States that American forces with heavy earth-moving equipment had buried thousands of Iraqis alive after failing to dislodge them from their positions.

One of the Iraqi army's greatest strengths, in theory at least, was the experience of its artillery personnel, who had played a vital role in the Iran–Iraq war, and the high quality of their large guns, which had greater range and a faster firing-rate than the best American artillery. The Iraqi guns were also capable of firing shells filled with chemical munitions, though these were not used. The guns were arranged in a wide arc behind the Kuwaiti border with Saudi Arabia, placed so that any coalition artillery close to the border would be within range of the Iraqi guns, but would not themselves be able to fire on Iraqi positions.

As the ground offensive began, much of the coalition artillery was moved forward. The Iraqis had no means of spotting the positions of coalition batteries until they opened fire, because the Iraqi Air Force had withdrawn. The coalition, on the other hand, could use both manned and unmanned aircraft to identify Iraqi positions. As soon as one Iraqi battery was attacked by coalition guns, others which had not been spotted would return fire. Before firing, the Iraqi gunners had to switch on the radar devices linked to their guns. Signals from the radars were picked up by American electronic systems, which used them to provide coalition gunners with the exact locations of the Iraqi batteries. The Iraqi positions would then be destroyed by a combination of Multiple Launch Rocket Systems (MLRS) and artillery fire. These operations were so rapid and accurate that Iraqi batteries were often destroyed within minutes of switching on their radars. Surviving Iraqi gunners said that in some cases they had time to fire only one round before their positions were wiped out. Although at a disadvantage in terms of range, the American guns and rocket systems were far more accurate, usually hitting their targets with the first shell or salvo of rockets.

A further factor in the coalition's favour was that the Iraqis were unable to move their guns quickly, partly because the trucks used for towing them were tied up with other duties, and partly because their tactic was to conceal the guns behind sand barriers, so far as possible. The coalition guns, on the other hand, could be moved after firing to avoid Iraqi return fire. The coalition's electronic position-indicators, using beams from satellites, made it possible for guns and MLRS to be kept on the move without losing accuracy. Elements of the artillery took part in the sweep through the desert, covering as much as 150 kilometres in twenty-four hours, and destroyed three Iraqi artillery battalions in one engagement on 26 February.

Another factor which contributed to the rapid pace of Operation 'Hail Mary' was that American, British and French forces were equipped with night-vision equipment. These systems, combined with the satellite position-indicators, enabled coalition forces to keep moving twenty-four hours a day and enhanced their ability to take Iraqi forces by surprise. However, the advanced technology was subject to human error, and there was a constant risk that coalition forces would accidentally attack each other. During the battle for Khafji, nine British troops were killed when their truck was attacked by an American aircraft.

By the third day of Operation Desert Storm the remaining Iraqi forces in Kuwait were virtually cut off from Iraq. Helicopter crews attacking the trapped tanks and trucks began to describe the slaughter as a 'duck shoot'.

General Schwarzkopf had intended to use Arab forces to retake Kuwait City, but this proved unnecessary because the 150,000 Iraqi troops based in the city had made their escape before coalition forces arrived. The first Western television crews arrived to find the city seemingly empty, though what remained of the population was in a euphoric mood. Meanwhile hundreds of oil wells outside the city were belching smoke and flames after being set on fire by the departing Iraqi troops.

One of the last escape routes to be reached by coalition forces was the road from Kuwait City to Basra. Thousands of Iraqis attempted to reach Iraq via this route, but found the way blocked because bridges had been bombed. Coalition air forces discovered a huge traffic jam at Mitllah, with hundreds of vehicles ranging from buses to tanks. Virtually all were destroyed, and burned-out vehicles filled with corpses were shown on television throughout the world. British government officials later disclosed that some pilots involved in the massacre objected to killing people who were trying to flee, and that this was taken into consideration in deciding when to halt the fighting.

On 28 February President Bush announced that the coalition would suspend the offensive pending a formal ceasefire. Operation 'Hail Mary' and the liberation of Kuwait had taken 100 hours, much less than the three weeks General Schwarzkopf had expected. Later, many in the West argued that the suspension was premature, and had allowed Saddam Hussein to keep substantial forces intact. Schwarzkopf hinted that he would have preferred to continue the offensive for another day, but praised Bush's decision as 'very courageous' in that it saved many lives, but at a political cost. Schwarzkopf's view aroused scepticism in the Arab world, where it was felt that Bush was far too pragmatic to have taken such a decision for humanitarian reasons. The US leader, it was widely believed, stopped the slaughter only because he realised that allowing it to continue would damage American relations with Arab governments in the coalition. The Arab world was shocked by the degree of force used and the scale of destruction, and any further massacre would have backfired against Washington.

The Western media hailed the outcome of the war as a great victory, and on 7 March 1991 President Bush was given a standing ovation by a joint session of Congress. When General Schwarzkopf returned on 9 June, New York City laid on a tickertape parade reminiscent of the welcome given to General Eisenhower at the end of the Second World War.

Many in the Arab world considered this rejoicing exaggerated. The defeat of a Third World army by vastly better-equipped forces could not be compared with the Allied victory over Germany, Italy and Japan. The Iraqi government had been wrong to invade Kuwait, but most Arabs thought that its punishment was excessive. News of the extent of Iraq's casualties strengthened that feeling. Somewhere between 30,000 and 60,000 Iraqi soldiers and over 22,000 civilians had been killed. With few exceptions, the Arab world found little reason to rejoice over the outcome.

12

The Aftermath

At the time the decision was taken to halt the offensive, Western and Arab members of the coalition believed that the Iraqi government and its leader were spent forces. Norman Schwarzkopf said the Iraqi army had been 'routed', a view strongly supported by the Western media and generally believed in coalition countries. Damascus advised Washington that once the fighting in Kuwait was over, Saddam Hussein would face an army insurrection and a revolt in the Ba'ath Party, in addition to an uprising by Shi'ites in southern Iraq which had already begun. Sectarian fighting around Basra was reported as early as 2 February, almost three weeks before the beginning of the ground offensive. The situation in northern Iraq was calm, but American and British special forces had infiltrated Kurdish areas to assess the prospects of using the Kurds to put further pressure on Baghdad.

This was the background to President Bush's decision not to use further force to topple the Iraqi leader. Better, he thought, to allow the *coup de grâce* to come from the Iraqis themselves. In his speech on 28 February announcing the suspension of the offensive, the US president said that the coalition had done its duty and it was now up to the Iraqi people to rid themselves of their 'evil dictator'.

Under a plan arranged with the United States, Saudi Arabia had been entrusted with making preparations for installing a provisional Iraqi government, selecting suitable Iraqis according to agreed criteria. This was based on the assumption that Saddam Hussein would fall, or be swept away, leaving a power vacuum which the provisional government would fill. The leader chosen by Riyadh came from Takrit (like Saddam Hussein), was a Sunni, and was a former member of the Ba'ath Party. The new government as a whole was intended to be a mix of Ba'ath Party and army figures.

In early March 1991 events in Iraq appeared to be developing much as the coalition had hoped. Within days of the ceasefire a

Kurdish uprising began in the north, while the Shia revolt in the south flared into a civil war, encouraged by the previously suppressed Dawa opposition party and by hardline elements in Iran. Between one and three thousand members of the Iranian Revolutionary Guards joined ranks with a militia formed by Iraqi Shi'ites, and began rioting, looting and cutting communications lines. Heavy fighting was reported, with much loss of life. In the north there was little bloodshed in the early stages as there were practically no government troops in the area. Kurdish groups stormed Iraqi government offices and brought large areas under their control.

As the two conflicts progressed, the Shi'ites gained authority in the governates of Basra, Karbala and Myssan, while the Kurds dominated D'houk, Arbil and As-Sulaimaniya. Two weeks after President Bush's announcement, the Iraqi government's area of authority had been reduced to only three of Iraq's eighteen governates – Baghdad, Mosul and Anbar. Then, in late March, the tide began to turn in Baghdad's favour. As Shia and Kurdish forces were driven back, it became clear that the Iraqi army had suffered less damage than Schwarzkopf had thought, and that Saddam Hussein and the Revolutionary Command Council were still in charge of the central government. If the two uprisings had been truly motivated by a desire for radical changes in the structure of Iraq, they might have succeeded; as it was, many of those involved were merely trying to exploit a chaotic situation, for reasons of greed or revenge.

The reassertion of the Iraqi government's authority showed that the coalition had made several serious miscalculations. Washington overestimated the number of divisions Baghdad had committed to the fight for Kuwait. Between eighteen and twenty-five divisions had been kept in central Iraq as a precaution against any coalition attempt to seize the capital. Secondly, the coalition was unaware that Iraqi forces had been ordered to withdraw just before the ground offensive began, and that some divisions had escaped with only light damage. Thirdly, the fact that most Iraqi soldiers are Shi'ites, while the officer corps is predominantly Sunni, led many in the coalition to expect large-scale desertions from the Iraqi army during the civil war. As it turned out, nationalism generally proved stronger than factionalism within the army. Among units which retreated from Kuwait in chaos, there was a breakdown of discipline, and many soldiers deserted or went on the rampage, but units which left in a more orderly fashion generally remained loyal to the central government. Fourthly, President Bush's incitement to Iraqis to rise up against Saddam Hussein led to an assumption, both inside and outside Iraq, that Washington would help the rebel movements. Although there was some American assistance, it was mainly directed to the Kurds. In the south, American forces turned a blind eye to the looting by Shia rebels of Iraqi military stores at Nasserieh air base, but on the other hand they allowed the Iraqi army to use helicopters in fighting the rebels. The coalition had ordered Iraq to keep its aircraft grounded, but an Iraqi military delegation which met General Schwarzkopf at Nasserieh on 3 March requested that an exception should be made for the helicopters, arguing that they were essential for administering the return of Iraq to normal life, as communications had been disrupted by the bombing. However, it was obvious that the Iraqi government was also likely to use the helicopters in the civil war.

Schwarzkopf's decision to grant the request reflected pressure from the Saudi government, which was growing alarmed at the large amounts of Iranian aid being given to the Shia rebels. It would not be in Saudi Arabia's interest for Iraq's government to be weakened to a degree which would disturb the internal status quo. Riyadh's worry was that any sudden change in the sectarian or ethnic structure of Iraq would encourage unrest among Shi'ites throughout the Gulf, including the Eastern Provinces of Saudi Arabia. Before August 1990 the composition of the Revolutionary Command Council was generally understood to be eight Sunnis, two Shi'ites and two Kurds (although the sectarian identity of individual ministers was not always made public). After the civil war there were a number of ministerial adjustments, but the balance seemed to stay unchanged.

The main surprise in the reshuffles was the dismissal of Dr Sa'adoun Hammadi, the deputy prime minister, on 13 September 1991. The reason given was that Hammadi attracted no votes in RCC elections in the first week of September. Although Hammadi was the highest-ranking Shi'ite in the RCC, his dismissal could not have had sectarian motives, since he was replaced by another Shi'ite, Mohamed Hamza al-Zubaidi.

By the end of March, after heavy fighting interspersed with civilian riots and looting, the central government had largely regained control of Shia areas. Some of the rebels fled into marshland around Basra and remained there in hiding for months afterwards. Other Shi'ites had sought refuge earlier in the wide strip of southern Iraqi territory which the coalition continued to hold for several weeks after the ceasefire. The civil war in the south was over, and nothing appeared to have changed, apart from a worsening of the chaos and suffering caused by the air campaign.

The northern rebellion had little in common with the Shia revolt. The two main Kurdish leaders, Gallal El-Talabani of the National Front of Iraqi Kurdistan, and Massoud El-Barazani, of the Democratic Kurdish Party, had assured Baghdad before 17 January that they would do nothing to exploit the Kuwait crisis. This enabled the Iraqi army to withdraw from the north. When fighting in Kuwait ended, the Kurds (in common with many others) thought that the central government had either collapsed or was about to do so. They felt freed from their promises, and old Kurdish fighters emerged from hiding in the mountains, or returned from Turkey and Iran, to join the political leaders in filling a vacuum of authority. For a few days it seemed that a Kurdish provisional government was about to be installed in northern Iraq, then the Iraqi army began to move, and any such dreams were shattered. Rumours that the army was preparing to use chemical weapons to re-establish control caused panic and led to a huge exodus from the towns to the mountains. Kurdish guerrillas attempted to block the army's advance but were no match for its military power. Kurdish political groups, however, made no attempt to rally the Kurdish population or to arouse general armed resistance. The first priority of some Kurdish politicians was to secure influential positions in post-war Iraq; once it became clear that the central government had not collapsed they had little interest in defying Baghdad. Talks between the Kurds and Baghdad opened on 20 April and continued for several weeks. By this time the army had regained control and normality might have returned within two or three months, but for outside pressures.

President Bush and John Major, who had replaced Margaret Thatcher as Prime Minister of Britain in November 1990, at first appeared to pay little attention to the Kurdish exodus. In fact they were biding their time, waiting for Iraq's central government to collapse. Disappointed by the American and British attitude, Kurdish groups staged protests to draw attention to their cause, including the occupation of the Iraqi consulate in London on 5 April 1991.

By early May it was clear that American and British hopes that Saddam Hussein would fall without further intervention on their part were destined to be disappointed. At about the same time Bush and Major began to pay attention to the Kurdish issue, and the media in both capitals aired the possibility of creating an enclave in northern Iraq under international control. The stated aim was to protect the Kurds from the Iraqi leadership, but the creation of such a zone would also convince the Iraqi army that American pressure would continue so long as Saddam Hussein remained in power.

The plight of the 600,000 Kurdish civilians fleeing from Iraqi forces was receiving huge attention in the Western media. The Kurdish issue is one which tends to be periodically 'discovered' by Washington and London as a useful instrument of pressure against Baghdad, only to be forgotten soon afterwards. With this in mind, many in the Arab world were sceptical about US intentions when President Bush announced, on 16 May, that he was sending forces to northern Iraq. 'I am not going to have the fate of the Kurdish people in the hands of that man,' the US leader said. About 4000 Americans and something less than a thousand British troops were sent to areas of the Turkish–Iraqi border to monitor the conditions of the refugees. These forces gradually moved south, entering Kurdish towns which were then reoccupied by their inhabitants. There were no clashes with Iraqi forces, and the Americans and British quietly withdrew. In August 1991 it was confirmed that they had all left Iraq.

The American and British decision to send forces to northern Iraq formed part of a wider campaign of sustained pressure on the Iraqi government. President Bush was under continuing pressure from Gulf leaders to use further force to dispose of Saddam Hussein, but he still hoped that the Iraqi people would do it for him, once they realised that their lives would remain unbearable so long as the Iraqi leader continued in office.

The United States and Britain played leading roles in bringing about a series of UN Security Council resolutions imposing stringent and intrusive inspections of Iraq's nuclear and chemical weapons programmes, and in ensuring that the UN ban on Iraqi oil sales was not lifted.

On 18 April, in response to Security Council demands, Iraq provided what it said was a list of its chemical weapons. The list gave details of five factories which produced nerve gases, and five depots where bombs and shells were filled with chemicals. All of them had been destroyed in the bombing campaign. It also mentioned substantial stockpiles, including 6620 chemical-filled shells for 122mm artillery, hundreds of tons various nerve-gas products, and 134 missiles with chemical warheads. When the list was later proven to be incomplete, Iraq provided some more information, but this did not add much to the original list. Over the following months Iraq was subjected to the most rigorous regime of inspection and surveillance ever imposed by the United Nations on a member country. UN inspectors had authority to go almost anywhere and look at almost anything.

The first UN inspection teams arrived in Iraq on 14 May 1991, acting under the authority of Resolution 687, which gave Iraq forty-five days to make its weapons of mass destruction available to be dismantled under UN supervision, and required that this process should be completed within a further forty-five days. The deadline proved to be unrealistic. A United Nations report on 24 October 1991 said that Iraq had thousands of chemical weapons, and that it would take two years to destroy them all. No evidence of biological weapons was found.

On 22 June sixteen experts arrived to investigate Iraq's nuclear research programme. They were followed on 3 July by a further twenty-one officials sent to supervise the destruction of medium-range missiles, and thirty-seven experts to monitor the dismantling of Scud missiles.

The information Iraq provided about its nuclear programme omitted certain details which the Americans were determined to obtain, including the names of the scientists involved. On 12 July, a dissatisfied President Bush threatened to resume the bombing campaign unless Baghdad co-operated fully with the UN inspectors. On 27 July a further fifteen experts resumed the search for nuclear information. Baghdad, feeling that its sovereignty was being eroded by the constant UN presence, tried to insist that the inspectors should use helicopters provided by the Iraqi army rather than by the UN, but dropped this demand when Bush said he was losing patience and hinted that the use of B-52 bombers might be imminent.

The breakthrough the Americans had been hoping for came in September when the CIA learned from an Iraqi defector that the Social Insurance Department at the Ministry of Labour in Baghdad contained the official files on scientists working in the nuclear programme. This information resulted in a further mission by forty-five UN officials, led by David Kay, an American. On 22 September the team seized huge quantities of documents from the ministry, but they were stopped as they left the building and detained, spending long periods in their buses in the ministry's car park. After a five-day stand-off, during which Bush made further threats, Iraqi officials catalogued the documents before the UN inspectors took them away. The files revealed the scientists' names, addresses and details of their education and training. The team gave these details to Washington before passing them to the UN in New York, a move which brought strong criticism from several quarters at the UN. Baghdad accused the team of acting as American agents.

Sadruddin Aga Khan and a team of experts visited Iraq from 29 June to 13 July to assess needs for humanitarian assistance arising both from the effects of the bombing campaign and the aftermath of the Shia and Kurdish revolts. The UN Secretary General issued the Sadruddin report on 17 July. It revealed that the suffering of the Iraqi people was on a far greater scale than the rest of the world had imagined. After much discussion in New York, on 15 August the Security Council passed Resolution 706, authorising Iraq to sell a quantity of oil to the value of US$1.6 billion under UN supervision. The proceeds were to be spent as directed by the UN on food and relief work. Iraq regarded this as an interference in its affairs and refused to comply, with the result that no oil was exported and the humanitarian crisis worsened.

Iraq could have resumed exporting oil on a more orthodox basis, but it would have had to contribute 50 per cent of the revenue for a decade or more to a UN compensation fund to pay war reparations. An appeal by Baghdad for a moratorium of at least five years on the start of its payments into the fund went unheeded. Baghdad wanted to use all oil revenue for its own reconstruction and recovery projects before beginning the reparations.

In September 1991 Baghdad said in a report to the Security Council that if it resumed exporting oil promptly, its revenue between 1991 and 1995 would be about $65 billion, before any contributions to the compensation fund. Iraq's basic requirements for foreign currency over the same period, to pay for essential imports and debt-servicing programmes, amounted to $214 billion. It therefore faced a deficit of $149 billion even if it paid no reparations during that period. This was based on the optimistic prediction that Iraq could export 600,000 barrels of oil a day in the second half of 1991, rising to 2.95 million barrels a day in 1995.

Seven months after the fighting ended Iraq seemed as far as ever from being able to resume oil exports. There must have been considerable bitterness in Baghdad on 27 September when two fully-loaded oil tankers sailed out of the port of Ahmadi, marking the resumption of Kuwait's oil exports. According to Dr Hammud El-Rakaba, Kuwait's Minister of Oil, the war cost Kuwait $75 billion in lost oil production and damage to wells and facilities. Nevertheless, the damage was much less than that suffered by Iraq, and the repair work was carried out faster than expected, with the help of large numbers of Western engineers. Two American companies undertook the huge job of extinguishing the 730 oil wells set on fire by the Iraqis, while the ecological disaster caused by oil flowing into the Gulf provided another task for American technology and expertise. The clean-up was expected to take many years.

These contracts reinforced Kuwait's already heavy dependence on the United States and Europe. Before August 1990 Kuwait had tried to keep up an appearance of independence, but this was no longer possible. As Western forces had played the leading roles in Kuwait's liberation, the Kuwaiti government was unable to resume the foreign policy it had pursued before the war, and there were no complaints when the United States and Britain left some of their forces in Kuwait after the war (although the bulk of the troops were withdrawn quickly). The Kuwaiti opposition called for the principle of full withdrawal to be accepted, but did not make it a major issue.

There was also a continuing Western military presence in Saudi Arabia, though its size was not disclosed because the matter was politically sensitive in Riyadh. On 29 April 1991 Dick Cheney, the American Defense Secretary, repeated the promise he had given King Fahd on 6 August 1990 that US troops would leave when Saudi Arabia asked them to do so. Silence then fell on the issue.

International attention gradually moved away from the West's military presence in Saudi Arabia and Kuwait, and the focus returned to prospects for convening a conference on the Arab – Israel conflict. Diplomatic efforts by the United States, the Soviet Union and the European Community to promote such a conference had been interrupted for seven months, partly because the Americans were determined to avoid any suggestion of a link with the Kuwait issue. As soon as the war was over, however, President Bush wanted the Arabs to feel that the United States was making a serious effort to bring about an Arab – Israel settlement. Between March and October 1991 James Baker made eight tours of Middle East capitals, searching for terms acceptable to both Arabs and Israelis for holding talks. A solution was in the US's interests and in those of Bush as a statesman, but the lack of any significant change in US policy towards Israel initially aroused scepticism among Arabs about American motives. Washington's view was that the war had created a new situation, in that Egypt and Syria had fought alongside the United States, while Israel, by not responding to Iraqi missile attacks, had abstained from actions which might have wrecked the coalition.

Baker's mission was not the first attempt to settle the Arab–Israel conflict through international talks. After the 1948 Arab–Israel war, the UN created what it called the Conciliation Committee, involving the US, France and Turkey, and meetings were held in Lausanne. The committee's terms of reference were based on General Assembly Resolution 181, which called for the creation of two states in what had been Palestine, one for Palestinians, the other to be Israel. No conciliation was possible, however, because Israel took possession during the 1948 war of an area greater than that given to it by the resolution. Israel, which had come into existence shortly before the war, complained that the Arab countries were working together with the intention of destroying the new state. The committee continued reporting to the General Assembly until 1957 and still exists officially as a UN body.

A second peace attempt was made after the UN Security Council had passed Resolution 242, which followed the 1967 war. The resolution emphasised 'the inadmissibility of the acquisition of territory by war and the need to work for a just and lasting peace in which every state in the area can live in security', and stated that the following principles should be applied: 1) Withdrawal of Israeli armed forces from territories occupied in the 1967 war; 2) 'Termination of all claims or states of belligerency, and respect for and acknowledgement of the sovereignty, territorial integrity and political independence of every state in the area and their right to live in peace within secure and recognised boundaries free from threats or acts of force.' Among other aims, the resolution referred to the need for 'a just settlement of the refugee problem'. The wording, a compromise reached after much diplomatic haggling, was unsatisfactory to many in the Arab world.

Gunnar Jarring, Swedish Ambassador to the UN, was appointed as a special representative of the UN Secretary General and toured the Middle East. Meetings were held in New York between representatives of the US, the UK, the USSR and France and representatives of countries which accepted the terms of Resolution 242 (Egypt, Jordan and Israel). The meetings were intended to resolve Israel's earlier complaint that Arab countries were conspiring to destroy it. The intention was that after this question had been settled, a peace conference would be held within the framework of the Security Council, but Israel blocked the process because it was not ready to withdraw from the Occupied Territories and did not trust the UN, with its majority of Third World and non-aligned countries, who tended to side with the Arabs.

A conference sponsored by the US and the USSR was convened in Geneva after the 1973 war. Egypt, Jordan and Israel took part, and Syria authorised Egypt to negotiate on its behalf. This conference did not succeed because Henry Kissinger (then Secretary of State) and the Israelis had a different agenda. Israel's aims were to squeeze the Soviet Union out of the talks and to persuade Egypt to sign a separate peace. The conference set up a military committee, which held a number of secret meetings without inviting the Soviet delegate. In these talks the Israeli military representatives tried to persuade Egypt to attack Libya, proposing that Israel would not interfere in anything Egypt did in Africa if Egypt agreed to give Israel a free hand in Asia. The tension increased when Moscow discovered that meetings were being held behind its back. Andrei Gromyko, then the Soviet foreign minister, threatened to send Soviet officers to break up any further meeting which was convened without a Soviet representative.

Although the Israelis and Americans eventually achieved their aims (the exclusion of Moscow and the 1978 Camp David accords), the outcome was not peace but rather an absence of war.

Many further attempts were made in the 1980s to convene a peace conference, but they made no headway. In view of the discouraging precedents, no one was surprised when Baker initially found little enthusiasm on the part of the countries concerned.

Israel had always said it wanted face-to-face talks with its Arab neighbours, but equally it had always insisted that it would not talk to the PLO. Tel Aviv demanded that PLO members should be banned from the conference and that Palestinian delegates should be chosen according to criteria defined by Israel. Tel Aviv also wanted the role of other participating powers and organisations (the US, the Soviet Union, the UN, the Gulf Co-operation Council, the Maghreb Council and the European Community) to be limited to that of attending an opening session, which would be followed by talks involving only the parties directly concerned. Israel largely secured these terms.

The Arab countries, on the other hand, wanted other participants in the conference to be fully involved, and felt that the conference should have powers to take decisions which would be binding on Israel. The PLO had always insisted on direct participation in any peace conference, and Syria wanted advance assurances that Israel would give up the Golan Heights (one of the territories captured by Israel during the 1967 war). All these demands were gradually dropped, partly because no one wanted to be the first to refuse to attend the conference.

The Maghreb group of north African states agreed to take part, but without enthusiasm. Muammar Gadaffi argued that the conference should be boycotted because nothing would come of it but Arab surrender to Israel. A senior Libyan official conveyed Gadaffi's view during a Maghreb summit in Casablanca on 15 September 1991, but he was told by other Arabs that the Americans would regard any country which refused to attend as obstructionist, and that in any case boycotting the conference would be an empty gesture.

The last Arab country to give way to Baker's mild arm-twisting was Syria. President Assad, normally suspicious of US intentions, told his cabinet shortly before the conference: 'This is the first time I have felt that the US was serious and willing to reach a solution.' He added: 'There is no way we can stay away – what would that achieve?'

Many Arabs were now ready to regard the conference as a brave attempt to find peace, but had misgivings about the rushed manner in which it had been arranged. All the important details were settled in the last few weeks of the Baker mission, reminding some Arabs of a scene depicted in many Egyptian temple sculptures of Ramses II dragging his Canaanite and Hittite prisoners by their hair to an unknown destiny. The preparations were felt to be inadequate, and the idea that Arab – Israel meetings could create their own dynamic seemed optimistic. Baker's strategy for bringing the parties together had been to concentrate on procedural problems, without attempting to resolve questions of substance before the conference.

The Secretary of State was partly deflected from this approach by a row over an application which Israel was preparing for a $10,000 million loan guarantee from the United States. The money was to be used to help pay for the resettlement of Soviet Jews, and Arab countries feared that this would mean an increase in the construction of Jewish settlements in the Occupied Territories. In the first week of September the United States asked Israel to delay its application until after the conference, because of Arab concerns. Tel Aviv ignored the request and went ahead with its application. On 12 September President Bush announced that if Congress approved the application, he would use his power of veto. American commentators could not recall any American president confronting the US Jewish lobby in so direct a fashion. As it turned out, Bush's veto was not needed, because the House of Representatives decided to delay consideration of the application until after the conference. In the Arab world any appreciation of these moves was tempered by the fact that the loan guarantee had merely been delayed, not rejected. Bush might seem marginally firmer with Israel than his predecessors, but US policy as a whole remained massively weighted in Tel Aviv's favour.

Earlier, some Arabs had felt encouraged when Washington announced in May 1991 that Jewish settlements in the Occupied Territories were an impediment to peace. It had taken the Americans two decades to reach a conclusion which most Arabs considered obvious.

On 18 October James Baker and Boris Pankin, the new Soviet foreign minister who had been appointed after the failed Soviet coup in August, met in Israel to conclude the preparatory negotiations. Yitzhak Shamir, the Israeli prime minister, held out until the last for the optimum Israeli terms for attending the conference. After a meeting between Shamir and Baker the Americans thought the process had collapsed, but Pankin, who met Shamir immediately after Baker, was more successful. It appears that Shamir finally gave way when Pankin reminded him that Moscow's offer to renew diplomatic links with Israel was conditional on Israel's attendance at the conference. Within a few hours Shamir announced Israel's decision to attend, to the astonishment of many of his supporters and the anger of small right-wing parties on which Likud depended for a working majority in the Knesset. The Soviet Union kept its promise to restore links, which were broken off after the 1967 war.

Invitations to the conference were issued by Baker and Pankin on behalf of their presidents, giving an impression of superpower partnership, though in reality the Union of Soviet Socialist Republics had ceased to exist in August and a new, looser federation had not yet been born, except as a frail patchwork stitched together with economic threads. The Soviet role might have been good for appearances and for Gorbachev's image, but it had little substance.

The opening session in Madrid on 30 and 31 October, which began with speeches by Bush and Gorbachev, was intended to set in train a long negotiating process. Some in the Arab world thought that Washington would try to keep the talks going for at least a year, in view of the impending US presidential elections. The Americans had suggested an interim solution involving a five-year transition plan; if agreement to such a plan were reached at a suitable moment it might strengthen Bush's prospects of a second term. Such views were not as cynical as they might seem, as Middle East affairs had long been part and parcel of US presidential campaign politics.

The Arabs would have felt more confident if the organisation of the conference had been put in the hands of the United Nations, once Baker and Pankin had persuaded the parties to attend. As it was, many Arabs felt their countries had been talked into attending a dazzling Spanish fiesta of hope and emotion without adequately considering what pitfalls might lie ahead.

Epilogue

Since the Gulf war, many intellectuals have reflected on the prospects of the region on the threshold of the twenty-first century. They have been concerned not so much with immediate questions of reconstruction and humanitarian aid as with finding a path to reconciliation and unity. Some have felt daunted by the scale of the problems and divisions, the urgency of the need for remedial measures, and the paralysis of decision-making from which the Arab world has long suffered. Prince Hassan, the Crown Prince of Jordan and younger brother of King Hussein, argues that the Arab world is pursuing what he calls 'the politics of despair', and must find a new way forward. Aided by a think tank, the prince produced a paper after the Gulf war suggesting ways of achieving this goal. The paper spoke of the need to amalgamate the security arrangements and human and natural resources of Arab countries to create a more united society. It identified some specific goals: peace between Arabs and Israel, a plan for Lebanon, arms reductions, a regional economic plan, and a human rights charter. What was needed, the prince felt, was a political process involving people with the intelligence and mental flexibility to find solutions.

The prince's approach might work if the Arab world had well-established political institutions and a tradition of respect for state constitutions. The difficulty in the Arab world, and the Third World generally, is that secure institutions are possible only when the various groups within society become strong enough to make their presence felt, thus opening the door to dialogue. Until society reaches that maturity, any plan for the future is bound to be imposed by a ruling minority on the majority, not necessarily against the majority's wishes, but without genuine popular participation.

Another possibility is that the Middle East could set up its own version of the European Community. In the early 1950s Jean Monnet, Robert Schuman and Sicco Mansholt, the founding architects of the

Community, were primarily concerned to heal European divisions left by the First and Second World Wars. Their approach was to begin by strengthening economic links (starting with plans for the European Coal and Steel Community in 1951, followed by the Treaty of Rome in 1957), progressing gradually towards elimination of trade barriers and harmonisation of industrial and fiscal legislation, and later social and foreign policy. Of course all the EC countries were full democracies before that process began, but this need not prevent the Arab world from adapting the European experience to its own requirements. An attempt to undertake a co-ordinated programme of Arab development was made in 1980, with the aims of reducing the gap between rich and poor areas and creating an all-Arab infrastructure of roads, communications and pipelines. The programme was not implemented, but it could be revived and modified. A good starting point would be an agreement on using and sharing water supplies in a rational and fair manner. By the beginning of the twenty-first century the Arab population, currently around 250 million people, is expected to have risen to 350 million, increasing the pressure on water supplies still further. Even Egypt, which receives 55 billion cubic metres of water a year from the Nile, will be hard-pressed to cope with its expected population of 77 to 80 million (compared with about 57 million now). Iraq, Syria and Turkey are competing for the same water sources, and many fear that this rivalry could lead to war in the next twenty years.

What is certain is that the Middle East urgently needs a new sense of direction. Dr Ibrahim Abu-el-Lughd, of Georgetown University, Washington, believes that the Arab world is condemned to follow one of two bleak scenarios, unless present trends are halted. His first scenario is based on a Latin American model, with states ruled by rich oligarchies kept in power by the Americans. In effect, the Latin American oligarchs have a licence from the Americans to make money, on the condition that nothing is done to disturb the strategic balance of the region. His second scenario is based on an African model and envisages the rule of chaos, with all its concomitant evils, including poverty, hunger and disease.

The flaw in the first scenario is that the Latin American oligarchies were a product of a very different history and culture. Limited parallels could be made with the Gulf sheikhdoms, but the Latin American model is in no way comparable with Egypt, Syria, Iraq, Jordan, Palestine, Lebanon, Yemen, Sudan, Algeria, Tunisia, Libya, Morocco or Mauritania. In Latin American oligarchies, small cliques tend to retain permanent control of both political and economic power. The Arab sheikhdoms are similar in this respect, but more stable, with fewer changes of government figures. The other Arab countries differ from Latin America in that political and economic power are not necessarily in the same hands. The rulers of the two kingdoms, Jordan and Morocco, have ultimate political power and substantial personal wealth, but do not dominate the entire business life of their countries. The leaders of the six post-revolutionary governments (Egypt, Syria, Iraq, Yemen, Algeria and Libya) generally have less personal involvement in business activity than their counterparts in Latin America, because the oligarchies are based on huge family enterprises handed down from father to son for generations. The remaining Arab countries – Palestine, Sudan and Mauritania – are even further removed from the Latin model. After twenty-three years of Israeli occupation, Palestine shows a clear separation between political and business activity. Sudan's military government is based on a political pact between the army and the Islamic fundamentalist movement, and Mauritania's leadership is also strongly influenced by fundamentalist pressures.

The second scenario is also improbable, because the Arab nation is an ancient society, richer in history and culture than most African countries, and has lived through periods more difficult than the present without falling into chaos. Some would contend that Arab history and culture is so powerful as to inhibit freshness of thinking. The revivalist movements, including the Muslim fundamentalists, base their call for a return to the past on the fact that in earlier centuries there were periods when Muslim society was more cohesive, and perhaps less discontented. The counterpart to this argument is that the Arab world has also had periods of renaissance, such as that begun in Egypt in the early nineteenth century by Mohamed Ali, who was inspired by the ideas introduced by the French during the Napoleonic period. There was a further renaissance during Nasser's revolution.

When the history of the Arab world in the twenty-first century is written, its pages may well be stained with oil, water and blood. The near future seems certain to be influenced mainly by the struggle to keep at least partial control of oil supplies in Arab hands, the shortage of water, and the immense tensions and frustrations in the Arab world today. The current ruling generation has both a duty and an opportunity to resolve these problems, and should not assume that the future will be determined by forces beyond its control. The Gulf war demonstrated that Arabs could not prevent the United States intervening when it thought oil supplies were threatened; Arabs can, however, ensure that no apparent threat to oil supplies arises in the future. One way of achieving that goal would be to create a new body bringing together oil producers and consumers to discuss oil prices and supplies. There is a need to move away from one-sided attempts by producers or consumers to regulate the market. Their respective interests might seem incompatible to an Arab finance minister trying to balance his state budget, but in the longer term greater co-ordination would suit both sides.

It should not be beyond Arab political skills to manage the problems of water and oil. The third element, blood, presents much greater problems. Nothing is more urgent than the need to contain and defuse the anger of the Arab world, yet nothing could be harder to achieve.

The causes of the tension are many and complex, but many Arabs feel that an important element is the American military presence in the Middle East and Washington's influence over a number of Arab governments. The continuation of a high US profile in Middle East affairs during the months after the Gulf war was the opposite of what the region needed. With the exception of a few tribal sheikhs, most Arabs wanted foreign forces to depart. The events of August 1990 to March 1991 left wounds which will take years to heal — wounds of the soul as much as the body. A profound sorrow over the destruction of Iraq was felt, in countries which participated in the coalition no less than in those which did not, and a sense of humiliation caused by the American management of the crisis overwhelmed all other aspects of the war. Americans assumed that Arabs were glad of protection against Iraq's ambitions to dominate the region, and against its vast chemical weapons capabilities, without realising that the whole affair was wounding to Arab self-respect.

The constant feeling of being infiltrated by Western interests of all kinds tends to undermine Arab self-confidence. Western governments were closer to their long-term goals of securing Middle East bases after the war than before it. The US will no longer have to worry that it might be refused access to Saudi bases in the event of a crisis, and the US, Britain and France reinforced their bonds with Kuwait. John Major underlined the importance Britain attached to this link by visiting Kuwait on 5 March, only five days after the end of the ground offensive. James Baker was four days behind, arriving on 9

March, and Kuwait quickly entered into a defence agreement with the US, Britain and France. The pervasive influence of Western experts, engineers, managers and salesmen is another aspect of the same problem.

Forty years of tension or war with Israel and Washington's economic and military support of Tel Aviv have had a devastating effect on Arab relations with non-Arabs. When Westerners accuse Arabs of being over-suspicious, they tend to forget that the West has never shown even-handedness on issues which affect the survival of the Arab nation. Washington's double-standards as regards Arab and Israeli weapons programmes are a source of great danger. While condoning, or at least not preventing, Israel's reported possession of between 100 and 300 nuclear warheads, the US destroyed Iraq's nuclear research facilities by using bombs and missiles equivalent in their combined explosive power to a small nuclear bomb.

The disclosure that Iraq's nuclear weapons programme was larger and more advanced than previously supposed made no difference to the Arab attitude. In Arab eyes, these were Arab weapons directed against Israel, rather than Iraqi weapons directed against fellow Arabs, and an Arab country was entitled to try to catch up with Israel's military technology. Saddam Hussein's mistake was not the development of such weapons but rather his statements that he was prepared to stand up to Israel before Iraq was in fact ready for such a battle.

The war brought feelings of shock caused by Iraq's invasion of Kuwait, followed by feelings of guilt among Arabs who participated in or condoned the devastation of an Arab country by an American-led coalition.

Washington wanted Arabs to feel that the US was defending them against an aggressor: the reality was that the US defended its own interests, and used methods of divide and rule to achieve its aims after the invasion of Kuwait. Playing on the fears of weak, rich, tribal societies surrounded by oceans of poverty and need, the Americans had no difficulty in convincing kings and sheikhs (who had long been conditioned to accept the need for American protection) that Baghdad was planning to seize their thrones.

Such men were almost as suspicious of their own people, and of other Arab forces participating in the coalition, as they were of Iraq. Kuwait and Saudi Arabia might have been expected to show gratitude for the roles played by Egypt and Syria, even if only as proof of their commitment to Arab solidarity. As it was, Kuwait and Saudi Arabia seemed more interested in relations with Britain and France. Other Arabs were made to feel second best to Western countries, to the point that Cairo took offence and began withdrawing Egyptian forces from Kuwait on 8 May, which was sooner than expected. The Egyptian withdrawal was completed by the end of July, while Syrian forces began leaving on 2 June and had gone by 28 July. Soon after the war Egypt asked Saudi Arabia for a grant of $500 million, a moderate request in relation to the backing Cairo had given by providing an Arab partner. Riyadh initially offered $200 million and only later (in October 1991) paid the full amount requested. There was a feeling among Egyptians of having been used by rich Gulf states and then neglected when they were no longer needed. Many in Syria, too, thought that their country had been treated like a hired guard rather than as a partner.

These resentments would not have arisen if links between the heavily populated states at the centre of the Arab world and the sheikhdoms of the Arab periphery had been as 'brotherly' as their governments claimed. The war brought to the boil tensions between Arab cities and tribes which had been simmering since the 1970s. An overlapping and complicating factor was that throughout the Arab world people were abandoning the countryside and moving into the cities, which were already grossly overpopulated. The frustration and hopelessness of millions of unemployed people in vast twilight belts around Arab cities was made worse by their awareness of the wealth of the oil-producing states. The cities can only be a time-bomb for the future unless something is done to address this anger. The fact that much of the oil revenue of the last twenty-five years has been invested in the West, rather than used to raise standards in the poorer parts of the Arab world, is bitterly resented in urban areas. Equally, the heavy spending by many Arab governments on unnecessary arms, even in countries which are never likely to be combatants in a war with Israel, has provided further fuel for that discontent. The last twenty years have seen the creation of Arab armies which could only be used to fight other Arabs, and whose purpose, in most cases, is to defend the privileges of ruling families.

A further source of rich – poor tension was the decision by most of the oil producers in the late 1980s to reduce their contributions to the PLO and the front-line states of Syria, Jordan and Lebanon. The Gulf war also contributed to the alienation of the Palestinians from the richer countries. Tens of thousands of Palestinians who moved to

Kuwait in search of security before the war found themselves crushed between conflicting forces in the Arab world.

No source of frustration is more fundamental than the limited participation of the Arab people in deciding their own future. Many believe that even if Arab governments manage to agree on joint policies on social justice, development and defence, the policies will have limited popular support, because of a consistent failure to involve and consult the people.

Political participation depends on the ability of social groups to grow and act and voice their opinions, which in turn depends on freedom of expression. Freedom of the media remains an unattained goal, although Egypt is slightly more liberal than other Arab countries. Every regime has fortified itself against challengers with technological defences purchased from the United States, Europe or Japan. Some of the poorest countries have spent millions of dollars on advanced telephone-tapping systems to monitor suspected opponents. Until the Arab world develops a tradition of open dialogue to articulate issues there can be no hope of developing policies by consensus, nor of making governments responsive to the popular will. As matters stand, it takes a riot to make Arab governments aware of popular discontent. The usual response to such expressions of frustration is the imposition of harsh emergency laws, which further erode the rule of law, together with severe limitations on rights to express complaints and grievances. A generation of old, tired leaders is suffering from a progressive hardening of its political arteries.

Without exception, the countries of the Arab world are ruled on a paternalistic basis, though that paternalism has several forms. In Egypt and Syria, governments were able to rule by popular consent in the Nasser era, but they subsequently handed power to their successors without consulting the people (unless in the form of rigged elections). In these countries, when the people lose confidence in the regime, the regime tries to change the people, because it is incapable of changing itself.

In the Gulf, sheikhs and kings are trying to perpetuate forms of government that were appropriate for tiny desert societies two centuries ago. Many wondered in 1991 whether the long-expected power struggle in Saudi Arabia had begun when Prince Khalid, commander-in- chief of Saudi forces, resigned only weeks after the end of the war, and when King Fahd repeatedly delayed going on holiday because of tension within the kingdom. The usual assumption that the succession will be decided among the 6000 quarrelling princes is not necessarily correct, because greater political awareness is spreading through the population as a whole. Some 120,000 Saudis have attended universities or other educational courses in the United States, and many are impatient for change, finding it intolerable that one of the world's richest countries should continue to be run like a private estate. Nothing could illustrate this more clearly than the fact that the country is named after the king who unified it.

In Kuwait, a limited measure of democracy in the 1960s and seventies was eroded when the ruling family suspended the National Assembly from 1976 to 1981 and again from 1986 to 1990. The emir's decision in July 1990 to take control of the composition of the National Assembly caused serious tension. After his return to Kuwait after the war, on 14 March 1991, Sheikh Jaber met eight opposition leaders, but made no concessions. On 15 May he declared that elections would be held in October 1992, but the opposition felt that elections would have little meaning without reform of the electoral process.

Some Arab countries have created make-believe institutions in the hope of presenting a democratic face to the world, while continuing to take all the main decisions without reference to these institutions. An inevitable side-effect is that all serious opposition is conducted on an underground basis, without involving the parliaments.

All these tensions and frustrations have combined to create confusion, bitterness and divisions beyond anything experienced in the Arab world this century. Unless there is a conscious effort to make a new start, Arabs can look forward only to years of despair, confusion and political stagnation.

Against this bleak background there are a number of more hopeful factors which might eventually transform the picture. The highly-educated and politically conscious bourgeoisie of Kuwait seems likely to resume agitating for greater democracy, and if it wins its struggle with the al-Sabah family a precedent would be created which could lead to change throughout the Arab world. Apart from Kuwait, there is also a substantial middle class in Egypt, Syria and Saudi Arabia.

Secondly, although the regimes have no enthusiasm for greater democracy, they may come to see it as a safety-valve for releasing sectarian tensions. Egypt, with its tradition of setting the pace of social development in the Arab world, would be a natural cradle for

Arab democracy. For the present, Egypt is governed through a disguised form of paternalism under which political parties are permitted a degree of free expression. Although less restrictive than most of the Arab world, the Egyptian system lags far behind the aspirations of its people. It is inconceivable that greater popular participation can be delayed much longer in a country with 3 million university graduates and a further 7 million receiving other forms of education, 3 million women working in paid jobs, 17 million workers belonging to trade unions and with a level of literacy high enough for about 250 new book titles to be published every month.

As the Arab world prepares for the twenty-first century there is an urgent need to bring its forms of government into line with the expectations of younger people. Some 60 per cent of Arabs are under the age of eighteen: by the turn of the century 100 million people in their twenties will be asking why their parents and grandparents failed to provide them with the basic tools of civilised government. The present generation of rulers could secure their place in history by beginning a long-overdue process of reform, but they seem more likely to be remembered as the Brezhnevs of the Arab world. The leaders may delay change, but they cannot prevent it. Men of greater imagination will eventually lead the Arab world out of its stagnation.